Requiem for
the Sudan

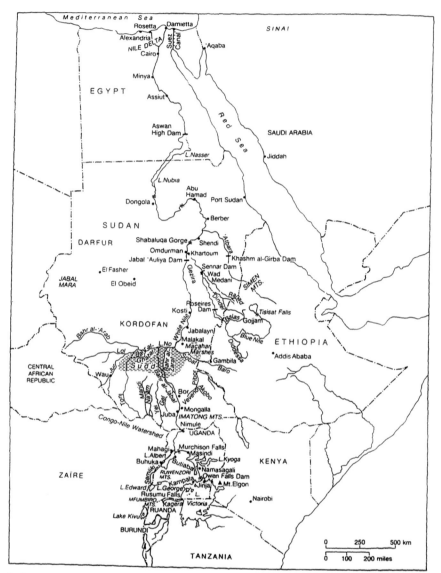

Nile basin

REQUIEM FOR THE SUDAN

War, Drought, and Disaster Relief on the Nile

———————— ■ ————————

J. Millard Burr
Robert O. Collins

Westview Press
BOULDER • SAN FRANCISCO • OXFORD

Copyright © 1995 by Westview Press, Inc.

Published in 1995 in the United States of America by Westview Press, Inc., 5500 Central Avenue, Boulder, Colorado 80301-2877, and in the United Kingdom by Westview Press, 36 Lonsdale Road, Summertown, Oxford OX2 7EW

Library of Congress Cataloging-in-Publication Data
Burr, Millard
    Requiem for the Sudan : war, drought, and disaster relief on the
Nile / J. Millard Burr and Robert O. Collins
        p.   cm.
    Includes bibliographical references and index.
    ISBN 0-8133-2120-4 — ISBN 0-8133-2121-2 (pbk.)
    1. Sudan—Politics and government—1985–   . 2. Disaster relief—
Sudan. I. Collins, Robert O.   II. Title.
DT157.5.B87   1994
363.3'48'0962409048—dc20

                                                                94-18552
                                                                CIP

Printed and bound in the United States of America

The paper used in this publication meets the requirements
(∞) of the American National Standard for Permanence of Paper
    for Printed Library Materials Z39.48-1984.

10   9   8   7   6   5   4   3   2

Contents

Illustrations

Tables

Photos (following page 203)

John Garang de Mabior, leader of the Sudan People's
  Liberation Army in the Equatoria province of Sudan, 1990
Roger Winter, director of the U.S. Committee for Refugees,
  meeting with John Garang
An old Sudanese woman walking between Bambouti
  and Bassiqbiri
Refugees seek food in the bush of the Equatoria province
Unidentified bodies near the Ethiopian border
Burned shell of a hut destroyed by civil war
Flooded village of the Nuer, Upper Nile province
  of Southern Sudan, 1992

Maps

Preface

J. Millard Burr began his investigation of drought in the African Sahil in 1982, working in the Office of the Geographer, U.S. Department of State. Robert O. Collins has written on the history of the Sudan for more than thirty years. This book is a collaborative effort in every sense, in that we have brought together the specialized knowledge from different perspectives and disciplines in an attempt to illuminate the complex and tangled course of events over the past troubling decade in the Sudan.

In 1988 the late Charles Gladson, director of the Africa Bureau, U.S. Agency for International Development, invited Millard Burr to take the position as logistics director in the USAID-Sudan mission. Gladson was incensed that the international response to the devastating 1988 famine in Southern Sudan had been so tardy and so inadequate. With the inception in March 1989 of UN-sponsored Operation Lifeline Sudan—an entirely new approach to the distribution of humanitarian assistance in a nation at war with itself—Millard Burr accumulated a massive amount of material on the famine itself and on the markedly successful relief effort. When the civilian government of Sadiq al-Mahdi was overthrown by a military coup in June 1989, we began to follow closely the activities of the Revolutionary Command Council and of those civilians who supported its totalitarian aims. Many unpublished U.S. Foreign Broadcast Information Service transcriptions and translations of Sudanese radio and news reports were collected. Meanwhile, beginning in 1988 the Agency for International Development scanned the domestic and international press daily and for nearly two years provided news reports on the Sudan to its USAID mission in Khartoum. In Khartoum employees of various international nongovernmental organizations (especially UN personnel) and private voluntary organizations provided copies of studies, minutes of meetings, trip reports, and a multitude of ephemera. Many individuals continue to send reports on a variety of Sudanese issues.

Writing the dark history of the famine and civil war recounted here was largely possible because of our access to such documents, most of which are unlikely ever to be made public. They graphically revealed the tragic human consequences of the failure of conflict resolution, of organizational mismanagement, and of a government hostile toward its own people.

We wish to acknowledge the many Sudanese who have provided us with support, information, and a knowledge of their cultural aspirations and hopes for a better future in a land plagued by war and drought. We would also like to thank our editors at Westview Press, Barbara Ellington, who championed the project and offered many useful suggestions, and Shena Redmond, who shepherded the manuscript through the production process with care and finesse. We are particularly grateful to Sharisse Baltimore and Alverta Scott, whose computer skills were essential in preparing the manuscript for publication. We also wish to acknowledge the splendid cartography of Brett Buyan, Keith A. Farnsworth, and Stephen Kirin of the University of California, Santa Barbara, Digital Cartographic Laboratory under the direction of Professor David Lanter, whose maps are contained in this volume. Finally, we must thank Roger Winter, director of the U.S. Committee for Refugees, for making the committee's photographic library available to us; thanks also to Renee Bafalis for the photos she provided.

Politicians, bureaucrats, military officers, Sudan People's Liberation Army officials (past and present), and scores of employees of indigenous, international, and U.S. aid organizations provided material for this book. Nothing would give us greater pleasure than to identify our benefactors. Very soon, *inshallah*, we will all celebrate the return of peace to the great nation, Sudan.

J. Millard Burr, Sonoita, Arizona
Robert O. Collins, Santa Barbara, California
July 1994

Acronyms

ABS	Agricultural Bank of Sudan
ACROSS	Africa Committee for Refugees from the Southern Sudan
ADRA	Adventist Development and Relief Agency
AICF	Action Internationale Contre la Faim
AID	Agency for International Development
AISS	Agencies Involved in Southern Sudan
CARE	Cooperative for American Relief Everywhere
CART	Combined Action Relief Team
CRS	Catholic Relief Services
EC	European Community
EEC	European Economic Community
ESF	Economic Support Fund
FANA	Food Aid National Administration
FAO	Food and Agricultural Organization of United Nations
FBIS	Foreign Broadcast Information Service
FEWS	Famine Early Warning System
GOS	Government of Sudan
ICF	Islamic Charter Front
ICRC	International Commission for the Red Cross
IMF	International Monetary Fund
INTERAID	International Assistance for International Development
LICROSS	League of Red Cross Societies
MALT	Management and Logistics Team
MENA	Middle East News Agency
MSF-France	Medicines San Frontiers—France (or other country)
NCA	Norwegian Church Aid
NGOs	nongovernmental organizations
NIF	National Islamic Front
NPA	Norwegian People's Aid
NSRCC	National Salvation Revolution Command Council
OAU	Organization of African Unity
OFDA	Office of Foreign Disaster Assistance
OLF	Oromo Liberation Front

OLS	Operation Lifeline Sudan
OXFAM	Oxford Famine Relief
PC	Popular Committee
PDF	Popular Defense Force
PLO	Palestine Liberation Organization
PVOs	Private Voluntary Organizations
RCC	*See* NSRCC
RRC	Relief and Rehabilitation Commission
SAT	Southern Air Transport
SCC	Sudan Council of Churches
SCF	Save the Children Federation
sitreps	situation reports
SPAF	Sudanese People's Armed Forces
SPLA	Sudan People's Liberation Army
SPLM	Sudan People's Liberation Movement
SRC	Sudanese Red Crescent
SRRA	Sudan Relief and Rehabilitation Association
SSRO	Southern Sudan Relief Operation
TCC	Technical Coordination Committee
TMC	Transitional Military Council
UNDP	United Nations Development Program
UNEOS	UN Office of Emergency Operation in Sudan
UNHCR	United Nations High Commissioner for Refugees
UNICEF	UN Children's Emergency Relief Fund
UNLO	United Nations Labor Organization
UPDA	Uganda People's Democratic Army
USAID	U.S. Agency for International Development
USAID-Sudan	U.S. Agency for International Development Office in Sudan
WFP	World Food Program
WHO	World Health Organization
WRO	Western Relief Operation

Introduction

The Republic of the Sudan is the largest country in Africa, encompassing more than a million square miles—approximately the size of the United States east of the Mississippi River. It spans over 35 degrees of latitude and embraces topography ranging from arid deserts to tropical rain forests. Over 450 ethnic groups live in Sudan, most of whom are farmers and pastoralists living at a subsistence level, subject to the vagaries of nature in a harsh environment. The remaining population, probably not more than ten percent, are "elites" who primarily inhabit the urban centers and as merchants, professionals, or learned scholars have prospered by their acumen, political activism, and education.

Since 1983, over a million and a half Southern Sudanese have perished in a prolonged and bloody civil war, fueled by the fratricidal and ideological fanaticism of those who have claimed to lead the people of Sudan. No one can give an accurate count of those who have died from bullets, malnutrition, or neglect on the part of the government of Sudan, many of whose leaders have been pleased to see the demise of their Sudanese African brothers. Nor can we know how many others, weakened from starvation, have chosen to die with a degree of dignity in the bush rather than be buried in mass and impersonal graves. At the same time, the children and the women of Southern Sudan have been reduced to slavery: The children tend to the livestock of their Northern Sudanese masters; the women are expected to provide sexual services in exchange for a meager sustenance.

But the Sudanese, having grown to adulthood in a harsh land, are great survivors; they will continue to persevere. They remain in the bush and the shantytowns and ghettos surrounding the principal cities of the Sudan—Khartoum, Omdurman, and Khartoum North. They are an embarrassment to the Northern Sudanese Muslim elite who have dominated professional and political life since independence on January 1, 1960, and who have no tolerance for the non-Muslim Southern Sudanese

1

whose antecendents are African and who have deep attachments to their own indigenous culture, religion, and history. The refugees, who have fled to the urban areas of Northern Sudan to escape from the depredations suffered in their homelands in the South, find no solace in or sympathy from their government.

The cultural, religious, and ideological differences among ethnic groups in Sudan are well documented in the enormous anthropological and historical literature. But those works have not explained the killing fields, the "ghost houses" of torture, the deaths in the detention camps, or the public spectacles of amputations for petty crimes. President Numayri and his successors may denounce individuals as dissidents, infidels, and enemies of the government, but few Sudanese of any ethnic group or religious persuasion would agree. Renowned as warriors who destroyed the British square at Tamai on 13 March 1884, the Sudanese of whatever ethnic group have been precisely that—warriors, not torturers in the "ghost houses" of Khartoum.

The magnitude of the human destruction in Sudan since independence makes the conflict one of the most savage of our time. Millions of Sudanese have fled under the most arduous conditions to seek status as refugees, destitute and unwanted. Millions have died; more will ultimately perish. But in contrast to conflicts elsewhere in the world, the atrocities in Sudan have been largely ignored. Occasionally an article has appeared in the national press—usually nothing more than a report on the camps of the displaced population, mostly the young and the aged—written by a courageous journalist who has managed to slip over the southern border for a mere few hundred kilometers. This is all the information available to us because the media, particularly television, has been prohibited by the government of Sudan from recording the devastation of the country and its people. In Sudan, a most remote country, this prohibition has not been hard to enforce, despite the most sophisticated technology of the international media.

For over a decade civil war has raged in the Sudan, but the coup d'état of 30 June 1989 changed the nature of the conflict. The coup was carried out by unsophisticated brigadiers of the Sudan army, supported financially by members of the National Islamic Front. They were soldiers, but the policy decisions were made by the Islamic politicians and polemicists led by Hassan al-Turabi, the principal Islamic fundamentalist leader in Sudan and the theological leader and politically dominant figure in the National Islamic Front.

The 1989 coup was not a spontaneous outburst of Islamic anger. It was a response to the failure of the Numayri government to assist the starving Muslim peoples of the West and East in 1984–1985, which had brought international media attention. Indeed, Sudan was scrutinized as never before, and Numayri—whose government depended greatly on the West and the United Nations for financial and material assistance—was eventually forced to accept the subsequent proliferation of Western nongovernmental agencies (NGOs) and private voluntary organizations (PVOs), as well as personnel from the United Nations. As expected, the corrupt and ineffective Numayri government could not last, and in typical Sudanese fashion a popular uprising deposed his government during his state visit to Washington in 1985. The leader of the coup was Chief of Staff General Abd al-Rahman Siwar al-Dahab, who formed a transitional military government that sought, only half-heartedly, to end the civil war. The ensuing elections, which did not even include the Southern Sudanese, whose territory was regarded as a war zone, were indecisive. Subsequently a coalition government was formed by Sadiq al-Mahdi, but his intransigence in moving to resolve the critical political and economic issues confronting the Sudanese left the country adrift at a time of great crisis. Although many Western agencies were eager to provide assistance to all needy Sudanese, Sadiq repeatedly failed to act decisively, no doubt cynically aware that humanitarian relief would assist precisely those who were rebelling against his government. Ultimately, seeking a resolution to Sudan's instability, the Revolutionary Command Council for National Salvation (RCC-NS), led by Brigadier Umar Hassan Ahmad al-Bashir, took power on 30 June 1989 and imposed an Islamic republic.

The devastation wrought by two well-armed combatants during a decade of civil war resulted in major social upheaval in both the Southern and Northern Sudan. Both the interminable conflict and social upheaval were made worse by repeated cycles of drought, accompanied by starvation and disease, all of which escalated the number of civilian deaths and contributed to the dissolution of the state. The crucial role played by Western humanitarian relief agencies also must be counted in what proved a continuing and controversial effort to provide aid to the long-suffering Sudanese. Finally, war, drought, and relief must be seen as intimately connected to the policies of the government of Sudan, the United Nations, and the Western donors.

Throughout the 1980s annual rainfall in Sudan was far below the average for the twentieth century. The first serious crisis occurred in Western Sudan in 1983 and resulted in the terrible famine of 1984-1985. During that period drought also spread to the Red Sea coast and Eastern Sudan and brought scores of foreign aid agencies to Sudan. By mid-decade drought had struck the South, where crop failures and the scarcity of forage were made more painful by the depredation of the Arab Baqqara militias from Kordofan—the *murahileen,* who had previously been armed by the Sudan government but were now uncontrollable.

Together drought and war caused the death and displacement of hundreds of thousands of Nilotic peoples, particularly the Dinka. The introduction of sophisticated weaponry on both sides greatly increased the intensity of the conflict. Even more terrifying was the employment by the Sudan government of the *murahileen* and other ethnic militias in support of its armed forces, which led to atrocities the professional officers of the Sudan army could not prevent and which was instrumental in provoking the displacement of millions of Southern Sudanese. The survivors of this irregular warfare were then threatened by a series of droughts that plagued the South, and the famine that followed resulted in even more deaths and displacement than those from battle. Once villages were burned, once villagers experienced debilitating drought, once herders suffered the destruction of countless of their beloved cattle, the Nilotes were forced to flee or starve. They sought food and refuge beyond their devastated homelands, mostly in the greater Khartoum area where they were greeted with hostility and prejudice by their fellow Sudanese and their government.

As the Southern Sudanese became acutely aware, disaster relief efforts faced almost insurmountable obstacles. On the political level, these ranged from blatant government corruption to simple bureaucratic inefficiency. Official insensitivity and programmatic derelictions cannot be avoided in this narrative because they were not trivial and were responsible for unnecessary loss of life and the deterioration of Southern Sudanese cultures and traditional Sudanese ways of life. Whether in the Southern or Western Sudan, relief for the displaced and the starving came almost solely from the foreign humanitarian agencies, a fact many Northern Sudanese found difficult to accept because of the paradoxical, historical conflicts between the traditions of hospitality—even to one's enemies—and the racial and religious animosity toward the Southern Sudanese, long regarded as inferior or heretical.

Expatriates during the colonial era used to remark that "Africa begins at Malakal"—the city where tropical Africa first appears. One rarely hears that expression today, but it remains an undeniable truth. Until the penetration of the Sudd in the nineteenth century, the great swamp of the Nile in Southern Sudan was one of the most isolated regions in the world, and so it remains today. The vast region of swamps, plains, forests, and mountains is a landscape hardly conducive to the conduct of conventional warfare, but it is ideal for guerrilla war. When the relief agencies were finally permitted to move food aid throughout the South, including territory controlled by the rebel forces, they were continually frustrated by the terrain and isolation of Southern Sudan, unable to overcome formidable geographical obstacles even by modern means of transport. Certainly, relations between the relief agencies and the Sudan government, which were ambiguous and often hostile, were continually strained by the interminable struggle to move commodities by means of a limited and crumbling infrastructure.

By 1986 the Western humanitarian agencies in Sudan numbered over one hundred and represented all ideological and religious persuasions—many nondenominational, others nonnational, and some simply philanthropic. The purpose was to assist the many thousands threatened by famine or privation; most expatriates, the *khawaja*, soon found, however, that the very nature of their work made it impossible for them to escape either physical or philosophical involvement in the civil conflict. Although organizations might remain neutral, few individuals could do so; thus the mantle of altruistic humanitarianism the relief agencies donned was often deeply suspected by the government of Sudan, which had become increasingly convinced that it would be victorious in the long and bitter war.

Operation Lifeline Sudan (OLS), the disaster relief program inaugurated in April 1989 under the auspices of the United Nations and funded in large part by the United States, was a unique response to the terrible year of drought in 1988 during which hundreds of thousands of Southerners died. OLS introduced a policy of food aid neutrality throughout Sudan that could serve as an example for disaster assistance programs elsewhere in the world, and it valiantly tried to overcome the political and geographic obstacles to effective delivery. Nonetheless, its success has not been replicated.

After al-Bashir and the Revolutionary Command Council assumed power, there was no interest in continuing Operation Lifeline Sudan, the last major international aid effort initiated in the 1980s. It soon atrophied. With Bashir, the era of Sadiq al-Mahdi—characterized by indecision and deception—came to an end, and a new epoch of military dictatorship began. All negotiations to end the civil war failed. In Khartoum, the Bashir government began to question the motivations of the expatriate aid agencies, the "neocolonialists," and then enjoined many restrictions upon their operations. For the *khawaja*, the Western aid workers, there was little choice but go elsewhere, even though the unhappy history of the decade was about to repeat itself. The scarcity of rain in the northwest in 1989 triggered the memory of the aid workers, who feared Darfur and Kordofan would once again be threatened by severe famine. When a fierce drought struck the Sudanese Sahil in 1990, Bashir, like Numayri had before him, denied its existence. War in Kuwait and the subsequent UN offensive against Iraq led the humanitarian agencies to hasten their departure from the Sudan. When a few returned in 1991, a famine in Darfur and in parts of the Bahr al-Ghazal was taking its toll, with tens of thousands dying. Throughout 1991 the drought and civil war dragged on. Even more debilitating was the infighting among the leaders and their followers in the Sudanese People's Liberation Army in August 1991. By 1992 there was a virulent civil war within a civil war raging in the Southern Sudan. By 1993 disaster relief was little more than a band-aid applied to a suppurating wound that only the Sudanese could heal.

In the North, affairs appeared in equal disarray. Bashir, as head of the Revolutionary Command Council, dissolved the council to clear the way for the assumption of power by Hassan al-Turabi and the National Islamic Front, both committed to establishing an Islamic Republic to which a third of Sudan's population could have no allegiance.

As the government of Sudan now seems poised to dominate the country politically, ideologically, and militarily, the many people and organizations that have sought to alleviate the devastating distress in Sudan have been saddened and have fled a land where interminable warfare and natural disasters combined to crush the aspirations of those who had hoped to bring some relief to the beleaguered, but much beloved, Sudanese.

The following is a sad tale of brutality, despair, and the desperate search for a solution—particularly by the many around the world who have a deep affection for the Sudanese.

ONE

■

The Death of a Dream

The mutiny was local; it occurred in one battalion, and it was restricted to one province. The mutiny has ended completely, and it has not spread at all in the south.
—General Joseph Lagu, Khartoum, March 1983

At approximately 5:00 P.M. on 27 February 1972 in Addis Ababa, Ethiopia, Ezboni Mondiri Gwonza, representing the Southern Sudan Liberation Movement, and Dr. Mansour Khalid, minister of foreign affairs of the Sudan government, ratified the Addis Ababa Agreement and effectively ended civil war in the Republic of Sudan. The agreement halted a conflict that for over seventeen years had devastated the South and caused the deaths of an estimated half million southerners. The region's population had been scattered like chaff in the wind; some two hundred thousand Sudanese were found in neighboring countries and five hundred thousand of those displaced had burrowed into the hinterland, or bush, of Southern Sudan.[1] The agreement was hailed by the international community as a triumphant example of how a nation could resolve a debilitating and divisive dispute through negotiation, compromise, and mutual respect. The president of the republic, Jaafar Numayri, an army colonel who had seized power in October 1969, basked in the glow of his role as peacemaker.

Aftermath of the Addis Ababa Agreement

The terms, but not the spirit, of the Addis Ababa Agreement were subsequently implemented. Refugees were repatriated, and the South's indigenous military movement, the Anya-Nya guerrilla fighters, were offered posts within the Sudanese army, police, or game warden system. By the end of 1976, 6,000 Anya-Nya officers and troops had been integrated into the army's Southern Command. Unfortunately, the expectations of a new era based on peace, equality, and social justice—not only

7

8

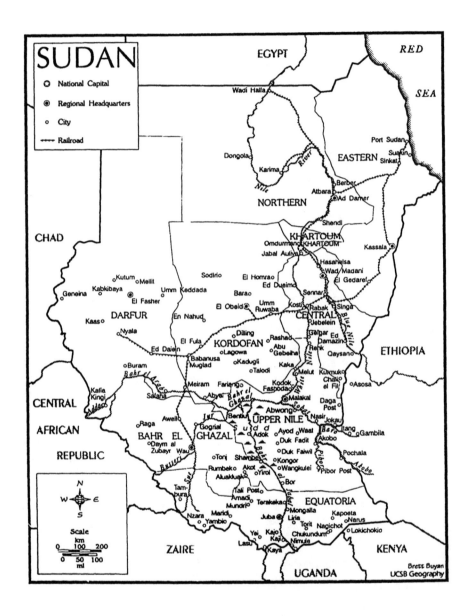

in the South but in all of Sudan—did not materialize. Large-scale development schemes made possible by peace and the infusion of Middle East capital were invariably located in Northern Sudan. Moreover, in the distribution of social services—schools, hospitals, communications—the South did not receive its proportionate share. Still, the South did achieve a large measure of regional autonomy complete with a southern legislative assembly and a High Executive Council.

Arabic remained the official language of Sudan, but English was declared the "principal language" for the southern region, "without prejudice to the use of any other [regional] languages."[2] Soon, however, the southern politicians were squabbling among themselves, frequently maneuvering and manipulating for personal gain at the expense of public good. Gradually, the spirit of Addis Ababa expired. The hundreds of different ethnic cultures split along the great divide between the North—oriented to the Arab, Muslim world of the Middle East—and the South, whose peoples identified with the African, non-Muslim region stretching far to the south and west. It was this enormous difference in culture, religion, and mutual perceptions that the Addis Ababa Agreement had sought to resolve, and the great experiment failed when President Numayri ceased to believe in a political creation he himself had sponsored.

An attempted coup in 1975 and another in July 1976 swung Numayri and the Sudan's only party, his Sudan Socialist Union, irrevocably to the political right. Numayri turned to old foes in the Muslim Brotherhood, the Ikhwan al-Muslimin, for support and rebuilt bridges to the traditional sectarian political parties he had once prorogued. In 1977 he achieved a reconciliation with his principal opponents—the Umma, the Democratic Unionists (DUP), and the Islamic Charter Front (ICF, later renamed the National Islamic Front, or NIF), which were collectively known as the National Front. Although the National Front had sought to overthrow Numayri in the abortive but bloody 1976 coup d'état, the president was prepared to purchase their support at the expense of the South. He yielded to National Front demands to revise the Addis Ababa Agreement and eliminate what Arabs in the North regarded as the South's privileged status. Certainly, the Islamic Charter Front, the party representing the Muslim Brothers, cared nothing for Numayri or for southern aspirations; instead, it used the National Front to accumulate power for itself and its members.

From 1977 onward, the National Front abetted President Numayri's relentless ambition to undo the Addis Ababa Agreement, and in 1978 Front members were brought into the government and Numayri's Sudan Socialist Union. Subsequent events convinced the president that not only should he gut the Addis Ababa Agreement but that the surgery could best be accomplished through his espousal of Muslim ideology. Nevertheless, in 1980 Numayri suffered a reverse when united southern opposition forced him to abandon his scheme to redefine the border between North and South so as to arrogate the oil fields of the Upper Nile province. Numayri's fury increased when southern representatives in the National Assembly published a small pamphlet, *The Solidarity Booklet*, in which they criticized him personally and northern political figures in general. The last straw was the student riots that erupted during his visit to the South's prestigious Rumbek Secondary School in December 1982. From that point there was no turning back, and the split between North and South was irrevocable.

The Relocation of the Integrated Southern Forces

The Southern Sudanese armed struggle was precipitated by the mutiny of the 105th battalion of the Sudan army in March 1983. The battalion was composed of former Anya-Nya officers and enlisted personnel who had been "absorbed" into the army's Southern Command as part of the Addis Ababa Agreement. The absorbed forces, however, were not immune to the deteriorating relations between President Numayri and the southern Sudanese elite. To be sure, most soldiers of the 105th were illiterate, and their horizons were limited; their world was their homeland south of the Sudd, the great swamps of the Nile north of which lay the hostile environment of Sahil, Muslims, and Arabs. They were only vaguely cognizant of the political machinations in Khartoum and of the various grievances expressed by the southern intelligentsia; their officers were aware, however, that no army recruitment had taken place in the South since 1974 and that southerners comprised less than 5 percent of those attending Sudan's prestigious military college. Moreover, they observed with great anxiety that retirement and dismissals had drastically reduced the number of southern Sudanese officers.

Although President Numayri had incarcerated twenty-four prominent southern leaders in December 1981 and the speaker of the regional assembly and the vice president of the High Executive Council of the South in February 1983, in his efforts to disestablish the Addis Ababa Agreement it was clearly more important to neutralize the Southern Command than to imprison a handful of fractious politicians. To immobilize the only possible armed resistance to his abrogation of the Addis Ababa Agreement, he ordered the relocation of most of the absorbed forces out of the South. In doing so Numayri demonstrated that he was suffering from acute political amnesia and had forgotten the lessons learned during nearly two decades of civil war in postcolonial Sudan. In August 1955 the Equatorial Corps of the Sudan Defense Force headquartered at Torit had been ordered to Khartoum to take part in the celebrations accompanying the departure of British troops from the Sudan. The Equatorial Corps, established in 1910, consisted solely of southerners under British officers; English was the language of command, and the religion, if any, was Christianity rather than Islam. As had occurred with the absorbed forces in 1983, the rank and file had intermarried with local families surrounding their posts. They established farms, reared families, and enjoyed the routine of garrison life. Thus a transfer to Northern Sudan was perceived as a removal from a friendly to a hostile environment. On 8 August No. 2 Company was on parade at Torit when it suddenly broke ranks and rushed the armory. Armed mutineers massacred Northern Sudanese officers, merchants, and their families, and rebellion swept Equatoria. Peace would not return until the ratification of the Addis Ababa Agreement in March 1972.

By 1983 President Numayri had dissipated the goodwill generated by the Addis Ababa Agreement. The pittance spent on economic development in the South, combined with Numayri's efforts to appropriate for the North the benefits of both oil discoveries in the South and the Jonglei canal construction in the Upper Nile, devalued and demeaned southern aspirations. Given the numerous personal and petty controversies among southern politicians, he considered the South an impotent giant. By far the most discordant political issues were the question of redivision, which could destroy the 1972 Addis Ababa Agreement, and the treatment of southern units in the Sudanese army. Eventually, the latter would be his undoing.

Most southern officers were absolutely opposed to the government plan to transfer the absorbed Anya Nya battalions to the North where they would be integrated into northern units. Nevertheless, Numayri was convinced that he had little to fear. He ordered the relocation of battalions 105 at Bor, 110 at Aweil, and 117 at Kapoeta in 1982 to 1983. Battalions 104 at Nasir, 111 at Rumbek, and 116 at Juba would move in 1983 to 1984. The Aweil unit received orders to relocate first but only after considerable persuasion departed for Darfur in December 1982. In contrast, the battalions at Bor and Rumbek refused to move, and only after the intervention of the High Executive Council at Juba did Numayri agree in January 1983 to postpone their transfer until later in the year. Although the concession temporarily mollified the 105th at Bor, the government, alleging mishandling of past payrolls, refused to reimburse the personnel. This transparent ploy, for there were no irregularities, only infuriated the Bor garrison. In retaliation the 105th and its units at Pibor, Ayod, and Pachalla mutinied. Units at Bentiu, the Upper Nile region, and Rumbek in the Bahr al-Ghazal region followed suit; and southern soldiers at the Raga garrison, a district headquarters located 225 miles northwest of

Wau, refused orders to transfer to El Fasher, capital of Darfur, and "fled with their weapons."[3]

The Revolt at Bor

The National Defense Council in Khartoum concluded that discipline in the Southern Command had disintegrated. Thus an example would be made of the Bor garrison, and the Southern Command in Juba was ordered to disarm the 105th at Bor and Pibor. Government troops under the command of Dominic Kassiano, a Zande from Western Equatoria, were harassed on their march from Juba to Bor, and—eager for a fight—Kassiano's force attacked the 105th at dawn on 16 May. The attack was met with fierce resistance from soldiers commanded by a redoubtable southern soldier, Major Kerubino Kwanyin Bol. By sundown each side had sustained many casualties. At daybreak Kerubino, outnumbered and outgunned, led his troops into the bush and began the long march to the sanctuary of Ethiopia. In June the 105th's second in command, Major William Nyuon Bany, led a unit from Ayod to Ethiopia and joined rebel units from Bor and Pibor. There Kerubino and Nyuan Bany placed themselves under the overall command of Lt. Colonel John Garang de Mabior, who had been asked by President Numayri in March 1983 to try to resolve the most dangerous of the many festering disputes troubling the southern garrisons.

Garang had seemed the ideal choice, as he was from the Bor region and had served in the 105th. Still, as director of research at army headquarters in Khartoum, he had closely observed the corruption in the government and had watched with dismay Numayri's maneuvers to unravel the Addis Ababa Agreement. Born in Wangkulei north of Bor in Upper Nile Province on 23 June 1945, he had been sent to school at Rumbek by Protestant missionaries. Before he was able to graduate from secondary school, General Ibrahim Abboud, the Sudanese dictator from 1959 to 1963, initiated a campaign absolutely to destroy the thin stratum of educated Southern Sudanese. Garang was forced to flee to Ethiopia, and when an extradition treaty was signed between Abboud and Ethiopian Emperor Haile Salassie, Garang and other Sudanese made their way south. Garang eventually settled in Tanzania, where he obtained a scholarship to attend Magambia secondary school. He then left for Grinnell College in Iowa, where he earned a bachelor's degree in economics.

Upon returning to the Sudan in 1971 he joined the Anya-Nya—despite the reservations of its commander, Joseph Lagu, that he was overly educated. Following the signing of the Addis Ababa Agreement, he was commissioned a captain in the 104th battalion of the Sudan People's Defense Forces. Garang returned to the United States in 1977 and in 1981 earned a Ph.D. in agricultural economics at Iowa State University. After returning to Sudan, Garang was a popular lecturer at Khartoum University and the Sudan's military academy. Garang was deeply opposed to the monopoly of power exercised in Khartoum by Arab notables and their sectarian parties and to the diminution and political impoverishment of those Sudanese on the periphery—Muslim and non-Muslim, Arab and African.

When it became known that the Sudan army at Juba had been ordered to disarm and detain the mutineers, Garang was approached by the officers and troops of the Bor garrison and was asked to lead them in rebellion. Evidently, Garang did not take part in the fighting at Bor on 16 May, but the following morning he collected his family and following a long and tortuous route arrived in Ethiopia where he soon joined the troops of the 105th. From this nucleus Garang formed the Sudan People's Liberation Army (SPLA) and soon incorporated within its political arm the nascent Sudan People's Liberation Movement (SPLM).

In Khartoum it first appeared that the revolt at Bor was but another spontaneous mutiny that had been easily handled. Sworn in for his third successive term as president on 24 May, Numayri casually claimed that it "had been resolved sternly and forcefully."[4] In fact, Garang was already galvanizing his forces in Ethiopia into a formidable revolutionary army, and by his own account more than 60 percent of those comprising the SPLA's first five battalions were battle hardened former Anya-Nya. Garang's first and most important political act was to publish a Manifesto on 31 July 1983. It spoke against the separation of the southern region from the Sudan and argued forcefully that the SPLA was fighting "to establish the united socialist Sudan, not a separate Sudan."[5]

As Garang sought to build a revolutionary army, he found himself challenged by the Anya-Nya II for leadership of that army. The Anya-Nya II was led by Samuel Gai Tut, a Nuer from Waat in the Upper Nile, and was made up of former Anya Nya who opposed the Addis Ababa Agreement. In 1975 Gai Tut, who had received training in Israel, had led a short-lived mutiny of the Akobo garrison after it received orders to prepare to move to the North. The southerners mutinied, shot their commander and seven men loyal to him, and, with their arms, headed for Ethiopia. Once reconstructed, the Anya Nya II forces reappeared in significant numbers in the Upper Nile region in the early 1980s. The dissidents made contact with Libya in 1981, and their movement began to receive arms in 1982. At first many villages opposed the rebels, but, according to one Westerner who knew the region well, by 1983 "this attitude had changed" and villagers "around Nasir spoke favorably of the guerrillas, contrasting their discipline with the lack of it among the Army."[6] In early 1983 missionaries and international relief workers in Southern Sudan reported that they had "run into Anya Nya II road blocks where they saw military equipment as sophisticated as that used by the regular Sudanese army."[7]

Gai Tut was a confirmed secessionist who sought to entice Garang's followers to his standard, arguing that secession was the only way for the South to preserve its cultural integrity. The issue of unity versus secession was debated vigorously in the rebel camps until February 1984 when Gai Tut was killed during a confrontation with the SPLA. Thereafter, an Anya-Nya II faction joined the SPLA, and a remnant, under the command of William Abdullah Chuol, retired to Malakal where it was soon reconstituted as a militia and used by the army to fight the SPLA. Although Garang consolidated military control, few Southern Sudanese politicians rallied to the SPLA, and most questioned the movement's aims. Some opponents supported separation, whereas others abhorred the SPLA's frequent use of revolutionary Marxist jargon; the split also reflected the deep differences that existed between the Dinka—which dominated the SPLA leadership—and other Southern Sudanese ethnic groups. The South, which contained about 25–30 percent of the nation's population, was a melange of at least forty tribes. Unlike the first civil war, spearheaded by Anya-Nya soldiers born in and operating from Equatoria, the second civil war would be led by Dinka from the Upper Nile and Bahr al-Ghazal. The Dinka were regarded with suspicion by the peoples and politicians of Equatoria, for they comprised about 40 percent of the South's population and contained by far the largest number of highly educated individuals in the South.

Unlike Joseph Lagu, the unsophisticated leader of the Anya-Nya I, Garang was quick to adapt the precepts of modern guerrilla warfare to the Sudanese bush.[8] He could not be bought with offers of political power as Numayri had bought Lagu. Moreover, Garang did not consider the movement a regional revolt; rather, it was a national rebellion opposing Numayri and the northern politicians unwilling to share power with the South. He soon won over many Nuer and Anuak in the Upper Nile and some Taposa of eastern Equatoria—all tribes long considered enemies of the Dinka.[9] The SPLA also attracted some Nuba from South Kordofan and occasional Fur from Darfur. It eventually attracted some Muslims, the most important being Mansour Khalid, who had served in the United Nations and in Numayri's cabinet and who would serve as an SPLA spokesperson. Garang approved the use of Arabic as the national language as long as the Northern Sudanese political leaders rejected claims to racial and religious superiority. The SPLA was obviously a threat to the sectarian parties that dominated the Nile littoral and that held power in Khartoum—power they had been unwilling to share with former slaves (abid) from the deep South.

What appeared to be an isolated mutiny of the Bor garrison soon turned into a terrible civil conflict, and *The New York Times* reported that a wave of forty thousand Sudanese had congregated at Itang, Ethiopia, to escape army attacks on southern villages. A UN official commenting on their growing numbers noted, "The refugees tell much the same story. ... They talk of villages being strafed, crops being burned, women being raped, and the cutting off of hands and torture."[10] Most of the refugees were from the Dinka, Anuak, and Shilluk tribes, and many had walked for up to ninety days to reach Ethiopia. They were the first to flee a conflict that would cause the death of *more than 1.5 million southerners* in a decade distinguished by persistent warfare, drought, famine, and disease.[11]

The September Laws

Numayri began by dismissing the Bor mutiny, and his vice president, the politically ambitious southerner Joseph Lagu, contemptuously referred to it as a local nuisance. Numayri then enacted Presidential Decree Number One of June 1983, which redivided the South; it effectively destroyed the 1972 self-government act and, thus, the Addis Ababa Agreement. Three regions were created—the Upper Nile, Bahr al-Ghazal, and Equatoria—and in what was an obvious political payoff, Lagu emerged as the South's political kingpin. Administratively, redivision was senseless because there were insufficient personnel to administer even a single region. Public services were woefully understaffed. In 1983 Khartoum funded fewer than fifty government doctors and twenty nurses for a population of 4 million people, and areawide there were more than fifteen thousand vacant civil service positions.

Most important, the president's promulgation of the September Laws of 1983 produced an irreversible break with the southern insurgents and solidified the hostility of the southern elites and masses. Government injustices, real and perceived, were encapsulated by Numayri's interpretation and imposition of the Shari'a—the "comprehensive system of personal and public behavior which constitutes the Islamic religious law."[12] The September Laws sanctioned the use of the *hudud*—physical punishments such as flogging, amputation, stoning, and execution—for crimes, which in most Muslim societies was rarely invoked. They also prohibited the sale of alcohol and the collection of interest on debts. The laws were introduced at a time when the Iranian revolution continued to shock the Sudanese because of the depth of its religious commitment and the rejection of Western democracy, and there was growing fear in the South that Islamic fundamentalism would force the same course on the Sudan.

Numayri's first use of the September Laws was utterly bizarre: He ordered the release of thirteen thousand prisoners on the grounds that "they had not been convicted in Islamic Courts in accordance with

Islamic law."[13] Public flogging and amputations followed, much to the disgust of Southern Sudanese accustomed to a more humane secular criminal code and of Muslims who argued that the penalties were contrary to the Quran and to Islamic jurisprudence. Sadiq al-Mahdi, the great-grandson of the nineteenth-century religious leader Muhammad Ahmad ibn Abdallah, called the Mahdi, the divinely guided one and Imam of God, objected strongly. Putative leader of the Ansar, his family's conservative followers, and the leader of the powerful Umma Party, he challenged Numayri's decrees while simultaneously defending the Shari'a: "We believe that organizing the public on the basis of Islam is a popular demand which we believe in and the masses of the Sudanese people believe in. Islamic penalties are matters by which the legislators intend to protect the Islamic system itself. They will be [employed] only as pillars for protecting the Islamic system itself, and are just and wise components of the equations and conditions which Islam has set forth."[14]

Sadiq argued that the September Laws were designed not so much to protect Islam as to ensure and enforce the dictatorial rule of Jaafar Numayri. He soon had ample time to contemplate his opposition, for he and twelve other Islamic notables were arrested for criticizing the president.

Southerners of every ethnic and political persuasion decried the specter raised by the laws of a "rising tide of Muslim fundamentalism" that "threatened to unsettle the spirit of tolerance characteristic of the Addis Ababa decade."[15] The SPLA declared that it would fight until the September Laws were revoked, a condition as important as any found in the SPLA *Manifesto*. And fight it did. Battalions 104 and 105 formed the nucleus of the SPLA and were joined by soldiers from fourteen southern garrisons and Anya Nya II forces. Many southern officers stationed in the North vanished, only to reappear in Ethiopia. The SPLA besieged Nasir and Akobo, fought its first fire fight at Malwal Bar—inflicting heavy casualties—and skirmished with the armed forces at Malakal, Aweil, and Rumbek. By February 1984 the army was "on the defensive."[16] The SPLA routed government forces protecting the Sobat River camp of the Campagnie de Constructions Internationales, the French company digging the vital Jonglei Canal designed to increase water supplies in Northern Sudan and Egypt. The French hastily withdrew, and excavation ceased. To the west an attack on Rub Kona by a rogue element of Anya-Nya II killed four employees of the Chevron Oil Company and caused the termination of the company's successful drilling program in Southern Sudan. River traffic between the North and the South was disrupted, which virtually isolated the southern region except from the air. Government steamers, tugs, and barges were destroyed, and Nile services south of Malakal were paralyzed. Truck routes were harassed and interdicted, particularly the important track from Kosti to Juba, and routes to the Sudan army garrisons were denied to all but the most heavily guarded military convoys. These in turn had to traverse mined roads and ford rivers where bridges had been blown. Finally, the rail line south of the Bahr al-Arab was mined, and a strategic bridge between Aweil and Wau was destroyed.

At first SPLA soldiers possessed only their own weapons, but these were soon augmented with weaponry seized during engagements at Rumbek, Yirol, and elsewhere. Colonel Muammar Qadhafi, the Libyan strongman, was pleased to purvey arms, particularly if doing so would embarrass his enemy, President Numayri. Major Arok Thon Arok, commander of the SPLA's Locust (*Jarad*) battalion, later claimed he was included in a delegation that had traveled to Libya and "obtained large quantities of arms." They ranged "from hand guns to SAM-7 anti-aircraft missiles, with many light weapons in between," and from December 1984 through April 1985 they were shipped through Ethiopia to Garang's headquarters in the Baro Salient.[17]

As the SPLA's firepower increased, some analysts surmised that additional weaponry must have been provided by yet another regional strongman, Ethiopia's Mengistu Haile Miriam.[18] Although Garang continually denied the allegation, the SPLA had no difficulty purchasing small arms in Ethiopia, given the huge quantities provided by the Soviet Union, and Mengistu was happy to discomfort Numayri for harboring Eritrean and Tigrean rebels in the Sudan. Certainly, the SPLA was free to recruit Sudanese refugees in Ethiopia, but more important was Mengistu's willingness to permit SPLA leadership to use Naru, near Addis Ababa, as its headquarters and center for its "clandestine" broadcasts.

Radio SPLA, which began to broadcast short-wave programs in English, Arabic, and Nilotic languages in October 1984, was an effective weapon. It aired during the afternoon "siesta" hours, and it soon won a large audience among northerners because it covered happenings in Khartoum that were never reported in a media under Numayri's control. Radio SPLA reiterated ad extremum that the movement was national in scope, open to all, and free of racial, religious and regional prejudice. The goals expressed in the SPLA-SPLM *Manifesto* were reiterated until most Sudanese were aware that the SPLA opposed the partition of Sudan, favored regional power sharing in the political and economic life of the country, and proposed greater autonomy for the South in administrative and military affairs, the end to military agreements with the Sudan's Arab neighbors, and an end to the September Laws. The radio pounded away at Muslim extremists and their obvious efforts to create an Islamic

Republic of the Sudan and to make Khartoum an Islamic city. If the September Laws were applicable in Khartoum, the nation's capital, Radio SPLA warned they would perforce apply to other regions as well.

In counterpoint, Muslim extremists branded Garang a Marxist—to be destroyed along with all Sudanese Communists. Despite Garang's denials and efforts to address this issue on Radio SPLA, analysts both within and outside the Sudan, including those who had no use for the Muslim Brothers or their movement, questioned his ideology. Clearly, the Ethiopian connection necessitated a certain amount of Marxist rhetoric, but Garang was never the Marxist or socialist ideologue his enemies, including enemies he would make within the SPLA, made him out to be. In time the arguments were vitiated, as Garang's economic philosophy expanded with the times and melded aspects of socialism and capitalism. Even Joseph Lagu, who had come to detest and fear Garang, denied that his former protégé was a Communist: "He has been with me and been one of my students before and I didn't see that Marxism and Communism very clearly defined in him at the time. Well, after launching his movement, for matters of convenience, he could have as well associated himself with Communists or pretended to do so, if by that he could gain anything from them. That is what I would say [is] the type of Communist he may be. I still doubt if he is a Communist really by conviction."[19]

Civil War

Trained as a regular army to fight conventional wars, the Sudan army was ill-equipped to combat the highly mobile and elusive insurgents. Following a series of defeats in 1984, General Swar al-Dahab was appointed defense minister and was charged with reversing the deteriorating military situation "in the civil war in the south."[20] Swar al-Dahab armed existing troops and created new militias from among the Baqqara Arabs of southern Kordofan and Darfur provinces. In the 1980s these traditional enemies of the Dinka tribe had greatly expanded the southward movement of their herds, and by 1984 armed bands threatened Dinka pastures and villages south of the Bahr al-Arab River—a physical feature that for more than two centuries had divided North from South and the Baqqara from the Dinka.

During the later years of the Anglo-Egyptian Condominium, peace was imposed on the frontier thanks to the great Baqqara and Dinka leaders, Babu Nimr and Deng Majok. Acts of violence were tempered by negotiation, and fines were imposed on transgressors. By 1984, however, the region was devoid of thoughtful leaders, and there was a reversion to a predatory state of nature in which the better armed Arabs seemed certain to prevail. Young, unruly, and trained to fight, the Baqqara had been the shock troops of the nineteenth-century armies of the Mahdi, and his successor Khalifa Abd Allahi. Now, in the twentieth century, Numayri and his instrument, Swar al-Dahab, re-created that whirlwind of destruction. The rough equilibrium that had existed for more than half a century along the Kordofan-Bahr al-Ghazal frontier was shattered almost overnight when the Baqqara were provided with automatic weapons. Equipped with new weaponry and driven by drought, the *murahileen*, as the Baqqara Arab raiders were called, surged into the Bahr al-Ghazal and the northern Upper Nile during the winter of 1983–1984. Scores of villages were destroyed and thousands of Dinka were slaughtered. Cattle were rustled, and women and children were carried off to the North. Within a year the *murahileen* were raiding as far south as Wau in Bahr al-Ghazal and Bentiu in the Upper Nile and as far east as Nile villages north of Malakal.

Through 1984, the *murahileen* of the Rizayqat and Missiriya Baqqara plundered and killed with impunity. It was indiscriminate slaughter, and acts of rapacity, little short of genocide, were rationalized by the need to destroy the SPLA's support base. Simplified, government thinking went as follows: John Garang is a Dinka; if John Garang is a Dinka, then all Dinka are SPLA supporters; thus, the Dinka homeland must be laid waste and the people extirpated. In 1985, in response to pleas from his fellow Dinka for assistance, Garang strengthened the SPLA units in Bahr al-Ghazal. By year's end they had severely mauled an ill-disciplined *murahileen* band operating southeast of Abyei, and for the first time the raiders were driven back across Bahr al-Arab. But the damage had been done. The land from Malakal to upper Bahr al-Arab lay devastated, the populace was decimated, the cattle were stolen, the soil was uncultivated. The stench of death hung heavily over the land, and the tragic scene was compounded by a killer drought.

Drought and Famine in the Southern Sudan

Simultaneous with early raids by Baqqara militia into Bahr al-Ghazal, a famine of incredible magnitude was sweeping across Africa's Sahilian belt. A prolonged drought had struck a score of African nations and placed at risk more than 150 million people. The catastrophe shocked the world community although scientists had been studying the effects of drought and desertification in the Sahil region for more than three decades. A UN Conference on Desertification concluded in 1977 that traditional herding practices were rapidly removing the desert cover, and it predicted that considerable financing would be required to halt the encroachment of the Sahara Desert. In 1980 a "Plan of Action" for Africa emerged from a meeting in Lagos, Nigeria, in which it was argued that drought and desertification were Africa's worst enemies.

Ironically, in that same year Sudan's Sahil suffered the first of five consecutive years of minimal rainfall. Even the harvest of millet, a drought-resistant crop hardier than dura, the Sudanese sorghum and staple food for millions, failed throughout much of northern Darfur and Kordofan. Without rain, the camel nomads living on the margin of the Sudan's Libyan Desert and the pastoralists in the northern Sahil pressed south into Baqqara pasture land. The Baqqara, in turn, began their southward migration earlier than usual; south of Bahr al-Arab they came into conflict with the Dinka, and to the west, in Darfur, they encroached upon the cultivation areas of the sedentary Fur.

In northern Darfur rainfall measured in El Fasher in 1983 was "down to 83 mm" compared with an average of 380 mm from 1941 to 1980.[21] Regional officials and international monitoring agencies warned Khartoum that if no food aid was forthcoming, a catastrophe was certain. Numayri ignored the drought, but the Sudanese public was shown "a nightly film of starving Ethiopians, with a commentary attacking the Addis Ababa Government for not feeding its people."[22] Although the government stalled, in January 1984 the U.S. Agency for International Development office in Sudan (USAID-Sudan) sent a team to investigate reports of crop failures. It found that the situation in Darfur and Kordofan was desperate and urged USAID leadership in Washington (AID-Washington) to ship emergency food aid. AID-Washington, which was the first institution in the West to respond to the drought, approved the shipment of some 82,000 tons of sorghum. Unfortunately, the first ship did not arrive in Port Sudan until November 1984, and only a trickle of food aid had been delivered to the needy by year's end.

In 1984 the rains that initiate the planting season in Equatoria and move slowly northward through the Savannah to the Sahil failed almost everywhere. In western Sudan some 6 million inhabitants of Kordofan and Darfur began to experience the most severe drought and famine conditions village elders could recall. Families had sowed their crops of millet and sorghum. They planted once, then again, and yet again; when forced to surrender to the drought, thousands of households had no food reserves. Nor could families survive by selling their livestock because when drought had struck the West in the late 1970s, and then persisted, herders and camel nomads had sold their stock for a pittance. The money evaporated as the price of cereals began to soar, and the widespread slaughter and death of much of the nation's livestock created tremendous dislocations within the economy of the western provinces.

The drought was implacable not only in Sudan but in eastern Chad as well; it propelled an army of starving Chadians across the border in search of food and aggravated the already perilous situation in westernmost Darfur. The 1984–1985 harvest (basically, October 1984 through

January 1985) was a disaster. Drought had also spread through Sudan's rain fed and mechanized rain fed cultivation areas, which accounted for some 80 percent of cereal grains harvested. They, too, were vulnerable, given the annual variations in rainfall, which precluded the extensive use of hybrid seed and chemical fertilizers. Rather than a yield of 3 million tons of cereals, which would have guaranteed self-sufficiency, only 1.5 million were harvested.

The governor of Darfur, Ahmed Ibrahim Diraige, who had submitted to Khartoum "and to all embassies and international organizations as early as October 1983" a comprehensive report of the impending disaster, resigned in 1984 to protest and publicize Numayri's "clamp down and persecution" of conscientious Sudanese "who called for publicity and international help."[23] By December 1984 some 300,000 people were on the move, and village and nomadic societies in Darfur and Kordofan slowly began to disintegrate. In the rural councils of Bara, Sodiri, and Umm Ruwaba in northern Kordofan, existing grain supplies were calculated in days and weeks, and desperate families fled to El Obeid and Omdurman where they congregated in large settlements of displaced persons. Still, Numayri remained impassive, seemingly oblivious to the widespread misery and death. It was not until late 1984, when some 50,000 starving people were encamped around Omdurman, that the effects of the unyielding drought were made manifest to the outside world. Thereafter, no one could protect Numayri from the acid pens of the international press once journalists learned that he was absolutely unmoved by the tragedy. By March 1985 international private voluntary organizations (PVOs) such as the Cooperative for American Relief Everywhere (CARE) and Oxford Famine Relief (OXFAM) were at work in the West, and they reported that in Darfur a million people faced starvation since they could no longer employ traditional survival strategies.

International Aid Efforts

This catastrophe, plus the lack of a strategic reserve, virtually demanded international assistance if famine deaths on a mammoth scale were to be prevented. Goaded from all sides, Numayri turned to what was then his most generous benefactor, the United States. Prior to 1977, the relationship between the two countries had been barely civil, and only $138 million in U.S. foreign aid and military assistance had been disbursed between 1956 and 1978. As Sudan joined with Egypt and the United States to thwart Libyan ambition, the policy reversal did not go unrewarded. Once Numayri—alone among leaders of other Arab states—supported the Camp David Accords ending the state of war between Egypt and Israel, the Carter administration opened the foreign aid floodgates.

Support arrived at a time when the Sudanese economy was in serious trouble. During Numayri's tenure the government budget deficit had risen from 3 percent of national income in 1970 to 15 percent in 1980; its balance-of-payments deficit "rose from $25 million to $500 million," and the country's foreign debt "rose from $85 million to $8 billion in the same period."[24] The economy was granted a reprieve when it received approximately $1 billion in U.S. foreign aid in the period 1979–1983. Specifically, an Economic Support Fund (ESF) administered by USAID-Sudan provided $506.3 million in the period 1980–1985. Funds were disbursed in cash transfers and commodity import financing—some of which were allocated for the purchase of petroleum imports. U.S. largesse continued despite a General Accounting Office finding that Sudan had not complied with AID's condition to assist private enterprise: Commodity imports were supposed to stimulate the private sector, but in 1983 and 1984, $99 million of $122.3 million provided had been allocated to government parastatal enterprises. As far as some AID-Washington officials were concerned, ESF was viewed "primarily as a means of political support for a friendly government rather than as a vehicle for initiating economic reforms."[25]

USAID-Sudan advised Washington in 1984 that Sudan was undertaking economic policy initiatives designed to reduce its domestic subsidies. Certainly, the government had slightly reduced the bread subsidy and had instituted export production incentives, but such actions were negated by government tinkering with foreign exchange rates. In fact, Sudan's foreign debt was approaching $10 billion, and its internal debt was staggering. Optimism that the Sudanese economy would improve was not based on any objective reality. The heart of the Sudanese economy was agriculture, and world prices, especially for cotton, were markedly depressed. Also, as the army had been forced on the defensive in the South, the military budget had been increased, and funds had been subtracted from the agricultural sector. Numayri's plan to use oil revenues to encourage agricultural productivity had been frustrated by war in the South, and for that reason more than any other, the promise of at least $6 billion in loans from Arab banks was not realized.

Despite a large infusion of foreign aid since 1980 and its support for Numayri in the face of Qadhafi's threats to Darfur, in 1984 the United States still enjoyed little economic leverage in Khartoum. When AID-Washington and the International Monetary Fund (IMF) insisted that Numayri reduce his bloated bureaucracy and divest its many unproductive parastatals, the dictator refused. Numayri was able to ignore his critics so long as his government was comfortably endowed with loans and grants from Asian, Arab, and Western sources and UN agencies and also received significant remittances from Sudanese working abroad.

Indeed, Sudan's economic development projects portfolio was sufficiently large in 1984 to ensure massive inefficiencies and corruption. Ironically, as drought raged in Sudan's Sahil the United States was extending a direct grant of $38 million in 1984 for balance-of-payments purposes (and it dispensed millions of dollars from 1984 through 1986 to enable Sudan to purchase petroleum products).

Often lost amid the military and economic development packages is the fact that, in 1984, AID-Washington first began to program substantial food aid for Sudan. Shipments were filtered through USAID-Sudan by means of the Agricultural Trade Development Assistance Act of 1954, better known as Public Law 83-480 (PL-480), a billion-dollar annual aid program that from its inception has accounted for about 10 percent of U.S. foreign aid. A PL-480 program is suggested by USAID missions, approved by AID-Washington, the U.S. State Department, and the U.S. Department of Agriculture, and reviewed by the U.S. Congress. The latter organizations maintained an oversight capacity to ensure that food aid served one or several priorities—economic development, humanitarian assistance, export market development, or a vague category that incorporated almost anything—foreign policy goals. PL-480 commodities were then distributed through the U.S. Food for Peace Program and in accordance with approved country proposals. Tangentially, the program helped to reduce U.S. farm surpluses, maintained adequate price supports to U.S. farmers, and built export markets for U.S. farm products.

In the 1980s, PL-480 was utilized in two important ways in Sudan. Through PL-480 *Title I*, USAID-Sudan offered the government wheat and wheat flour at bargain prices through a government-to-government sales program. Sales were based on easy repayment terms—usually a ten-year grace period with forty years to pay and interest rates of 2–4 percent per annum. This aspect of PL-480 helped to speed a dietary metamorphosis in the Sudan because Khartoum and the northern cities reduced sorghum consumption and began to consume cheap subsidized bread made from imported wheat. The conversion was inexorable, and the insatiable demand for wheat bread defied thousands of years of traditional dietary tastes. Through PL-480 *Title II*, USAID-Sudan provided commodities to various PVOs and UN agencies for needy Sudanese.

For USAID-Sudan two dark clouds were visible on the Sudanese horizon. The first was the problem of the South. By 1984 the fighting had forced an end to USAID-Sudan projects for road construction and agricultural development in Equatoria. Plans to improve transport in the Upper Nile region were deferred and field surveys terminated as the SPLA roamed through the countryside with increasing impunity. With more reason than foresight, USAID-Sudan still argued that "despite a gloomy short term prognostication, the South must become the seat of an expanded program that [will command] a major portion of our attention when a political reconciliation is achieved."[26] The second dark cloud was the severe drought in the Horn of Africa. In 1983 the United States had shipped 400,000 tons of food aid to Ethiopia as part of an international effort to assist some 10 million people threatened by starvation. No sooner had that program been implemented than USAID-Sudan had received scattered reports that Sudan's 1983–1984 crop harvest would fall well below the average and responded with shipments of sorghum. Most families had survived to plant another crop in 1984, but again the harvest had failed. Practically no food reserves remained in Kordofan, Darfur, and the Red Sea provinces. Even before the first ship carrying U.S. PL-480 sorghum arrived in Port Sudan in November 1984, USAID-Sudan was considering yet another program. It contracted with CARE to supervise the distribution of its food to the West, and U.S. red-hulled sorghum, which contrasted with the white dura consumed by most Sudanese, was soon making its way. To many starving Sudanese this sorghum assumed mystical properties, including those associated with fertility and sexual prowess, and in time came to be called "Reagan dura," a nickname that spread throughout Sudan.

In some of the more stricken villages, such as those in the Bara district of northern Kordofan, families had no food, but they did have funds to pay for it. In such cases food aid was sold at greatly subsidized prices, and the funds were used to pay the enormous expense of transporting food by means of an antiquated railroad system or unimproved roads. As the disaster relief program evolved, about half of the USAID sorghum was sold at cost less transport, 35 percent was given out free, and 15 percent was discounted. At El Obeid the UN Children's Emergency Relief Fund (UNICEF) and OXFAM established a Drought Monitoring and Nutritional Surveillance Unit to direct food supplies to the neediest towns, villages, and congregations of displaced persons. El Obeid itself was among the most needy, and between 25 November and 11 December over eight thousand people were registered at its displaced camp alone. The encampment soon exceeded 60,000 displaced persons and panic ensued among the townspeople when the municipal water system was nearly drained. Among the displaced persons, more than 50 percent of the children were diagnosed as either moderately or severely malnourished, and infant feeding programs were introduced and a health clinic established. Elsewhere, at Umm Ruwaba and En Nahud, thousands more settled into displaced camps; UNICEF and the Sudan Ministry of Health provided essential vaccines and pharmaceuticals, and the Sudanese Red Crescent distributed all of its available tents. In Darfur inaccessible communities along the southwestern border with Chad were supplied by cargo helicopters and a C-130 cargo plane funded by the

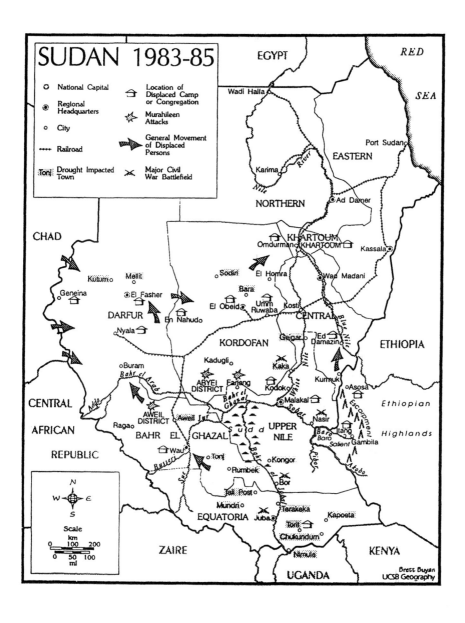

SUDAN 1983-85

National Capital

Regional Headquarters

City

Railroad

Toni Drought Impacted Town

Location of Displaced Camp or Congregation

Murahileen Attacks

General Movement of Displaced Persons

Major Civil War Battlefield

EGYPT

RED

SEA

Wadi Halfa

Port Sudan

EASTERN

Karima

Nile River

Ad Damer

Kassala

NORTHERN

KHARTOUM
Omdurman KHARTOUM

CHAD

Kutum o   Meliit

Geneina

El Fasher

DARFUR   En Nahudo

Nyala

Sodiri   El Homra

Wad Madani

Bara

El Obeid   Umm Ruwaba   Kosti

CENTRAL

Blue Nile

Buram

Kadugli

Bahr el Arab

ABYEI DISTRICT   Fanjang

CENTRAL

AWEIL DISTRICT

AFRICAN   Ragao

Aweil Isr

Geigar   Ed Damazin

ETHIOPIA

Kaka

Kodoko

Kurmuk

Asosa

Ethiopian

Malakal

Highlands

BAHR EL   GHAZAL

REPUBLIC

Wau

Sudd   UPPER NILE

Nasir

Itang

Baro   Boro

Gambila

Salient

Toni

Kongor

Rumbek

Bor

N
W—E
S

Scale
km
0 100 200
0 50 100
ml

Jali Post

Mundri

EQUATORIA   Juba

ZAIRE

Terakeka   Kaposta

Toni

Chukundum

KENYA

Nimule

UGANDA

Brett Buyan
UCSB Geography

European Community; a food airlift was also used to relieve Geneina in westernmost Sudan, where it was reported in July 1985 that one hundred famine-stricken people were dying daily.

Although the 1984 drought had not spared the South, the disaster relief program operated solely in Northern Sudan. It was complex and very expensive, but it did succeed in getting food to the needy despite major obstacles to transportation in Africa's largest nation. By June 1985, 220,000 tons of food in Port Sudan were awaiting shipment West, and another 200,000 tons were jammed in the pipeline between the port and the western provinces. USAID had misplaced much of its hope for transporting food shipments on the railroad, but ancient rolling stock, inefficiency, and corruption slowed movement by rail to a crawl. A once efficient, reliable and comfortable means of transporting people and goods, one in which the British builders had taken enormous pride, had been replaced by a government parastatal characterized by a bloated bureaucracy and the Railway Worker's Union's unrestrained featherbedding. After utilizing the rail system for two months in December 1984 and January 1985, the Sudan Railways Corporation "abruptly ceased honoring its contract" with the donor agencies despite its "doubling of normal freight rates."[27] The corporation insisted that the government needed the freight cars to transport wheat from Port Sudan and sugar throughout the North. The ensuing slowdown in 1985 ended any USAID hope that it would be able to stockpile sorghum in the west before the onset of the spring rains, if indeed they came.

In Port Sudan 15,000 tons of food could be off-loaded on a normal day, but rail capacity inland rarely exceeded 2,000 tons. Thus, when 400,000 tons of Reagan dura arrived at Port Sudan in May and June 1985, the transport system was completely overwhelmed. When the railway service stalled, thirty-ton trucks were loaded at the port's warehouses and sent to Kosti; there, commodities were reloaded aboard hundreds of five to eight ton market trucks ("*suq* lorries") for distribution in northern Kordofan or were sent by rail to Nyala in southern Darfur. Trucking contractors, not surprisingly, raised their freight rates, because there was great competition for their use for other purposes. When trucking slowed and could not keep pace with ship discharges, USAID-contracted warehouses literally overflowed with PL-480 grain. Finally, when train service improved, corruption followed. In one notorious example, sugar rather than sorghum was surreptitiously moved to Nyala. In another, a freight train arrived in Nyala completely empty at a time when the situation in Darfur had become so desperate that the European Community was airlifting food to the region at enormous expense.

The Sudan drought and famine, the loss of life, an expensive disaster relief program, and the media claims of mismanagement all combined to create a powerful magnet that attracted U.S. politicians and congressional staff. As had occurred in Ethiopia during the 1983–1984 drought, Sudan became a popular place to visit and to be photographed. In November 1984 Senator Ted Kennedy and his entourage, complete with a personal photographer—which, like diarrhea, was a mandatory accompaniment for politicians and VIPs—became the first of many U.S. senators and representatives to arrive in Khartoum to see for themselves what was occurring in Sudan. When Senator Kennedy asked if he could stay overnight in a Sudanese village in order to gain a better understanding of the drought and its effects, his request was politely declined for reasons of "security." Thereafter, "security" was the common rationale employed by government officials to prohibit or limit the access of curious politicians, prying journalists, and aid workers to those sensitive areas most severely affected by drought and famine.

Both the climax and the denouement of the drought in the North occurred in 1985. The rains returned to the western provinces and the Red Sea Hills, and the displaced quickly departed for their villages. To the west the rains were also good, and the camps were soon depopulated. Perhaps as many as 250,000 people died—no one will ever know for certain—but the disaster relief program had still managed to save tens of thousands of lives. In certain instances the miraculous did indeed occur. If trucks could not move helicopters, camels, and donkeys were employed. Where the decrepit narrow-gauge railroad failed, it was repaired. When truckers were not interested in making long hauls, they were paid premium rates to change their minds. When the government ran out of diesel fuel, USAID-Sudan imported it. The USAID program alone cost a quarter of a billion dollars, and even its detractors were forced to admit that it was a major miracle that so much was accomplished in so short a time. It was not a pretty program nor was it efficient—or so the auditors complained. They were unimpressed with USAID-Sudan's accounting—at one time in 1985 some three hundred freight cars carrying 8,000 tons of food were "lost" somewhere along the 600 miles of rail between Port Sudan and Nyala.[28] Although USAID-Sudan received the brunt of the criticism, it in fact had only arranged for the receipt of commodities and then paid for their onward shipment. Logistics were actually supervised by the government's nascent and inexperienced Food Aid National Administration and USAID contractors. Given the urgency, USAID had cut every corner imaginable; USAID-Sudan Director Dr. William Brown was fanatically committed to saving lives and so was his staff, and in the end they did just that. USAID-Sudan, the principal donor, accounted for more than 425,000 tons

TABLE 1.1 1985 USAID-Sudan Food Aid Program Commodity Deliveries and Transport Costs (in $000)

	Sorghum (Tons)	Other (Tons)	Cost of Commodity	Cost of Transport	Total Cost
North Region					
Darfur (SCF/UK)[a]	188,000	5,970	47.6	78.5	126.1
Other					
(CARE,UNWFP)[b]	231,000	17,920	67.1	94.3	161.4
Total North	419,000	23,890	114.7	172.8	287.5
South	6,000	510	1.8	–	1.8

[a] Managed by Save the Children Foundation of the United Kingdom.
[b] CARE International, and the UN/World Food Program.
Source: USAID-Khartoum, 1986.

of food aid, and the relief program itself had provided essential rations for an estimated 2.5 million people at a time of desperate need (see Table 1.1).

The End of the Numayri Era

Amidst the frenetic bustle of relief activity and to the great relief of most Sudanese, President Jaafar Numayri was overthrown on 6 April 1985. His relentless imposition of the *hudud*; his abrogation of the Addis Ababa Agreement; his unilateral decrees that led to the renewal of the civil war; his continuation of the state of emergency and the increase in the malevolent activities of the security service; his condoning the spiraling inflation, the devaluation of the Sudanese pound, and the reduction in subsidies; his expulsion of the Muslim Brothers from the Sudan Socialist Union in 1985; his demoralized and discontented army; and, finally, his inept handling of the 1984–1985 drought and famine—each contributed in its own way to his downfall. Indeed, given the litany of his abuses and failures, the fact that he remained in power as long as he did is probably best explained by U.S. financial support and the stoic patience for which the Sudanese are well-known. His fall came as he was on a visit to the United States to mend political fences and to request an increase in foreign aid. In his absence the Union of Engineers initiated a general strike on 3 April, and for three days students, professionals, and the discontented took control of Khartoum. When the army refused to intervene, Numayri was washed away by a tide of enemies demanding the return of civilian rule. For the time being this was not to be, because the army joined the popular revolution only in order to dominate it. Led by General Swar al-Dahab, Numayri's chief of staff, a Transitional Military Council (TMC) took control; cognizant of the popular will, which had coalesced as the National Alliance for National Salvation, the TMC promised that it would rule for only one year before returning the country to civilian government. The generals were, in fact, reluctant to pick up the pieces from the wreckage that Numayri had left behind.

The TMC efficiently dismantled the cumbersome edifice of the Sudanese Socialist Union but appeared to have few other policies, either domestic or foreign. It restored civil liberties, press freedom was guaranteed, political prisoners were released, and the secret police was disbanded. Political parties were permitted to re-form in anticipation of 1986 elections. The army, however, would let no one take advantage of the ebullient atmosphere in order to disturb law and order. When the Muslim Brothers demanded the retention of Shari'a, the TMC dealt harshly with street demonstrators and arrested their leader, Dr. Hassan al-Turabi, who was campaigning "for the full restoration of Shari'a law," an action the TMC knew "would rule out any reconciliation with the South."[29] Yet even though the generals would not impose the *hudud*, they refused to abandon the September Laws and rejected the SPLA demand that they do so. Instead, the TMC proposed a national conference on the South, but nothing ever came of it. The TMC failed to improve relations with Ethiopia, Egypt, or the United States, and relations with the latter cooled rapidly as the army turned to Colonel Qadhafi and played the pan-Arab card in its search for weapons. Qadhafi ceased to support the SPLA and began to woo the TMC with oil and arms.

Although the United States was very concerned about a military protocol signed with Libya in June 1985, it still continued its substantial foreign aid program. The TMC's humanitarian response to the disaster relief program offered an immediate improvement over the Numayri regime, and in July AID-Washington announced it would continue the program for which it had already earmarked 940,000 tons of PL-480 Title I and II commodities. Nearly 600,000 tons had been distributed or were stored in Port Sudan, and to improve future deliveries, AID-Washington pledged $200 million to purchase fuel and spare parts for the railways and offered to deliver one hundred trucks to transport supplies.[30] At an NGO conference held in Khartoum in July, interim Prime Minister Muhammad Dafa'allah blamed the regime for concealing the famine, "a fact that resulted in difficulties in distributing relief material sent by fraternal countries," and promised that his government would improve its performance and its relations with the donor agencies.[31]

Decrying the deaths "of thousands of citizens" and Numayri's admission, which "had come too late," Dafa'allah warned that many thousands of citizens were still at risk. However, fortune smiled on the TMC, the donors, and the West, as the early rains were good and there was the promise of the first good harvest in years. USAID distributed over seven thousand tons of seed grain, and it was soon noted that cultivation was extensive throughout the North. In Kordofan, where trucks could reach drought-impacted villages more easily, the situation improved rapidly, and displaced camps in El Obeid and Omdurman were soon empty. In northern Darfur, however, thousands returned to villages only to find that the first promise of good crops was followed by searing heat and no rain. NGOs cautioned that the 1985–1986 harvest would again be much less than the annual average and that an estimated 400,000 tons of relief grain would still be needed in 1986.

Disaster in the West Now Magnified by That in the South

The problem in Darfur, however, paled in comparison to the imminent catastrophe in the South. The war between the SPLA and the *murahileen* was the continuation of an epochal struggle between Arab in the North and African in the South for territorial hegemony. In its most elemental form, this struggle again pitted the most ferocious of the Arab tribes, the Baqqara cattle nomads of Kordofan and Darfur, against the Dinka, the largest of the African tribes in the Southern Sudan. By the fall of 1985 the SPLA had increased its presence along the Bahr al-Arab frontier—an area expatriate agencies termed the Transition Zone—and SPLA attacks began to exacerbate already existing food shortages in Bahr al-Ghazal and the Upper Nile. Indeed, the war could not have come at a worse time, because the South's population was growing faster than food production, and only western Equatoria and the northern Upper Nile were considered self-sufficient. In any year some part of the South could be expected to suffer severe food shortages, and Nilotes in need had customarily bartered cattle for Arab grain; thus villages in southern Kordofan and the northern Upper Nile had evolved into seasonal markets where Nuer, Dinka, and Shilluk exchanged goods with northern traders (*jallaba*). By 1985 the insurgency had greatly reduced commercial intercourse, and the South's population—youthful, rural, predominantly illiterate, and very poor—was truly ill prepared to withstand the combination of famine and civil war.

In 1984 the rains also failed throughout much of Southern Sudan. Officials in Bahr al-Ghazal recorded only some 20 percent of the average annual rainfall, and those in the Upper Nile reported little more. Crops withered, and the harvest was one of the poorest in memory. It was, of course, not the first time crops had failed, and over the generations the Dinka had evolved their own survival strategies—but those strategies, however, only served in time of peace. The 1984 drought in Kordofan and Darfur had led the Baqqara to spend much of that year south of Bahr al-Arab where their *murahileen* pillaged widely. From Tonj District the government received a report that "every member from that destroyed area ran away for safety," and no crops were cultivated.[32] It was an incredible situation, for in the twentieth century depredations had occurred on a relatively limited scale and were restricted by the presence of the Condominium government, strong Arab and African chieftains, and the rough equilibrium of strength between Baqqara and Dinka. Nilotes driven from their villages survived on wild plants, roots, and fish until order was reestablished. The *murahileen*, with their automatic weapons and the silent blessing of the government, not only destroyed the balance of power but also wreaked devastation on such a wide scale that the traditional means of survival proved inadequate. Villagers were forced to seek shelter with extended family members who had not been victimized by *murahileen,* and thousands of Dinka fled to towns and cities where they became dependent upon charity. When the Bahr al-Ghazal government received no assistance from Khartoum, many of these refugees congregated in miserable displaced persons camps where they hoped to receive food aid from Sudanese Christian charities or expatriate aid agencies. In order to survive, many of the most desperate chose to cross the Bahr al-Arab into southern Kordofan where they indentured themselves as menial laborers in the fields of the Baqqara Arabs.

In the Upper Nile drought and insecurity also ravaged the land and the people. By the summer of 1984 province administrators, like their counterparts in Bahr al-Ghazal, were certain that the harvest would be disastrous, but their warnings went unheeded in Khartoum.[33] Indeed, the rains failed, and the river levels dropped precipitously. Barges that could carry grain from Kosti, Rabak, and Renk to Malakal and the Sobat River region were unable to make the passage. Regionwide the SPLA had ceased to be an annoyance and instead had become downright dangerous. Its units sank a number of large river craft south of Malakal, and by 1985 the rebels had gained the upper hand in the battle for the Sudd. Still, as in Bahr al-Ghazal, thousands of Dinka and Nuer flocked into the towns seeking food and safety, and "approximately sixty thousand Sudanese" from the eastern Upper Nile fled to Ethiopia because of "unsettling political and economic conditions in southern Sudan."[34] By autumn 1984 food scarcity and insecurity produced the first significant movement of displaced persons to the North, and thousands of Dinka, Nuer, and Shilluk began to appear in Renk, Kosti, and Khartoum. Those who remained behind employed such traditional practices as breaking open anthills in search of grain and grubs and collecting minuscule amounts of edible grass seed.

Although less hard hit in 1984 than either the Upper Nile or Bahr al-Ghazal, Equatoria suffered a prolonged drought that had a severe impact on at least half of its population. East of the Nile massive crop failures were reported around Kapoeta where 100,000 Taposa required assistance. In Torit the groundnut crop withered; in Nimule the maize, groundnut, and bulrush millet crops were hard hit; over 30,000 hungry southerners were gathered at Ikotos. West of the Nile the rains ceased in September, adversely affecting that region's sorghum and cassava crops. To the north in Terekeka and Tali the seasonal rivers dried up early, and cattle therefore had to be driven long distances in search of water. By fall 64,000 displaced were congregated in Juba, 52,000 at Terekeka, and to the west another 53,000 in Mundri.[35]

Despite all of their pleas for food aid, none of the three southern provinces received help from Khartoum in 1984. Surrounded by misery, district commissioners and the regional governors warned that with having no regional food reserve, the months preceding the 1985 harvest would be difficult. On 4 January 1985 Aldo Adjo Deng, acting governor of Bahr al-Ghazal, reported to the Ministry of Agriculture and Natural Resources that deaths from starvation were occurring in Rumbek and that "as far as essential food stuffs are concerned, particularly dura, [regional supplies] are very meager indeed." He added: "What we have transported to Rumbek was the whole quantity we have in stock in Wau. ...We are strongly asking your excellency to put this case forward to the National Relief Committee to urgently send assistance, to Lakes Province, the only stricken part of our region."[36] Assistance did not arrive. By April 1985 starving people in Rumbek were "dying daily," and the commissioner of the Lakes District reported that "though the rains are now falling the people have no seeds for cultivation as there is nothing even to eat."[37]

The International Response

The reports of starvation in the South mobilized the relief agencies to action. The International Commission for the Red Cross of Geneva (ICRC) and UNICEF joined together in May 1985 to provide a first-hand report to donors in Khartoum. Ruedi Kueng, the ICRC director in Sudan, and Egil Hagen of UNICEF began at Torit where they met with Colonel Avelino Angaya, commissioner of eastern Equatoria, who demanded 40,000 tons of sorghum. Some villages in eastern Equatoria were unquestionably facing massive starvation, for there was little food and the spring rains were late. Thus, immediate food aid was urged by Kueng and Hagen but in more reasonable proportions. In Malakal, TMC Military Governor Major General Abd al-Salaam Ahmed Salih insisted that his town badly needed food and medicines. Concerned that he would be blamed for the famine in Malakal and for any deaths attributed to it, the governor urged the immediate shipment of food by barge from Kosti and medical supplies for the decrepit, rat-infested Malakal hospital. The hospital had once been one of the South's most modern facilities, capable of caring for five hundred patients a day; it had survived minus trained staff, pharmaceuticals, and nutritional products—all a testimony to southern neglect by northern governments. Kueng and Hagen promised to dispatch immediately five hundred tons of sorghum and medical supplies so long as the army provided protection and the Kosti tug captains were willing (or forced) to risk the passage.

On June 1 the team was in Aweil where at least nine hundred tons of food aid was urgently needed; it could be transported by rail from western relief stocks located in Babanusa if the Sudan Railways Corporation would provide the trains. The corporation had, however, only a handful of diesel engines for use on the narrow-gauge track between Babanusa and Aweil, and the aid donors found these engines always seemed to be in use somewhere else. Once the engines were available, the army would procrastinate until it could form a "convoy"—three diesel engines and ninety boxcars hauling a maximum of 2,700 tons of cargo—and then it would claim it had insufficient military personnel to escort the train convoy to Aweil. Thus, although relief food moved through Babanusa to the drought-stricken West, the hungry in Aweil were isolated, and the town was fast becoming a microcosm of the savagery unleashed in Southern Sudan because of famine, starvation, and war.

Situated at the center of the great arc of the Dinka people, which sweeps east to west and north to Bahr al-Arab, Aweil witnessed some of the most ferocious depredations of the Baqqara raiders. Unfortunately, the cruelty of the *murahileen* was often copied in Aweil by government officials and military officers, whose brutality was forged in ethnic and cultural prejudice unmitigated by their presumed professionalism. The most notorious of these was Colonel Isaiah Paul, a Zande from Yambio, who detested his people's historic enemy, the Dinka. A former Anya-Nya, Paul was the commander of the Aweil garrison from 1982 to 1985, during which time he was responsible for a series of atrocities, particularly when he was drunk—which he was frequently. One incident involved the brilliant Deng Akot, a graduate of Cairo University, who was in charge of the civil service. He was tied to the ground and run over by a tank. The atrocity precipitated a massive desertion of young Dinka from their homelands to the SPLA. Colonel Paul was saved from being cashiered for malfeasance and drunkenness by his uncle, Allison Magaya, who rose to the rank of major general and turned western Equatoria into his personal fiefdom after being named its army commander.

From Aweil, Kueng and Hagen continued on to Rumbek, where they were shocked by the famine conditions in the town and scenes of people "dying on the street due to hunger."[38] Children with match stick limbs were curled up in the dust to die, and their parents had barely enough strength to beg for food. This was a terrible portent of even more grisly scenes to follow. Rumbek was an important military garrison that the SPLA had besieged since July 1983. A series of battles had nearly destroyed the town and the famous Rumbek secondary school. The last engagement occurred early in 1985 when there were 20,000 people in town, half of them displaced persons. When the attack ceased, the dearth of food drove many to Wau, the shops closed, and only the army had adequate food supplies. The hungry began to die in March, and those remaining despaired of help, for the SPLA had mined all roads leading to Rumbek. The army commander urged an immediate airdrop; the investigators returned to Khartoum, where their report awakened the donor agencies to the fact that famine conditions in the South were as bad as those in Kordofan and Darfur. Nevertheless, the NGOs, enmeshed in a complicated western relief program, were slow to respond to the Keung-Hagen recommendations and the need for famine relief in Southern Sudan.

The Catholic Relief Services (CRS), a U.S. nonprofit NGO whose mission is to support Catholic Church charities abroad, was the first to react to the dreadful famine situation in Tonj and Rumbek. The Catholics had a long missionary tradition in Bahr al-Ghazal. Bishop F. X. Geyer had established the first Catholic mission station at Kayango thirty-five miles west of Wau in 1904. Still, in the summer of 1985, CRS officials in Kenya were appallingly naive about the difficulties of transporting grain to the deep interior of Southern Sudan. Their sense of urgency was undoubtedly stimulated by the report of Hagen and Kueng and perhaps contributed to their haste in entering a land in which nothing is ever accomplished quickly. After receiving a consignment of 390 tons of PL-480 food for emergency distribution in Southern Sudan, CRS launched its operation in July 1985.

To begin with, the CRS consignment was part of a much larger shipment that arrived in Mombassa on the SS *Cove Trader*. When Mombassa docking facilities could not accommodate the ship, its cargo was offloaded into two scabrous smaller ships, the *Taiwo* and the *King George*, which were crawling with vermin. Crucial days were lost when CRS was forced to fumigate the infected maize. Nevertheless, promised the premium rate of $150 per ton, Kenyan truckers finished the long haul to Juba by September. There, Sudan Ministry of Plant Protection officials found the shipment was infested by flour beetles, and by the time more fumigation finally allowed the release of the shipment, the direct route north to Rumbek was closed following its mining by the SPLA. Thus, a long and treacherous detour of 550 miles through Yambio, Tambura, and Wau was required. South of Tambura one of the Kenyan trucks crashed through a bridge, and its cargo was conveniently distributed among the nearby Azande. Three miles later the convoy lost two more trucks: one to a culvert, the second to a stream. The remaining seven vehicles promptly dumped their grain at Tambura, four hundred miles from the Rumbek destination, and retreated to Kenya. What occurred in Tambura is unclear, but most of the maize soon disappeared. Many weeks later, twenty tons arrived in Rumbek on small suq lorries, and Monsignor Pellegrino, the apostolic administrator in Rumbek, was grateful for even such a small favor.

Desperately in need of food in Bahr al-Ghazal the governor, Lawrence Wol Wol, pledged that if USAID could transport PL-480 food from Port Sudan to Kosti, he would personally see to it that Sudan railways would deliver it to Aweil and Wau. His deputy governor, Brigadier Albino Akol, readily agreed to coordinate shipments by truck to Tonj, Rumbek, and Yirol. USAID agreed to these terms, and within days 680 tons were dispatched from Port Sudan—only to disappear. Wol waited and waited, and in November 1985 his office in Wau laconically reported that twenty-two freight cars with 680 tons of food had been lost somewhere "on the way between Kosti and Babanusa."[39] A month later, the Food Aid National Administration, on behalf of the Sudan Railways Corporation, demanded £S268,000—the carrying charge for 680 tons of sorghum to an unspecified location in Bahr al-Ghazal. Never one to be put off, Wol fired a scathing memorandum to Khartoum:

> For the last eleven months from January to November 1985, Bahr al-Ghazal Administrative Area did not receive any emergency food assistance, and the entire region has been [required] to buy essential commodities at the black market price....With the floods and cattle raiding [Bahr al-Ghazal] will need more food assistance ...since their cattle are robbed by Murahileen from southern Darfur and southern Kordofan who also have destroyed crops in the field in mid August 1985....Now the towns of Aweil, Gogrial, and Wau are full of destitute and displaced people who are in great need of essential commodities....Dura, wheat flour, salt, soap, vaccines, and other medicines are so expensive as to be beyond the means of ordinary people.[40]

Concerned with the drought in the West, which had become a national problem of international significance, the TMC dismissed the governor's plea for 30,000 tons of grain as a local problem. After all, Lawrence Wol Wol was a Dinka.

Despite the *Cove Trader* fiasco and the problems in Bahr al-Ghazal, the Catholics did not give up easily. In Equatoria the Catholic Relief Services and Sudanaid, the relief agency of the Catholic Church in the Sudan, were the most active of all of the relief organizations, and in October 1984 they reported that given widespread drought, there would be a "general shortage of food in Eastern Equatoria" in 1985.[41] The warning was passed to representatives of the European Catholic donor agencies at a meeting held in Juba in November, and in early 1985 the Catholic Relief Services informed Khartoum that famine conditions existed in eastern Equatoria. The USAID-Sudan regional coordinator in Juba advised Khartoum that relief officials had already calculated that some 500,000 Equatorians would require food assistance in 1985. By May 1985, Catholic Church officials were reporting that people were dying of hunger in the Kapoeta District; in response, Sudan aid shipped five hundred tons of bulgur wheat to the Torit diocese. Trucks were then found in Torit to haul food to Kapoeta and Chukundum. This effort, however, was simply a palliative, as the Torit diocese reported in June that villagers living near Torit were starving and that destitute families had taken to the bush to harvest wild "greens" or anything edible. Fortunately, the cultivation of traditional crops throughout most of Equatoria dramatically improved when rains west of the Nile returned to normal and east of the river the rainfall was more abundant than it had been in two years. Shortages still existed in Chukundum and Kapoeta, but these were overcome by assistance from Norwegian Church Aid, which initiated a food-for-work program among the Taposa and Didinga of eastern Equatoria. By 1986 cultivation throughout most of Equatoria had returned to normal.

The Catholic relief agencies were also busy in the Upper Nile in 1985. In response to widespread famine they joined with the UN World Food Program (UNWFP) to organize a large relief effort. In the spring of 1985 the Upper Nile, like the Bahr al-Ghazal, had yet to recover from the drought of 1984. Villages as far south as Bor needed food, and with the escalation of fighting and the sinking of steamers in the major waterway, the Bahr al-Jabal, river transport had virtually disappeared. Malakal, the capital of the Upper Nile, experienced both an influx of destitute Nilotes and shortages of food. Perched on a high bank, with its waterfront lined by tall, shady trees in which clouds of egrets roost with their snow-white plumage illuminated against the blood-red setting sun, Malakal is where Africa begins. To the north, the Sudanese look to the world of Islam and the Arabs; to the south live the Africans with their own cultural traditions. By 1985 Malakal had been transformed into a military base with more storage space for tanks than for grain, and unlike Equatoria and the Bahr al-Ghazal region, it had made no attempt to organize a disaster relief program. Although the civilians suffered, the military garrison survived quite well. Many rumors circulated that the *jallaba*, northern merchants, and even military officers were hoarding grain for sale at Malakal on the black market.[42]

When reports of widespread deaths from starvation throughout the region reached Khartoum, the UNWFP and international donor agencies offered to assist Sudan aid. USAID-Sudan promised two thousand tons of grain from the huge inventory it had stockpiled for relief in Kordofan and Darfur. There was, however, no guarantee that the government would supply barges and tugs to move food aid between Kosti and Malakal. By mid-1985 most government garrisons in the Upper Nile were under siege. SPLA forces already exceeded 10,000, and by year's end their presence in large numbers in easternmost Upper Nile would force the evacuation of 18,000 civilians from Kurmuk, a Blue Nile town, which became the first district capital in the North to be directly threatened by the insurgents. Unlike Equatoria, the rains in the Upper Nile had been average to poor, and as villagers starved and those with seed began to cultivate crops, the TMC used "security" to roadblock the Upper Nile food aid program and the Sudan aid effort.

The 1984–1985 famine in Southern Sudan had at least one positive consequence. In response the NGOs met in Juba in June to coordinate their efforts to meet the growing need for food assistance in 1985. Representatives from OXFAM, BAND AID, African Committee for the Relief of the Southern Sudanese (ACROSS), Norwegian Church Aid, Sudan aid, and the indigenous Protestant-dominated Sudan Council of Churches (SCC) gathered in Juba to form the Combined Action Relief Team, or CART, which would solicit, receive, and distribute international food aid to the needy in Equatoria. Thereafter, the activities of CART and the achievements of the various NGOs, whether in Juba or elsewhere in the South, were almost unknown except to the small number of individuals who have contributed to charitable organizations that work overseas. The employees of these nongovernmental entities were often considered a nuisance by their own embassies and were scorned by the UN organizations until those organizations needed them. They did, however, "come from far and wide to brave dangers in a strange land and live a rough life in the bush."[43]

Certainly, the NGOs played a crucial part in the development of disaster relief assistance in Sudan as they did elsewhere in the world. They were occasionally threatened by irate villagers who wanted them to do more or by government officials who wanted them to see, speak, and do less. Malaria and hepatitis were common afflictions. The invalids were sent home; some were killed. Some were expelled for fatuous reasons, usually because they took their work very seriously. PVOs were occasionally threatened by Muslim fundamentalists, who labeled them

"Neo-Crusaders" who had no rightful place in the Sudan. Nevertheless, they pioneered disaster relief throughout the South at a time when nothing was forthcoming from the Sudan government and the international donors were preoccupied with the drought and famine in the North. Finally, in every disaster relief program initiated from 1984 through 1993 in southern Sudan, the NGOs were to play a pivotal role.

TWO

■

The Politics of Food

A new situation has arisen after the threats from the SPLA and the shooting down of Sudan Airways plane at Malakal. With the airspace closed in Southern Sudan there is not much more that can be done under present conditions. All sorts of technical solutions to get in food and distribute it have been tried. One after another seems to fail, all attributed to the civil strife.
—Staffan de Mistura, UN World Food Program, Khartoum,
August 1985

Although the Western relief program had been characterized by haste, improvisation, and inefficiency, results counted and all sins of omission were forgiven. A USAID review of the accounting practices employed by the Food Aid National Administration (FANA), which the government had charged with the supervision of foreign food aid and the maintenance of warehouse records, revealed that in Port Sudan, 14,250 tons of sorghum worth $4.6 million were missing. The loss was not so much the product of blatant corruption as it was simply one of just plain honest mismanagement. Port Sudan was too small to accommodate a mammoth relief operation. The arrival of huge ships, all simultaneously discharging grain (nearly all of which had to be bagged in the hold), overwhelmed dockside facilities, longshoremen, and port warehousing. Streets leading to USAID-Sudan-contracted warehouses were "littered with sorghum," and the delighted citizens were happy to clean up the mess.[1] Warehouse floors were awash in a sea of sorghum, and an accurate count of the amount of grain was nearly impossible because subcontractors possessed no scales, dealt with inadequately stitched bags, and stacked commodities haphazardly. By 1986 Reagan dura had so inundated the port that a fine film of sorghum coated Port Sudan's docks, streets, and rail yards.

In Washington, AID began 1986 by proposing a PL-480 Title III program for Sudan that would for the first time authorize the sale of food commodities at concessional prices over a multiyear (1986–1988) period. The intent of Title III was to support low-income countries in which agricultural production could be increased significantly and, unlike Sudan, in which governments actively stimulated the growth of the rural sector. Such programs were approved in countries with "progressive policy actions," but in the case of Sudan AID-Washington argued that Title III was essential because one in four Sudanese was "at risk" and food shortages would require a prolonged infusion of food aid. The U.S. Department of State was manifestly unimpressed and killed the proposal. Assistant Secretary for Africa Chester Crocker did try to protect other foreign aid programs, but he was overruled by Secretary of State George Shultz, who, after the U.S. Congress cut foreign aid to Chad and Kenya, stated that "he would later reinstate the funds by taking them out of Sudan."[2] With that, the diminution of the USAID-Sudan program was a foregone conclusion.

Food Requirements in Southern Sudan

Without a Title III program, USAID-Khartoum was satisfied to leave the South to the United Nations. It informed PVOs working in Equatoria that program funds and commodities for 1986 were "earmarked specifically for those people identified as suffering from continued drought and harvest failure," which meant people in Darfur and Kordofan.[3] USAID made no allowance for Equatoria, where some 200,000 people were known to need food immediately. Nor was an allowance made for Bahr al-Ghazal, where another 200,000 needy were located. Despite its large inventory, USAID responded to the Upper Nile governor's desperate pleas for help with the claim that given its program in the West, it had "no further stocks available at [that] time."[4] Indeed, when the drought in the West was broken, USAID-Sudan sought to ensure that it would never again be as directly involved in the management of a food aid operation as it had been in the years 1984–1985. To that end, it sought to enhance the capability of the nascent Relief and Rehabilitation Commission (RRC), which the new military government had created in May 1985 to coordinate disaster relief in Sudan. The RRC commissioner, who began with little more than an office and a secretary, approved all foreign food aid programs and reported directly to the TMC (and later to the Office of the Prime Minister).

As the Western agencies wound down their program in the West, in early February 1986 Sudan Council of Churches, the relief arm of the Protestant churches, warned that food shortages in the South had reached a critical stage. An estimated 1.5 million people (or about one in three southerners) were "experiencing or vulnerable to a deteriorating

TABLE 2.1   Affected Populations in Southern Sudan (January 1986)

Area	Needy Population	Source of the Problem
Equatoria		
Terekeka	22,000	War
Tindilo	5,000	War
Tali Post	7,000	War
Juba Town	5,000	War
Southern Bari	5,000	Persistent drought
Bungo	4,000	Drought
Torit/Kapoeta	130,000	War, cattle rustling
Bahr al-Ghazal		
Wau Town	10,000	War, *murahileen* raiding
Aweil/Gogrial	187,000	War, *murahileen* raiding
Rumbek	No Data	War, insect infestations
Tonj	15,000	War
Yirol	20,000	War
Upper Nile		
Kadok/Kaka	34,000	Drought, war
Malakal Town	40,000	War
Renk	4,000	War
Mayom/Bentiu	50,000	War, cattle rustling
Maban/Melut	4,000	War
Grand Total	542,000+ in need 1,000,000 vulnerable	

Source: Sudan Council of Churches, "Especial Report on Southern Sudan," Khartoum, February 3, 1986.

nutritional status."(See Table 2.1.) In the Ministry of Defense, Brigadier Osman Abdallah Muhammad acknowledged that eighty people were "dying daily from famine in the south," adding, "I hope Colonel John Garang will appreciate the gravity of the situation and understand that we are not deceiving him."[5] Garang was not deceived. The SPLA had already reported that famine was widespread in Bentiu, Rumbek, Terekeka, and Kapoeta, and deaths were occurring elsewhere throughout the South well in advance of the rainy season. In Khartoum the United Nations worried that as many as a million southerners would require some food aid in 1986, and UN-Sudan Resident Representative Winston Prattley, an official with twenty-five years' experience in the United Nations, met with the SPLA in February 1986 in a quiet but unsuccessful effort to secure free passage from Kenya to Juba for food aid convoys. The SPLA rejected the program because the United Nations would not promise to distribute aid to villages controlled by the SPLA. As Prattley fought a lonely battle to move food aid to the South, the association between the RRC and international aid donors (the United Nations, USAID-Sudan, NGOs, PVOs,) was greatly strengthened in April 1986 when the RRC was granted a corporation charter that gave it semiautonomous status. The commission was reorganized, and disaster relief programs were supervised by four regional desk officers. The commission then subsumed the existing Management and Logistics Team (MALT)—a team of European experts financed by the Netherlands to improve the government's ability to move food aid—and the Sudan "Early Warning System" unit, which had been created by the United Nations to predict natural disasters. The latter eventually received substantial support from Famine Early Warning System (FEWS) advisers funded by AID-Washington and its Office of Foreign Disaster Assistance.

The first RRC commissioner had been ineffectual and was soon replaced by the more energetic Kamal Shawki, an adept bureaucrat whose most significant characteristic was his ability to survive in perilous political times. Under Commissioner Shawki drought and famine in the South were directly addressed by an agency of Sudan government. The RRC evolved into a friendly club, and meetings chaired by the affable Al-Hilo often ambled along aimlessly. "Expatriates" (as foreigners residing in Sudan liked to call themselves) were expected to be both tactful and gullible, and those who endured were blessed with a leaden backside and the patience of a Baqqara nit picker. USAID-Sudan, which had hoped that a propitious 1985–1986 harvest in the West might permit it to return to what it most enjoyed—providing development aid—soon found itself hopelessly intertwined in RRC activities. Since it had food, or could get food quickly from the United States once the embassy issued a disaster declaration, it became the commission's principal participant.

Historically, most of the valuable information concerning the South's food requirements had been supplied by Sudanaid and Sudan Council of Churches. Consequently, when the SCC estimated in January 1986 that 1.5 million people in the South would soon be at risk of starvation, the RRC was forced to take the claim very seriously. Kamal Shawki warned "What must happen by the donor community [is] a radical revision of its assessment on the current situation and urgent action on the institutional, governmental and international arrangements necessary for responding to the crisis."[6] The demand seemed both presumptuous and premature until a group of PVO leaders calling themselves the Agencies Involved in Southern Sudan (AISS) warned Khartoum and the world in May 1986 that the situation was even more disastrous than the SCC had supposed. The movement had begun with OXFAM, which had called upon the government and the SPLA to agree to an immediate cease-fire to avoid what it called "the looming social and human catastrophe." When it received no response from either side, OXFAM along with seventeen leaders from various agencies created AISS. In July it stated that massive starvation threatened 3 *million* southerners and pleaded for an immediate "food truce in South Sudan."[7] Using commendable political acumen, AISS members including Sudanaid, SCC, and World Vision formed an Emergency Support Committee in Bahr al-Ghazal and invited the RRC to provide a chair. In accepting the invitation the RRC was given its first real opportunity to work closely with the PVOs in Khartoum and in the field. This gave the PVOs a conduit to the highest circles of government, but it also opened them to direct supervision by a series of agencies that would expel individuals or organizations whose work or opinions they considered prejudicial to official policy. Indeed, the PVOs were forced to become increasingly circumspect during the tenures of both the Transitional Military Council and its successors.

Aftermath of the 1986 Elections

As Sudan prepared for elections in the spring of 1986, the Transitional Military Council appeared happy to return government to the civilians. The South was famine-plagued, and despite his expressed (and questionable) concern for the displaced and distressed Sudanese, TMC Chairman Swar al-Dahab agreed with "urban Sudanese [that] it was a crisis best left to the *khwajas*."[8] The war was not going well, although the army, with the aid of Libyan bombers, had recently driven the SPLA from Rumbek. Still, a major campaign to clear the road between Juba and Bor had failed, and many units were demoralized by the increasingly hostile environment. Some—particularly the Fur and the Nuba, who were sympathetic to the SPLA—had "mutinied in their barracks" at Omdurman in what was an ill-conceived and unsuccessful attempt to oust the TMC.[9] The economy needed even more reconstructive surgery than the army. The war consumed a million Sudanese pounds a day—$400,000 at the official rate of exchange—and its cost was increasing. The 1985 drought had cost some $300 million in export earnings, and foreign currency holdings were scanty. The foreign debt was mounting, and Finance Minister Abd al-Magid resigned in December 1985, casting a jeremiad that Sudan was "retreating into the Middle Ages, like Albania."[10]

In April 1986 democracy enjoyed a renaissance in Sudan as more than 1,000 candidates from forty-two parties competed for office. Nevertheless, the campaign was virtually devoid of serious debate. The strongest party, the Umma, appeared complacent, and only the National Islamic

Front and the Communists bothered to debate the central issues—the war and the economy. Although the economy might be too recondite a subject for many, the war was an omnipresent reality upon which all other problems were dependent. Prior to the elections the National Alliance for National Salvation, which had played a decisive role in the downfall of President Numayri, sought to open discussions with John Garang and his lieutenants at Koka Dam in Ethiopia. Representatives of the Umma Party, the Southern Sudan Politicians Association (comprising most of the southern leaders in Khartoum), trade unions, and the professional associations explored the possibility of peace. The talks were extremely positive, and after five days of deliberations the participants signed the Koka Dam Declaration outlining the conditions necessary to open negotiations to end the war. Both sides agreed to hold a constitutional conference in Khartoum during the third week in June to determine the configuration of the new Sudan.

In May voters went to the polls, with the Umma Party receiving a plurality of the 4.5 million votes cast and ninety-nine of three hundred and one seats in the Constituent Assembly. (Elections could not be held in thirty-one of sixty-eight southern districts.) After forming a governing coalition, Sadiq al-Mahdi became prime minister. It was a remarkable comeback for Sadiq, who had been prime minister in 1966, was arrested by Numayri on charges of high treason in 1969, exiled to Egypt, returned to Sudan in 1972 where he was arrested and jailed for two years, and then was exiled again. In Libya he had helped found the National Front that had united exiled politicians in opposition to the Numayri dictatorship. In July 1976 Sadiq had charted an armed attempt to overthrow Numayri that had nearly succeeded. In the following year he had met with Numayri in Port Sudan and made peace with the dictator. Sadiq had not joined the Numayri government, but he did refrain from publicly criticizing it until Numayri moved far to the right of the political spectrum. During the TMC interregnum Sadiq worked hard to rebuild his political base.

During the election campaign, Sadiq encountered unexpectedly strong opposition from the National Islamic Front (NIF). NIF was especially strong in Khartoum, where it received 40 percent of the votes cast and gained the strong support of professionals and military officers. It won fifty-one seats in the election and was victorious "in every constituency in which there was an army barracks."[11] In his campaign Sadiq promised southerners "a share of the 18 Cabinet portfolios proportionate to the southern population," supported the Koka Dam Declaration, and indicated that the proposed constitutional conference would take place as scheduled in June.[12] He also agreed—momentarily—to curtail the activities of the Islamic Call Organization, the *Manazzamat al-Da'wa*

Islamiyya, which was devoted to the propagation of Islam and Muslim charitable works and had received significant funding from Saudi Arabia and the Gulf states through the Faisal Islamic Bank in Sudan. However, when Swar al-Dahab was named chair of the Islamic Call Organization, the restrictions were soon withdrawn, and the Da'wa fell increasingly under the influence of Sadiq's brother-in-law and NIF party leader, Hassan al-Turabi.

Sadiq's promises to southern politicians appeared to create a climate for peace, but within weeks he began to undo the Koka Dam agreement. He postponed the constitutional conference, using the excuse that he would meet with Garang at Addis Ababa during the July summit meeting of the Organization of African Unity. They met and formed an instant dislike for one another, and their talks rapidly degenerated into a "tense confrontation" whose only outcome was to be the continuation of the war.[13] Sadiq lost interest in the peace dialogue, and when he refused to repeal the September Laws or call a constitutional conference, the National Alliance for National Salvation was unable to maintain momentum, and its connection with the SPLA withered and then died.

Famine in Southern Sudan

As prospects for peace receded, famine relief became even more necessary. Sadiq was, however, entirely indifferent to the plight of the South. This reaction was not entirely unexpected, because prior to the 1986 elections Sadiq had revealed to American journalist Robert Kaplan an "alarming lack of interest" in the famine in Kordofan and Darfur. "Providing relief for famine," Sadiq declared, "was the responsibility of the wealthy West, not of any Sudanese government." Kaplan added:

> More alarming was his attitude toward the non-Arab, non-Moslem southerners who accounted for roughly half the country's population. Like rulers in other countries, Mr. al-Mahdi never doubted his particular ethnic and religious group's right to dominate others. The Prime Minister's hesitation to accept a cease-fire in the war with the southern rebels, and his government's obstructionist attitude toward allowing food supplies into the south, very much reflected the reluctance of Arab-Sudanese to accept what is geographically obvious: that Sudan is only half an Arab polity; that it is also an African one.[14]

With the exception of AISS in Khartoum, PVOs in Equatoria, Sudan-aid in Bahr al-Ghazal, and SCC and Sudan aid in Upper Nile, no one appeared particularly interested in combating famine in Southern Sudan. USAID-Sudan, which had been evacuated after a U.S. Embassy employee was shot and wounded in Khartoum in an act of reprisal that followed the U.S. bombing of Tripoli, demonstrated minimal interest in famine relief when its staff returned. USAID was capable, but the management of an extensive famine relief program in the South would require "official" approaches to the SPLA—something the Department of State had discouraged since 1983. James K. Bishop, an energetic deputy assistant secretary of state who was driven by humanitarian concerns, had opened contact with the SPLA's representative in the United States in 1984; however, this effort to create a working relationship with the SPLA had moved little beyond an exchange of letters and a press report of what proved to be an innocuous meeting in a London coffee shop.[15]

The International Red Cross persevered, but despite months of quiet diplomacy its representatives failed to find a formula acceptable to both the insurgents and the government by which food aid could be distributed simultaneously to SPLA-controlled villages and government-controlled garrisons in the South. Sudan government did agree, however, to respect the neutrality of an SPLA camp at Narus, south of Kapoeta, where the ICRC provided hospital services and humanitarian assistance without attendant publicity. Norwegian People's Aid (NPA), a new PVO, also appeared at Narus and was the first to work directly with the SPLA. NPA, the humanitarian arm of the Norwegian trade union movement, had begun to provide humanitarian assistance during the Spanish Civil War; in Sudan it began by funding the movement of food aid from Kenya to Narus. The operation was directed by Egil Hagen, a Norwegian who had left UNICEF shortly after reporting on starvation in Southern Sudan in 1985. Hagan made no effort to be quiet or self-effacing, and the activity of NPA trucks and small, unmarked and uninsured airplanes—in sum, his rogue operation—proved irresistible to the media. Hagan moved through the rebel landscape with ease, and to a score of journalists his bravura, can-do approach to disaster relief created something new—the modern soldier of misfortune.

War in Southern Sudan

As Hagan was aware, if the donors wanted a program in the South, John Garang could no longer be ignored. The army's restrictive policies had resulted in ever more crowding in garrison towns and the exponential growth of the displaced population. To Garang the southern city was no longer "a productive city, but a consumptive, exploitative, cancerous growth on the rural areas." He felt government forces were responsible for "making both the cities and the rural areas unproductive and inducing famine the magnitude of which has never been experienced in Africa."[16] By 1986 the SPLA roamed the countryside at will, interdicting food shipments to garrison towns and urging all rural displaced persons found therein to return to their villages. It began the year by threatening to shoot down cargo planes, and soon afterward "several civilian and military" aircraft were reported to have been "damaged by SPLA fire or even brought down."[17]

The SPLA siege strategy was simple but effective in smaller towns and villages, but it failed in the larger urban centers serviced by a good airstrip and defended by a large army contingent. When the SPLA did besiege Juba, Wau, and Malakal, visiting journalists and aid workers accused the insurgents of using "food as a weapon." As the war continued and more southerners died of starvation and related diseases this allegation became more pronounced. When asked why the SPLA only seemed to add to the suffering, Garang responded: "In 1986 a BBC reporter came to me in Kapoeta and asked me the same question, and I said we are not refusing relief. It is the relief that is not coming."[18] Virtually nothing was reported about heavily armed government convoys that moved food to the military (and the black market) but not to needy civilians. In contrast, there was only rare criticism of an army policy to create hostages of those who had sought refuge in the cities but later wanted to return to their villages. Both the SPLA and the government mined the approaches to garrison towns, and civilians seeking to leave found their escape perilous; however, on various occasions the SPLA offered to clear a secure path out of a besieged town or to impose a momentary cease-fire if the government would permit the displaced persons to leave. On no occasion did the army release its captives.

The Plight of the Dinka

By 1986 the famine conditions in the South had become most severe among the Dinka of Bahr al-Ghazal. *Murahileen* assaults along the rail line north of Aweil had forced the Dinka to evacuate at least fifty villages, with most of the dispossessed fleeing south to Aweil. Sudan aid reported that 250,000 to 300,000 Dinka in villages located north of the Lol River had been forced south by Rizayqat militia after dry-season raids. The Baqqara raiders continued their destruction of a pastoral way of life; cattle were killed or rustled, and Dinka villages lost a quintessential source of protein and calories, which accounted for much of their diet during the months between the depletion of the cereal supply and the beginning of the harvest season.

Hundreds of thousands of cattle were taken or destroyed by the Baqqara. In one study carried out in the 1970s, the cattle population of Bahr al-Ghazal and the western Upper Nile was as high as 3.5 million, and cattle densities between the Bahr al-Arab and Lol Rivers were among the highest in Sudan.[19] A decade later at least half of the cattle in that region had been slaughtered, run off, or rustled for later sale in the Omdurman cattle market.[20] Dinka leaders estimated that by 1988, the

Dinka had lost over 5 million cattle, and although in Khartoum these claims were regarded as highly exaggerated, government officials privately admitted that Dinka losses probably exceeded 2 million head. Completing the cycle of destruction, Dinka crops were stolen, trampled, or burned in the field, thus ruining a primitive but effective subsistence agriculture system. The end product was the flight of tens of thousands of Dinka in search of food and security.

Northern Aweil District was particularly devastated, as bush wars and the cattle raids had displaced entire villages. The Twic Dinka, attacked by Missiriya *murahileen* on many occasions in 1985, had suffered especially heavy losses of people, cattle, and *tukuls* (huts). They were, thus, the first Dinka to flee to the North in large numbers. Many settled on the outskirts of Babanusa, and some traveled as far west as Nyala in southern Darfur. Most important, for the first time since the outbreak of civil war, large numbers of southerners began to appear in Khartoum.[21]

South of Aweil a number of skirmishes were fought along the road to Wau between increasingly active SPLA units and army outposts. At Tonj an estimated 20,000 Dinka left for Wau in search of food after the meager 1985 harvest was exhausted. In Wau itself, there was virtually no grain for sale, and the black market price for sorghum rose six fold in less than four months. In January 1985 the governor of Bahr al-Ghazal calculated that he would need 45,000 tons of sorghum to feed some 1.5 million people from February through July 1986. (A normal adult ration was calculated at one pound of sorghum per person per day; ideally, 45,000 tons would have fed 1.5 million adults for about two months.) He also requested from the RRC 1,250 tons of sorghum for seed distribution to impoverished farmers. By July 1986 famine was rampant in Wau. Dinka who arrived from Aweil, Rumbek, and Tonj with cattle to exchange for grain found none except that which was hoarded by the *jallaba* and sold at unaffordable prices. In a bizarre occurrence, in early May 1986 the last military convoy to reach Wau before the SPLA closed the Aweil-Wau road mysteriously delivered fifty-five tons of sorghum to the Wau Relief Committee. The relief food was consumed almost immediately. Given the number of starvation deaths, on 28 July the governor appealed directly to Sadiq al-Mahdi for help, and the prime minister issued a directive to the RRC and Sudan Railways to respond immediately with a relief train. Nothing happened.

When no food arrived in Bahr al-Ghazal, many displaced Dinka moved into the SPLA safe haven that stretched east and west of a diagonal line connecting Tonj with Mashra al-Raqq, where the SPLA had re-created a local administration, and village chiefs and local courts were active. The haven, however, had no great surplus of food, little seed, and minimal health and educational services. Thus the influx of more than

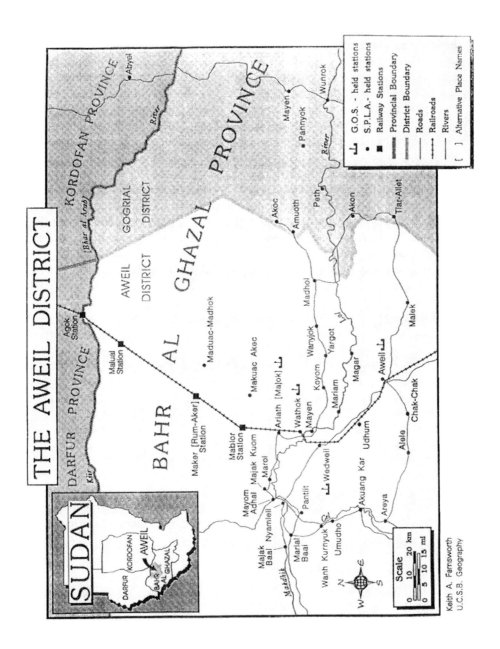

Keith A. Farnsworth
U.C.S.B. Geography

40,000 Dinka and some Nuer in early 1986 resulted in severe shortages of land and pasture. Elsewhere, thousands of Dinka who had melted into the bush after the SPLA captured Rumbek in March 1986 (and held it for more than a month) made their way toward Yirol. Following its capture, rumors circulated in Khartoum that people and supplies were being air-lifted from Ethiopia, and heavy equipment flown into the town was used to extend the local airstrip. The SPLA turned Yirol into a base of opera-tions for southern Bahr al-Ghazal and northern Equatoria.

In northern Bahr al-Ghazal, Aweil was being harassed almost daily by rebels commanded by the talented Daniel Awet Akot, SPLA commander for that region. Akot's troops fought furiously to rid Bahr al-Ghazal of *murahileen,* and in 1986 they began to make life miserable for the army in the town of Aweil, an overgrown and picturesque African village of 30,000 inhabitants. Aweil was filled with SPLA supporters, and its army contingent of 600 troops, commanded by the brutal Isaiah Paul, con-ducted itself like plunderers in a conquered land. When nearby villages were entered and suspects picked out by military intelligence, the cap-tives tended to disappear.

By 1986 Aweil's hospital was in ruins, and schools were closed on the pretext that students were taught pro-SPLA doctrines, which was proba-bly true. In the market the northern merchants demanded exorbitant prices in cash or cattle for grain. In May a bad situation worsened over-night when an army vehicle struck a mine on the Aweil-Wau road, killing two soldiers. Seeking vengeance, the soldiers promptly sacked Aweil while their officers remained indifferent to the pillage, which lasted nearly a day. Over fifty Dinka were killed, much of the town was burned to the ground and nearly all of the Dinka population fled to the bush in terror.[22] Ironically, five days later Medicines Sans Frontiers/France (Doctors Without Borders, or MSF-France), the renowned PVO, arrived in Aweil to rebuild the local hospital. With its customary efficiency, the team reported that the nutritional and health status of Aweil's popula-tion was rapidly deteriorating and that the number of displaced persons would undoubtedly increase because the 1986 rainy season had begun poorly and drought was already widespread.

Hostilities Beyond the Nilotic Plain

Despite the early hopes that a civilian government could bring peace to Sudan, by July 1986 the Koka Dam agreement had proved to be a fleet-ing commitment, and there was little hope for an early peace. Fighting had escalated in Bahr al-Ghazal, and, according to one report, the "army policy of concentrating rural dwellers in towns" meant that little food was planted for the autumn harvest. OXFAM Director Mark Duffield warned that there was very little food in the South, and an ominous

OXFAM field report warned "It looks as if the whole area is sliding into chaos."[23] In June and July the SPLA attacked near Wau, besieged Bor, and attacked army outposts at Fanjak and Bentiu in Upper Nile.

Security in Equatoria likewise deteriorated rapidly. In January 1986 regional security was aggravated when the regime of Uganda's General Tito Okello was deposed by Yoweri Museveni. A schoolmate of John Garang's, Museveni was a nationalist who had been fighting a succession of parochially based, corrupt governments in Uganda since 1981. Okello's undisciplined rabble, the Uganda National Liberation Army, fled northward, and, like the armies of Idi Amin and Milton Obote before it, sought sanctuary in Equatoria. The Acholi, whose homeland straddles the Sudan-Uganda border, played a prominent role in Okello's army and promptly set up a rebel training camp inside Sudan. It was attacked by Garang's forces, and fleeing Acholi sought refuge among their kin in the frontier towns of Nimule and Parajok, where they thrived as bandits who harassed villagers regardless of their political sympathies and targeted merchant convoys that moved supplies to Juba from Kenya and Uganda.[24]

A much more serious threat to the SPLA was the Uganda People's Democratic Army (UPDA). Its units were employed by Sudan government to defend garrison towns, and "in return Sudanese army provided it with food, shelter, and transport."[25] The UPDA also attacked Ugandan refugees who had fled from the Obote or Okello dictatorships and settled in Equatoria. In April and May 1986 seventeen refugee camps located east of the Nile were precipitously abandoned after attacks by "unidentified" armed gangs. The government blamed the SPLA, but Garang had no reason to antagonize Museveni, nor did the SPLA ever claim responsibility for the flight of more than 60,000 refugees back to Uganda. Indeed, "unidentified raiders" became a catchall phrase to describe pillaging by UPDA and Ugandan National Liberation Army (UNLA) bandits. Their influence was not significantly reduced until the SPLA became active in Sudan-Uganda border-towns some months later.

With the southern frontier in turmoil, in the spring of 1986 the SPLA launched offensives in Equatoria both east and west of the Nile. In the west it overran villages in the Terekeka District, and their inhabitants—mostly Bari families—fled to Juba and settled at Jabal Kujur, the first of the capital's camps for the displaced. East of the Nile SPLA activity precipitated the exodus of the Lokoyo and Lolulobo to Juba, and in April the SPLA attacked Kit 1, sixty-six miles from Juba, and then overran Palotaka and looted a Norwegian Church Aid (NCA) site. In March the Adventist Development and Relief Agency (ADRA) began to advocate a Juba airlift, but a reevaluation was required after the SPLA reportedly fired two heat-seeking missiles at civilian aircraft.

The SPLA Takes the Offensive

The SPLA next targeted Liyangari and Liria ten miles east of Ngangala and then Ngangala itself. As fighting intensified in eastern Equatoria, the NCA, one of the most successful PVOs in Sudan, was forced to reduce its local staff from 1,200 to 170 and the number of expatriates from twenty-two to seven.[26] West of the Nile the SPLA drove the Mundari militia from the field, and it, too, sought safety in Juba where undisciplined remnants "resorted to indiscriminate killing" among the city's Dinka community.[27] The militia's action was almost predictable, because an anti-Dinka graveman had been quoted in February by Governor Peter Cirillo, who barely disguised his distaste for people he called "bad elements in town."[28] As the SPLA tightened the noose around Juba, "incipient food riots" were reported. The market price for staples rose precipitously, and the U.S. Embassy warned that "if town needs are not met soon, breakdown of law and order can be expected as well as substantial increases in malnutrition."[29] Food shortages soon exacerbated ancient ethnic animosities, and in July there were "more reports of Dinka being killed in Juba town," and approximately 3,000 Dinka were "gathered into an area providing protection."[30] Protection for the Dinka, however, was sporadic.

The USAID-Juba representative, Charles Fields, who was about to close operations in the South, reported that it was no longer safe to move food into the rural areas without a military escort. He reported that CART was having trouble distributing food in Equatoria, and the chaos was complicated by a "series of food wars between conflicting tribes" in villages dominated by neither the SPLA nor the government.[31] When Torit was nearly overrun and the Catholic Mission on the outskirts of town was looted, Bishop Paride Taban and most of his parishioners moved into the town center, and the Kiltegan Fathers moved to Juba. Many villagers fled at the time when the cultivation of their crops was the most critical, and intensification of the conflict around Kapoeta and Terekeka caused an estimated 80,000–100,000 displaced people to leave their villages and seek shelter in garrison towns, either with extended family members or in sites created for them. Then, when the market price of staple cereals in Kapoeta and other towns exceeded the purchasing power of the displaced, some 50,000 desperate southerners fled eastern Equatoria for Uganda and Kenya.

By July 1986 Juba's population had increased to an estimated 170,000 inhabitants, double the 1983 census figure, and the capital of the South had developed almost overnight into "a refugee city of tented camps."[32] A month later the SPLA had succeeded in closing all roads into Juba, and commercial trucks were attacked on both of the major routes from

Nimule and Yei. CART reported that drivers were "reluctant to accept trips to Juba," and it warned potential food donors that if the situation did not improve the city would eventually require airlifts from Khartoum or East Africa to replenish its food supplies.[33] The Juba airport, never particularly safe, was closed for a few days in July after the SPLA occupied Jabal Lado ten miles north of the city. Panicked, the Relief and Rehabilitation Commission informed donors that if widespread starvation were to be avoided Juba would require 2,000 tons of food aid a month—a total approximately equal to the monthly movement of *all* commercial supplies previously trucked to the city.[34] Juba was indeed surrounded, but it was hardly on the verge of starvation. CART advised that "the number of cattle in and around Juba is enormous," because huge herds had accompanied pastoralists, particularly the Mundari.[35] As CART was aware, cattle would not be slaughtered or sold until their owners became absolutely desperate. Thus, anyone who could—including members of the last regional assembly of the South, which met for a short time in 1986—left for the North or went into exile. The war had finished off "romantic old Juba," and its subsequent physical and political decline was ugly, demeaning, and demoralizing.

Efforts for Food Relief for the South

In Upper Nile conditions in 1986 were similar to those in Equatoria and Bahr al-Ghazal. Shilluk and Nuer from the Kodok District north of Malakal fled drought and insecurity to settle down river in the mechanized and rain-fed agricultural schemes between Kosti and Renk. Thousands more sought to escape the intense fighting in the Sobat and Jonglei Districts, and Malakal attracted tens of thousands of displaced Nuer. Rivers and roads to Bentiu, Bor, and Nasir were under constant SPLA attacks. A mass of humanity piled into the thirteen wards (*hillas*) of Malakal Town, camping in makeshift *tukuls* wherever they could find space.

After suffering through many delays, in July 1985 Sudanaid succeeded in barging more than 500 tons of sorghum to starving Nuer and Dinka in Renk, Wadakona, Melut, and Malakal. The next month 525 tons reached Geiger, Renk, and Wadakona, and in September an additional 400 tons were distributed in Renk, Kaka, Melut, and Malakal. The tonnage delivered was, in fact, much less than the amount required in northern Upper Nile, and Sudanaid could only guess at the severity of the famine situation south of Malakal. In Malakal itself, in 1985 Sudanaid had, joined with Colonel Pio Yukwan, commissioner of the Sobat Province and a Shilluk, to found the Malakal Relief Committee. Underfunded and with a part-time staff, the committee was overwhelmed by the exponential growth of displaced persons and reported to the RRC in December 1985 that the number of displaced people in dire need exceeded 30,000 and that the food supply was nearly exhausted. It waited in vain for some government assistance as the displaced poured into Malakal faster than the committee could count them.

After the SPLA paralyzed river traffic on the White Nile, Yukwan, who was then acting governor of Upper Nile, contacted the relief agencies and requested a new food aid program for his region. UNICEF pledged 700 tons of food and thirty tons of medical supplies, and the European Community and Sudan Red Crescent Society offered food and other assistance. Sudanaid took charge of the operation and used its own funds to purchase sorghum in the North for shipment to Malakal. It contacted USAID-Sudan in December 1985, but USAID inexplicably claimed that its entire stock of food had been "pre-programmed" for Western relief. It flatly turned down Sudanaid's modest request for 160 tons of sorghum, maintaining that it had "no further unprogrammed stocks in Kosti" and had "already allocated all stocks of grain in Port Sudan."[36] Ironically, in mid-1985 USAID-Sudan had given UNWFP 900 tons of sorghum for inclusion in Sudanaid shipments to Upper Nile and then complained that UNWFP had not acted "with the same urgency as was contained in the initial request from the Regional government."[37] Despite the greater emergency unfolding in 1986, USAID-Sudan decided to program its food for a relief operation in western Sudan whose needs had already been oversubscribed.

In December 1985 Sudanaid leased a small barge and a privately owned pusher tug in Khartoum. The *Moghren*, flying the UN flag, shoved off on New Year's Eve. In Kosti it was joined by four barges loaded with 1,600 tons of Sudanaid commodities. Once the *jallaba* discerned that the barges would move under the protective cover of a UN flag, they were quick to join the convoy, and Sudanaid's four relief barges were joined by barges transporting a merchant cargo of some 5,500 tons of sorghum. The SPLA observed the convoy but made no effort to impede its movement or attack government troops that covered its flanks.[38] When the barges docked at Malakal on 10 February, the Catholic bishop of that city reported to Khartoum that food shortages had created "conditions worse than anything" he had ever seen.[39] Kevin O'Rourke, a Sudanaid monitor wrote "It is a Christian town but the 5 percent or so Muslims enjoyed the late Christmas as much as the others."[40]

The February convoy provided a six-month reprieve, but despite its success—or perhaps because of it—the government refused Sudanaid's request to participate in a military escorted commercial convoy that left Renk for Malakal on 4 April. When the SPLA learned that some barges carried military cargo, it retaliated with desultory sniping. The convoy arrived safely, but no new convoy was formed for months. Blocked from the river route, Sudanaid and Sudan Council of Churches paid truckers to move 250 tons of food from Kosti to Mayom south of Malakal in March and April and 150 tons to Bentiu in April and May.

By July 1986 the population of Malakal exceeded 80,000 (almost three times its pre-war population) and included 30,000 displaced persons. One out of four children was malnourished, and the February food aid was nearly exhausted.[41] The *jallaba* still possessed considerable stocks, hoarding their supplies to await even higher prices. When Acting Governor Peter Mabiel, a Dinka from Abwong, announced that all grain would be confiscated and be sold to the public at the official price of £S85 a sack, he was swiftly removed. His successor, Colonel Gordon Kong, the Anya-Nya II leader who had helped to arrange the transfer of that entity's allegiance to the government following the death of Gai Tut, did not make the same mistake. No grain was confiscated even though the rains were late, seed was short, cultivation was sporadic, and the late summer harvest could not possibly relieve the growing food shortage in Malakal.

Fearful that a disaster was imminent, Sudanaid began the laborious process of leasing barges and tugs for yet another trip upriver. Seven hundred tons of food supplies and thirty-two tons of seed were loaded in Kosti and Renk, but when another commercial barge convoy left Kosti in late July, Sudanaid was specifically forbidden to join it. When the *jallaba* barges reached Malakal, the food "was sold immediately to the Army or was put into hidden stores."[42] The cost of a sack of sorghum in Malakal soon reached £S510, and by October that price had doubled. By that time thousands of hungry southerners had ignored military threats to kill all those who attempted to escape from the city and had disappeared into the bush.

In August the Ethiopian office of the UN High Commissioner for Refugees reported that 102,000 Sudanese refugees were already registered in Ethiopian refugee camps and warned that their numbers were increasing rapidly. Indeed, almost everywhere throughout the South, the food supply situation had become critical. Fearful that tens of thousands of people might die if aid were not quickly forthcoming and frustrated in their attempts to move food into the South, Sudan Council of Churches and Sudanaid practically begged the RRC to support a "food aid truce" in Southern Sudan. The plea was taken up by UNICEF, UNWFP, and nearly a score of PVOs including MSF France and OXFAM. A further refinement in donor-government coordination and cooperation occurred in May when a Technical Coordination Committee (TCC) was created through which RRC representatives, UN participants, foreign embassy personnel, and representatives of both domestic and foreign NGOs could meet on a formal basis, as often as needed to review and discuss disaster relief and food aid issues. Although the RRC promised little, the PVOs and the European Community enthusiastically favored a relief program in the South. Shortly thereafter, the UN Office of Emergency Operation in Sudan (UNEOS) took charge of expatriate efforts and was given executive responsibility for what it called the Southern Sudan Relief Operation. The TCC members then declared: "Neutrality is agreed upon by donors and agencies as a necessary basis for relief operations in the area because of armed conflict that prevails. In practice, neutrality means that no relief consignments will be dispatched to areas or situations that CART cannot monitor. No dispatches of food movements will be undertaken by CART with military escort."[43]

Using the TCC to good effect, UNEOS began by organizing food airlifts for the CART operation in Juba. Air shipments began in late June and continued through July. The expense of air freight, however, was enormous, and wherever possible the donors favored overland transport. Roads were hazardous and insecure, yet the donors managed to truck 200 tons of food from Kenya to Juba compared with 120 tons flown in from Khartoum. The totals were inadequate, accounting for less than a week's supply of food for displaced persons in Juba. The price of sorghum spiraled upward and soon reached £S1,200 for a 90-kilogram sack. With that, authorities threatened to confiscate all black market and hoarded grain. When prices still did not fall, two government sweeps "found and reported" small quantities being hoarded, but they were instantly "confiscated by the military for 'military' use."[44] There was a curious aspect to market pricing, and one investigator noted that "relief and commercial supplies reaching the South did not seem to have much impact on prices."[45] Once scarcities occurred, the *jallaba* were allowed to set the price for grain. They were protected by senior army officers, and together the two groups made a profit in the grain market, a situation they regarded as fair compensation for having to live in Southern Sudan.

The SPLA Retaliates Ruthlessly

After a month of effort, during which only 320 tons of food were delivered, the Southern Sudan Relief Operation (SSRO), no matter how well-intentioned, seemed certain to fail. The UN World Food Program estimated that 20,000 tons of grain were urgently needed just to feed the "reachable" population in the South, but the funding required to carry out such a program exceeded the amount the major donors—USAID and the European Community—were willing to commit. As SSRO sputtered, UNEOS received an unexpected shock when Radio SPLA warned on 15 August that within twenty-four hours, all airplanes using southern airfields would "be doing so at their own risk."[46] The SPLA, which had issued such warnings before, was convinced that just as it was tightening its efforts around Bor the army was using civilian aircraft to equip army forces for "a new military offensive."[47]

The following day the SPLA used a SAM-7 missile to shoot down a scheduled Sudan Airways passenger flight from Malakal to Khartoum. Some sixty-three Sudanese died. This ruthless act halted all relief agency flights to the South for weeks and no flights went to Malakal for four months. The attack was unquestionably the greatest error in judgment the SPLA had made in its war with the government, for although the explicit SPLA warnings had been disregarded, it could not justify shooting down a passenger plane. Congratulatory messages on Radio SPLA were astonishingly tactless, especially one sent to John Garang by Major Arok Thon Arok, a member of the SPLA Political-Military Command.[48] John Luk, the SPLA representative in London, provided only lame and unsatisfactory excuses. He explained that the SPLA was "very sorry about the people who died" but argued that the government was using civilian planes for military purposes. Luk employed a rather convoluted argument: "It is true that the plane was carrying passengers to Khartoum, but we did not know what it was carrying from Khartoum to Malakal."[49] He closed by warning that if a government plane were to penetrate the same airspace again, it would also be shot down.

The SPLA's enemies claimed that the SPLA was trying to terrorize the international relief agencies into halting their food aid flights, an allegation John Garang vehemently denied. In a BBC interview he "refuted claims by some foreigners" that the SPLA forced citizens to join the rebel movement. "If that were the objective," he argued, it "would never have survived nor would it have attracted mass support." Garang argued that "war had its own rules" and pointed out that although "an enemy was not [usually] warned of an impending attack," the SPLA had done just that.[50] Regardless of Garang's justification, the Malakal incident could not have come at a worse time for the southern Sudanese. Sudanaid, Sudan Council of Churches, UNICEF, UNWFP, OXFAM, and MSF-France all warned that half of the South's 2–3 million people would need some food assistance, which they seemingly could not presently transport. AID-Washington Administrator Peter McPherson reported that the scarcity of food was acute "for 700,000 people clustered in such government-held garrison towns as Wau, Malakal and Juba." *Arab News* added that little grain would arrive from the countryside, because "an army policy of concentrating rural dwellers in towns [meant] that little food [was] being planted for the autumn harvest."[51]

Despite the famine warnings, the SPLA refused to open southern air space and claimed it would not do so until an agreement was reached "as to the respective proportions of relief supplies" to be divided between the SPLA's relief arm, the embryonic Sudan Relief and Rehabilitation Association (SRRA), and "the Khartoum government."[52] The SPLA was also determined to prevent the movement of food aid by truck as long as the shipments were likely to fall into the hands of the army. The SPLA did not ask for parity, but it wanted at least a portion of the donor food its SRRA was to distribute to the needy. The SRRA had been founded in September 1985, and its directorate of fifteen people was a composite of Southern Sudan, with members from the Latuka, Nuer, Anuak, Azande, and Dinka tribes—none of whom had much experience in relief work. It was never quite the "independent humanitarian organization, formed and manned by the refugees and displaced citizens," it made itself out to be; consequently, Western donors had little confidence that it could coordinate a successful relief effort.[53] AID-Washington registered its reservation, and McPherson noted in an interview with *The Washington Post* in late August 1986 that "the experience of the international community in past relief efforts has shown that there must be monitoring to ensure that the food is distributed properly."[54] McPherson's creed was sorely abused within days, however, as an army airdrop to relieve the Bor garrison missed its target and PL-480 wheat was parachuted into the eager arms of the SPLA; this was a curious distribution—certainly without monitoring—of food whose shipment to Sudan had been approved by the AID director's own Office of Food for Peace.

Despite donor protests that SPLA policy was endangering thousands of civilians, Garang and his lieutenants continued to insist that humanitarian food aid had only helped the government. They warned expatriate aid agencies and civilians alike to leave Juba, Wau, Malakal, and Bentiu. The International Red Cross took the threat seriously and postponed an airlift of 300 tons of grain from Entebbe, Uganda, to Wau. In Wau a Red Cross team had surveyed two camps of displaced persons and reported that 36 percent of the people were severely malnourished and 35 percent moderately malnourished and that the city's food aid was nearly gone. USAID-Sudan, however, was unconvinced. It cabled AID-Washington: "Previously no, repeat, no, nutritional data received by [us] has indicated the situation in the South no worse than that in selected northern areas." Without having investigated the situation in Wau itself, USAID-Sudan questioned AID-Washington funding support for the International Red Cross: "Both the [government of Sudan] and the [PVOs] who have historically been the recipients of our assistance will be alienated if the ICRC receives a misappropriate amount of the resources/publicity if they work alone."[55] For USAID-Sudan the specter of the Western relief operation was still fresh in its collective memory, and its leaders feared that UNEOS and, by extension, the International Red Cross were about to drag the donor community into another quagmire.

Operation Rainbow

Indeed, UNEOS pressed forward with plans to move food to the South in any way possible. One suggestion was to use personal diplomacy, approach the SPLA directly, and gain its permission to move commodities. To sweeten the offer the UN considered a "food aid neutral" program to provide food to both sides simultaneously. The planning for such a radical scheme, one that seemed certain to discomfort Sadiq, involved several high-ranking UN officials who frequently considered their personal involvement more important than the operation itself. One representative of the UN World Food Program was Staffan "the Count" Domingo de Mistura, who was a Swedish nobleman or an Albanian charlatan or perhaps both. To some he was an inspiration, to others the evil incarnation of what came to be known as "Operation Rainbow." He was new to Sudan but hungered for the fame—properly managed through the media—the food crisis in Southern Sudan could bestow upon him. His superior, Winston Prattley, was the head of UNEOS and the personal representative of the UN Secretary-General who suddenly, on the verge of his retirement, found himself clutching a tiger by the tail in the guise of the charming, multilingual, effervescent de Mistura. In the middle was Kamal Shawki, the director of the Relief and Rehabilitation Commission. Shawki, who had been a UN employee for fifteen years, quickly understood that the South had replaced the West as the nexus of donor interest. Working closely with the United Nations, he staffed a Southern Sudan Relief Operation office within the RRC and informed Sadiq al-Mahdi of the possibility of widespread famine in the South.[56]

The key to any meaningful relief program for the southern region was the SPLA. Prattley had been in contact with the SPLA in February 1986, when he tried unsuccessfully to arrange safe passage of UN food convoys from Kenya to Juba. Following the Malakal incident Prattley and de Mistura met with the SPLA in Addis Ababa to discuss a trade-off whereby in return for the use of certain roads or neutral "corridors" into the South, food aid to both sides would be provided simultaneously. Shawki's role in this proposal is somewhat obscure. He worked closely with de Mistura to create Operation Rainbow, a food aid program that received wide publicity and international donor support, yet he was "eager to cover his own involvement in negotiations with the SPLA."[57] Often lost amid the bureaucratic infighting that came to characterize Operation Rainbow was the fact that it was the first program in Sudan that attempted to give equal importance to the problem of disaster relief in both the North *and* the South. Internationally, Operation Rainbow was significant because each side appeared ready to accept the principle of the neutrality of food aid—something unheard of in the history of warfare.

Neither Staffan de Mistura nor Kamal Shawki was born to shun the limelight. Indeed, they waxed in the glow of media attention. Each called himself the father of Operation Rainbow, but de Mistura had the better claim. Within hours of the Malakal tragedy the SSRO Technical Coordination Committee met to discuss the reaction of the donors. De Mistura not only chaired the meeting but took charge of it as well. He invited the participants to suggest new ways to move food to the South. USAID suggested a donor petition asking Sadiq to declare the South a national disaster area. De Mistura liked the idea but wanted deeds instead of words. He argued that the famine required a massive airlift of food aid, one the United Nations could fund and promote. To ensure the inviolability of cargo aircraft, some sort of food aid parity would have to be worked out with the SPLA, an idea originally suggested by the International Red Cross the previous April. The donors bought in, and with Kamal Shawki aboard, de Mistura "invented, organized and promoted" Operation Rainbow.[58] The scheme was a palliative rather than a panacea, and even de Mistura recognized that airlifts could not offer a long-term solution to the food aid dilemma. They were expensive and were only a stopgap until more substantial means of transport—trucks, barges, and the railroad—were functioning on a regular basis.

It is unclear whether de Mistura and Prattley or Prattley alone persuaded the SPLA to permit the donor agencies to airlift supplies to Wau, where people were on the verge of starvation, in return for the delivery of food to a town controlled by the SPLA. In either case, the SPLA accepted the proposition, and on 3 September the U.S. Embassy cabled Washington that Garang had offered to call off the air blockade and had "proposed a compromise." If UNEOS wanted Operation Rainbow to service Wau, where over 50,000 displaced persons had crowded into the town and famine seemed imminent, the SPLA wanted food airlifted to Yirol where the same problem existed on a smaller scale. The parties agreed to airlift "16 tons of relief food first to rebel-held Yirol and then 48 hours later to government-held Wau." The SPLA gave "assurances" that relief planes "would not be shot down in airspace it controlled" and that SPLA units would not fire at planes "that passed over their areas without permission."[59] Whether Kamal Shawki seized on Operation Rainbow as a way to resolve the problem of starvation in Wau or whether he actually believed in the concept of food aid parity, he quickly disparaged the Wau-Yirol airlift when the government rejected the plan. An SPLA attack near Wau had lasted for the period 23–26 August, and subsequent food riots in the city resulted in the pillaging of the remaining stocks of food aid and precipitated heavy fighting and casualties between "the army on the one hand" and the Dinka "police, prison wardens, and game wardens on the other."[60] Given the fierce fighting between the two groups and the growing number of persons who had died from starvation, the last thing the army wanted was a host of reporters in Wau writing of the ravaged town and their irrepressible photographers recording the agony of starvation and death—and there was plenty of both. Thus, a "done deal" was undone and Shawki informed UNEOS that Yirol was off-limits because of "military operations." The army then refused to allow chartered aircraft to land anywhere in Bahr al-Ghazal.

With food aid deliveries suspended, in late August Shawki countered with a government program "to alleviate the situation." The army would clear SPLA insurgents from a five-to-six mile radius around the various airports; the railroad to Aweil would be improved; barges would be given military escorts from Renk to Malakal; the government would "appeal to friendly countries to help with food and funding to reach the South through river, rail, and air corridors."[61] Donors would fund civilian aircraft moving relief supplies to Malakal or Wau, but no mention was made of the parity agreement the United Nations had arranged with the SPLA. In sum, Operation Rainbow would not cost Sudan a piastre, and the RRC could take the credit if it were successful.

UNEOS was trapped. UN officials could hardly return to Addis Ababa to renegotiate an aborted agreement with the SPLA, and Prattley and de Mistura could only pray that the SPLA would not shoot down UN-insured planes should Operation Rainbow ever get off the tarmac at Khartoum airport. Something had to be done, because the movement of relief supplies had ceased and Malakal, Wau, Aweil, and Juba were all pleading for help. De Mistura then reversed his field and announced at the next TCC meeting that Operation Rainbow would be "the international community's response to the RRC's appeal for an airlift to the South." It would last one month and cost $1 million, and the operation would "come under the RRC umbrella."[62] The Embassy of the Netherlands immediately pledged $200,000, UNICEF and UN/WFP did likewise, and Canada offered $300,000. In contrast, USAID-Sudan was skeptical: A dramatic, highly publicized airlift would not solve the long-term problem of famine relief in Southern Sudan, nor would it be much of a stopgap, as de Mistura had declared, until overland transport could operate in the South. USAID also had little confidence in the players, especially the RRC and the UNWFP. Its protests were soon overruled by the Department of State, which was also caught in the riptide of media coverage, and USAID pledged five hundred tons of food aid and the equivalent of $200,000 in Sudanese pounds to pay for local expenses.[63]

Incredibly, despite jettisoning the policy of food aid parity, UNEOS reported: "We expect that the SPLA will consider its requirements met and not attempt to shoot down the plane."[64]

The RRC opened an operational office manned by European logisticians at Khartoum International Airport, and donor supplies began to arrive. On 15 September UNEOS announced to a host of journalists invited to Khartoum for the event that Operation Rainbow was ready to fly. They were promised seats on the first relief plane, as was Mother Teresa, who was in Khartoum. A chartered C-130 was painted with a bright rainbow logo, and the first flight to Malakal was scheduled for 21 September. A chartered C-130 was loaded and then grounded after Garang warned against any plan to move commodities to Malakal without receiving prior approval from the SPLA and insisted that the SPLA was still negotiating with "relief officials."

Despite government restrictions and SPLA intransigence, Operation Rainbow began to influence the thinking of the relief agencies caught up in de Mistura's exuberance. On 18 September the European Community office in Sudan (EC) proposed a contingency plan whereby the International Red Cross would coordinate a relief program to move food to the South by "all means possible." Food would be distributed free of charge to the needy displaced in garrison towns, sold at cooperatives at subsidized rates, or distributed in villages in order to halt the flood of displaced persons moving to garrison towns. Infant feeding centers would be created, medical teams would be employed, and survey teams would study problem areas. Throughout the South discontinued economic development projects would be revived. The RRC would be asked to provide technical support, and its office would be strengthened. In return, the government would allow the donors to use government river and rail transport, and it would provide other transportation services and financial and technical assistance as required. The proposal was, in fact, Operation Rainbow writ large, and if Sadiq's government accepted the program, the EC was prepared to pledge more than $9 million to carry it out.

The EC plan was based on wishful thinking, because in effect, it required a cease-fire at a time when both Sadiq and the army were in no mood to seek a truce. Without explanation, on 20 September, a day before the inauguration of Operation Rainbow, the government announced that it could not guarantee the security of the airports in Southern Sudan. Pilots and crews who had agreed to take part in Operation Rainbow suddenly had second thoughts, and the program ground to a halt. Less than a week later, the government, which had interpreted the UN and EC programs as overbearing and arrogant, openly rejected the principle of parity and protested any donor arrangement that involved the SPLA. On 26 September the government announced that Operation Rainbow was dead. After weeks of waiting, the international media fired its big guns at the Sudan government. *The Washington Post* was especially indignant. Its representative claimed that "Civil War and the politics of starvation... have again derailed a two-month-old international attempt to fly emergency food into famine-stricken cities in southern Sudan."[65] In the United States, where many citizens—including influential members of the U.S. Congress—had followed the progress of Operation Rainbow with great interest, the media made clear for the first time that it was far too simplistic to blame the SPLA entirely for the starvation occurring in Southern Sudan.

Weary of waiting and bombarded by editors for copy, of which there was none, the press soon departed. Nevertheless, Kamal Shawki still had $1 million in donor pledges that he was determined to spend. He began by making the outlandish suggestion that food be flown to Malakal, from where it would be shipped by *truck* to Juba and Wau.[66] He next proposed the use of UN-flagged C-130 aircraft to transport 40 tons of food a day to Juba, where CART would distribute the commodities through a program managed by OXFAM. With luck the plane could deliver 1,000 tons in a month (at 20 tons a flight), at which point the money would be exhausted. Unfortunately for Shawki, the UN's London insurers demanded not only an exorbitant insurance payment but a written guarantee as well from both the government and the SPLA that flights carrying food aid would be respected.

Operation Rainbow was again stopped, but the donors agreed that something had to be done. CART reports were frightening: In Juba's makeshift camps for the displaced, 15 persons died every week, and PVOs predicted that the number of displaced would reach "90,000 by the end of October." On 2 October relief food and fuel supplies were exhausted, and "little or no consignments [were] expected via overland routes in the immediate future."[67] Donor fears were at their zenith and Operation Rainbow was practically moribund when a mysterious French DC-8 slipped into the Khartoum airport on the night of 12 October. It was promptly loaded with 32 tons of food and took off for Juba—the only airport in the South capable of servicing jet airliners. Immediately painted with the circus colors of Operation Rainbow, the jet was a *cadeau* from the government of France, which had pledged $600,000 to defray the cost of charter insurance. The cargo jet made just seven flights in three days before its mission was completed. Given conditions in Juba, even a few hundred tons of food was better than none, but the airlift offered very little very late, and in the end it cost France and the other donors about $1,400 per ton to airlift the food from Khartoum.

Because the United Nations is preternaturally cautious, when the DC-

8 took off for Juba everyone assumed that the United Nations had received an SPLA promise not to shoot it down. *The Washington Post* reported, however, that there was no indication that "a deal had been struck,"[68] which, indeed, was the case. Instead, the United Nations had gambled and won, counting on the possibility that the SPLA would not be foolish enough to bring down another civilian plane, particularly one with UN sponsorship and painted with the colors of the rainbow. The DC-8 made quick work of its task and returned to France; with its departure it was time to shut down Operation Rainbow. The RRC appropriated twenty-seven tons of food left over at Khartoum airport; which was "distributed" by a senior government official who toured Juba in December.

Nowhere was there greater disappointment with Operation Rainbow than at Malakal. Its relief committee was both empty-handed and angry. It had registered 13,000 displaced families, and it felt that Operation Rainbow's organizers "should have made certain of their facts before raising expectations of the people."[69] This reaction was understandable, but the committee could not visualize how hard Prattley and de Mistura had worked to sell the idea of food aid neutrality. Indeed, it could be said that Operation Rainbow's denouement occurred on 30 October when the government accused Prattley of meddling in Sudan's political affairs and declared him *persona non grata*. It was an act unprecedented in the history of the United Nations and was hardly a fitting end to Prattley's distinguished career. Moreover, it had a chilling effect, attenuating the relations between the Sudan government and the relief agencies for months to come. UN bureaucrats and expatriate aid officials had been given an object lesson in how far they could go in discussing relief assistance with the SPLA. A European diplomat remarked angrily: "The international community took that lying down.... No one stood up for Prattley: not the United States, not the European Community—nobody." According to OXFAM-Sudan's Mark Duffield, "It was a big blow to everybody's confidence." To all expatriates the message was clear: "If the government could expel Winston Prattley, it could expel any humanitarian organization—and it would."[70]

Winston Prattley's replacement arrived in December 1986 as Kamal Shawki was turning over most of the RRC administration to his new deputy, Dr. Al-Hag Al-Tayeb. De Mistura spent a few more months, manipulating his way back into the UNFAO and winding down UNEOS operations. He was aware that Operation Rainbow had been an expensive failure. The cost per ton of cargo moved was prohibitive, and only hundreds of tons had been moved when thousands were needed. In 1987 the United Nations was still trying to collect pledges from the tightfisted donors, and USAID-Sudan did not deliver the local currency equivalent of its $200,000 pledge until June 1987.

Although Operation Rainbow never became the program Prattley or de Mistura had envisioned, it did manage to focus world attention—if only for a few weeks—on the drought, famine, and implacable and merciless Sudanese civil war. The U.S. Congress in particular the nascent Select Committee on Hunger of the House of Representatives and its chairman, Mickey Leland, were especially attentive. Operation Rainbow had placed the plight of the Southern Sudanese on the world map and had highlighted a civil war of which few in the West had been aware and few governments had noticed.

The Remnants of Operation Rainbow

The SPLA was bitterly disappointed that Operation Rainbow had failed to accomplish its humanitarian purpose. The population under its control suffered the same deprivations as did displaced persons in the Sudan army's garrison towns, and the insurgents had much to gain through the principle of parity. Reporters based in Kenya who managed to visit the SPLA base camp at Narus in eastern Equatoria observed starvation and hundreds of children dying from measles and malnutrition. The United States, however, still refused to deal directly with either the SPLA or it's humanitarian agency, the SRRA. Incensed by the muddle that was made of Operation Rainbow, Garang had some caustic words of advice for Washington: "Before Numayri fell, the U.S. had its money on the wrong horse. It still has its money on the wrong horse. They should shift the money to the winning horse."[71]

Garang denied both claims that his health was failing and media reports that the SPLA was disintegrating. Nevertheless, news reports, which were later substantiated, indicated correctly that Garang and Kerubino Kwanyin Bol had fallen out, evidently over strategy. It had nothing to do with "personal gain," as the Sudan government had eagerly suggested.[72] Instead, as with most major disagreements that surfaced within the SPLA, sooner or later the issues were distilled to the fundamental differences between separatists and unionists. Many SPLA members were secessionists at heart, and few of Garang's lieutenants were as convinced as he that Sudan should remain one nation. Still, despite the differences that existed within the rebel high command, as a fighting force by 1987 the SPLA was stronger, larger, and better armed than it had ever been. With the exception of Kapoeta, Torit, and a few small garrison towns, an area equal in size to Uganda was under SPLA control, and the SPLA officer corps had been expanded to add Equatorians into the predominantly Nilotic leadership. As its military successes mounted, the SPLA gained the loyalty of hundreds of small settlements along the rivers, creeks, and streams of eastern Equatoria, where cattle could still find water and small-scale subsistence agriculture could be practiced. The SPLA leadership had made peace with the Toposa chiefs and elders in the Kapoeta area and with the Toposa who had migrated to the Ethiopian borderlands in search of water.

The situation was somewhat the same in Upper Nile, where only Malakal, Bentiu, Bor, Nasir, and a few smaller towns remained under government authority and the SPLA ruled the bush. In 1986 it had particular success in the Sobat basin, halting the devastation the army had been inflicting on the Anuak inhabitants since 1983. When the SPLA increased its activity around Pochala, the army responded by attacking Ajika village, home of Agada Akwai, the Anuak paramount chief. Agada Akwai was captured and held captive for six months until he was freed by SPLA forces. By 1987 most of eastern Upper Nile was in the hands of the SPLA. Pochala and surrounding villages were being rebuilt, and Anuak in exile were returning to their villages from refugee camps in Ethiopia. The SPLA moved without fear of the army between Narus in the south to Kongor in Upper Nile and Yirol to the west in southern Bahr al-Ghazal. Morale was high among the SPLA commanders, who were optimistic that Torit, Bor, and Kapoeta would soon fall.

In Malakal the failure of Operation Rainbow allowed Sudanaid and Sudan Council of Churches no alternative but to use government convoys to move food. After weeks of effort, Sudanaid received permission to hitch its barges to a government convoy, which subsequently arrived in Malakal on 6 November—six months after its barges had been loaded and nearly nine months after the donor food had arrived at Kosti. In Malakal itself, the displaced were delirious with joy because many had felt that as inhabitants they would soon die. Sudanaid also nearly gave up hope when the Malakal stevedores demanded £S5 per bag (about $1.25 for a ninety-kilogram sack) to unload the barges. Arab truckers then insisted upon charging £S8 per bag to move the commodities a mile from the quay to Sudanaid warehouse. When Sudanaid ran out of money, they then had to pay demurrage for commodities that began to rot in the barges. Fortunately, the military commander intervened because the 1,200-member military escort, fearing an SPLA attack, was anxious to return to Kosti. The food was quickly unloaded, and in late November the barges—weighed down by an estimated 16,000 displaced—began their return trip to Kosti.

As long as the SPLA was precluded from receiving donor food, the convoy was in great danger while proceeding on the White Nile. SPLA snipers fired from the thick vegetation along the river banks north of

Malakal, and near Melut the army escort barely succeeded in beating back a determined SPLA assault. The escort suffered heavy casualties, and the army was forced to use helicopters to evacuate the wounded. The barges finally reached Renk on Christmas Day, and an estimated 5,000 of the harried passengers disembarked to seek employment in the local sorghum fields. Three days later the convoy docked at Kosti, and the remaining displaced persons disappeared into the towns and cities of Northern Sudan. The harrowing return from Malakal in December was more than sufficient to convince the barge and tug operators of the danger, and they suddenly lost all interest in moving supplies to Upper Nile.

Once again all eyes turned to the skies, but SPLA commander Major Arok Thon Arok warned the Sudan army in November 1986 that if "the relief planes carry supplies, food, and medicine to only one side, we shall consider them hostile to us." Arguing that "relief should be distributed to all areas," he added the warning: "We believe the government is making use of civilian aircraft to carry soldiers and military equipment to its forces in the south."[73] The army had indeed begun to use Sudan air to fly military supplies to Juba, but the SPLA, perhaps still smarting from the universal outcry that followed the Malakal incident, confined its firepower to unsuccessful attempts to harass the airports rather than the airplanes.

The displaced persons in Aweil fared little better than those in Malakal. North of Aweil *murahileen* raids virtually halted cultivation and forced the Dinka into town. Aggressive SPLA activity in August caused large numbers of displaced persons, some from villages as far south as Tonj, to move to Aweil. In Aweil itself, Catholic Father Rudolf Deng reported that in 1986, "nearly 100,000 persons were at one time in Aweil and or neighborhoods in search of relief food."[74] By September no food remained, and the displaced could only await the arrival of a train convoy that left Babanusa 220 miles to the north on 16 August. After crossing Bahr al-Arab the military escort skirmished with the SPLA; for the next sixteen days the train moved at a snail's pace, and train crews were forced to repair miles of sabotaged track. Originally, two wagons with sixty tons of food aid had been attached to the train at Babanusa and consigned to the Aweil Relief Committee, but they disappeared en route. Thus, the train brought only army personnel, food, arms, and munitions for the military. As the trains were being unloaded, the army sent a punitive patrol toward Udham, a Dinka village considered friendly to the SPLA and located alongside the rail line twelve miles north of Aweil. The village was sacked, many civilians were killed, and village leaders who surrendered were handed over to military security at Aweil, only to disappear.[75]

The exchange of troops was completed quickly. The train was unloaded, and on 14 September it returned north with 700 military personnel aboard. With no food for civilians in Aweil, more than 10,000 Dinka crammed into and on top of the empty boxcars for the journey north. An additional 35,000 displaced persons had already begun to walk south in the forlorn hope of finding food in Wau.

The northbound train stopped at Meiram, a small town located just north of Bahr al-Arab, where it uncoupled empty cars overflowing with famished Dinka and hitched on loaded wagons that were waiting. Consequently, thousands of displaced Dinka had no recourse but to follow the rail line and walk toward an uncertain future in the North.

A second train convoy reached Aweil on 7 November, after which three quarters of its cargo was trucked to Wau. Ostensibly, it carried no relief goods, even though USAID had informed Washington in September that the government "continued to focus efforts on getting the relief trains through to Aweil" and there were still forty-eight wagons of EC food aid at Babanusa.[76] When the freight cars were unloaded, *mirabile dictu*, three carloads were discovered that contained ninety tons of Reagan dura. The cargo, which was delivered to the Aweil Relief Committee, was another part of the lost USAID shipment that had been loaded at Port Sudan on 23 October 1985. After more than a year it had resurfaced, infested with mealy bugs and flour beetles—which the needy displaced persons devoured without complaint.

Beyond this pittance, the Aweil Relief Committee had virtually no food and no prospects. Father Deng advised the donors that although much sickness and death had occurred in 1986, the next year would be much worse if a substantial relief operation were not soon undertaken.[77] To the south, food stocks had been exhausted in Wau's markets, and the inhabitants "went on a rampage," stealing what food they could find, including the little relief food stored in the town.[78] Wau airport remained closed, the population of the city surpassed 170,000 people, and the displaced persons were reported to be starving. Rough statistical data gathered by Sudanaid and SCC in the autumn of 1986 painted a dismal picture of the depths to which the war had impoverished the human and material resources of Bahr al-Ghazal. Half of the population of Aweil District was on the brink of starvation.[79] Brigadier Albino Akol, governor of the Bahr al-Ghazal, acknowledged that from 1984 through late 1986, the *murahileen* had displaced 600,000 people—and thus, at least one in three citizens from that region had been uprooted. SCC and Sudanaid reported significant movements of Dinka toward Ed Daein in southern Darfur and Muglad and Babanusa in southern Kordofan. In Khartoum the Bahr al-Ghazal regional office registered displaced Dinka residing in the capital; its first census enumerated 52,621 Dinka, most of whom were living in wretched poverty, but the office estimated that the number in Khartoum probably exceeded 75,000.[80] In October *Sudan Times* predicted that in 1987 famine would be widespread in Bahr al-Ghazal; Sudanaid and SCC estimated that in 1987 Upper Nile would need 7,000 to 10,000 tons of food for 175,000 displaced persons.[81] The two private voluntary organizations, which had been in the forefront of providing aid to the South, seemed to be fighting a losing battle, but they continued their warnings that more food would be needed in 1987 than had been delivered to Upper Nile since the renewal of civil war in 1983. For the 1986–1987 crop year, food production estimates in the South were gathered by Sudan Early Warning System Group. Its report in December 1986 predicted a famine as bad as, if not worse than, that caused by the 1984–1985 drought in the West. When their estimates were questioned by government officials as well as donors, the analysts admitted that they were not sure of what was occurring in much of the region. But then, who was?[82]

When USAID-Sudan closed its books for the year 1986, it did have reason to be proud of the effort expended in the West. It had been the major food donor in the 1984–1986 period and in 1986 alone had provided 340,000 tons of PL-480 food commodities (65–70 percent of all food aid), two-thirds of which went to Darfur and Kordofan.[83] (See Table 2.2.) The Western drought faded from official consciousness when summer's "heavenly rain" rejuvenated the grasslands and cultivation's of western Sudan. By November 1986 a bumper harvest seemed likely throughout much of the North. Grain prices dropped to one-tenth of the black market prices in 1985, and the government even prepared to export 200,000 tons of sorghum. When EC officials tried to focus RRC attention on Bahr al-Ghazal and suggested that the outstanding donor commitments that were not needed in Darfur be transferred to that region, the RRC politely ignored the suggestion.[84]

Despite being satisfied that the objectives of the Western relief program had been met, USAID-Sudan still demonstrated no interest in becoming directly involved in a disaster relief program in Southern Sudan. While it had provided funds for Operation Rainbow, USAID still possessed sufficient local currency to pay the air freight costs to move 10,000 tons of sorghum from Khartoum to Juba.[85] The program's denouement had, however, given it the reason it was looking for to shun any new program involving the government and, tangentially, the SPLA. USAID had learned through experience the difficulties of managing a relief program in Western Sudan, and its failure to move expeditiously a small quantity of food from Port Sudan to the railhead at Babanusa and then to Aweil only buttressed the argument of USAID naysayers against its involvement in Southern Sudan. Despite having food and funds, USAID-Sudan acted hesitantly in the face of the many problems existing

TABLE 2.2   USAID Emergency Food Aid Program by Private Voluntary
Organization and Region, Fiscal Year 1986

Region	Tonnage	Commodity Cost (millions)	Transport Cost (millions)
Darfur—SCF U.K.	48,000	11.1	4.5
Kordofan—SCF U.S.	47,700	14.3	4.2
CARE	97,700	26.9	8.4
Central—World Vision	24,100	8.6	0.6
ADRA	3,700	1.8	0.4
Northern—ADRA	900	0.4	0.1
Total	222,100	63.1	18.2
Southern—ICRC-General	3,000	0.3	1.3

Source: USAID-Khartoum, 1986.

in the South—despite the fact that throughout much of Bahr al-Ghazal
the 1986 harvest was less than the poor 1985 crop and in the face of the
desperate situation that existed in Wau. Its new mission director, John
Koehring, shuddered at the thought of becoming mired in some swampy
program in the South. Nevertheless, to satisfy Washington's concerns,
the government's RRC would have to be strengthened to take on the
tasks that would relieve USAID-Sudan from any moral or material obligations vis-à-vis Southern Sudan.

Peace was only a distant possibility. Following the failure of the
Addis Ababa talks in August 1986, Radio SPLA and Garang continued to
insist that if Sadiq wanted peace, it would have to be achieved, "within
the framework of the Koka Dam initiative."[86] Garang did, however, leave
the door ajar for discussion. Following talks with Juba's Archbishop
Paolino Lukudu in December 1986, the prelate reported that Garang had
expressed a willingness to meet with Sadiq and open a new round of
peace talks as long as meetings were not held in Khartoum.[87] The government called the proposal "vague," and a few days later Sadiq formally rejected any discussions with the SPLA or dialogue with the rebels
until they freed themselves from "Ethiopian domination and foreign
intervention."[88]

Ethiopian domination was thereafter a common theme as were government claims that Cuba, Israel, East Germany, Kenya, Uganda, Chad,
and even South Africa were aiding the SPLA. When an excuse was
required to explain an army defeat, one or more of the SPLA's friends—
real or imaginary—were blamed. Sadiq assured Sudanese that he was
determined to carry on the war "as long as the rebels continue to receive
instructions and orders from Ethiopia and refuse to negotiate with

Sudanese Government." He criticized President Mengistu in particular and vowed that Sudan would "continue to support the Eritrean resistance movement" until Ethiopian support for the SPLA was withdrawn.[89] For domestic consumption the government declared that the SPLA was disintegrating and the rebellion "receding." Minister of the Interior Ahmad al-Hussein grandly pronounced that the South was gradually being opened for government relief supplies and that land, river, and air communications were free and clear. He added disingenuously that "the rebellion has now been reduced to a faction of the Dinka tribe to which rebel leader John Garang belongs."[90]

THREE

— ■ —

Battering the Dispossessed

A strada or a minor road—they know not which is which; they cannot camber, do not patch and will not even ditch.

—E. A. Balfour,
"The Rolling Raga Road," Sudan Verse

By New Year 1987 the gravest famine conditions in the South existed in Bahr al-Ghazal. Baqqara militia raids, SPLA incursions, drought, and locusts had reduced the 1986–1987 harvest by half the normal amount. The governor's appeals for food were ignored, and the desperately hungry had gone to the bush to seek anything edible. With Wau slowly starving, the Relief and Rehabilitation Commission (RRC) finally proposed a program to move 38,000 tons of food by truck—even the most sanguine admitted that, without parts or maintenance, the railroad was out of the question—before the spring rains closed the roads into Wau. Kamal Shawki first turned to USAID-Sudan, but it stubbornly maintained that its primary role was as an agency for economic development, and its new director, John Koehring, was a career development man who had no interest in stopgap food aid programs. Although USAID-Sudan had more than 20,000 tons of food in its inventory, Koehring was convinced that a Wau program would invite truckers to demand exorbitant prices, rob USAID blind, and greatly reduce his local currency account as had occurred in 1985. The 1986–1987 harvest far exceeded expectations in the North; it was 60 percent higher than average production for the previous five years. Also, USAID-Sudan preferred to work with the Ministry of Finance to create a national strategic grain reserve.[1] The effort, however, had no chance of success, because the harvest "soon disappeared into private hands," and much of it was exported.[2] Nevertheless, USAID-Sudan sought to redirect RRC requests in the direction of the UN World Food Program and the European Community.

Famine in Wau

Koehring's reluctance was one thing, and Washington's reaction was another. AID officials wanted no repetition of the 1984–1985 famine, and following Operation Rainbow they felt vulnerable to sniping from both the international press corps and congressional watchdogs. They were also being pestered by UN agencies and U.S. PVOs to do something in the South. Consequently, a harassed AID-Africa Bureau agreed to provide 50,000 tons of PL-480 food in support of southern relief, and its mission in Khartoum was instructed to facilitate the program at once. USAID-Sudan joined the new relief effort for the South, but it still tried to limit its involvement by insisting that the RRC take responsibility for the delivery of 20,000 tons of food for Bahr al-Ghazal, 10,000 more for Upper Nile, and 20,000 tons of maize to be purchased in Kenya for delivery in Equatoria. It offered to pay some transportation costs if other relief agencies did the same. USAID-Sudan offered to release immediately 12,000 tons of sorghum it had stored in Port Sudan and elsewhere but stipulated that CARE would supervise the sorghum's transfer to the RRC Management and Logistics Team (MALT). USAID next demanded that in Wau its food aid be delivered to a consignee of its choice, either World Vision International or Sudanaid. In effect, the United States would assume the role of provisioner and banker, and the RRC, MALT, and private voluntary organizations would provide the individuals needed to make the program work.

Kamal Shawki was not pleased. He did not want the food aid consigned to private aid agencies over which he had no direct control because he had his own constituency to consider. He reminded USAID that "since the Governor of each region is a member of the RRC Board of Directors, and also its representative in his region, he is the designated consignee of all food aid and other relief materials"; more ominous was his soothing promise that security would be provided "by the army authorities, according to the need and the prevailing circumstances."[3] USAID-Sudan balked, and Shawki—desperately in need of the quantities of food that only the United States seemed ready to provide—was forced to backtrack. He saved face by agreeing that Wau was a special case and that USAID sorghum could be consigned to either Bishop Nyekindi or World Vision.

No one has ever been "at home" in Wau. Situated on the fringe of the Dinka country, it is surrounded by a host of disorganized and diverse peoples. The British occupied Wau on 17 January 1901 but never knew whether it was a Dinka town, an Azande village, or the abode of the Sudanic cultivators crushed between these two dynamic African peoples. Malakal and Juba, situated on the right and the left banks of the Nile, respectively, were explicable polities, but Wau was an aberration. It was and remains a town belonging to no single ethnic group, deriving its importance only from its position as a commercial and administrative center at the confluence of the Busseri and Sue Rivers. Located in the midst of the vast Nilotic plain hundreds of miles from nowhere, it was miserable under the best of circumstances and it was a wretched and pitiable place in January 1987. Three mutually antagonistic elements were prepared to loot and kill for food and vengeance: The army controlled the barracks, the railway depot, and the airport; the Fertit militia—armed by the government, made up of the hodgepodge of Sudanic peoples, and in large part Muslim and committed to oppose Dinka expansion—controlled half the city; and finally, the Dinka dominated the police force and the *suq* (market), *markaz* (administrative headquarters), and half of the residential area. In January the Fertit militia took advantage of food riots to kill their Dinka adversaries and burn their living quarters. Into this maelstrom of ethnic, cultural, and religious turbulence plunged the humanitarians.

The EC argued in January that the most urgent task facing the donors was to move food to Wau as soon and as fast as possible. This was a facile argument that veiled a formidable task. The direct route to Wau was by railroad from Babanusa through Meiram and Aweil, but that route had been closed after the SPLA blew up bridges and mined railroad tracks south of Aweil. The only alternative required a thousand-mile journey that began with the movement of food aid from Kosti by truck or train to Ed Daein in southern Darfur; there, commodities were loaded aboard *suq* lorries whose drivers used a variety of roads to reach upper Bahr al-Arab. Thereafter they used uncharted paths that crisscrossed the infamous western district of Bahr al-Ghazal to reach Raga. It was, as both herder and trucker knew, an arduous journey, and in spring it could be made even more treacherous by the early arrival of rains that nearly always halted all vehicular traffic from June to October. Sudanese truckers are among the most determined, resourceful, and greedy in the world. They know their vehicles, the terrain, and their customers. Consequently, owners of the ubiquitous six-ton *suq* lorry charged £S1,000 per ton from Ed Daein to Raga and usually made a 100 percent profit on each shipment.

At Raga local truckers controlled the traffic to Wau and utilized a road built by the British during the Condominium. Leaving Raga with or without an escort, the *jallaba* were forced to pay the military a flat fee per truck. Arriving in Wau, they paid the military again merely to unload their vehicles. Given the obstacles of nature, unrepaired bridges, and the vulpine stare of the military authorities, a driver was fortunate to complete two round trips a year from Raga to Wau. Customarily, only four or five convoys moved during the dry season and usually no more than one, if that, during the rains. A convoy normally consisted of hundreds of commercial trucks, many from Darfur. In 1986 the first convoy left Raga in February consisting of 280 merchant trucks and a military escort. It also included four trucks whose costs were paid by Sudanaid. Of these, one loaded with twenty five barrels of diesel fuel arrived empty; another carrying a generator delivered its cargo in pieces. A third truck had half of its load of infant food supplement stolen. The thefts occurred even though the convoy was escorted by 400 soldiers who, despite the RRC admission that they had cost "a lot of money," helped themselves to the commodities along the way.[4] When the donors found that shipping costs included protection money, they protested to the RRC. In turn, Shawki complained to the governor of Bahr al-Ghazal, and the subject then died a quiet death.

In late March another convoy left for Wau, but it was attacked by unknown assailants at Daym Zubayr and promptly turned back to Raga. By April no convoys were moving from Raga, and the program to relieve Wau had collapsed. As the stocks of food in Raga grew higher, so did the market price for cereals in Wau. Truckers were unable or unwilling to move a growing pile of food grain, and even the RRC had to admit that it was increasingly difficult "to interest transporters to go to Raga."[5] On 18 April the skies opened over Raga, and warnings were issued that the Raga road was also impassable beyond Daym Zubayr and that the Kuru River bridge was impassable. Although noted for their daring, the Sudanese drivers—many of whom owned their vehicles—were not about to risk losing them on bridges weakened by rising waters on the Sopo and Kuru. The assurance the RRC had given in January that the Raga road was passable all year was a fiction, which the donors should have known. Miraculously, a small convoy hauling 178 tons of relief food arrived in Wau in early May; it was forced to turn twenty-four tons over to the military and then beat a hasty retreat to Raga. It would be the last convoy to reach Wau from Raga until the Kuru River bridge could be repaired.

Raga: A Community Always In Crisis

As Kamal Shawki was misleading the donors, he was also extending and cementing his authority. Despite Operation Rainbow and the fiasco looming at Raga, he could count on the support of Prime Minister Sadiq al-Mahdi. In April 1987 Sadiq designated the Relief and Rehabilitation Commission the "official" government agency for liaison with nongovernment and private voluntary organizations concerning all matters dealing with relief, rehabilitation, drought relief, and desertification control.[6] Ironically, on the day of Shawki's greatest triumph, USAID-

Sudan agreed to reimburse the RRC at once "for all reasonable costs" it had incurred in the transport of 4,000 tons of food from El Obeid to Wau—despite an existing agreement with the RRC that payment would only be made upon delivery in Wau. USAID thus paid £S4.4 million up front, or the equivalent of $1 million at the official rate of exchange, to move 4,045 tons of food to Raga, where donor grain was stacked in the open and few truckers were willing to chance the road to Wau.

Despite the mounting problems in Raga, Commissioner Shawki was optimistic. For reasons more mystical than rational, he explained that there had been a slowdown in deliveries but that "local knowledge will play an important role in ensuring the onward delivery of food."[7]

In 1987 the commissioner of Raga District was Azraq Nataki Azraq, a Banda from Sopo whose father had taken refuge in western Bahr al-Ghazal after the French had defeated Sultan Sanusi of Ndele in 1911 in the present-day Central African Republic. Azraq was reported to have used his authority to profit from government price controls on basic commodities such as tea and sugar while the inhabitants suffered numerous shortages of food and medicines. In 1987 he was accused of not assisting villagers along the Boro River, where it was later rumored that "400 people starved to death."[8] Certainly Raga was not a safe place for displaced persons. In addition to the Fertit militia, the town had seen a recent influx of Rizayqat traders, Fallata from West Africa, and Habbaniya Arabs—all looking for land and trading livestock. Most were well armed. To add to the growing ethnic tensions, western Bahr al-Ghazal had suffered from drought in 1984 and 1985, and July 1986 the SPLA began its campaign against the Fertit militia. In turn, the Fertit continued to destroy the villages of their historic enemies, the Dinka and the Luo, several thousand of whom sought refuge in Raga. More Dinka, many bound for Darfur in search of work, arrived as a result of the calamity emerging in Wau. Thus, by early 1987 about 60 percent of the district population had congregated in Raga town, the size of which had doubled in three years.[9] The combustible relations between the Nilotes and the Fertit, and the Fertit militia and the SPLA reached a flash point with the growth of the displaced population.

Raga, like other garrison towns in the South, was controlled by the army. Civilian officials had not been paid in months, and those who could not profit from collusion with the military wanted to leave what they regarded as a miserable posting. The price of food had soared. Education and health care were marginal and were nonexistent for the displaced residents. When the rivers began to rise and the creeks overflowed, the truck drivers headed north for Darfur, leaving more than 8,000 tons of sorghum behind in Raga, most of it donated by USAID-Sudan; it was a severe temptation to the greedy and the hungry. In April the U.S. Ambassador Norman Anderson met with Minister of State for Defense General Fadlallah Burma Nasr to request protection for the relief food stockpiled at Raga. He also protested the £S1,000 fee "levied by local military commanders" on vehicles transporting food aid to Wau.[10] Burma Nasr was noncommittal, and neither he nor the governor of Bahr al-Ghazal seemed disposed to assist the dispossessed in Wau despite the numerous reports of starvation inside the city.

By late April conditions inside Wau were horrible. Outside the city limits a twenty-mile "security zone" ringed the municipality, and the nearby fields and villages were deserted. The east bank of the Jur River was empty, where in the previous year settlements and cultivators had dotted the landscape. The roads were dangerous, devoid of maintenance, and strewn with land mines. To the west cultivation was taking place only in secure villages protected by the Fertit militia. To the north and east the SPLA defended the cultivators and the few herds that remained. The center of the city was packed with an estimated 55,000 displaced persons. There were innumerable incidents involving the militia and the Dinka police. A curfew was enforced from 6 P.M. to 6 A.M. by an army command whose contempt for the relief agencies—the Sudan Council of Churches, Sudanaid, World Vision—was as obvious as it was pernicious. Military security agents routinely investigated reports that the agencies had provided food to the SPLA when, in fact, they had no food in Wau to give to anyone.[11]

In June the army command informed Khartoum that the Raga-Wau route would remain closed until the Kuru River bridge could be repaired, thus ending any prospect of relief food arriving in Wau until after the rainy season. Despite their persistent requests, Kamal Shawki was in no hurry to arrange for the donors to visit Raga to see what had become of their food. Although USAID-Sudan and EC officials finally managed to obtain seats on a 12 June military flight to Raga, they were informed just before takeoff that the flight was canceled "due to security reasons."[12] Thereafter, every time they received permission to fly to Raga, the military plane either left early or the flight was canceled without reason. As the donors fumed, Commissioner Shawki suggested a new plan—a sorghum airlift from Raga to Wau using an unknown airline Al Sahib Air Cargo and Trading Services. When Shawki told the agencies the price—£S50 million, or approximately $12 million, to move 8,000 tons of grain—they respectfully declined the offer. With each passing day, however, they were receiving reports from a number of sources that their food in Raga was disappearing. Most of the 8,843 tons of sorghum shipped to Raga had been stored in a military compound, and 30 percent had been stacked in the open, where it was deteriorating rapidly following the heavy rains. No one seemed able to explain why fifty rolls of plastic sheeting trucked from Darfur to Raga in April had not been used to cover food stacked outdoors.

Appalled by the news from Raga, Sudanaid urged the donors to send a "relief coordinator" there as soon as possible to straighten out the mess. Paul Symonds, an Australian with a background in food relief projects, accepted the thankless job; after a harrowing nine-day trip by vehicle from Ed Daein, he reached Raga at the end of June 1987. Symonds immediately caught the army loading its trucks with donor sorghum stored in the army compound. The military lamely explained that one shipment was for a nearby leper colony and another was to pay the Raga Relief Committee for the work its members had performed. Indeed, wherever donor sorghum was stored in the open, Symonds found the stacks aswarm with Fertit and Arab pilferers. He wrote to Khartoum: "The people believe this food is going to feed their enemies and [go] directly [to] the SPLA who are feared and hated. This belief is fostered by army personnel who in my presence told a large group of Raga residents that I had come to take the food to the SPLA in Wau and that they should come and take the dura."[13]

Symond's work was made more difficult when the SPLA attacked Khor Shammam, twelve kilometers from Raga, which was home to the SPLA's inveterate enemy, the Fartak family. The Fertit leadership was afraid of what might happen should the SPLA overrun Raga, and it could expect no pity because the SPLA seemed determined to exact vengeance for the numerous atrocities perpetrated by the Fertit militia. In fear and retaliation the military declared a strict curfew, which it used to load hundreds of tons of sorghum onto military vehicles for movement to private warehouses, shops, and traders' homes. Ironically, some local merchants, who had paid the high costs and sack taxes to move legally purchased sorghum from Ed Daein to Raga, were as angry as Symonds when they discovered that the price they had paid for sorghum in Darfur could not compete with the sorghum stolen by the military and sold at bargain prices to the *jallaba*. The town was so awash with stolen donor sorghum that a few Arab traders from Wau surreptitiously reached Raga, bought sorghum at discount prices, and shipped the grain *north* to southern Darfur. When Symonds complained bitterly to Commissioner Azraq Nataki Azraq, nothing was done, and the military continued to methodically pilfer the grain. When his principal assistant reported that he had received death threats from military and local officials, Symonds found the military was suddenly pleased to give a donor representative a seat on a military aircraft.

Confronted by a pack of furious donors, Kamal Shawki used the Technical Coordination Committee meeting held in Khartoum on 6 July to dismiss their complaints that the situation in Raga was actually worse than Symonds was reporting. The commissioner admitted that the grain was "indeed the responsibility of the Government of the Sudan," but the donors had to understand that, as he put it, "we are doing all possible to regularize the situation in Raga, but you will appreciate that difficulty of access and irregular communication does not make our task any easier."[14] Embarrassed and angry, the donors were desperate to get their food out of Raga. USAID-Sudan and the other donors frantically tried to find a trucking company willing to undertake transport to Wau. There was only one bidder, Camp Services, which had already moved USAID food to Raga at unconscionably high prices. Its new offer was even more startling—£S2,000 per ton and a million-pound advance. With no other truckers interested, the donors were left with Hobson's choice: They could use Camp Services or watch their food disappear or rot. Paralyzed by the ransom they were being asked to pay and by the question of the availability of the Kuru bridge crossing, the donors procrastinated. They finally rejected the proposal, even though the *Sudan Times* had broken the story of the Raga imbroglio on 23 July with the headline: "EEC and USAID Food Rots in Raga While Population Starves." In despair, Symonds left for Khartoum on 21 August, at which time there were still 4,900 tons of donor dura left in Raga which methodically disappeared. By the time the Kuru bridge was repaired by the government's Department of Roads and Bridges, there was no food left to move. Nearly 9,000 tons of sorghum had been pillaged.

The Continuing Deterioration in Wau

Although the Khartoum donors failed to truck food to Wau, World Vision succeeded. In February 1987 it loaded 500 tons of USAID food in Kenya and trucked it along the same general route the ill-fated trucks carrying Cove Trader food had used. The SPLA was informed well before the World Vision trucks reached the Equatoria–Bahr al-Ghazal border that they were transporting food to the Wau Relief Committee, and its soldiers did not molest the convoy. Impressed with the effort— and with the unexpected arrival of food aid, which helped to reduce tensions inside Wau—USAID-Sudan agreed to fund the rebuilding of the bridges along the 300 miles of road from Yambio to Wau in the hope that the route could be used by relief convoys even after the rains came. The proposal was blocked by the governor of Equatoria, Peter Cirillo who refused to allow USAID to use earth-moving equipment it had brought to Juba for that purpose. Nevertheless, World Vision succeeded in transporting 200 tons of food aid to Wau in June but was forced to halt shipments when the Bo River bridge had to be repaired.

By late June 200 to 300 emaciated southerners were arriving daily in Wau, and at midyear World Vision estimated there were perhaps as many as 70,000 displaced persons who required help. What food the Wau relief committee had was delivered to children and the neediest; by late July less than fifty tons were left, "with 5,000 being fed but many more in need."[15] Stocks were exhausted before World Vision could repair the Bo River bridge at its own expense. Before shipments could be resumed, the famine and fighting around Wau had generated even more displaced persons, and many new arrivals were "too malnourished to utilize the food they were given."[16] It was a gruesome summer, and the starving in Wau died quietly and in large numbers. Expatriate volunteers from World Vision and the International Red Cross, who had remained in town despite the shortage of food, as well as Medicines Sans Frontiers–Holland personnel, who were trying to restore the dilapidated Wau hospital, witnessed a terrible famine.

The Massacre at Ed Daein

As SPLA units pushed deeper into western Bahr al-Ghazal in 1987, they were equally aggressive to the north along the Bahr al-Arab. As the Baqqara militia raided south of the river, with the Rizayqat destroying the villages of Acho-ro and Ajok in January, the *murahileen* became more circumspect. Once the SPLA had crossed the Bahr al-Arab River, the days of unopposed *murahileen* plundering were over. In January 1987 a member of parliament from Ed Daein, southern Darfur, complained to Bona Malwal, editor of the *Sudan Times*, about the SPLA presence near Safaha, a traditional dry-season watering hole on the upper Bahr al-Arab for both the Rizayqat Baqqara and the Malwal Dinka. A few days later a company of SPLA insurgents trapped a Rizayqat militia force from Ed Daein District that had been raiding Dinka villages south of the Bahr al-Arab. It killed over 150 Baqqara and recaptured 4,000 head of cattle.[17]

In an attempt to reduce the insurgency in the Transition Zone, in February Prime Minister Sadiq al-Mahdi appointed General Fadlallah Burma Nasr to be minister of state in the Ministry of Defense. The general, a Baqqara from Lagowa in southern Kordofan, was the godfather of and arms purveyor to many Baqqara militia, and it was on his suggestion that Sadiq agreed "to give an unprecedented level of modern firepower to the Arab militia."[18] The general and the prime minister were thus the *imperium in imperio* of a savage policy that not only destroyed hundreds of Nilotic communities in the South but also caused hundreds of thousands of the displaced persons to flee to the North.

By 1987 a steady stream of dispossessed were flowing into and through Darfur and Kordofan. The Nilotes, however, were hardly strangers, as the Dinka and the Luo had first begun to migrate across the Bahr al-Arab in large numbers during the early 1960s. Prior to the outbreak of civil war, the Dinka were tolerated but not accepted by the Baqqara Arab community. In Darfur and Kordofan they found work in the fields, as housekeepers, or at construction sites, and by 1964 a large number had taken up residence in Ed Daein Rural Council in southern Darfur. By May 1986 a census, "conducted by an Islamic group for the purpose of Islamisation and relief work," found 16,970 adult southerners in the township.[19] In Ed Daein they built a church that served as both a place of worship and a social center. In 1986 Rizayqat leaders tried to force town officials to destroy the church, but their petition was rejected by the local court. Just prior to the SPLA's crushing victory over the Ed Daein militia, the National Islamic Front had been active in the town, and religious and ethnic tensions were being inflamed by town leaders.

The local church remained the focus for the ascending discontent, and church gatherings were regarded as subversive meetings. The solar panels used to light the church were considered by some a magic and dangerous innovation, perhaps a means to communicate with the SPLA. On Friday, 27 March, when the defeat of the Rizayqat was still fresh in the Arab's memory, a group of fifty Rizayqat attacked some thirty Dinka who had gathered on the church grounds following a prayer service and forced the Dinka to scatter. Swollen by latecomers, the mob then attacked the neighboring Dinka quarter. At least five Dinka were killed and hundreds more took refuge in the nearby police station. The mob mushroomed, and the police—fearing they could not protect the Dinka—moved hundreds to another compound located close to the railroad station. The Ed Daein massacre had begun, but it would not reach its climax for another twenty-four hours.

The following morning the atmosphere was febrile yet quiet, and the police moved even more Dinka to the railroad station. The intent was to move them from the town to the relative safety of Nyala by means of a freight train that had just arrived. As the Dinka were loaded into wagons, the train was blocked by an Arab mob, which set fire to the wooden wagons and lit fires beneath metal wagons crammed with southerners. In the ensuing holocaust, hundreds suffocated or were burned to death. The horde, consisting of hundreds of people then ran amok through the town killing and mutilating any Dinka found. By 6:00 A.M. the bloodletting had run its course. The Dinka who survived were trucked to Nyala, where the local government, fearing the massacre might be contagious, moved them to Kaas, two hours away. UNICEF was the first expatriate agency to describe the massacre, and it reported that it had "cost the Dinka between 300 and 1,500 lives," most of whom "were women, children, and the elderly" who had been collected and buried in a mass grave.[20] A detailed investigation published in Khartoum in July 1987 provided evidence that more than a thousand Dinka had been immolated or slaughtered.[21]

Two weeks after the massacre the RRC reported that "large numbers of displaced" were "coming into Aweil due to Ed Daein incidents."[22] On 13 April members attending the RRC Technical Coordination Committee meeting received information that two trains loaded with Dinka who had left Ed Daein "due to tribal fights" were about to arrive in Khartoum.[23] TCC members were left to wonder what sort of "tribal fight" would lead to a mass migration of hundreds of Dinka to a northern town.[24] It was later reported that 800 to 900 Dinka adults had arrived at the Khartoum train station. Many were severely dehydrated or in a state of shock.[25] Exhausted from the long journey, like thousands before them they took shelter where they could find it or moved to existing sites on the outskirts of Khartoum and Omdurman where the displaced congregated.

In June USAID-Sudan staff visited Nyala to investigate "the plight of displaced people after the Ed Daein massacre."[26] They found about 2,500 survivors, with the majority having taken refuge in an army compound where they felt relatively safe, although they received no government services and living conditions were execrable. Many of the 1,250 displaced Dinka found at Kaas asked for transport to Aweil "and a chance to restart among their own people."[27] The Dinka in Nyala left as soon as they could, and by July an OXFAM survey found only 384 Dinka families from Ed Daein still camped there. Incredibly, when the time came to clear their fields for planting, the landowners of Ed Daein offered the Dinka work if they would return.

For months the government denied that the massacre had occurred, and on 20 June the minister of the Interior informed the Constituent Assembly that the total number killed "in the [Daein] incidents was not more than 183."[28] The Sudanese whose investigation had forced the government to respond were vilified by National Islamic Front members; they had reported not only on the massacre but also on aspects of slavery in Sudan, including the traffic in captured Dinka children occurring in the Bahr al-Ghazal, southern Darfur, and Kordofan borderlands. Their account of events was circulated widely through the North by citizens who were tired of war and who were aware that as the economy deteriorated, approximately one-third of the national budget was being spent on the military for no apparent good purpose.

Food Aid to the South After Ed Daein

There was war weariness in the South as well. The militias, the bandits, and the SPLA had spread chaos throughout the vast region. The

SPLA had effectively blocked the movement of food into all of the major regional and district headquarters by destroying bridges, mining roads, and attacking government land and river convoys. Critics of the SPLA, both Northern Sudanese and expatriates, claimed that the insurgents were consciously using food as a weapon of warfare. The SPLA's siege tactics were judged merciless, inhuman, and counterproductive and its leadership willful and elusive. No one seemed able to corner Garang because he moved through the bush to direct the fighting personally. Eventually, Bona Malwal of the *Sudan Times* caught up to Garang and asked him to respond to the government's assertion that the SPLA had willingly prevented the transport of humanitarian aid. Garang did not deny having obstructed relief work, but he declared that the SPLA, "as a movement and by its very composition, could not be indifferent to the plight of the people of the Southern Sudan." Nevertheless, he revealed an obvious mistrust of the major international aid organizations and claimed that certain routes were closed because "the only thing that the Sudan government and the international agencies that work for the Sudan government would move through these routes is weapons and materiel and not food for the people."[29]

Garang was bitter because only two major humanitarian organizations had considered providing some relief support through the SPLA's Sudan Relief and Rehabilitation Association (SRRA). The first was the International Red Cross, which had been trying for years to respond directly to the growing human crisis in the South; the other was UNICEF, which had a mandate to provide assistance to children regardless of location or political circumstance. The United States remained aloof, and after the Prattley affair, the United Nations shunned Garang, as did the European Community. Major PVOs, such as CARE, were active in the North and would not jeopardize their status in Khartoum by working with the SRRA, regardless of the need.

Only Julia Taft, the dynamic and irrepressible director of AID's Office of Foreign Disaster Assistance, made any attempt to interest the U.S. government officials in the plight of the Southern Sudanese. In June 1986 she had met with Mansour Khalid, then deputy director of the UN World Commission on Environment and Development stationed in Geneva, and had gathered first-hand information on the SPLA. Khalid, a prominent Khartoum lawyer, had signed the 1972 Addis Ababa Agreement on behalf of Sudan but ten years later had broken relations with Numayri because of his corruption and religious fundamentalism. When civil war erupted again, he secretly joined the SPLM. Brilliant, sophisticated, and charming, he was a Garang confidant. He gave Taft the names of the woefully underfunded SRRA representatives operating in the United States, a background paper on the history of the organization, and a list of its medical and food aid requirements for 1986. When Taft returned to Washington, she began to consider the idea of a neutral food aid program to benefit the needy in both North and South. She was effectively stonewalled by the State Department's Africa Bureau. After the departure of James Bishop, it wanted no part of John Garang, the SPLA, the SRRA, or, by year's end, another Operation Rainbow. Taft continued to apply pressure behind the scenes and eventually played a predominant role in providing humanitarian assistance to Sudan.

In early 1987 the RRC estimated that approximately 1.2 million southerners were in need in government-controlled areas. In contrast, the SRRA stated that there were actually 2.95 million "hunger stricken" southerners. It also claimed that it could reach 1.165 million people approximately double the number it had claimed it could service in June 1986.[30] Unmistakably, the SPLA was winning territory and in doing so had inherited an immense number of southerners affected by war, drought, and famine. As it attacked on the ground, it also scored points on the air; Radio SPLA poured forth a stream of propaganda, pounding Sadiq and his government. The SPLA Political-Military High Command reminded the Sudanese that it was Sadiq who had rejected the "language of peace which had been agreed upon at Koka Dam" and that if he wanted peace, Sadiq had only to accept the precepts of the Koka Dam Declaration that his Umma Party representatives had signed.[31]

While Radio SPLA employed the Koka Dam theme, the government's propaganda machine was also busy. Ironically, despite the combined failures of Sadiq's foreign policy, Sudan's economy, and the government's war aims, as the rebels grew stronger the army had become less inclined to sue for peace. The *Sudan Times* explained: "A deal can't be struck with the SPLA when it has the initiative... nor is there any value in striking a deal when the national army is on the march because victory is on the horizon."[32] Despite the paradox, Sadiq al-Mahdi began 1987 by calling it the "year of peace." He created a Ministry of Peace and Constitutional Conference Affairs and uttered surprisingly pacific statements. In *Renewal*, the newspaper of the Catholic diocese of Juba, he asserted that it was "high time for us to launch a new peace initiative," because a military solution was unthinkable when neither side "will win the war."[33] And when Minister of Peace Dr. Muhammad Ahmad Yaggi was asked when the constitutional conference would be convened, he replied amiably, "As soon as preparations currently underway are completed."[34] Those preparations took an inordinately long time, and the ministry, soon obscured by the *habub* or sandstorm of Khartoum politics, was quietly dissolved.

Government propaganda next portrayed the SPLA as a defeated and demoralized rabble—despite SPLA attacks very near Malakal and Mongalla; propaganda had it that Garang had been "liquidated" by his own forces, and when the rumor proved false, he became the "prisoner of Ethiopia which hoped to establish a Marxist-Leninist republic in southern Sudan."[35] The radio trumpeted fictitious victories, but what Sadiq was selling neither the sophisticated residents of Khartoum nor his potential allies among the Arab states would buy. Saudi Arabia, which had responded sympathetically to Sadiq's return, was utterly dismayed. Having invested heavily in Sudan, Saudi bankers were concerned with failing ventures and objected strenuously to the grotesque Sudanese economic policy. Consequently, Sadiq received neither the arms nor the economic aid he sought from either Saudi Arabia or the Gulf States, and even Qadhafi reduced shipments of war material.

Sadiq al-Mahdi: Maneuvers to No Avail

Although Sadiq spent little time in 1987 seeking to resolve the civil war, he did concern himself with the DUP challenge to his leadership and the need to reconstruct the Umma Party in order to offset the growing strength of the National Islamic Front in Khartoum and in the Upper Nile and Kordofan electorates where the Umma had always run strong. *Al-Tadamun*, a London journal, described the process: "The fact remains that the Umma Party and the National Islamic Front have benefited from the [DUP Party's] past weakness. It is also a fact that the Umma Party, with the new directions it is following under the leadership of Mr. Sadiq al-Mahdi, has succeeded in penetrating the positions of modern forces in Sudanese cities after a period during which the party's influence had been confined to areas where old sectarian loyalties prevailed."[36] Nurtured by his family's rural roots and haunted by the specter of the Shari'a, Sadiq was pushed one way by historical traditions and pulled another by his Western education. In a February 1987 interview in Cairo's *Al-Mussawar*, he acknowledged the unfortunate consequences of *hudud*: "They were one of the aspects of a barbaric experience the Sudan went through in the [Numayri] era, and we are intending to review them. However, it is difficult for that to be done with the stroke of a pen, because we have institutions, and no one can eradicate what he wants in the twinkling of an eye. The matter must be subject to study and the submission of a proper alternative before what exists is eliminated. The alternative is now being presented to the Council of Ministers, and the matter will be presented to the Constituent Assembly for the issuance of further laws. "[37]

Still Sadiq procrastinated. As his government continued the interminable task of studying the Shari'a, he was free to play politics in Khartoum. Sadiq's politics did not, however, put food on the table. Most

Sudanese continued to suffer a decline in personal income and held Sadiq responsible for not reversing a decade of deterioration in Sudan's economy. Transfers of funds from Sudanese working abroad were less than expected; following a series of debilitating strikes, an inflationary cycle seemed destined to continue, as did periodic severe shortages of basic commodities. In July 1987 a harried government declared a state of emergency giving it extensive powers of arrest and detention—although the state of emergency that had existed during Numayri's final months had never been abrogated.[38] After fifteen months in office, the fortunes of Sadiq and the Umma Party seemed in serious disarray. In Washington the government was seen as "indecisive to the point of paralysis because of the enormity of the problems it faces, the fragility of the coalition which supports it, and the conflicting international pressures to which the Sudan is exposed."[39] Sudan's foreign debt was enormous; annual payments amounted to $800 million, an obligation it could not possibly meet. In fact, Sudan was bankrupt. Critics contended that no progress could occur until the war in the South had ended.

In the Last Futile Search for Peace

In the South John Garang seemed prepared to continue fighting as long as the resolutions of the Koka Dam Declaration remained unrealized. In fall 1987 there was, however, some movement after the SPLA met in Addis Ababa, Kampala, and Nairobi with representatives of the resuscitated National Alliance composed of members of the six major parties active in Southern Sudan. This was an unexpected development, and following Garang's discussions with James Surur, spokesperson for the southern politicians, a tentative agreement was concluded to resume peace talks. After admitting that "I don't come out of the bush very often," Garang supported renewed efforts to achieve peace and offered a two-step approach to initiate negotiations. First, a meeting of both sides would be called to formulate an agenda to guide the proceedings of a National Constitutional Conference. Second, once the agenda had been agreed upon, the two sides could move directly to convene the conference.[40] Garang insisted, however, that the agenda would have to address the Koka Dam preconditions, which included canceling military pacts with Egypt and Libya and abrogating the September Laws. Surur returned to Khartoum with a vision of peace, and President Yoweri Museveni of Uganda, whom Sadiq had previously asked to become involved in negotiations with the SPLA, offered to mediate. Sadiq responded by offering a plan to employ the Shari'a only within the Muslim community; predictably, Garang stated that only the abolition of the September Laws and the enjoyment of a single legal code by all

Sudanese was acceptable. It was not a promising start, but at least the two sides were talking to, rather than at, one another.

The Plight of the Sudanese Displaced

As talk of peace was in the air, the number of displaced persons in the temporary dwellings and shantytowns that had grown up on the outskirts of Khartoum was a living reminder to the capital's residents that the civil war had unexpected consequences. The first wave of displaced persons, which arrived from the West during the 1984–1985 famine, had been followed in 1986 by a tsunami composed of southerners fleeing warfare, starvation, and *murahileen* raids. When food became scarcer and widespread starvation was threatened in 1987, they made their way north by the hundreds of thousands.[41] Unlike the Arab wave, the southerners were barely tolerated by Arab residents of the capital's metropolitan region (Khartoum, Khartoum North, and Omdurman). They were not permitted to settle within residential areas, and the only land they could generally invade with impunity was on garbage dumps or other wasteland. The first major displaced persons settlement, Hag Yusif "Carton," was a collection of thousands of shacks built from cardboard and whatever refuse could be scavenged. Founded in 1981 by the most wretched of the newcomers to the capital area, Hag Yusif was located on a sterile landscape thirteen kilometers east of Khartoum North. It had no essential services—no health clinic, no school, no clean water. Males found jobs in the growing construction industry and usually took up residence on or near the construction site; others walked long distances to their work. The women brewed sorghum beer *(merissa)*, a highly competitive business that showed a poor profit and that, given the September Laws, was also a dangerous vocation.

In November 1985 Sudanaid and the Islamic African Relief Agency began to work among the impoverished southerners living in the capital. Sudanaid and the Sudan Council of Churches established camp committees in the growing number of settlements. Sudanaid undertook surveys in various sites despite government objections that they were "squatter settlements and thus illegal in the eyes of the law—it being illegal to settle on unplanned and unsurveyed land."[42] By October 1986 Hag Yusuf had grown to encompass 100,000 displaced persons, and within the camp itself new quarters or small towns (Takamul, Wehda, Barona, Shigla) were evolving. Sudanaid worked with camp committees to provide newcomers with a dry ration sufficient for two months—enough time, it was hoped, to tide them over until they could obtain work.

By 1987 the problem of the Khartoum displaced persons was out of control. Practically and metaphorically they were orphans, and every set-

tlement suffered from a dearth of services, high rates of child malnour-
ishment, and an astronomical purchase price for water that was nearly
always of poor quality. Of the capital's twenty-three largest sites, seventeen had large numbers of the unfortunate living in squalid "carton" villages, where slightly more than half of the children who died did so from
preventable diseases such as diarrhea and measles.[43] In February 1987
SCC—working in cooperation with the government's Department of
Maternal/Child Health, the Commissariat of Health Services for the
Khartoum region, and UNICEF—organized and conducted the first professional health survey of Khartoum's displaced camps. The results
were published in April and attracted considerable donor attention.
Sudanaid and SCC also generated many enemies among the government
bureaucracy, especially among the Muslim Brothers who dominated the
government's Ministry of Health and objected to their findings: The
major source of water in all sites was the ubiquitous donkey cart; latrines
were few; little more than half of the people ate three meals a day; 20
percent of the children were undernourished, one in three suffered from
diarrhea, and only one in ten had been inoculated for measles.[44] Infant
mortality for children under age five was 165 per thousand, a figure that
begged comparison with a Ministry of Health survey in South Kordofan
that found the rate an "unacceptably high" 86 per thousand.[45]

In response to a problem that could no longer be hidden, the Commissariat of Health Services for Khartoum allocated eight of the capital's
worst slum sites to the Sudan Council of Churches. The SCC then
employed a strategy to provide an initial ration of food, blankets,
cooking utensils, and plastic sheeting to new arrivals. Thereafter, most
Khartoum displaced persons often went hungry, but few starved. By
June 1987 the SCC had created a health program designed for 200,000
displaced residents. Other PVOs became involved and expanded the
donor effort site by site and spontaneous settlement by spontaneous settlement. As the number of displaced persons increased, some PVOs were
granted permission to truck water to camps, where it was placed in large
rubberized storage tanks. However, when the government wanted a
spontaneous settlement to move, it would simply reduce the amount of
water available to the drivers.

Slowly and grudgingly, the Sudan government was forced to confront
the issue of displaced southerners in Khartoum. Drastic steps were
undertaken in April 1987 when the government began a campaign of
forced expulsions (kasha). Many displaced persons were driven from the
city, and such documents as they had were sequestered. Rape, looting,
and some deaths occurred. In July USAID-Sudan reported that removals
were occurring "in small numbers and in diverse areas."[46] Prime Minister Sadiq al-Mahdi denied that a campaign of harassment had focused on

the southerners, but the U.S. State Department's 1987 report on human rights stated that there was "a widely held perception among Northerners that the large number of displaced Southerners in Khartoum is a potential security threat. Furthermore, representatives of pro-Islamic political groups hold the view that refugees, most of whom are non-Muslim, dilute the religious purity of Khartoum and other northern regions."[47]

In July 1987, when the Bahr al-Ghazal office in Khartoum tried to involve the RRC in its program, it was advised that the displaced persons were the responsibility of the commissioner of Khartoum—although the commissioner was doing his best to expel as many southerners as possible from the capital.

Following the publication abroad of a spate of articles dealing with the plight of the Khartoum displaced persons, Pacifico Lado Lolik, a southerner and a member of the Council of State, requested a meeting with representatives of USAID-Sudan, the Netherlands Embassy, UNWFP, UNICEF, and the European Community. He criticized the RRC unjustifiably for not assuming a role in assisting the displaced persons in Khartoum, and the RRC responded blaming the commissioner of Khartoum. Lado Lolik continued his jawboning until late July, when the commissioner finally approved an ambitious Sudanaid project for the Khartoum displaced persons and a minor distribution through the Bahr al-Ghazal office. The displaced persons problem was further stimulated following a freak downpour that struck Khartoum on 11 August. The fear that the settlements would spawn a massive epidemic in the three cities led the RRC to urge that more NGOs be allowed to work among the southern displaced persons.[48] In September the RRC enumerated the displaced persons in the capital area, and after a count of 687,000 was reported, PVOs that had previously been discouraged from providing assistance were asked to expand their role. By year's end fourteen PVOs were at work in twenty-two settlement sites, and the larger ones (Zagalona, Hillat Kusha, Abu Saed) received assistance from more than one expatriate aid agency. Meanwhile, in the South the devastation from famine and war continued to exact a doleful toll.

Civil Strife in Wau

In summer 1987 Wau's agony continued without surcease. At night the sound of small arms fire was punctuated by the occasional thump of artillery. Little money was in circulation, and government officials had not been paid in months. The wealthy and influential had bought their way out on a military flight or had escaped by devious routes to Raga. The hospital functioned irregularly because the staff, like everyone else, spent hours scavenging for food to feed their families. Grain was still available in the market, but prices were beyond most people's reach. To make matters worse, Wau Town had fallen into a state of veritable anarchy. Civilians disappeared at night and were found dead the next morning; corpses, many riddled with bullets and showing signs of torture, were dumped along the town perimeter. Armed by the government and led by Missiriya Baqqara, the Fertit needed little excuse to attack the Dinka, particularly the Dinka police. The new regional commander, Major General Abu Gurun, did nothing to curb the excesses of the Fertit militia. He was given the *nom de guerre* "the butcher of Wau" because of his willingness to provide weapons and ammunition, including 80 mm mortars, to the Fertit militia. Thanks to Gurun's dispensation, the militia roamed through Wau, throwing grenades into Dinka huts and murdering Dinka civilians in the streets. In June a score of Dinka were killed and mutilated in the Lokoloko quarter; after a government C-130 was hit by an SPLA SAM-7 missile over Wau airport on 3 August, General Abu Gurun supervised a search of the Dinka quarters that resulted in the deaths of more than 100 persons. Additional hundreds were taken to the river, shot, and thrown to the crocodiles.[49] Later, in a single evening the Sudanese army lobbed nearly a dozen mortar shells into the Dinka quarter, creating confusion and death. Contemptuous and deeply suspicious that the representatives of World Vision, Richard Stueart and his wife, were sending reports of the Wau massacres to the media, the army confiscated all relief agency radios in Bahr al-Ghazal.[50]

On 6 September the military clashed with Dinka police, leaving twenty-five dead in the heart of Wau. The killing continued, and a shootout—again between the army and Dinka police—resulted in the deaths of more than 300 civilians when army tanks attacked the Dinka sector of town and burned or destroyed nearly six hundred Dinka *tukuls*.[51] From March through September 1987, thousands of Dinka, hundreds of Fertit, and scores of soldiers and police were killed in a city at war with itself. As the *Sudan Times* reported in late September: "Wau is presently a divided town with the northern part, from the railway station to the airport and Grinti, in the hands of the military. The southern part of the town, the main market and the government offices and quarters are under the control of the police. However the lynching of civilians is going on unabated."[52]

Despite the civil war raging inside Wau, in late August World Vision succeeded in moving a convoy with 700 tons of USAID maize from the Bo River to Wau. Around 5,000 people on the verge of death were fed, and some food was provided to thousands more emaciated displaced persons. The shipment seemed, however, only a palliative, and the civilian government was powerless to stop Abu Gurun's troops from torching the Dinka quarter or the massacre of civilians by the Fertit militia; it was equally powerless to rescue the donor food stolen in Raga that now began to appear in small amounts on the Wau black market. In November another World Vision convoy arrived from Tambura, this time with 166 tons of maize for the Wau Relief Committee, and more trucks were waiting to cross the Bo River. Miraculously, World Vision succeeded where the Khartoum donors had failed. It was, however, a Pyrrhic victory. Although it had completed plans to move 6,000 tons of food from Kenya to Bahr al-Ghazal, without warning the Sudan government ordered World Vision to leave the country, using "security reasons" to justify its action.[53]

World Vision's demise, along with the expulsion of three other important Western relief agencies—ACROSS, Catholic Relief Services, and Church World Services—stunned international relief personnel almost as much as the expulsion of Winston Prattley. Prattley had been replaced, but when World Vision left Wau there was no organization—indigenous or expatriate—able to continue the flow of food aid to the beleaguered city. Within days of the expulsion, a satisfied General Abu Gurun was recalled to Khartoum to become commandant of the Sudanese Military Academy. After his departure the new acting governor, Darius Bashir, cabled Khartoum in December: "There is still much hunger in our Region, people from rural districts are pouring into Wau town." Beshir added, "The little food grown by natives this year was destroyed by locusts during November 1987." He concluded, "Urgently send us some relief items and money for transport of dura from Raga to Wau."[54] For the year the Wau hospital reported 833 deaths from starvation, but this figure represented a small fraction of those who died quietly in their *tukuls*, crawled into the bush to die alone, or died in a desperate effort to escape the city.[55]

Death in Aweil

Although conditions were bad in Wau, famine conditions in Aweil District were even worse. A train hauling 240 tons of USAID and EC sorghum arrived in early 1987, but half of the USAID consignment was unfit for human consumption, and the EC donation was taken by the Aweil commissioner and never reached the Relief Committee. Moreover, EC officials were never able to locate nineteen additional wagons of food designated for Aweil that were lost somewhere en route. By April 1987 the Relief Committee was virtually begging Khartoum for help. There were 18,000 displaced persons in Aweil town, and the number was increasing daily. The committee was impoverished, but its chairperson,

Father Rudolf Deng, vowed that "in the best African tradition [it] stood ready to help as long as it had food." Father Deng added: "One still has to reckon with the remaining [nearly] 1 million inhabitants of Aweil Area Council, let alone the population of Gogrial, Tonj, Wau, Rumbek, Raga, etc., who now look to Aweil for food, security, and other amenities of modern life. Where are they? They too have been displaced but for their own good reasons, they have opted to face life as it is with dignity and courage in the bushes feeding for the most part on roots of plants, leaves, and wild fruit. They too are object-subject of our care and concern."[56]

As was the case in Wau, Khartoum had received numerous warnings of the incipient famine in Aweil. One was sent by the manager of the European Community's once promising Aweil Rice Development Project, who warned that starvation was "imminent."[57] The problem was exacerbated when a second train arrived in April; it delivered only three wagons (ninety tons) of food aid, sufficient to feed the displaced residents for a week, but the news that food aid had arrived spread quickly through upper Bahr al-Ghazal. When a donor team reported in May that Aweil "was potentially the most seriously affected area" in Bahr al-Ghazal and that children were seen "scavenging on weeds," the donors finally decided to criticize the government for its lack of concern.[58] USAID, the British Embassy, the Netherlands charge d'affaires, and the EC all pressed the Sudanese Railway Corporation to move the train convoy from Aweil to Babanusa as quickly as possible to load food aid. The convoy finally began the return trip on 24 May. Its boxcars overflowed with thousands of starving southerners who used the train to escape the Aweil death trap.

To secure a rapid turnaround from Babanusa, the donors met with General Fadlallah Burma Nasr, minister of state for defense, to protest the inadequacy of "delivery facilities for relief supplies to the South."[59] The general brushed aside the protests and assured the donors that three trains moving 108 wagons would soon leave for Aweil. USAID-Sudan then began a frantic venture to locate the sorghum it had previously stored in Babanusa; eventually, 10 wagons—loaded at an indeterminate date and for purposes unknown—were found at a railroad siding at El Fula and were transported sixty miles to the Babanusa railhead. Despite USAID's effort, the convoy preparing to depart included only seven boxcars of relief aid.

The lack of progress in moving food southward led the Bahr al-Ghazal Relief Office in Khartoum to bitterly criticize the RRC: "News of deaths of hunger will certainly be reported from Aweil area this year, but there are no preparations ... to avert the catastrophe. Our experience in the Relief Office is that even if the Southern leaders take the matter up with the RRC authorities ... nothing will be achieved. It seems that

North/South politics has made its way [into] humanitarian fields."[60] The Relief Office was prophetic. When a convoy of three trains guarded by the military left for Aweil in late June, only three wagons of Italian rice donated by the EC went along. Despite the number of trains leaving Babanusa in the first seven months of the year, only 300 tons of food and other humanitarian relief had reached Aweil to provide for an estimated 100,000 extremely needy people. In one egregious case, a number of boxcars loaded with UNICEF medicines for the Aweil hospital were left behind while a wagon load of pharmaceuticals was delivered to the Aweil police; by mid-July there were no essential medicines in the hospital and not even an aspirin, in the market.

The donors were understandably outraged that relief food was the last item to be transported, but despite their anger they invariably used the RRC, a deficient venue, to vent their grievances. They were notoriously loathe to confront openly either Sadiq or his ministers, and none threatened to leave Sudan or raise their concerns with the international media—which in the case of USAID-Sudan was impolitic and in the case of the United Nations was impossible.

In July the commissioner for Aweil informed the *Sudan Times* that 50 people had already starved to death. The toll was, in fact, much higher, and Father Deng reported that by August eight to ten people a day were dying, and Aweil's grave diggers were "so weak from hunger" they could no longer "bury the dead."[61] Thus, when the train returned to Babanusa in August, thousands more undernourished Dinka scrambled aboard to escape the town. On a single day in August around 500 new arrivals from upper Bahr al-Ghazal were registered in Khartoum; despite their wretched physical condition, the RRC argued that not everybody coming from the South should be considered to be displaced or starving because "people are moving freely for their own business, some of them coming for holidays and so on."[62]

In August the Aweil Relief Committee husbanded its supplies carefully, cooking only sixteen drums of rice daily for distribution. In Khartoum the Embassy of the Netherlands responded to the crisis by donating £S1 million to the committee to purchase whatever sorghum might still be held by the Aweil *jallaba*. Nearly 200 tons (2,000 bags) were purchased from merchants, who charged up to ten times the price paid in Khartoum. This was only a fraction of what was needed for the 100,000 displaced persons registered from July through September, and by autumn 1987 Aweil Town had begun to die. The governor reported that the young men whose families had lost their cattle or been forced from the land were either joining the SPLA or attempting to reach Ethiopia, 500 miles to the east. The UN World Food Program reported that a "large number" of displaced persons had been living on roots for some time and that 1,100 deaths had recently been registered.[63] Older males, women, and children scattered in all directions—to Wau, to Abyei and other towns and villages in Kordofan and Darfur, and even to Khartoum.

Although the trains had made more trips between Babanusa and Aweil than in any year since the outbreak of the civil war, they continued to carry few relief goods. In late October another train was sent from Babanusa, and it reportedly pulled *eight* wagons of relief food (240 tons) and the ton of UNICEF medicines that had previously been shunted aside. The train, which was carrying its usual component of troops and military supplies, was ambushed between Ariath and Malwal twenty-five miles north of Aweil. The SPLA claimed that more than 150 soldiers, including the commander and 5 officers, were killed in a seven-hour battle and that twenty rifles and six machine guns were captured. It denounced the government for transporting military supplies under the guise of relief food. Ironically, when the convoy limped into Aweil on 5 November, only *five* wagons (150 tons) of EC-donated rice were delivered to the relief committee.[64]

When food first became scarce in Aweil District in early 1987, tens of thousands of Dinka began the trek north into southern Kordofan in search of food. Many traveled through Safaha and arrived at Ed Daein. Many more passed through Abyei in southern Kordofan, where they stayed seeking food from their Dinka brethren and any work available. By February the displaced Dinka were so numerous that the governor of Kordofan pressed the RRC to send food relief for Abyei. When approached, USAID-Sudan avoided any commitment; given the existing problems in Raga and Wau, it promised to consider the government's request only when it knew "more about the numbers of displaced, their origin, where they are currently located, their exact food needs, how this food would be distributed and by whom."[65] The RRC responded that in Abyei District there were at least 35,000 displaced Dinka—25,000 from Abyei District and 10,000 from elsewhere in Bahr al-Ghazal. When USAID investigated on its own, it found that security in Abyei Town was "precarious" and that local Arabs had just burned many Dinka *tukuls*. USAID beat an undignified retreat, covering its flanks by employing the most tortuous bureaucratic prose imaginable: "While the Kordofan Government would like the population of this area to return, and for the Meseryia peoples to form a buffer zone against the incursions of the SPLA, waiting for the rains to allow regrowth of the building materials to reconstitute the burnt down huts is probably sensible. When the security situation in this area is stabilized, so that we could ask a PVO to supervise or monitor food distributions, we will reconsider [the RRC] request."[66]

Starvation and Death Beyond the Bahr al-Ghazal

The Abyei problem was overlooked for the rest of the year as the donors grappled with problems surfacing in Wau and Aweil Districts. Elsewhere in southern Kordofan the European Community managed to ship 360 tons of food to Meiram, a Missiriya village located in southwestern Abyei District a few miles north of the Bahr al-Arab, where 10,000 displaced Dinka had congregated.

Elsewhere in the South, Upper Nile region was little better off than Bahr al-Ghazal. In 1987 the Nuer living south of Bentiu began to spread a story of a silver airplane that had circled lazily in the sky for several of hours and then suddenly plummeted into a swamp in the sparsely populated Sudd. Following the crash a tall plume of white smoke was reported. Later, when the first rains arrived, great numbers of villagers in the area began to sicken and die. Entire families were taken, as were their cattle. The scourge was blamed on the mysterious plane, which was used to explain an extensive outbreak of kala-azar (visceral leishmaniasis), a potentially fatal disease, that began in Upper Nile south of Bentiu and soon spread throughout the region and to Khartoum. Kala-azar was not new to Upper Nile; what was new was the frightening incidence of a disease that had previously been occasional but never pandemic. Leer was hit particularly hard, as was Bor; one of John Garang's sons came down with the disease and was treated by Western health volunteers who had begun to work in SPLA-controlled Southern Sudan. The disease was spread by thousands of Nuer who fled Upper Nile and eastern Bahr al-Ghazal to escape the civil war and the 1987 famine. Moreover, the problem of kala-azar was exacerbated by an outbreak of meningitis. The diseases soon spread to Khartoum, causing great uneasiness in the capital and resulting in the demand for an immediate program of vaccination. The panic was used by Muslim fundamentalists to insist that southerners should be prohibited from settling inside greater Khartoum.

Face to face with the four horsemen of the apocalypse—war, famine, plague, and death—the RRC began in 1987 by hurriedly loading food aid in barges for delivery to southern villages along the White Nile and to Malakal. It had received pledges for a total of 2,700 tons of food from USAID—Sudan, Canada, Italy, the UN World Food Program, and other donors. UNICEF provided blankets and infant formula for children; USAID agreed to pay the cost of tugs and barges. A large convoy including six barges of food aid arrived in Malakal in March, creating an inventory of about 3,100 tons of rice, sorghum, and vegetable oil for the usually harried Malakal Relief Agency. The barges had brought their own stevedores, and they gouged the relief agencies for £S9 (more than $2.00) to carry a sack the short distance from barge to *jallaba* trucks waiting on the quay. Once emptied, the barges remained at quayside for months. In the meantime nothing arrived by truck, and the airport received only military supplies. By June 1987 the 70,000 displaced persons had devoured about half of the March shipment, and the food ration of one pound per person per day was reduced to stretch the food supplies at least through October.[67]

Sudanaid, the persistent good Samaritan to the inhabitants of Malakal, sought to relieve the food shortage by securing land on the open outskirts of the town for cultivation; it also purchased seed and hoes for distribution to the displaced persons. It was nearly always frustrated by the military, which flattened squatter camps on the edge of town to create open fields of fire against the inexorable encroachment of the SPLA. Eventually, 4,000 farmers participated in the plan, only to be thwarted when summer rains did not materialize. Indeed, in hundreds of Upper Nile villages the maize crop failed, and in July the governor requested food for the hard-hit villages located along the Sobat River. However, the convoy remained in Malakal, where by September its population had ballooned to an estimated 130,000 people. With rising food prices and virtually no food aid remaining, the displaced Dinka were forced to seek refuge elsewhere. Thousands joined the stream of Dinka who had already begun to move from Bahr al-Ghazal to Ethiopia. Alarmed by a smattering of reports that seemed to indicate that much of the populace of northern Bahr al-Ghazal and Upper Nile was on the move, AID-Washington asked USAID-Sudan to report on drought conditions in the "Malakal/Bor/Nasir triangle." The mission provided only sketchy data on rainfall and livestock conditions and offered the lament that no "more detailed information" was available.[68]

From Malakal, others began to trek northwest to southern Kordofan and north to Khartoum. On occasion they faced four-legged predators as well as the customary two-legged ones; one large group reported that it had been attacked by lions—something unheard of for many years—that devoured at least eighteen people.[69] Thousands who remained in Malakal swarmed on to the barges, which, after being tied up for six months, began their return journey to Kosti in October. For many the choice was to leave or to starve. At least 15,000 passengers disembarked at Renk, where the district had begun in 1987 with more than 20,000 displaced persons desperately seeking work. Few barge passengers found work in Renk, and most continued on foot toward Kosti and Khartoum. Despite the hardships endured they were still better off than the displaced Dinka left behind in Malakal; despite severe rationing, by year's end 140,000 displaced persons had consumed nearly all of the relief committee's food supply.[70]

Of the three southern regions, in 1987 Equatoria was the least affected by war and famine. Still, the numbers of displaced Dinka—which had fluctuated as a result of SPLA, government, and bandit activity—had evolved in Juba and the principal towns into a permanent population. The relief agencies and their CART operation had been severely tested as insecurity increased. In January 1987, CART estimated that Equatoria's displaced population numbered 90,000 and warned that their numbers in Juba would soon double. (See Table 3.1.) Within months, eastern Equatoria suffered from drought, insect infestations, and warfare, and more than 125,000 displaced persons were added to the total. The problem of security was complicated by the numbers of armed militia who had taken to banditry. Near Juba the army command found it increasingly difficult to control the Mundari militia it had armed to defend the northern approaches to the capital. Badly mauled by the SPLA around Terekeka, they had retreated into Juba Town despite all attempts by Sudanese officers to keep them in the field. East of the Nile the government-armed militia spread banditry like a plague; along the Torit road the Catholic Diocese in Juba reported that the militia "waged inhuman acts against civilian"; in a specific case, "at Lowqoi village, they hunt down men and women, especially those who work in the fields."[71]

In response to the CART appeal for more aid and to the appeals of the governor and Kamal Shawki as well, a large convoy with a three-month supply of food aid arrived in Juba in May 1987. By July CART was distributing about 1,600 tons of commodities a month that had come from cross-border programs. The truck route from Zaire to Juba was, however, becoming increasingly problematical, and the road from Yei to Juba was downright dangerous. In addition, the route through eastern Equatoria, from Kenya and Uganda through Torit to Juba, was very insecure and was often closed by SPLA units. In June the army garrison at Juba, reinforced by its Murle militia, launched a major offensive to open the vital Juba-Bor road only to be thrown back in defeat by a stubborn SPLA defense. The Murle lost heavily, and those who were not slaughtered fled for refuge in Juba. Throughout the late summer and fall, the SPLA stepped up its hit-and-run tactics, moving freely in the countryside and tightening the noose around Torit and Juba but avoiding the army's concentrated firepower.

It was not until southerners other than the Dinka began to suffer from famine and war that powerful Catholic Church leaders in Equatoria were motivated to excoriate both sides—rather than just the SPLA—for the numerous depredations befalling their parishioners and their people. When over 200 Christian leaders from Southern Sudan congregated in Juba for an ecumenical conference in July, they castigated the government's "current plan and programme of Arabisation," declaring "that the Muslim Government in Khartoum" was using every means, "sometimes

TABLE 3.1   Equatoria Region—Displaced Persons, February 1987

Displaced from	Displaced to	Population
Jebel Lado, Mongalla, Juba rural-East Bank	Juba	11,000
Terekeka District	Juba	28,000
Torit/Kapoeta District	Juba	20,000
	Total in Juba	59,000
Yei, Wandi, Kediba, Amadi Mvolo, Bahr el-Grindi	Mundri	6,000
Ibba, Nguande, Kazi, Woko	Mundri	4,000
Wau	Yambio	2,000
Wau	Tombura	4,000
Torit District	Torit	10,000
Kapoeta District	Kapoeta	5,000
	Grand Total	90,000

Source: Combined Action Relief Team Report, Juba, 23 February 1987.

even inhuman ones, to subdue the Christians and the southerners to Islam." They added, "The [conference] participants are aware of this and they have decided to inform the rest of the people." In a joint prayer that ended the conference, Catholic Archbishop Paolino Lukudu Loro asked the quintessential question that had not been raised in Juba since the Addis Ababa Agreement: "Is it a crime to be an African in Sudan?"[72] This was strong stuff from the church leaders, many of whom had previously straddled the fence between the SPLA and the government. A few weeks later the government retaliated by sharply criticizing the Sudan Council of Churches for providing "tickets and facilities" that allowed members of the Southern Sudanese political parties in Khartoum to attend meetings in East Africa whose admitted objective was "to facilitate the unity of the parties in an effort to bring about a negotiated settlement of the conflict in the South" and that had led to discussions with John Garang. The meetings did little to move the government, but "to the chagrin of Khartoum," the South's political leadership finished the year more united than it had been in years. For once, "All the African Parties represented on the trip supported a united Sudanese African approach to the problems facing the country."[73]

The SPLA on the Offensive

In counterpoint, SPLA activity in Upper Nile and Blue Nile regions in late 1987 did much to unite Khartoum's conservative Muslim factions. From 1985 through 1987 the army and the SPLA had campaigned for control of a strategic region parallel to the Ethiopian frontier from Kurmuk in Blue Nile to Jokau in Upper Nile. In April 1987 the SPLA, supported by a host of Uduk from the Ingessana Hills, had overrun the garrison at Tali Post before slipping over the border into Ethiopia. Desultory fighting continued until 11 November, when an angry Sadiq al-Mahdi announced in Khartoum that the SPLA had taken Kurmuk and complained of heavy shelling "from inside the Ethiopian side of the border."[74] The fall of Kurmuk—which southerners had since the Addis Ababa Agreement contended formed part of the South—was a thunderbolt that had an enormous psychological impact on the government and the Arab jingoists: "There was panic in Khartoum. Rival Northern political groups rose to the occasion, seeking to make political headway from the incident. The SPLA advance was represented as a slight on the integrity of the North, a threat to the hydro-electric power stations at Al Damazin ... a precursor of some future attack on the capital itself."[75]

In Khartoum the government counterattacked with a hysterical campaign characterized by racism and religious bigotry that precipitated an increase in racial and religious tensions in the capital. According to the Islamic African Relief Agency, the SPLA offensive generated 52,000 displaced persons.[76] This time, however, it was the Arab population that was forced to flee. Most settled at Damazin, where local officials quickly provide a daily sorghum ration. The Agricultural Bank of Sudan pledged 1,500 tons of sorghum from its stocks, and the RRC provided powdered milk, sugar, vegetable oil, beans, and 3 tons of clothing.[77] Government representatives were dispatched to the capitals of the Arab world to request funds to win back an "Arab" town captured by Africans and infidels with the help of "Ethiopian and Cuban troops."[78] The government asserted that it was threatened by an "African invasion," a claim so preposterous that it was repudiated by President Hosni Mubarak of Egypt.[79]

After holding Kurmuk for a few weeks, "the SPLA withdrew quietly, having made their point." Still smarting from the loss, Sadiq refused to attend the December meeting of the Organization of African Unity in Addis Ababa. Characteristically, he changed his mind and met with Ethiopian President Mengistu Haile Miriam in what some hoped would be a move toward ending the war, since Sadiq had frequently maintained that the SPLA-Ethiopian connection was the key to peace. Nothing came of their discussions except an innocuous agreement to form a joint commission to discuss bilateral issues. Simultaneously, government representatives met with Mansour Khalid in London, but their talks first foundered and then sunk on the granitic pinnacles of the September Laws. Nevertheless, these talks signaled to some—and buoyed the hopes of optimists—that the differences between the Sudanese belligerents were narrowing and the prospects for peace expanded despite the increased flow of arms to Sudan from Iraq, Libya, Egypt, and Saudi Arabia.

In fact, whereas Kurmuk had been a propaganda victory for the SPLA, it only led an embarrassed military and a furious prime minister to fight the SPLA with greater vigor. Sadiq's Umma-DUP coalition, which had been ready to submit a new legal code to the Constituent Assembly, now held back, and the so-called alternative laws were not submitted until July 1988. Moreover, Sadiq tried to push a bill through the assembly that would have legitimized the existing militias. He argued that "paramilitary forces" were needed and with others employed the specious argument that "the idea to set up the forces arose from SPLA attacks in the provinces of South Kordofan and Blue Nile."

In Parliament the Umma and the DUP split, with the DUP opposing the militia bill "on the grounds that the force would rival the armed forces."[80] Some government officials admitted privately that arming the militia had been a "defensive" strategy that had gone wrong. Others countered that the use of the militia, as practiced by some military personnel, including General Burma Nasr, was the most efficient means of extirpating the Dinka and replacing them in northern Bahr al-Ghazal with Baqqara Arabs. Southern assembly members, even those who disliked the SPLA, considered the plan revanchist—surfaced by conservative forces in the Umma Party and backed by the NIF and the Muslim Brotherhood to drive the Dinka from the land. In classic guerrilla terminology, once the Dinka were scattered, the SPLA— the fish—would not be able to swim in a sea of Dinka villages.[81] A Dinka from Gogrial and an official of a Western relief agency warned that there were already "too many arms and there is no law. The Gogrial district ... is being emptied of people and cattle. It has never been like this before."[82] The bill was shelved temporarily, but not before it had become evident to most Sudanese that a civil war fought by southerners to effect political and economic parity among all regions had become a war to the death, a war that verged on the planned extermination of a culture.

In Khartoum many people were sick of the interminable war between the North and the South, and a number of politicians had already concluded that Sadiq was the reason no progress was being made to end it. Consequently, in December 1987, a Sudan Transitional Charter which professed the Arab and the African nature of the state was signed by the members of all major political parties except the National Islamic Front. The charter also called for a Constitutional Conference, new legislation to reduce the enormities of the September Laws, and an equitable distribution of funds derived from the nation's natural resources. Sadiq could not reject the charter out of hand, because too many Umma Party leaders supported it. He could, however, ignore it, which he did in order to continue the war. John Garang's New Year's message directly blamed Sadiq for the war's continuation: "Peace had not come to our country because the government of PM Sadiq al-Mahdi is seeking a military solution, and has rejected the Koka Dam Declaration as the basis of the proposed National Constitutional Conference. He has worked out his own version of the Declaration—a weaker one—which, in essence, is a deviation from the one signed by his party before he assumed the premiership of our Country.[83] Sadiq al-Mahdi and John Garang, were as far away from agreement as they had ever been, and an end to the terrible destruction in the South appeared as far removed as ever.

FOUR

■

Starvation in the South

The major problem now is in the Aweil area, around Maryal Bay and Gom Masher.
Fighting in this area [between the Dinka and the Rizayqat Arabs] has flared up again
right up to the south bank of the Bahr al-Arab. The harvest in this area has totally col-
lapsed and most livestock have been stolen. Large numbers of people are moving out of
this area.

—UN World Food Program–Sudan telex,
22 January 1988

As 1987 drew to its gloomy conclusion, the relief agencies began to
project Sudan's need for food assistance in the coming year. Food aid
was required in the east, where lingering drought persisted in the Red
Sea region; in the west the governors of Kordofan and Darfur, ready to
bend the truth if doing so would result in more food aid, began to ask for
ridiculous amounts and shamelessly employed 1983 population data that
had been invalidated by years of drought and dislocation. The European
Community, which had already staked out a major role in the economic
development of Darfur, agreed to take the lead in sponsoring a Western
Relief Operation (WRO). The WRO began, however, only after considerable discussion—which was not without acrimony—and only after the
Relief and Rehabilitation Commission had reduced its demands for
Darfur by half, to 55,000 tons of food aid, and lowered its demands for
Kordofan to 71,000 tons of aid.[1] In contrast, the RRC paid little attention
to, and had no program in mind for, the South, even though it did
request 31,800 tons for the three southern regions.

The Western Relief Operation

USAID-Sudan had only reluctantly agreed to support the WRO and
did so only after the Ministry of Agriculture announced that given the
excellent 1987–1988 harvest, the government's grain reserves were prob-

ably sufficient to meet any regional shortage. It was further reassured when the Ministry of Finance informed donors that they could "purchase food locally for relief" and promised to sell sorghum from the Agricultural Bank of Sudan (ABS) at the official price of £S45 a ninety-five kilo bag.[2] For USAID-Sudan, the government's optimism could not have been more propitious; it had submitted no request for emergency food aid for 1988, and a government solicitation—whether approved in part or in full by AID's Food for Peace Office—would have arrived in Sudan well into 1988. The donors accepted the fact that "adequate stocks existed in Sudan for the WRO, and ... imports were not required. The choice was to purchase grain on the open market by tender, or to buy from ABS stocks. In line with the principle behind the WRO of relying as much as possible on GOS [Government of the Sudan] institutions and contributions, it was agreed to purchase from ABS who were at that time holding very large stocks."[3]

Although the European Community began its WRO planning, USAID-Sudan was unwilling to take a direct part. It believed the media had unfairly criticized the agency for the various lapses in performance that had plagued the 1984–1985 program. Having once rushed into the breach to manage a large-scale relief program in Kordofan and Darfur, it had thereafter maneuvered relentlessly to avoid playing a major role in the administration of any food relief operation. To protect itself from criticism in Sudan and Washington, USAID-Sudan created a Disaster Preparedness Committee, which was to coordinate future relief activities, and then it tried to avoid entanglement in RRC programs. USAID-Sudan was pleased to see the EC take over the WRO program and agreed to provide from its Trust Fund Agreement Account nearly £S15 million (about $3.5 million) to help defray expenses. It also pledged to assist in programs that would develop WRO disaster relief infrastructure. This idyllic solution was, unfortunately, deeply flawed, and USAID soon found that its funds and its energies could have been better spent elsewhere than in the West, where rains had fallen from above average to very good and most villagers harvested a decent crop in the 1987–1988 season.

The Western Relief Operation began well enough when foreign donors agreed to an initial allocation of 10,000 tons of food aid for Darfur and 20,000 tons for Kordofan. It was soon mired in bickering, however, when the government claimed in January 1988 that despite news to the contrary, the 1987–1988 harvest in Kordofan and Darfur could be the worst in a decade and that the nation's sorghum harvest might not exceed the unbelievably low total of 1.3 million tons. A USAID team was sent to Darfur, where it found that farmers in the Jabal Marra district had harvested a bumper crop; thus, the problem of food shortages throughout that region was resolved. Cereal production had been particularly good in southern Kordofan, and Darfur had enjoyed "two good years of rain" despite a few pockets of drought in the north.[4] Camel and cattle prices were stable, and there was no sign of herdsmen having to sell their animals. Sudan, in fact, was benefiting from a 650,000-ton cereal surplus—of which 85,000 tons were in Kordofan. Because donors had one set of expectations and the government had another, the surplus evaporated almost overnight. Sorghum was exported pell-mell, with government officials employing the usual excuse of a hard-currency shortage to explain the pervasive corruption that accompanied export sales. Agricultural Bank stocks were rapidly depleted, and all thought that any strategic reserve was forgotten. The donors had been gulled as usual, but they deserve forgiveness because they believed the government was finally placing the welfare of its citizens above the export of sorghum.

When AID received conflicting signals on conditions inside Sudan, it pressed the somnolent USAID-Sudan mission to review its food policy for 1988. In response, USAID Director John Koehring cabled Washington in unintelligible bureaucratese that the mission was "continuing emergency requirements in Southern Sudan." Despite conditions in Sudan Washington was informed that large numbers of Ethiopian refugees, fleeing from drought conditions in that country, might enter Sudan and would require food assistance "of amounts difficult to quantify, but assuredly in excess of food stocks USAID had in Sudan."[5] No extensive analysis was provided of the growing famine conditions in the South; although Washington offered USAID-Sudan 50,000 tons of U.S. sorghum, Khartoum replied that given the good 1987–1988 harvest, 25,000 tons would suffice. It added disingenuously, "If not needed, this stock can be allocated to a national strategic reserve."[6]

The donors expended considerable effort investigating conditions in Kordofan and Darfur; in the northern Sahil, where rains had been sparse, ample food aid was delivered in a timely fashion. In doing so, however, attention was diverted from signs and omens that a massive disaster was building in the South. Although USAID policy in the West appeared reasoned and political, its unwillingness to take part in another relief program for the South may have been sagacious but was hardly noble. The agency was still angry over the Raga debacle. Before visiting Raga in January 1988, an RRC-UNICEF team had been told that 1,300 tons of donor food "were still in the stores" and then found that all the food was gone.[7] USAID was not about to chance its local currency on another expensive trucking scheme to Bahr al-Ghazal, yet the Raga incident fails to explain the reluctance of USAID-Sudan and the U.S. Embassy to ignore the evidence that a major famine would have a dreadful impact on the South in 1988. World Vision had reported to Khartoum that in November and December 1987, around 75 of 471 children and adults registered at a single center for the malnourished in Wau had died.[8] Famine conditions existed in Wau, and USAID informed Washington in January 1988 that displaced persons arriving in Khartoum reported that "the situation there is grave" and that "food shortages caused by the multiple problems of drought, locust damage and civil unrest" meant that cereal prices throughout the South had risen to "prohibitively high" levels.[9] The RRC's TCC was aware that no relief supplies had arrived in Wau since November, that relief stores were empty, and that a sack of sorghum was selling for twenty times the Khartoum price. There was a 60 percent mortality rate among children admitted to the Wau hospital and a 20 percent rate among displaced children visiting the only operating feeding center.[10] Elsewhere in Bahr al-Ghazal, there was famine in Aweil and the surrounding countryside. In Upper Nile the crop harvest around Malakal was one-fifth the normal amount. The "eastern corridor" from Kurmuk to Pibor suffered almost complete crop failure, and Dinka fleeing to Ethiopia to escape the drought and the *murahileen* in Bahr al-Ghazal found no food in the villages along the way. Thousands starved before reaching a refugee camp.

North of Bahr al-Arab in late 1987, the arrival at Meiram of 10,000 Dinka, nearly all of whom were "in very bad physical condition," was visualized in Khartoum as an isolated phenomenon and certainly not the apex of a massive wedge of southerners moving north in search of food.[11] In February 1988 OXFAM reported from southern Darfur, where it had worked for years, that the influx of southerners had alarmed local officials. Many displaced persons were Dinka and Luo from as far east as Tonj and Rumbek. Finding no food in Wau and a poor harvest in the villages to the west, they had pressed on to Raga and then north to Darfur. Darfur was little more hospitable than Raga, but the Dinka appeared more willing to take their chances with the enemy they knew—the Baqqara—than with the strangers and the dreaded tsetse fly to the west in the Central African Republic. The Red Crescent Society–League of Red Cross Societies (LICROSS), an umbrella organization that included indigenous Sudanese Red Crescent representatives working with representatives of Red Cross societies in the United States and around the world, seconded OXFAM's warnings and added that the *murahileen*, taking advantage of the dry season, were once again killing and looting in Aweil District, and the UNWFP reported that thousands of Dinka were on the move.[12]

A typical attack was made upon the inhabitants of Udum village, most of whom were SPLA sympathizers. Fleeing toward nearby Mareng Akuar, they were methodically massacred: "The *Murahileen* surrounded the village the following night, attacking at dawn. Some of the raiders were wearing khaki uniforms. They herded about 170 people, mainly men but also including some women, into a byre which was then set on fire. Those who escaped were shot. Captives outside the byre then tried to flee but were shot down. Others were thrown down a well and then shot."[13]

Despite numerous warnings of drought and pillaging in Bahr al-Ghazal and Upper Nile, the relief agencies still seemed unable to grasp the fact that a catastrophe was building in the South. At the weekly TCC meetings, conditions there invariably came up for discussion, but little was done except to "deplore" the government's inactivity. In January the TCC received a copy of a "very urgent" letter from Darius Beshir, acting governor of Bahr al-Ghazal, to Sadiq al-Mahdi informing the prime minister and the minister of defense that he was very alarmed by the gravity of the famine in his region. Bashir wrote, "Right now, citizens are starving to death in the villages. Wau town has run out of essential food items like grain." The governor practically begged for help in order "to avert a very devastating human tragedy."[14] Beginning in January 1988, the PVOs reported at weekly TCC meetings that the situation was calamitous inside Wau and was alarming elsewhere in the South.

Following up on the proposal it had sent to Washington, USAID-Sudan met with the Ministry of Finance to suggest a government-to-government swap of PL-480 Title I wheat for Sudanese sorghum stored in the Agricultural Bank of Sudan warehouses. Despite the bank's previous unreliability, the USAID-Sudan director was convinced that sufficient sorghum was held by private traders and the ABS "to meet the needs [in Sudan] until the 1988/89 harvest."[15] Inexplicably, the mission proposed in February that although the swap arrangement could be finalized at once and shipments of U.S. wheat would follow shortly thereafter, USAID would not require the government to deliver its sorghum until August 1988. It proceeded with the swap, although it admitted that the Sudan government might be "unwilling or unable to be responsive to potential emergency needs in the South and elsewhere" and seemed in no hurry to build its food aid inventory.[16] The decision to permit the government to postpone the swap of sorghum until August was to have a decisive and negative effect on USAID planning and on its ability to react to emerging food requirements in the South.

As the RRC pressed on with its Western Relief Operation (and USAID Title I wheat arrived in March), famine spread relentlessly throughout Bahr al-Ghazal. Drought struck everywhere, and a report from Lakes Province claimed that "nearly all the towns in the Province have been deserted totally ... and their residents have effectively been displaced and left in destitution."[17] Disease killed those impoverished who did not die of starvation. In Upper Nile, where half of the strategic reserve set aside by the Malakal Relief Committee had been confiscated by the military, a heavily escorted convoy of barges reached Malakal in February.[18] They brought only a sixty-day supply of relief food, and soon, gaunt and hungry, "the displaced people roamed the streets in search of food." By July it had been reported that an exodus of some 30,000 displaced persons struggled down river where, near Kosti, they congregated at the Cumbo and Leiya encampments.[19]

The catastrophe building in the South did not escape the attention of the outside world. In February *The Times* of London, published a scathing report on famine conditions in Southern Sudan.[20] Despite appeals from the U.S. ambassadors and the EC representative, Minister of Defense General Burma Nasir promised nothing and did nothing to move relief trains to Aweil and barges to Malakal. The heads of mission approached Prime Minister Sadiq al-Mahdi on 27 February. Their discussion involved little more than an exchange of opinions, but it motivated U.S. Ambassador Norman Anderson to declare a "Civil Strife Disaster" in Sudan. The declaration was precisely what Julia Taft, director of AID-Washington's modest Office of Foreign Disaster Assistance, had urged in Washington, and it eventually enabled her office to take charge of the disaster relief program for the South.

The Exodus to Ethiopia

Not only were there reports of thousands of people moving toward southern Kordofan and Darfur in late 1987, but by early 1988 tens of thousands of walking skeletons from Bahr al-Ghazal were arriving in Ethiopian refugee camps. In August 1986 some 120,000 Sudanese refugees were registered in Ethiopia, and a year later around 165,000 Sudanese were located in three camps, Itang, Dimma, and Asosa. (See Table 4.1.) Itang was the largest and was as old as the civil war itself. A new camp at Dimma was opened in June 1986 with only 5,000 people, most of whom were Toposa males who had lost their cattle to the army, the bandits, or the SPLA. A third camp, Asosa, was established in April 1987 with 20,000 refugees. A fourth camp, Fugnido, was constructed in November 1987 within an Ethiopian game park. It soon became notorious for the thousands of very young boys, many of them orphaned, who were more dead than alive by the time they reached the camp from Bahr al-Ghazal. "Many newly arrived refugees talk of a one to four months walk to Ethiopia with a little sustenance en route due to passage through famine stricken areas. As a result, not only are the new arrivals critically nourished, but also the existing health and supplementary feeding programs can hardly respond to both the nutritional and medical needs of

TABLE 4.1 Sudanese Refugees in Ethiopian Camps

	Itang	Dimma	Asosa	Total
March 1983	10,000	na[a]	na	10,000
June 1986	–	5,000	na	5,000
August 1986	–	–	na	120,000
June 1987	130,000	15,000	2,000	165,000
April 1988	–	35,000	–	255,000

[a] Not applicable.

Source: USAID-Sudan.

the new arrivals and at the same time provide required services to the existing populations."[21]

Special emergency assistance—including medical supplies, feeding kits, and tents—were desperately needed. So were funds for the Ethiopian Red Cross, which was overwhelmed by the problems faced in the four camps. Disease accompanied malnutrition, and pellagra, scurvy, and anemia were prevalent in all the camps. When maize was distributed, many Dinka, accustomed to a diet high in animal fat and protein, became ill from a regimen dominated entirely by cereals and vegetables. By February 1988 malnutrition was so pervasive at Itang that about 25 percent of the patients treated in the camp hospital died. When a delegation from the U.S. Embassy in Addis Ababa and Michael Priestley, the UN resident representative in Ethiopia, visited Fugnido in early 1988, they gazed upon a chilling sight, one "more than most people could deal with without severe emotional reaction." Visitors "broke down and cried," and Priestley "described the situation as the worst he had seen in 37 years with the UN."[22] There was a shortage of drugs and laboratory equipment in Dimma and Fugnido. At Dimma the emergency ration of 2,400 kilo calories had been reduced for more than six months, since the flow of food aid had been disrupted by the deplorable condition of the road between the camp and Babecka. More than eighteen trucks had been lost in a year and a half while trying to navigate the tortuous route down the Ethiopian escarpment into the camp.

By spring 1988 the movement of thousands of people from Bahr al-Ghazal to Ethiopia had received substantial publicity. A *Sudan Times* "Special Report" published on 5 May noted: "Statistics from the usually reliable United Nations sources known more for their conservative estimates, some would call them underestimates, show that of the 100,000 people who have left Bahr al-Ghazal during the last three months, 40,000 of them have gone into Ethiopia.... The pattern of migration of southern Sudanese refugees and displaced persons has become well established;

the strong and young, mainly men and boys, go to Ethiopia and the weak, mainly women, children, and the aged come into northern Sudan."[23] One Dinka boy, who trekked for four months and a thousand miles before arriving at Fugnido, described that in his village near Winejok, Dinka adults had been rounded up and burned alive and the village razed to the ground. The cattle were commandeered, as were the children old enough to be sold as slaves in southern Kordofan. Infants too young to travel were pounded to death.[24] At Fugnido, seemingly every orphan had a tale to tell of death and destruction by the *murahileen*. Mawut Madol from Bor related stories much like those coming from Bahr al-Ghazal: "Sudanese Army took the cows, they took the grain, then they burned the houses, then they dispersed the people. They killed so many people, I saw people falling, and I ran." When asked where he was headed, he answered, "To the place where people are going— Ethiopia. I don't know if it is far or near."[25] Relief workers estimated that of every ten people who began the great trek to Ethiopia, four perished along the way; of those who made it, 15 percent died after their arrival.[26] In December 1988 The United Nations Commissioner for Refugees (UNCR) feared the number of Sudanese refugees in Ethiopia might soon exceed 420,000. British Minister for Overseas Development Christopher Patten was not far wrong when, upon returning to London after a tour of the Sudanese refugee camps, he declared that Southern Sudan was "being turned into a graveyard."[27] What, then, would be the response of the United States?

The American Response

The same rationale that had guided U.S. State Department policy toward Sudan in 1983 remained unchanged in 1988. Lying astride the Nile, the lifeline of Egypt, and with eight land frontiers and a long coast-line on the Red Sea, the strategic position of Sudan appeared, as it had to the Victorians, self-evident—a conclusion arrived at by military minds in London in 1888 and in Washington a hundred years later. In the nine-teenth century two particular demons, Germany and France, threatened British interests in the Nile Valley. In the twentieth century there were different devils—Libya and the Soviet Union—but analysts felt the inter-national and domestic affairs of Sudan had a direct bearing on the secu-rity of Egypt, Chad, the Nile basin, including the East African states, the Red Sea, and the Horn of Africa. If Sudan were friendly to the West, it would counterbalance its more radical neighbors—Libya, Ethiopia, and South Yemen. Although its economy was in disarray, the government was elected, the press was the most free of any in Africa, and Sudanese were charming and eminently likable. Politically, the Parliament was composed of a number of greater and lesser groupings that masqueraded as national parties, but none was sufficiently dominant to rule the country without enlisting strange alliances and entering into unholy coalitions. Politics meant compromise, and Sadiq was the great compromiser. The war continued in the South, and although the U.S. State Department deplored the civil conflict, it was careful not to give any encouragement to the SPLA lest it endanger its relations with Khartoum.

Despite the fact that there was sympathy in some quarters of the U.S. Congress for these African freedom fighters, the overwhelming majority of its members were nearly as uncomfortable with the movement as was the Department of State. Garang had been blamed for rejecting Sadiq's ephemeral offer of a cease-fire in April 1987. The Kurmuk incident had made Washington uneasy and thereafter frustrated when it could not influence the SPLA's war aims—perhaps forgetting that they had remained consistent since they were first enunciated in 1983. Curiously, this consistency, usually regarded as a virtue, infuriated a succession of State Department officials who thought Garang should compromise his principles when offered mediation, conciliation, negotiations, or arbitration. There was ambivalent arrogance in Washington's attitude toward John Garang. On the one hand he was considered something of a gangster, an intellectual lightweight; on the other the Department of State knew little of John Garang and the SPLA, with which its officials had made only furtive contacts, and any analysis of the leader and the movement was more opaque than clear. In a paper prepared for Congress in March 1988, a State Department analyst betrayed this ambiguity: "Colonel Garang portrays himself principally as a Sudanese nationalist determined to address problems of Sudan. He admits to Socialist economic views, but not to doctrinaire Marxism.... He and his organization are certainly beholden to President Mengistu of Ethiopia; however, it remains unclear how much latitude they have for independent action."[28]

In March 1988 the U.S. Congress opened its annual spring hearings on Africa. Various members had already come to the ineluctable and obvious conclusion that peace, security, and economic development in Sudan depended upon the resolution of the civil war. Even before the hearings, AID-Washington had been cautioned that Congress was dissatisfied with the Sudan program. In February 1988 a Famine Early Warning System Report—funded by AID/OFDA (Office of Foreign Disaster Assistance) and distributed widely in Washington—warned its readers:

> The population of the Southern Region continues to be highly vulnerable to a food emergency. The security situation there limits information.... There are reports that food aid is increasingly being used as a tool

for the control of civilians in the Southern Region. Relief vehicles have
been commandeered for military use in Equatoria Region. Increasing
numbers of displaced people from the Southern Region are arriving in
South Darfur and South Kordofan Provinces. Newspaper correspondents
continue to report massive exploitation of Southerners in these
provinces.[29]

In Khartoum the report was not well received by either USAID-Sudan
Director John Koehring or the U.S. Embassy, and the latter tried to
dismiss the reference to apparent human rights violations with the egregious obfuscation "FEWS reports of newspaper correspondents saying
that there is a massive exploitation of Southerners do not clarify whether
this is occurring in the North or South."[30] This was tantamount to
begging the question, and both the mission and the Embassy knew it; so
did the Congress. In late February congressional leaders Howard Wolpe
of the House Subcommittee on Africa, Mickey Leland, chair of the House
Select Committee on Hunger, Paul Simon of the Senate Subcommittee on
Africa, and Ted Kennedy signed a joint letter to both Sadiq al-Mahdi and
John Garang informing them that to permit the continuation of the existing situation in Sudan was unconscionable. The letter expressed concern
that according to the "best available information," starvation threatened
the areas of Wau, Malakal, Juba, Kapoeta, Kongor, Yirol, and Pochala;
and the signatories asked the recipients to "agree with the donors on an
'open roads' policy" to permit the movement of donor food aid through
contested and insecure areas. They also requested that priority be given
to relief rather than military cargo going to the South and added, to the
bewilderment and anguish of Sudanese officials unfamiliar with the
sanctimonious and patronizing side of U.S. politics, that "we have been
encouraged by the increased contacts, in recent times, between the government and the SPLM with a view toward achieving a political settlement of the current conflict.... We have urged our government to do all it
can to facilitate these negotiations."[31]

Congress was convinced that the best assistance the United States
could provide, and indeed its only leverage with the Sudan government,
was to tie military and economic aid for the rest of fiscal year 1988 and
fiscal year 1989 to the progress made by the government of Sadiq al-
Mahdi toward reaching a settlement with the SPLA. The U.S. Congress
left little doubt that it was unhappy with Khartoum's failure fully to
support relief efforts in the South, especially in Equatoria where the
British press was reporting that the Sudan army had blocked the movement of fuel supplies, commandeered relief vehicles in Juba, and refused
to give relief convoys sufficient protection. The State Department was not
happy with congressional clarity but could do little in the face of congressional insistence. For once, the U.S. Congress was sufficiently deter-

mined to ensure that Sadiq could not escape the conclusion that if he expected U.S. foreign assistance to continue at existing levels, he would have to seek peace.

Sadiq's policies would also have to change if he expected to continue to receive British foreign aid. A firestorm of protest had erupted in the British press in February 1988 when twenty OXFAM trucks, valued at $600,000 and used to deliver food aid in Equatoria, were seized in Juba by the army in order to transport troops eastward for a counterattack on Kapoeta, which had just fallen to the SPLA. The trucks were taken from the CART compound by order of "the local military commander." When OXFAM protested, Governor Peter Cirillo claimed the action was the result of "a direct order" from Khartoum.[32] Unfortunately for Sadiq, the incident occurred just after the British government had announced that an additional £25 million in foreign aid was to be added to the £20 million already pledged. In London a government spokesperson reminded Sadiq that "the British taxpayer had been very friendly to Sudan" and called the Juba incident an "intolerable" imposition.[33] The trucks, after all, had been purchased by a grant from the British government's foreign aid agency. It was not the first time the government and the private voluntary organizations had disagreed over the use of the trucks. *The Independent* wrote: "The Government and aid agencies have clashed in the past over whether food convoys should have armed escorts. The aid agencies rightly feared that the convoys could then be used as a cover to transport weapons. An OXFAM worker was expelled in December 1986 over the issue. Other aid agencies have been cautious about importing new vehicles which could tempt the army. Last year a new fleet of vehicles donated by the Italian government is believed to have been taken by the army, at least temporarily."[34] The outcry from the British press did not go unrewarded. The trucks were returned within the week; Khartoum called it a misunderstanding and buried the matter. Nevertheless, the issue of aid to Sudan could no more be buried in Britain than it could in the United States.

In response to growing congressional concern, Charles Gladson, AID assistant administrator for Africa, was questioned closely about disaster relief during an appearance in March at congressional hearings to review the agency's annual appropriation. Gladson was convinced that it was no longer possible to view disasters as natural phenomena that have temporary consequences. AID's Africa Bureau argued that in Sudan there was no guarantee that the situation would improve when the rains returned, when the floods abated, or the insect hordes receded. Rather, it concluded that disasters in Sudan were abetted and their consequences prolonged by inept and inapt government policies.[35] Gladson, who had helped convince Congress to approve a Development Fund for Africa that rewarded nations whose economic policies showed promise of success, had been prepared to pull AID out of Sudan. Nevertheless, when faced by a House Select Committee on Hunger that wanted disaster assistance for Sudan, Gladson quickly reversed course. Gladson knew what the activist representatives and the increasingly vocal Mickey Leland wanted to hear, and he indicated that AID would become more directly involved in providing relief aid to Sudan. In the end, AID passed through the congressional hearings with few difficulties; the State Department was warned, however, that Congress would see to it that the Sudan aid budget would be cut further if Sadiq did not actively pursue peace, and AID was warned that food aid and disaster relief for Sudan would be the subject of continual congressional scrutiny.

Southern Sudanese Seek Refuge
from War and Famine

Even as congressional hearings were being held, tens of thousands of Dinka and Luo were making their way northward out of Bahr al-Ghazal into southern Kordofan and Darfur seeking anything edible. Some took the western route around the Fertit militia at Raga, then went north to Buram in Darfur and, finding no food there, on to Nyala. In Nyala, in February 1988 a government official made the rounds of displaced persons settled there and returned "visibly shocked" by the appalling condition of some 25,000 new arrivals.[36] Others struggled to reach the North by a more direct and shorter way funneled through Safaha to Ed Daein. The Twic Dinka from Aweil trekked northeastward to Abyei. They had no difficulty following the trails leading north, for they were littered with the dying, the dead, and the skeletons. For most this was the last resort, because to go north was to place oneself at the mercy of one's inveterate and historical enemy, the Baqqara Arabs, now better armed than ever because of the sale and distribution of Libyan arms throughout much of northern Darfur.[37]

In April an average of 700 Southern Sudanese reached the Bahr al-Arab at Safaha each day. There, as they waited to be processed by an army detachment, the Dinka settled into camps with little food, stagnant water, and no shelter and in which meningitis was epidemic.[38] The army enforced registration, formed the people in endless queues, interrogated possible SPLA sympathizers, and did little to protect the Dinka from *murahileen* lurking nearby. Desperate to survive, Dinka mothers sold their children for £S300 to Rizayqat buyers in order to obtain food for the remaining family members; the process, known as *pawning*, trapped illiterate Dinka women, who made their mark on a bill of sale written in Arabic conferring ownership to the Arab with the right to buy back the child from slavery at some future time—a time that almost invariably never came.[39] The PVOs, particularly OXFAM, worked feverishly to relocate the displaced persons at Safaha, who numbered more than 15,000 in mid-April. A consortium composed of Sudanese Red Crescent–LICROSS, OXFAM, and MSF-Belgium, which was created to help the southerners, was confronted immediately by Ed Daein officials overwhelmed by the influx of unwelcome guests. Fearful of a repetition of the 1987 massacre and uneasy over reports from Safaha of fighting between the SPLA and the Baqqara militia, the Rizayqat Arab leadership wanted nothing to do with the thousands of dispossessed people flooding into their prosperous market town. Local officials moved them on to Nyala, and from there they were sent to a makeshift camp at Abu Ajura, which had no water, food, or shelter. The consortium contacted the RRC and the aid donors in Khartoum to inform them that there were already some 25,000 Dinka around Nyala; the nutritional condition of the arriving Dinka was described as devastating.[40]

In February the 150,000 displaced Dinka who had gathered at Aweil had given up all hope of finding food and had begun to move northward in droves. When a train did arrive on 10 March, it carried only 400 tons of relief food, an amount sufficient to feed only 30,000 starving people for one month. By mid-April the starving Dinka in Aweil began to die in great numbers. Father Rudolf Deng and 7,000 displaced persons used the train to travel from Aweil to the North in April. The desperate people who were left behind—the Aweil Relief Committee had registered 36,000 families immediately prior to Father Deng's departure—used what strength they had to march north. They followed the rail line to Muglad or used the various paths that led to Abyei, where the new arrivals found no help. In February a UNICEF nutritional survey of Abyei displaced children found malnutrition rates so high that the regional government was forced to respond. The Food Aid Administration Office in El Obeid agreed in March to provide Abyei with 350 tons of sorghum—an amount sufficient to give 25,000 displaced persons a month's ration—of the 3,250 tons that had been unallocated during the first component of the Western Relief Operation.[41]

Most of the displaced, unable to eat promises and without resort to food aid, decided to continue north toward Muglad. By March more than a hundred Dinka a day were reaching the outskirts of Muglad and the barren encampment for the displaced, where the exhausted tried to gather their strength. They huddled together surrounded by a flock of human scavengers who stole Dinka children from their emaciated mothers. Rather than remain among their traditional enemy, those Dinka who had sufficient strength continued north and clambered aboard trains in Babanusa that were bound for the east and Khartoum.

Thousands perished. Some were ordered off the cars by police when the trains stopped at stations along the way. On a single occasion in April 1988, an estimated 7,000 southerners who had scrambled onto a train in Babanusa were periodically cleared away and "left behind between Babanusa and El Obeid."[42] Many dehydrated, sick, and starving people who clung to the cars lost their hold, fell from boxcars and carriages, and died by the tracks. Among the most tragic of those who arrived in Khartoum were the distraught mothers who no longer had the strength to hold their babies but who themselves had managed to survive.

Pressed by AID-Washington and OFDA to enumerate and locate the southern displaced persons, USAID-Sudan responded in late March that even though there had been "a recent influx of Southerners into southern Darfur," no one was able "to provide reliable estimates of their numbers."[43] USAID was short of food after delivering most of its supply to the Western Relief Operation. Also, it had insufficient funds to meet its anticipated transport costs because the government had failed to pay the £S30 million stipulated in an Emergency Food Transport project agreement signed by the Ministry of Finance and Economic Planning and USAID-Sudan in September 1987.[44]

The Red Cross Attempts a Rescue

As thousands of Southern Sudanese were dying from starvation, the officials of the relief agencies in Khartoum sought to limit their activity in Southern Sudan by turning the problem of disaster relief in that region over to the International Commission for the Red Cross (ICRC). The ICRC mandate could most recently be found in, and its international relief effort was justified by, Protocol I of the 1977 Geneva Convention, which made the provision of relief to civilians in time of war neither an unfriendly act nor an "interference in the armed combat." Headquartered in Geneva, its representatives remained rather aloof from the Khartoum diplomatic circle. In a somehow old-fashioned way, they were quiet individuals with strong opinions; they composed thoughtful programs and were determined never to quit as long as lives could be saved. Thus, it was not surprising that the donors wrote to Prime Minister Sadiq al-Mahdi on 27 April: "While we continue to believe a much more sustained effort on the part of Government agencies is in order to ensure food supplies, including those made available by donors, reach critical areas of primary concern, namely Wau, Aweil, Malakal and Juba, we also believe that the most effective manner of addressing the entire problem will be found through an arrangement with the ICRC."[45]

Encouraged by the donors, who would gladly supply food aid if the International Red Cross were to manage its transport and distribution, the ICRC revived the objective of the ill-fated Operation Rainbow to provide food to both sides in the South simultaneously. It could claim that its historic neutrality was based not only on Protocol I of the 1977 Geneva Convention but had antecedents in Article 3 of all four Geneva Conventions of 12 August 1949, to which Sudan was a signatory. In time of war, Article 3 permitted the Red Cross to "bring protection and assistance to persons taking no active part in the hostilities" and allowed it to help "authorities concerned to improve and preserve the dignity and way of life of the affected civilian population." Unlike the UN organization, the ICRC was a neutral entity and not the creation of governments of a community of nations. The director of a very active PVO in Sudan explained the difference with disarming candor: "The UN in Sudan has shown itself to be a sort of compromise institution. This is only to be expected since three quarters of its member states are Third World countries with a bad record on human rights."[46]

Pierre Pont, the ICRC director of operations in Khartoum, met with Sadiq al-Mahdi on 17 February, while at the same time another ICRC official met with the SPLA; both were asked to approve a tentative plan to allow surveys of food and health conditions in the South. Where food aid was found necessary, the surveys would be followed by the creation of a distribution plan to assist the needy.[47] For once both Sadiq and the SPLA agreed, and on 14 March a "Plan of Action for Southern Sudan" was delivered to the prime minister. When he appeared to ignore the proposal, which had received the tacit agreement of the SPLA, the EC delegate, G. D. Gwyer, met with Sadiq and urged him to move forward on the plan. He expressed general donor concern with regard to the large number of Dinka arriving in Safaha and asked the prime minister to encourage the army to provide escorts for food aid truck convoys from Raga to Wau and for trains between Muglad and Aweil.

When no action was forthcoming, the ICRC followed with a *Note Verbale* on 16 April requesting a response to the Plan of Action. The *Note Verbale* had received the support of the UNDP, which prepared a circular countersigned by the major donors that also urged Sadiq to approve the ICRC program. The prime minister, however, was deeply involved in a new political crisis. The erratic governing coalition had ceased to rule, and the interminable squabbling over the budget, the economy, and the war had virtually paralyzed the Constituent Assembly. In May Sadiq formed a new coalition that for the first time included the National Islamic Front along with the DUP in a broad-based government. Given NIF hostility to any rapprochement with the SPLA, the relief agencies assumed that the possibility of a food aid program in rebel-held areas was now remote.

Hassan al-Turabi, the NIF leader, was named attorney general; he continued his adamant opposition to negotiations with the SPLA and lobbied openly for additional funds for the war. He argued, "Defense can't be half-hearted. You either defend yourself effectively or you achieve peace."[48] There seemed no doubt which course of action Turabi would choose and the war continued. The NIF then proposed legislation—the so-called "alternative laws"—that was to replace Numayri's September Laws. Most legislators found the alternative laws little different from the existing statutes, and their consideration resulted in much acrimonious debate. Next, both local and expatriate attitudes toward the new governing coalition hardened following its inept handling of Palestine Liberation Organization terrorists who attacked the Acropole Hotel and the British Sudan Club in May. Both were popular sites at which foreigners, relief workers, and the press congregated. The injuries and deaths, especially the murder of a family involved in relief work in Sudan, deeply affected the expatriate community and excited new tensions between the donors and the government.

Amid the political turmoil in Khartoum, the ICRC persevered. It provided Sadiq and Garang with a redefined program that earmarked six sites—Kongor, Yirol, and Pochala in SPLA territory and Wau, Juba, and Malakal held by government forces—in which food deficits were thought to be severe and in which surveys should be carried out immediately. In Malakal relief supplies were exhausted, and the Relief Agencies Coordinating Committee claimed that the city was overflowing with an estimated 110,000 displaced persons. The committee pleaded for an airlift, which the ICRC agreed to fly but the military refused to sanction.[49] Meanwhile, a stream of articles appeared in the international media about the spreading starvation in Southern Sudan, and they seem to have been crucial in changing Sadiq's mind with regard to the ICRC program. By June the usual midsummer torpor had overtaken Khartoum, and the political storms that characterized the *habub* season in the capital were reduced to an occasional dust devil. Concerned with his own image and with that of his new government, Sadiq sanctioned the ICRC survey, and a Red Cross team began an assessment in Wau on 13 June. The ICRC continued in July and August with a systematic survey of food needs in Malakal, Juba, and the SPLA strongholds of Kongor and Yirol. Surveys, however, were one thing and food distributions were another and with each passing day time and lives were lost.

Duplicity Means Starvation

Throughout the spring, reports of drought, famine, and death had multiplied. Substantial information was obtained from witnesses north of the Bahr al-Arab, but it was also apparent that a similar disaster was occurring within all three southern regions. In eastern Equatoria the Torit Relief Committee reported that deaths from starvation in the besieged town had "risen to between 30–40 daily," and grain excavators were being used to dig tombs for the dead because "people have no strength." In Malakal the huge displaced population became more desperate each day. In May people were starving to death in Wau and Aweil. In Kosti MSF-Holland had assessed the health and nutrition needs of some 40,000 Upper Nile displaced persons in three camps. Most were Shilluk who had walked 250 miles from Kodok and had arrived emaciated and destitute. In Abyei, Muglad, and Babanusa, most of the Nilotes were fearful and were hesitant to remain in the displaced camps found in the land of the Baqqara. At the Khartoum railroad station, trains discharged more thousands of starving women and children, some of whom perished in the rail yard: "The indifference of the government in Khartoum and the molestation to which even these very weak refugees are subjected in the north, has become a source of bewilderment to many of these people. Nevertheless, the trek to the north continues, because for many it is better to die on the move than to wait for death in their war-ravaged homeland."[50]

Once the government began to receive such criticism—not only from its implacable antagonist, *Sudan Times*, but from other Khartoum newspapers and the international press as well—Sadiq acted quickly to diffuse the damaging reports. In June he not only revived the ICRC proposal but also asked the UN Secretary-General Javier Perez de Cuellar "to alert the international community" to the grave situation prevailing in Sudan and to appeal for emergency assistance. AID's Office of Foreign Disaster Assistance, which was already aware of the problem, forced USAID-Sudan to respond to the issue by sending an employee to Sudan to investigate famine conditions in southern Kordofan and Darfur. OFDA sent Michael Harvey, a young official with little experience, to Khartoum; he was joined by Thomas Staal, a hard-working former employee of World Vision–Sudan who had only recently been hired by USAID-Sudan. Unfortunately, neither man was very wise in the ways of the U.S. government bureaucracy or USAID missions, both had little reporting experience, and both could be influenced by USAID or the U.S. Embassy as long as they were in Sudan. For five days in June, the team traveled through southern Kordofan and Darfur. At Meiram, where MSF-France had arrived three days earlier, they found 6,000 displaced Dinka, 1,000 of whom were gathered around the nascent feeding center. Although it spent only a few hours in the village, the team later reported that MSF-France had the situation under control. It then visited Muglad and Babanusa but was unable to visit Abyei, where the onset of the rainy season had led UNICEF to withdraw its personnel and turn over its struggling supplementary feeding program to the Camboni fathers, who used all the money they had to purchase grain from the *jallaba* at inflated prices.

The team returned to Khartoum and on 21 June a cable, ostensibly drafted by the AID-OFDA team member, was sent to Washington. The first paragraph was highly misleading: "A recent field visit to southern Kordofan and southern Darfur by USAID/Khartoum and visiting OFDA staff has reviewed efforts to meet the needs of displaced persons fleeing southern Sudan. The visit confirmed the very bad condition of those who are arriving from the South, but also found that NGOs, in cooperation with local and regional governments, are addressing the problem."[51] The cable was an obfuscation, reflecting the embassy's resolution and that of the Department of State not to criticize openly Sudan government's southern policy as well as the determination of USAID-Sudan officials not to become involved in a relief program for southerners or the South. The situation of the southern displaced persons was wretched everywhere but according to the same cable it was "being addressed as best as can be expected at this time." Especially questionable was the cable's praise for phantom local and regional officials whose "surprising" support was commended. In reality, there was virtually no local government support for the displaced; there was none in Darfur, certainly none in Kordofan, and especially none in Khartoum. The cable might have lulled AID-Washington, the press, and the U.S. Congress to sleep if it were not for *The Atlanta Journal and Constitution*, which provided an entirely new analysis of the famine in Sudan. The newspaper, which was to become the most severe critic of U.S. policy, reported less than a week after the cable was received in Washington that "High-ranking U.S. officials have been briefed about Abyei, and they have seen reports that an additional 10,000 hungry Southerners have poured into two other towns in the area. But State Department officials, quoting a June 21 cable from the U.S. Embassy in Khartoum, said in interviews that the situation was under control."[52]

Surprisingly, this influential cable differed little from information disseminated two weeks later by the UN World Food Program in Khartoum; its 7 July situation report claimed: "The number of DP's mostly in the border areas between north and south Sudan is still increasing, but RRC assisted by NGOs and Donors is having the situation under control in those areas."[53] In fact, the doctors and personnel of MSF-France were furious because the army quietly and on four occasions used trains to resupply its garrison at Meiram without offering to carry relief aid for the hundreds who were starving to death. The organization was prepared to seek out the media to report the deplorable conditions and government inaction at Meiram but was "besieged" by UNICEF, the EC, and "various private organizations." All pleaded with the French not to go public for fear that not only MSF-France but other PVOs would suffer "the same fate as Winston Prattley, World Vision and others" who had protested conditions in Sudan.[54]

The Somnolent Media Begin to React

The first systematic effort to publish the story of this plethora of horrors was undertaken by Colin Campbell and Deborah Scroggins, staff writers for *The Atlanta Journal and Constitution*. In lengthy articles that appeared between 24 and 28 June 1988, the authors described the plight of women and children, the family separations, the towns without infants, regions without young men, the "tribesmen from southern Sudan who have grown so desperate for food money that thousands have sold their children to Arabs for as little as a dollar each."[55] They noted that Southern Sudan was as large as the U.S. South, and the numbers of dead, dying, and displaced were beyond simple calculation.

Officials at the USAID mission and the U.S. Embassy in Khartoum were not pleased with the authors' reporting. It was thought they had unfairly used the term *selective starvation* to indict the government of Sudan for instituting cultural genocide, to which Campbell and Scroggins replied that the United States was applying a double standard in Sudan. On the one hand, Chester Crocker, the assistant secretary of state for Africa, declared that "we intend to keep the spotlight of public opinion on the government of Ethiopia"; on the other, in Sudan—which Crocker admitted offered one of the few "essential strategic relationships in Africa," one that figured "prominently" in U.S. national security—a terrible famine affecting hundreds of thousands of Sudanese had "dropped into darkness."[56]

The articles by Campbell and Scroggins were snapped up by Cable News Network, whose headquarters were in Atlanta, and in July it began to provide detailed reports on Sudan. Next, the International Minority Rights Group provided a detailed analysis of the criminal activities perpetrated against southerners and condoned by Khartoum. Taken together, and in concert with articles appearing in *Sudan Times*, even Sudanese were made aware that tens of thousands of Dinka were dead and dying from starvation and that the unrestricted use of Arab militias had contributed to what was tantamount to state-sponsored genocide. Hopelessly embarrassed, the government hastily restricted the activities of the irrepressible television and newspaper photojournalists and prohibited them from visiting displaced camps.

In Khartoum, USAID-Sudan and the U.S. Embassy had plenty of time to perceive that they were involved in a terrible crisis, yet both wallowed in uncertainty. The State Department remained unresponsive, and in a June meeting with the House of Representatives' Select Committee on Hunger, Deputy Assistant for Africa Roy Stacy stuck to the administration's guns: "The United States," Stacy conceded somewhat vaguely, "has not been content with the pace of deliveries." He added that Sudanese authorities were "similarly frustrated with delays of relief shipments" and had assured the State Department "that an even greater effort will be made to secure timely movement." Campbell and Scroggins intimated that the assistant secretary had been hoodwinked: "Stacy's confidence in the Sudanese authorities' sincerity in saying they want to feed the south diverges radically from the assessment of some U.S. diplomats in Khartoum. One of these skeptics said of some Sudanese officials, 'Never doubt their ability to lie right to your face.'"[57]

The second article in the series went even further, charging Sudan government with attempting to cover up the existing famine by expelling World Vision, Catholic Relief Services, and Church World Service from Sudan and making it nearly impossible for journalists to visit the South or southern Kordofan and Darfur. It reported that the magnitude of the famine was so great that the United Nations was requesting food to feed 2 to 3 million Southern Sudanese, or about half the population of the South—an apocalyptic scene that was confirmed four months later by Bryan Wannop, the UN resident representative in Sudan: "As the situation in southern Sudan continues to deteriorate, the stream of people moving within the southern region seeking the relative safety of government-held towns or traveling north has reached an estimate level of 200 families [approximately 1,000 persons] per day. Some authorities estimate that as much as 80 percent of the population of the southern Sudan may have been uprooted by the war and resulting famine."[58]

The articles in *The Atlanta Journal and Constitution* and Raymond Bonner's perceptive piece in *The New Yorker* in March 1989 depicted a U.S. Embassy and a USAID mission that were incapable of action even after there could be no mistake as to the seriousness of conditions in Southern Sudan. Bonner reported that there was a kind of "gag rule" in the U.S. Embassy in Khartoum and that the reason it shunned journalists was "attributable in part to extraordinary deference to the Sudanese government."[59] There was another reason as well: USAID-Sudan had run short of food. The government had failed to deliver by June 1988 the 50,000 tons of sorghum from the Agricultural Bank of Sudan. When it could provide no more than 9,720 tons Washington terminated the wheat-sorghum swap. Thus, precisely at the time when starvation in Southern Sudan began to receive significant international media coverage, USAID-Sudan informed AID-Washington that its food stocks would be "severely constrained" for at least six months.[60]

U.S. Government Confusion

Reports of widespread destitution and deaths in the South were not matched by problems in the West. By March the European Community had enough detail from the field to indicate that its donors should place "very low credence on need figures established earlier for Darfur and Kordofan at 51,000 MT and 71,000 MT respectively."[61] EC members needed little convincing that the Western Relief Operation had been overgenerous in its support. Nonetheless, the RRC obstinately refused to reduce its estimates. PVOs that attended Technical Coordination Committee meetings responded with furious declamations, and after much heated debate the RRC reluctantly agreed on 31 March to a "reallocation" of sorghum from the West to Safaha. It was the first concerted effort to respond to the growing number of southerners fleeing the South.

Despite the bureaucratic victory, the donors, seemingly mesmerized by Khartoum's sleepy ambiance, continued to misjudge the extent of the famine in Bahr al-Ghazal. Sudanitis—a syndrome resulting from physical hardship commingled with human frailty—attacked the reasonable, trapped the romantic, ensnared the drifter, and impaled the humanitarian *khawaja*. This can be the only explanation for a July UN-FAO Food and Agricultural Organization report that insisted the RRC, assisted by NGOs and donors, had the "situation under control."[62] It can probably be blamed for a UN World Food Program report sent in July that noted: "Despite a continued influx into Southern Kordofan, Central Region and Khartoum, central and local authorities, multilateral, bilateral and NGO donors have continued to cover the most essential food needs of the displaced and pledges already made or being finalized are expected to be sufficient to cover identified requirements for the next 4–6 months."[63]

In reality, the donors were practically without food, and there was little likelihood of their purchasing grain in local markets or through the Agricultural Bank of Sudan. Ironically, the RRC had no trouble obtaining sorghum from the ABS and, regardless of the donors' predicament, gratuitously announced that it had purchased 5,500 tons of sorghum the bank had stored in Umm Ruwaba. When the grain was shipped to the West, the donors—whose members were devoted to making themselves as comfortable as possible while toiling in a notorious "hardship post" and by 1988 were members of a sleepy "old-boy's" club, hardly protested. Old Sudan hands had seen it all before, and ambitious expatriates were not about to "rock the boat." With the exception of the International Red Cross, the donor community was generally indecisive, and its leaders seemed to take an almost masochistic pleasure in explaining to their home offices how difficult it was to work with the government of Sudan.

When USAID-Sudan finally attempted at midyear to use its periodic situation reports ("sitreps") to inform AID-Washington that Sudan government, its institutions—including the Relief and Rehabilitation Commission—and its army were all hampering food aid, the U.S. Embassy warned USAID that no compromising cable or thoughtful appraisal of the government's abysmal performance in providing relief assistance for the southerners should leave Khartoum. One important cable was intercepted by the embassy's chief political officer; its most critical portions were deleted, and a USAID analyst with vast field experience was reprimanded. In the future, he was told, his cables were not to "imply criticism of the GOS" or substantially differ in tone from a diet of tapioca the embassy was feeding the Department of State.[64] Ambassador Anderson, the embassy's deputy chief of mission, and the political office all demonstrated a distinct distaste for USAID personnel, especially for USAID Director John Koehring who spent as much time as possible out of Sudan. Collectively the embassy distrusted the SPLA, southerners, or anyone who appeared to criticize the government of Sadiq al-Mahdi— although the embassy itself had few good words for the Sudanese prime minister. It demonstrated virtually no interest in disaster assistance, although it reported in June that "the government of Sudan has still not evidenced sufficient interest to organize itself to address the problem or decide which government agency is responsible for the displaced."[65]

The Great Flood of August 1988

USAID was thoroughly chastised and rather demoralized, and its cables evolved into laconic recitations of factual information that minimized analysis. Emotion-laden reports and pejoratives were left to the private voluntary organizations that began to voice their concerns in Washington, especially to Julia Taft and AID's Office of Foreign Disaster Assistance. Convinced that something had to change in Khartoum, AID-OFDA was about to demand a reconsideration of the USAID mission's relief program when a monumental rainstorm struck the city. Beginning in the evening of 4 August, eight inches of rain fell on Khartoum in fourteen hours. This was more rainfall than the capital had received in the previous two years, and based on historical data, the statistical probability of such a phenomenon occurring was "one in five hundred years."[66]

Downpours continued for the next two weeks and further paralyzed Khartoum, Omdurman, and Khartoum North; the work of relief agencies was diverted from the acute problem of starvation in the South. Eighty percent of Khartoum was covered by standing water, and the government declared the city a disaster area and announced a six-month emergency for the nation. The capital dried out very slowly, and an estimated

200,000 mud brick dwellings had washed away. For weeks the streets of Khartoum were a quagmire. Also hard hit were the breadbasket of Sudan, the Gezira between the Blue and White Nile south of Khartoum, and towns as far east as Kassala. The shantytowns scattered around the periphery of greater Khartoum and occupied by displaced southerners were inundated and destroyed, and they appeared to the government to be spawning grounds for a massive epidemic of contagious diseases. Although the flood was destructive, however, it was not the killer famine which had been devastating Southern Sudan. Fewer than 100 people died as a result of the massive rainfall; in contrast, a UNICEF report prepared in August 1988 and distributed a month after the deluge claimed that although food and medicine were being distributed in Khartoum, in southern Kordofan alone 20 to 100 southerners were dying every week in the displaced persons' camps. As UNICEF put it, "Due to the emergency in Khartoum and the Northern Region, other areas in the country were forgotten."[67]

Disaster relief for Khartoum arrived from around the world, especially from the Arab nations, within hours of the reported disaster. The Saudi Arabian air force, which seldom flew to Khartoum, provided as many as forty-two military planes, and nineteen civilian Saudi Arabian aircraft flew cargo to Khartoum. The government created a High Emergency Relief Commission chaired by the minister of finance to organize the relief operation, and a military unit coordinated the logistics of four Zonal Committees. The relief effort was politicized, and army distributions of aid supplies gave priority to sections of the city that supported the Umma Party. By September the Western embassies were aware that the army was setting aside one-third of all incoming food for its own use. Little went to the million displaced persons, or to children in seventeen major sites in which the rate of serious malnutrition ranged from 10 to 27 percent.[68] Nothing was done to help rebuild the slums, "among the grimmest, most impoverished urban areas of Africa."[69] PVOs reported that Khartoum authorities resisted the provision of health service in displaced sites until they were warned that diseases there "were a threat to the public health of Khartoum."[70]

The international response to the Khartoum flood had been immediate. USAID-Sudan issued yet another disaster declaration, and USAID provided 1,000 tons of sorghum to Sudan Council of Churches to distribute to the displaced southern persons in the capital. A U.S. Air Force C5-A flew in a load of plastic sheeting, the Center for Disease Control in Atlanta produced a team of epidemiologists for Khartoum, and OFDA "expressed its willingness to contribute toward a possible UNICEF relief effort."[71] By the time the flood had receded, USAID had delivered 7,100 tons of food to a consortium of PVOs involved in Khartoum relief programs—a much more positive response than its feeble reaction to famine in the South—and again had virtually no sorghum.

The Pathos of Meiram

Light years away from the State Department's home in Washington, D.C., lies the great Nilotic plain stretching from the Central African Republic in the west to the towering escarpment of the Ethiopian Highlands in the east. Through this plain meanders the Bahr al-Arab River, known to the Dinka as the Kiir, in a great arc along which are dotted villages and towns on the frontier between Arabs and Africans. Here, in spring and summer 1988, the tragedy of Safaha shifted eighty kilometers eastward to Meiram, a Missiriya town south of Muglad on the rail line from Aweil. Meiram was neither prosperous nor poor, but it was home to many newly sedentary Missiriya families who cultivated sorghum and groundnuts. As the Dinka exodus from Aweil staggered north along the railroad, 50 to 100 emaciated southerners—mostly women and children—managed to reach Meiram every day. By May some 6,000 Dinka had congregated in the *suq*, overwhelming the town and, by their very presence, inciting the Missiriya to rid Meiram of these Dinka *abid* (slaves). The antipathy was historic, but in May tensions escalated over the dearth of water at the height of the dry season, compounded by the shortage of food. There was food in the market, but the *jallaba* priced it far beyond the reach of the thousands of hungry Dinka who were tramping north or of the 7,000 unfortunates who had been pulled off the train at Meiram in April and left to the mercy of the Missiriya. By June the town had 12,000 destitute displaced persons; as in Safaha, the Meiram Baqqara preyed on the weak, and "several hundred children disappeared."[72]

Concern, an Irish private voluntary organization that had begun work in Sudan in 1985 and in 1988 operated from Babanusa, was the first to warn that there was an immediate need in Meiram. In May it shipped 220 tons of food to the town officials for distribution to the needy. UNICEF followed with a shipment of supplementary food rations to a hastily created Meiram Relief Committee composed of the leading Missiriya *shaykh* and the commander of the small army garrison. On 10 June MSF-France arrived in Meiram and with its accustomed competence quickly introduced a program of medical and nutritional assistance and took charge of what remained of the "Unimix" that had been supplied by UNICEF. Within hours it was feeding some 600 children.

During the dry season Meiram was less than a day's drive from Muglad, but after the rains began the wadis overflowed, the road became a quagmire, and by July the town could only be reached by rail. Under normal circumstances a mix of 12,000 adults and children would require about 150 tons of food a month to meet minimal nutritional needs. Without food the only options for the adults were to seek work in the fields of the Missiriya, sell their children into slavery and purchase food for those who remained, or keep moving north. MSF-France, which had arrived on 10 June, had wisely established a displaced camp more than a mile from the town, clearing the market of the Dinka to the great relief of town officials. Meanwhile, thousands of Dinka continued the struggle north along the railroad track from Aweil and arrived at the camp. As their numbers increased, the nervous Missiriya leaders did little to disguise their feeling that the French team should leave the town and somehow take the Dinka with them. The French refused, and they appealed to the army commander, who realized that the Dinka problem was more manageable with the health team than without. Thus, the French were allowed to remain as long as they maintained the lowest possible profile.

Less than a month after their arrival, the French doctors ran out of food just as a massive wave of new arrivals, most of whom were sick and emaciated, washed into town. In August Dr. Alan Campagnie of the French aid organization Action Internationale Contre la Faim (AICF) received urgent messages for help from MSF-France, and he passed this information on to the RRC, other government institutions, and the donors. The RRC at first refused to be hurried, but the AICF, founded in France in 1979 by the French journalist Francoise Giroud, believed in "direct action rather than ideological debate or abstract thinking."[73] It approached the donors for food and was joined in its appeal by Concern. USAID-Sudan immediately released 300 tons of sorghum it had previously received from the ABS—half the amount it had been readying for shipment to Aweil by train.[74] In addition, the UN World Food Program gave Concern cash for the local purchase and transport of sorghum. The RRC finally responded and requested funds from the donors to move an additional 150 tons of food by truck.[75]

At least 300 tons of food could have been transported by train from Babanusa to Meiram in a day if the Railways Corporation had provided a single diesel and a crew; when no train was made available, Concern managed to send 80 tons of food to Meiram by truck just before the track south of Muglad dissolved into a mud wallow. No more food could be trucked until the roads dried out in November, and the rest of the donor food remained stalled in Babanusa. In August OXFAM and Save the Children Fund (SCF) reported that thousands of living skeletons had left Meiram, and MSF-France remained caught up in a struggle that had become very personalized, with the doctors determined to salvage as many of the dying as they could. Whenever possible they sent reports to to Khartoum advising the donors of the deplorable conditions in the camp, which had swollen to the unmanageable numbers of 26,000 people, most of whom were dying. Forced to depend on the Meiram Relief Committee to distribute sorghum, MSF-France husbanded what little Unimix it had, but supplies would not last long because the group was feeding 3,000 children a day. The other displaced persons went hungry. When the Unimix ran out, the children died along with the adults. According to Cole Dodge, director of UNICEF for Sudan, "By the fourth of August, the weekly death rate was the highest MSF had ever recorded in any of its programs around the world." It was even higher than that recorded at the Korem "death camp at the height of the 1984–1985 Ethiopian famine."[76]

On 24 August the outside world learned in a BBC interview with OXFAM's Mark Duffield that hundreds of Dinka were dying at Meiram each day. Reports also appeared in the British press, and slowly the story began to emerge. As usual, adverse publicity or the threat of it was required to motivate the donors to move quickly, and as usual the private voluntary organizations were the first to visit Meiram despite the difficulty they had in obtaining travel permits. Nevertheless, a succession of visitors came, and they reported a scene from hell. Dead Dinka were scattered throughout the camp and beyond in the bush, rotting and mutilated by scavenging, bloated hyenas. Finally, on 25 August an RRC donor team visited El Obeid and convinced the governor of Kordofan, Ábd al-Rasoul al-Nour, to demand that the Railways Corporation provide a diesel locomotive at Babanusa to move 150 tons of sorghum to Meiram. Organized largely by Angus Finucane of Concern, the train was dispatched within the week and arrived at a time when CARE reported that camp deaths had increased from eighteen per day in July to sixty per day in mid-August.[77] Mortality was, however, woefully understated. MSF-France reported a mortality rate of *twenty-six per thousand per day*—a life expectancy of little more than a month for those found in the Meiram displaced camp. Upon the arrival of the train from Babanusa, the food was immediately seized—to the dismay of MSF-France—by the town's relief committee:

> A lot of food arriving is creamed off by the Army before it reaches the distribution point. On the 27th August MSF managed to stop the food distribution altogether when it was realized that most of the food was going directly into Arab hands. MSF recently obtained 600 sacks of Dura for the Dinka camp, but of these, 100 sacks were "mislaid." Upon inquiring as to the whereabouts of a load of sugar donated by Saudi Arabia, MSF was intimidated and told never to ask about it again.[78]

Beyond Meiram

Elsewhere in the lands astride the Bahr al-Arab, death was ever-present. In Abyei, where the displaced still waited for RRC food, the July mortality rate ranged from 5–8 persons per day and increased to 100 or more per day in August. Also in August, the number of deaths increased to 15 a day among the 15,000 displaced persons found in the Muglad camp and to more than a score daily among the 8,000 Dinka packed into the Babanusa displaced settlement. In En Nahud, where CARE was directly involved in a variety of programs, the number of displaced families had nearly doubled in a month and the population was increasing by at least 50 people per day. Most of the displaced were from Abyei, Aweil, and Mayenabun; uncounted numbers were also located in the nearby towns of Tibbun, Um Chak, and Um Bateekh. CARE reported that the food stocks "in all areas are low or exhausted" and pleaded with the donors "to assist these poor people as quickly as possible."[79]

On 6 September a team of donors and PVOs—including representatives from USAID, EC, UNICEF, UNWFP, the Dutch Embassy, the Ministry of Finance, RRC, and the governor of Kordofan—boarded a train at Muglad loaded with 300 tons of donor sorghum that was bound for Meiram. The train would not have moved if Chevron had not donated five barrels of essential lubricants for the locomotives. Upon arrival and without exception, the visitors described the scene as one from the Holocaust and listened with horror as living skeletons recounted events of destruction, capture, slavery, pawning, privation, famine, and death: "In stark contrast to the naked, emaciated Dinka [was] the relatively prosperous Arab community of Meiram."[80] The scenes of the dead and dying lying in the sun, of children tottering on matchstick legs or curled up waiting to die shocked the visitors and government officials. They were particularly offended when they learned that the town officials forced the displaced persons to walk more than a mile from the camp to the feeding center for their daily ration. Some never made it. The *Sudan Times* quoted a press statement released by the relief agencies in Meiram in which it was reported that the "crude mortality rate" had reached a high of 53.9 deaths per 10,000 persons per day, a number four times greater than the worst reported Arab death rate in western Sudan during the height of the famine in 1985.[81]

The donor representatives returned to Babanusa by train but not before stopping at Muglad—the capital of the Missiriya *Dar* and the heart of that Baqqara tribal homeland. In June the USAID-OFDA team had reported that only 60 or 70 displaced Dinka were present in the town, but it was in Muglad that the donors finally realized the enormity of the action taken by the Missiriya nazir, Ali Nimr, when he forced the removal of displaced persons to a site outside the town. Since June, Concern, like Sisyphus, had been faced with an impossible task: With limited means and few funds, it had struggled to provide assistance to as many as 15,000 displaced persons and had done its best to make livable a site at which an estimated 2,000 Dinka died in summer 1988. The number of permanent camp residents was growing rapidly, and Concern had just received news that a single group of 1,000 persons was on its way from Abyei. Inside the camp, "fathers deny food to hopelessly sick children or relatives so that others with better chances might survive," and "healthy men toil relentlessly outside the camp to build an enclosure where the sick can be isolated to combat the spread of disease."[82] All of the survivors had tales of Missiriya harassment and enslavement, which, when published, were vehemently denied in Khartoum. As one Baqqara disingenuously explained, the Dinka worked for him because "starving Southerners had implored him to take them in and feed them in exchange for work."[83] The donors learned that the death rate in the Muglad camp was now as high as 15 to 20 persons a day, and to add to the horror, the donors were further chastened when they later learned that among the 300 displaced persons who clambered aboard the donor train to escape from Meiram, at least 30 died within twenty-four hours of their arrival in Muglad.[84] From Muglad the team continued to Babanusa where, thanks to the energetic work of the governor of Kordofan, trains loaded with relief goods for Meiram were dispatched on 14 and 21 September. By mid-September the Meiram camp population had dropped to 13,000, but the camp at Muglad was receiving much of the spillover and was growing rapidly.

Babanusa, Muglad, and Meiram were visited again by a government-donor team on 30 September. Conditions were still very bad, and by chance rather than design, Concern had assumed a crucial role in assisting the displaced persons in southern Kordofan. It reported on regional conditions and was invariably involved in the requests for and receipt, storage, and transport of food for the displaced in Abyei, Meiram, Muglad, Babanusa, and other nearby villages where the Dinka had congregated. Muglad was accessible by road, rail, and air, and Chevron-Sudan had constructed a large base camp there equipped with an all-weather landing strip and had rebuilt the road between Muglad and Babanusa. Chevron provided at no charge a large warehouse at Muglad capable of storing 4,000 tons of food and made available to the donors and PVOs gasoline and diesel it had stored. With Chevron's support and Concern's abilities, Muglad soon became the center of donor operations in southeastern Kordofan.

Southwestern Kordofan was another matter, and the situation there escaped donor notice for months. Thousands of Dinka began to appear in Kadugli, where they were herded into camps located well outside the town. Some of those who wanted to continue north found they would either have to pay £S50 or voluntarily sell a child, a practice *Jeune Afrique,* which reported the story, called "an old Sudanese tradition."[85] Many of the displaced had arrived from Aweil District, where from 30 to 150 of those who had remained near their villages died each day in the period July through September. Over 7,165 registered deaths were recorded, and the starving "died outside the town or around it" in numbers greater than those reported in Aweil itself.[86] This desperate situation became known to the RRC as early as July, but the RRC was so certain the military would find an excuse not to deliver either planes or trains that on 1 August it asked USAID-Sudan if it "wished to organize an airlift." If it did, Al-Hag al-Tayeb, the acting RRC commissioner, offered "every assistance in obtaining the necessary permits from Civil Aviation and the military authorities."[87] Neither USAID nor the other donors seemed to grasp the gravity of the situation despite their visit to Meiram and a September report that had appeared in the Khartoum daily *Al-Ayyam,* which reported "mass deaths" in the town.[88] No interest was shown in the Aweil crisis until the donor trip to Meiram in September, after which the donors considered a flight to Aweil to study the landing strip but then canceled this effort when it seemed likely that a train might move from Babanusa.

Everyone seemed to ignore Abyei, which was off the beaten track, until journalist Carol Berger reported in June 1988 that the town was "teeming with 20,000 sick, emaciated Dinka refugees." She found that the Dinka were penniless and that the army refused to let them transport food given to them by the Camboni fathers outside the garrison town.[89] No attention was paid to the situation even after the RRC reported in August that to the best of its knowledge, none of the Western Relief Operation sorghum had ever been distributed in Abyei.[90] There was, in fact, very little food in Abyei in June, and there was none for the displaced three months later. The number of displaced persons continued to grow, and by September a major movement of displaced persons occurred at the height of the rainy season; thousands of Dinka headed north to Muglad, and in three weeks alone UNICEF reported that well over 500 people from Abyei had arrived at the El Adila displaced persons camp, which was well off the normal track used by persons moving north.[91] In fact, the South was in the midst of a cataclysmic event that was to take hundreds of thousands of lives, and the spindrift of a terrible famine was appearing everywhere and in significant numbers throughout all of southern Kordofan.

To the south, the governor of Bahr al-Ghazal, Lawrence Lual Akuey, informed Khartoum in September that 8,303 deaths from starvation had been officially registered at Aweil, and although the numbers of those who had died at Wany-Jok, Ariath, Paliet, and Paliou-Piny were unknown, they could have been in the "tens of thousands."[92] In Tonj, Gogrial, Rumbek, and Yirol, the governor did not officially know the number of the dead, but he thought it to be very great. In Wau he admitted that he was helpless to provide food for the starving and publicly accused the employees of Bahr al-Ghazal office in Khartoum of siphoning funds for their personal use. The Catholic Diocese of Wau reported that famine had even reached into the farmland of western Bahr al-Ghazal. In July 163 people had starved to death in Mboro, a village of 3,000 people located forty miles west of the capital. Bishop Nyekindi of Wau reported that war, flooding, and other disasters had left "the innocent surviving population in frantic search for food." In town many employees cared "for an average of thirty displaced in their homes in addition to their family obligations." The bishop added a sad footnote: "Nature had done its part by providing good rainfall and thereby enabling the trees to produce soft leaves on which these people have been feeding."[93] Thousands of displaced Dinka from Aweil and Gogrial as well as Fertit and Luo had sought food and shelter at four camps the Diocese had created in June, where over 200 people had died from malnutrition by the end of August. By September the markets in Wau were bare; the *jallaba* were escaping to Khartoum and those who remained sold sorghum on the black market for more than twenty times the prevailing price in Khartoum. The bishop had been buying food on the black market but was now £S100,000 in debt and was no longer certain he could find the money pledged to the black marketeers.

In early October Angelo Beda, the chair of the government's hapless Council for the South, visited Wau and informed the press that "62 people die daily of hunger."[94] For the commissioner, a Zande from Tambura and a graduate of the Rumbek secondary school, it was a terrible admission to have to make. In May 1988 Sadiq had appointed Beda to the post of chair of the Council for the South, although the council was little more than a sop presented to the southern politicians by the government and a pallid shadow of the old High Executive Council of the Southern Regional Assembly. Although he was a decent man, Beda's political life was hopelessly compromised by his efforts to work with the prime minister; to the southerners both he and the council were considered prisoners of Sadiq al-Mahdi and the Arab interests in Khartoum. Beda had spent five months trying to form an effective council as the northern political parties consistently vetoed the southerners he nominated to represent Upper Nile and Bahr al-Ghazal.[95] The council and the government's failure to respond to famine in the South were highlighted in a shocking story the Khartoum newspaper *Al-Usbua* published in July.

It reiterated charges raised previously by government and church officials in Wau and published photos of the dead and dying. It noted that the governor was about to free all prisoners from the Wau jail because he could no longer feed them.[96]

It was guessed but not learned until much later that conditions in the SPLA villages in Bahr al-Ghazal were as harsh as those anywhere in Southern Sudan. In November 1988 Akon and Leer, the SPLA-controlled villages included in the ICRC Plan of Action, were the last towns to be surveyed by the Red Cross team. At Leer the team members were met by their guide, Casito Omiluk Oduho, Sudan Relief and Rehabilitation Administration representative for Leer and Adok and son of the veteran southern politician Joseph Oduho. The drought had had an effect on Leer, but deaths from starvation were not nearly as great as they had been in Aweil. Akon, located between the Lol and Kuom Rivers twenty-five miles northeast of Aweil Town, was the SPLA stronghold for northern Bahr al-Ghazal. At the outbreak of the insurrection in 1983, Akon could boast of a police station, a primary school, a small health dispensary and a large market; in 1986 an especially violent raid by Baqqara militia had destroyed the primary school, the dispensary, and the *suq*. By 1987, however, the SPLA was well established, and in the aftermath of the continued raiding and drought that brought devastation to Malwal, Abiem, and the Twic Dinka villages north of the Lol River, some Dinka relocated near Akon rather than move to the North. In 1988 the SPLA received the allegiance of some fifty Dinka chiefs living within a twenty-mile radius of Akon, and in March hungry people began to arrive in Akon from every direction. When they learned there was little food to spare, most of the people moved on, and as supplies ran out the Dinka population shrank from 200,000 to 50,000 people. In June and July villagers buried many who had died from starvation, and the two SRRA men who had medical training could do little to help the dying. Malaria was epidemic, and with only one functioning pump, clear water was rare. The villagers who remained had literally nothing to spare, and the little good fortune they may have had was threatened by a major flood that struck the Lol River region in August and September and inundated the fields. To make matters even worse, disease began to destroy the few cattle that remained following *murahileen* incursions.

In Equatoria, 1988 was little different from the preceding war years. The displaced population continued to grow, and the donors continued to seek sufficient food to supply the displaced persons who had settled in Juba. The outlying areas were largely ignored. The food situation was more severe in Torit than in Juba; it was not until July 1988 that the first convoy to arrive since December 1987 limped into Torit Town with 150 tons of maize. Its passage had not been easy. Torit was a strategically important town; if it were to fall to the SPLA, the food aid lifeline through Kenya into eastern Equatoria would be lost to the government. As the SPLA tightened its hold east of the Nile, the army had been forced to supply Ikotos, Kiala, Farajok, and Nimule through airdrops, but it could not parachute food into Torit because the SPLA was too close to town. Thus, military supplies and food had to come overland, and the SPLA forces under the command of the former academic Kual Manyang were ready. They ambushed the Torit convoy of forty-six trucks, armored personnel carriers, and 1,000, troops inflicting considerable damage and casualties before the survivors struggled into the besieged town.

To the east, Kapoeta, a "spacious, well-laid-out pretty town with good water," had replaced Narus, whose water supply was inadequate, as the headquarters for food aid distribution within SPLA territory.[97] In June 1988, however, there were no crops, and food was scarce. The hospital had a single doctor and no medicines. Malnutrition was rampant, and it was reported that nearly 150 people had died from meningitis in the preceding two months. Still, once SRRA began to inoculate herds around Kapoeta, the SPLA was able to recruit successfully from the Toposa. Kapoeta was important to the SPLA, because a track led eastward from the town to the Boma Plateau and the SPLA sanctuaries in Ethiopia.

Whether in Juba, Akon, Kapoeta, or elsewhere, the terrible suffering occurring in the South could not possibly escape the notice of the SPLA. Indeed, of all the private voluntary organizations only Norwegian People's Aid—which under Egil Hagen's direction was said to be providing food aid to four SPLA camps near the border with Ethiopia—maintained cordial relations with the movement. The Western aid organizations claimed they had less luck with the SRRA than they had with the RRC, but in reality most of 1988 was characterized by unimaginative leadership and a complete lack of understanding of the catastrophic circumstances in the South. Consequently, when the flood receded and donor relief work returned to normal in Khartoum, it was almost too late to react to the great tragedy that had befallen the Southern Sudanese.

FIVE

— ∎ —

The International Response

We have no desire to choose sides in the Sudanese civil war, nor should we. There have been grotesque abuses on both sides. But the lion's share of the blame for causing this tragic conflict must rest with the extremist policies that have been adopted by the Sudanese government through three successive regimes over the past six years.
—Open letter from Representatives Wolpe, Leland, Ackerman, and Solomon to the Honorable Secretary of State George P. Shultz, 9 December 1988

In July 1988 reports reached Peter Schumann, chief of the emergency unit of the UN Development Program, that "a major human tragedy is in the making" in Southern Sudan. However, when floods struck in August, "all relief efforts centered on Khartoum."[1] In the wake of a spate of damning media reports, Sadiq had asked the UN Secretary-General to provide assistance, and Schumann along with the Ministry of Social Welfare formed a committee to review the displaced persons problem. The committee was joined by a team headed by UN Disaster Relief Coordinator for Africa Charles La Muniere, whose interest in Nilotic peoples was well-known. Upon arriving in Khartoum, La Muniere received a draft committee report that was long on platitudes and short on ideas.[2] Nonetheless, it served to involve both the Office of Foreign Disaster Assistance and Julia Taft. Taft had just received a report written by a Catholic priest and smuggled out of Abyei in August that indicated that thousands of Dinka were starving. An OFDA team brushed aside the dithering USAID-Sudan mission and joined La Muniere to take charge of a program to benefit the displaced Southern Sudanese.

Julia Taft and the Office of Foreign Disaster Assistance

Appalled by what she read and by what she already knew of conditions in Southern Sudan, Taft mobilized her limited Office of Foreign

Disaster Assistance (OFDA) personnel and used them to surmount the inertia that characterized the disaster relief policies of USAID-Sudan, the U.S. Embassy, and the Office of African Affairs in the Department of State. In August USAID Deputy Mission Director, Frederick Gilbert "had heard enough," and on 2 September a letter was sent from Ambassador Anderson to Sadiq al-Mahdi on behalf of the donor heads of the mission outlining the need to provide assistance to Abyei.[3] Wnen nothing happened, it was too much for Taft to bear. A dynamic and determined woman with deep roots in the Republican Party, Taft had extensive political contacts in the Reagan administration and on Capitol Hill. She was determined to focus attention on a terrible tragedy that had been ignored, deprecated, or dismissed.

Taft used with great effect both videotape and eyewitness reports supplied by Roger Winter of the U.S. Committee for Refugees, which found that the spreading famine in Southern Sudan transcended regions, tribes, ethnic rivalries, and political loyalties. Winter had visited Kapoeta in August, and after surveying conditions in that area, severely criticized U.S. government inaction. He had written: "Critics of U.S. policy... charge that the Reagan Administration's relative silence about the Sudan government's role in preventing aid deliveries is hypocritical. They point to the U.S.'s repeated denunciation of the Ethiopian government for using food as a weapon and say a double standard applies. The reason the U.S. doesn't censure Sudan, these critics say, is because Sudan is the strongest U.S. ally in the region. Ethiopia on the other hand, allies itself to the Soviet Union."[4]

Because the committee was a highly respected organization with a long-standing interest in Sudan, Winter's argument and committee reports distributed to the U.S. Congress and the Department of State could not be discounted. Taft also used a tape shot by a German television crew that showed grisly scenes of the dead and dying in southern Kordofan, and with the material from Abyei and that from Winter she almost single-handedly succeeded in reversing a policy of drift. She prevailed upon Secretary of State George Shultz to read a report on conditions in Southern Sudan and then to view a videotape. The explicit scenes of the dead and dying so outraged the secretary that he promised Taft his full support for whatever program she might propose. Her efforts particularly impressed members of the Subcommittee for Africa and Mickey Leland's Select Committee on Hunger. Many in Congress had already expressed that something was quite wrong with a policy that fostered subsidized bread to the Arab population in Northern Sudan while thousands of southerners starved.

Once the August floods had subsided and Khartoum returned to a semblance of normalcy, neither the U.S. Embassy nor USAID-Khartoum requested OFDA assistance, and Taft's effort to vault humanitarian concerns over the business as usual attitude that characterized relations between the U.S. Embassy and Sadiq al-Mahdi was resisted by the State Department's Africa Bureau.[5] The State Department later blamed the depressed economy, the crumbling transportation infrastructure, locust infestations, drought, and the Khartoum flood for hampering the relief effort in southern Kordofan and the South, but at no time did it openly challenge the government to help its own people or suffer the consequences. As southerners starved by the thousands, the Washington bureaucracy finalized the delivery of 200,000 tons of PL-480 Title I wheat, which arrived in 1989 and produced subsidized bread for northern city dwellers. Nevertheless, thanks to Taft, by late September a change in Washington's attitude toward Sudan was evolving. An opening was finally created for OFDA in late September when Ambassador Norman Anderson requested $2 million in funds for flood relief and locust infestations and another $1 million to assist the displaced persons in Khartoum. Because the funds had to be provided through OFDA, neither the embassy nor USAID could escape Taft's direct involvement, and she reacted quickly. AID funds were "found" and obligated, and on 28 September—two days before the end of the 1988 fiscal year—an OFDA representative arrived in Khartoum to set up shop within USAID-Sudan to supervise the distribution of disaster relief funds.

In early October 1988 a second devastating report, prepared by MSF-France, this time enabled Taft to change completely the focus of disaster assistance to Sudan. The PVO described in chilling detail the plight of thousands of starving southerners at Meiram. The document provided a history of a disaster that began with the arrival of thousands of Dinka in early 1988. It described food shortages, dwindling resources and a nearly impossible effort to save at least 3,000 women and children as thousands of starving displaced people died.[6] No help had arrived from the town, the region, or Khartoum, and the local military commander warned MSF-France personnel not to tally the dead or count the camp population. By September nearly all children under age five had died. As MSF-France begged the RRC for help, 100 miles away at Babanusa donor food rotted in a score of boxcars. When they learned of the catastrophe, southerners in Khartoum attributed government indifference to the Aweil exodus of April 1988, the death of thousands of starving Dinka en route to Khartoum, and the scenes of the dead and dying in the Khartoum railroad station. That flight had greatly embarrassed the government, and it was argued that Sadiq wanted no replication of the Aweil tragedy—even though the rail line between Babanusa and El Meiram was secure. The starving people would die in Meiram, not in Muglad or El Obeid and certainly not in Khartoum.

After reading the report on Meiram, Julia Taft instructed OFDA personnel in Khartoum to join with La Muniere and the UN team to survey conditions throughout southern Kordofan. Within days the professional disaster relief experts had created an entirely new set of priorities to stimulate the donors and the RRC to action. The U.S. media—which had sensed the possibility of a major story line—followed the OFDA team to Khartoum where the flood waters had subsided, the feared epidemics had not struck, and life had nearly returned to normal. They soon fastened on the tragedy in southern Kordofan and on the UN-OFDA team that was planning to visit Abyei, where it was rumored that a disaster greater than the one at Meiam was taking place.

The donors argued that Abyei could not be reached by plane, but the UN-OFDA team used an Iraqi helicopter left from the Khartoum flood relief program, and Joseph Gettier, an experienced professional with AID-OFDA, cadged the needed fuel. The visitors who flew into Abyei on 8 October included Charles La Muniere, the government's commissioner for the displaced, the governor of Kordofan, the deputy commission for the RRC, and the regional military security officer. Also included were representatives of World Food Program, World Health Organization, United Nations Development Program, the European Community, and MSF-Belgium. The ebullient La Muniere, an American who had previously served as the UN resident representative in Sudan, was well-known and had made many contacts. Among them was Kordofan Governor Ábd Rasul al-Nour. Born and reared in Muglad, he was an unusual Missiriya who was instrumental in finally moving food aid from Babanusa and worked effectively with the growing number of PVOs operating in Kordofan. Once on the ground the visitors found that the army had "supplied its troops in the town by helicopter but not the civilians."[7] They also found that Western Relief Operation food aid delivered to Abyei in 1987 and 1988 was provided "as fodder for cattle owned by Arabs" rather than given to "the African Dinka people" for whom it was intended.[8]

The professionals, many of whom thought they were inured to scenes of death and starvation, discovered a disaster such as they hoped never to witness again. Palsied children struggled to gain a share of the available rations. Overcome with pathos, Joseph Gettier helplessly watched those who were pushed aside sit or lie down "clutching their bowls, staring in a marasmic daze" waiting for death:

> The kids assemble outside a gate, with a guy inside like an Oliver Twist with a big ladle. The gate opens and the kids rush in. The stronger ones push and scratch and kick to get to the front and get their bowls filled. Perhaps 500 get fed, perhaps 200 don't. On the periphery are the

kids that didn't make it today. They won't make it tomorrow; they are effectively dead. All the while ... parents were crying out from behind the fence urging their children to get up and make it to the front. They are competing for life itself."[9]

The number of deaths in August averaged at least fifty per day, and in September 295 deaths were officially registered.[10] A month later there were few young men and virtually no children under six months of age still alive. There were, however, about 40,000 displaced persons in the town, all requiring some assistance.

The Airlift to Abyei

Upon their return to Khartoum, La Muniere and Gettier swung into action, the former the fixer and the latter the banker, to create a food airlift for Abyei. Both wanted a Sudanese agency to take the lead role in the distribution of food, and with the strong support of Dan Prewitt, the League of Red Cross Societies (LICROSS) director in Khartoum, the Sudanese Red Crescent (SRC)—which had extensive experience in Kordofan and a manager of proven ability in its director, Ibrahim Osman— was asked to lead this relief operation. SRC was the most active of the Islamic private voluntary organizations and was more acceptable to the southern leaders than was Al Da'wa al-Islamiyah (the Islamic Call Society) or the Islamic African Relief Agency, both of which were controlled by the Muslim Brothers and worked mostly within the Muslim community. Gettier prepared a new disaster declaration that allowed OFDA to provide a $1.5 million "umbrella" grant to support LICROSS and the PVO consortium operating in southern Kordofan and Bahr al-Ghazal. The declaration was purposely vague and open-ended and thereby allowed OFDA to "gain access to other areas with population in need in the South."[11] The RRC's Al-Hag al-Tayeb and Governor al-Nour concurred with the proposal, and despite donor fears that the government would not allow flights to affected areas, La Muniere immediately obtained approval for an Abyei airlift.

Contrary to government claims, the airstrip was in good condition, and an airlift was inaugurated on 15 October when a single Cessna was loaded at Kadugli and began to fly one ton of food at a time into Abyei. It was met by Sudanese Red Crescent personnel, who were soon joined by Save the Children Fund-U.K., OXFAM, and MSF-Belgium. The mini-airlift delivered ninety tons of food in eleven days. In addition, a UNICEF plane brought 13.5 tons of food, medicine, and other supplies and transported relief personnel, including technicians from the National Rural Water Corporation who repaired two desperately needed water yards.[12] Within days the international media had descended on Abyei *en masse*. They discovered that more than 10,000 Dinka and Luo had already starved to death: "In some ways, the airlift touched down too late for Abyei" because the "worst had already happened."[13] Journalists described and photographers captured scenes of children too weak to walk to the feeding centers, who huddled together in the dirt awaiting death. Food aid that had been sent to Abyei was found stored in the local jail, and "prosperous-looking Muslim merchants and soldiers sold food at exorbitant prices in the forlorn marketplace."[14] There had been a diabolic disregard for human life, and Richard Dowden, Africa editor of the *Independent*, wrote: "Nothing we have ever seen or heard from Africa—not Biafra, not from Ethiopia in the famine or Uganda under Amin and Obote—is as bad as what is happening now in Sudan."[15] The journalists could not help but wonder why neither the government nor the Western relief agencies had acted more forcefully to meet the Abyei crisis. What was happening there and elsewhere in southern Kordofan was, Dowden claimed, even more devastating than the Ethiopia catastrophe "during the worst years of its famine."

In response to a growing drumbeat of criticism, Sudanese officials claimed that the government had drawn up a plan to supply relief to about 224,000 southerners. In fact, the government had no plan. Yet the government could not be blamed entirely for the calamity at Abyei: "Some foreign aid workers said they knew before the rainy season began in earnest that the situation in Abyei as well as El Meiram and Muglad was very bad. They said they knew it would get worse because of the Dinkas fleeing into southern Kordofan and swelling the population of the remote and poorly supplied towns."[16] The fact was that despite the numerous adumbrations and a multitude of warnings—including those from Cole Dodge, the OXFAM team, Father Rudolf Deng, and various officials who lived in the South—the donors failed to react with the speed, the urgency, indeed, the outrage the situation demanded. A European diplomat tactfully explained that USAID-Sudan and other Western agencies had been reluctant to speak out publicly about the numerous deaths from starvation for fear of being censured by the government. As the diplomat put it, "They want to save lives and they need Government acquiescence as well as Government cooperation to do that."[17] In fact private enterprise in typical Sudanese fashion assisted the relief operation.

Fakki Nowatny, a Muglad trucking contractor with ties to the Nimr family, was contracted to move USAID sorghum to Abyei. In November 1988 Nowatny organized a convoy of twenty-four trucks that reached Abyei in two weeks. A month later the roads began to dry out, and his trucks made the round-trip from Muglad in three days. By December

Abyei's population had dropped to 28,000, and Sudanese Red Crescent feeding centers were operating efficiently. Thereafter, the number of displaced persons began to decline, and those who were sufficiently healthy headed north. Thanks to a *Wall Street Journal* article, Nowatny soon became a local celebrity whose hospitality to many visitors and ability to obtain trucks seemingly from thin air soon made him one of the richest men in Kordofan.

After Abyei, Aweil

When Secretary of State Shultz, the media, and a spectrum of members of Congress publicly deplored the famine and the neglect of the Southern Sudanese, the confluence of voices virtually ensured that the U.S. government would become involved in yet another program of disaster relief for Sudan. And once the OFDA was given a mandate to assist the starving, no one in Washington could deflect its operations. Funds magically became available, and UN agencies that needed money got it; so did the International Red Cross and a variety of private voluntary organizations. OFDA troubleshooters appeared in Khartoum and soon judged that USAID-Sudan had reacted slowly to the crisis and would probably continue to do so. A relay followed of OFDA and OFDA-contracted personnel to "assist" in the disaster relief program, and they persevered with such tenacity and used the media so effectively that the USAID mission was swept aside by the determined and energetic newcomers.

It was increasingly clear to Julia Taft that if her office were to fund an effective program in support of the displaced southerners it would eventually need the acquiescence of the SPLA. The SPLA could not be wished away, but the OFDA was prohibited from opening direct contact with its leadership in Addis Ababa or Nairobi, although Taft retained a channel of communication with Mansour Khalid in Geneva. Unable to deal directly with the SPLA itself, OFDA—over the objections of the State Department's Africa Bureau—turned to the PVO community to discern what interest it might have in working in SPLA territory if it received AID funding. This was the start of what would soon become a crucial breakthrough in the humanitarian delivery of food aid.

The enormous challenge, the resources at their disposal, and the support in the highest levels of the U.S. government led OFDA personnel to exert their influence in Khartoum with little sensitivity to what USAID-Sudan, the United Nations, or other donors thought. On 17 October Joseph Gettier attended the RRC Technical Coordination Committee meeting to inform the donors that OFDA would fund a relief operation to move food to both Aweil, where the extent of starvation was still subject to much conjecture, and Abyei. In October Taft was informed that efforts to relieve Aweil were "mired in indecision" and that no progress had been made "to mitigate conditions in the besieged town." The OFDA analyst added that up to 100 persons per day were dying "while the U.S. pursues the optimal, the technically correct relief option."[18] Ground surveys had determined that the Aweil airport was too small for large cargo planes, and for weeks OFDA tried to obtain government approval to schedule relief trains between Babanusa and Aweil. Time and again the government blocked its effort, and Aweil was to receive no direct assistance until December when MSF-France situated a team in Aweil after an absence of two years. Aweil received its first supplies on 3 December when a UNDP charter aircraft delivered emergency food supplies from Khartoum.

In all of the South, starvation was probably the most concentrated in Aweil Town, where 8,300 deaths were registered between April and September 1988. Even government employees and local police "died with their children." In satellite villages, deaths numbered in the tens of thousands, and "some families who struggled to cultivate perished completely leaving no single member to harvest the crops."[19] MSF-France and a UNDP team found that the death rate of children below age five had been 2.6 per 1,000 *per day*, "calculated over a period of 180 days between June and November."[20]

Frustrated on the ground, Gettier took to the air. OFDA allocated $1 million and contracted with Air Serv, a U.S. PVO, to airlift food aid for around 130,000 starving Dinka in Aweil. Air Serv quickly initiated one of the most amazing food airlifts in Africa's history. Light cargo planes were loaded with USAID sorghum and flown from Muglad and Meiram to Aweil. The first plane landed on 5 December, and within a few days an air bridge was operating at a frenetic pace. With that beginning, Gettier next obtained a $1.5 million OFDA grant to support a relief program for all of southern Kordofan. This umbrella project, managed by LICROSS, was augmented on numerous occasions and benefited nearly every PVO working in southern Kordofan—MSF-France in Meiram, Action Internationale Contre la Faim (International Action Against Hunger, or AICF) in Kadugli, and Concern and LICROSS–Red Crescent projects in Muglad and Babanusa.

Concern was also provided assistance in the management of the Muglad displaced persons' camp. Although Muglad had not received the publicity of Abyei, Meiram, or Aweil, it was a crucial way station on the track from Aweil to Babanusa. In October a small sample of displaced persons indicated that half of the children were undernourished—nearly 20 percent severely—and that in September at least one death had occurred in every household.[21] By December Concern was managing a camp staff of nineteen Arabs, twenty-one Dinka, and seven others assigned to sanitation and burial. The camp ran smoothly when left to itself, but because of the exponential growth of both the Muglad and Babanusa camps, the town councils threatened to shut down the relief operations. To resolve this dangerous situation and to mollify fearful and angry local officials, OFDA provided vehicles to the Relief and Rehabilitation Commission in Khartoum in return for its promise to place its personnel in the field to work as intermediaries between PVOs and hostile local governments.

In response to the stream of southerners moving north from Bentiu, Mayom, and other villages of Upper Nile in search of food, in early October the AICF began to help at a displaced persons' encampment at Kadugli. By month's end it was providing food and medical services for 2,500 displaced persons within the town and another 16,000 people scattered in the villages to the south.[22] In the Nuba Mountains relief for the displaced Nuba was hampered by the army, and the number of displaced persons in Kadugli was swollen by the army's destruction of the cultivations and villages in those hills (*jabals*) where the SPLA was winning converts.

In Meiram MSF-France was still providing treatment and supplemental feeding and carrying on its tendentious guerrilla campaign with the town council and the local military commander. In November 1988 an OFDA team visited Meiram and its report on the conditions there was circulated widely in Khartoum, prompting the USAID mission director and the EC delegate to send a joint letter to the RRC commissioner requesting that he investigate the charges. The letter specifically cited an attempt by Babanusa authorities to confiscate relief stocks consigned to Concern as well as problems involving government bureaucrats in El Obeid. In late November the donors were also forced to protest the order of the South Kordofan Commissioner, Abd al-Wahab Abd al-Rahman, that local councils take over all relief distributions despite existing agreements among the RRC, donors, and the PVOs, which had been negotiated in Khartoum.[23]

After spending weeks in the field, the OFDA team had gathered sufficient information on camp locations and displaced persons to inform Washington that the disaster relief program would require a long-term investment in personnel and funding and that the RRC and its new commissioner, Al-Hag Al-Tayib, would require the support of all donors for some time. OFDA personnel then began to attack the operational constraints that had previously hampered food distribution—diesel and jet A-1 fuel shortages, deficient communications, and inadequate supervision of food moved by road and rail. They purchased spare parts and marine radios for tugs and barges as well as radios, which were turned over to the RRC and to PVO working in southern Kordofan, Malakal, and Wau.[24] They purchased blankets and plastic sheeting for shelter. They pledged funds for the repair of the Babanusa airstrip and urged the use of Babanusa as the principal staging site for food distribution throughout southern Kordofan and northern Bahr al-Ghazal. They got UNICEF to inspect water supplies in Muglad and Babanusa because it was critical to the maintenance of around 500,000 head of cattle that roamed the area. When townspeople complained that tens of thousands of displaced persons were competing with them for the scarce resource, OFDA helped pay to drill wells to service both Muglad camp and Muglad Town.

The U.S. Response

In the United States a spate of articles on the Abyei airlift had taken Sudan from the anonymity of a column filler to page one. The press was on to a compelling story and it stayed with it for so long that the government was helpless to staunch the flood of negative reporting emanating from Khartoum. The *Sudan Times* began to republish reports appearing in foreign magazines and newspapers, and its editor, Bona Malwal, continued to inform the Sudanese about the tragedy of the Southern Sudanese:

> After almost a year of death from famine and disease, which have claimed tens of thousands of Dinka lives, the Sudan government has finally bowed to internal and external pressures and permitted a small airlift operation organized by relief agencies and financed by the United States government to the small Southern Kordofan town of Abyei.... The airlift operation into Abyei, small and probably not as effective as it should be, is thought to be a new beginning in a situation in which the Sudan government, which controls the town, has had an indifferent attitude to nearly a year of suffering by the people.[25]

A congressional delegation led by Mickey Leland visited Khartoum in October 1988, and other politicians were soon on their way. Many members of Congress were angry, particularly Howard Wolpe, who worked closely with Leland: "I've found absolutely extraordinary the passivity of the State Department diplomacy in the terrible disaster developing in Sudan.... Their concern for the famine has been secondary to their concern not to alienate the Sadiq government." Although Wolpe praised Julia Taft and the OFDA, other members of Congress expressed anger that the U.S. Embassy in Khartoum had been "lukewarm" to the idea of the Abyei airlift.[26] In Sudan, OXFAM and MSF-Belgium were emboldened by the international reaction, and in December they prepared a strong memorandum for the RRC protesting "the authorities' efforts to prevent Western relief workers from investigating the distribution of food."[27]

Sadiq al-Mahdi could hardly remain indifferent to all this activity, especially after an October meeting with Joseph Gettier and Walter Bollinger, AID-Washington's deputy administrator for Africa, during which an "OFDA proposed plan of action" was discussed and an *aide-memoire* was left with the prime minister that expressed U.S. government concern for displaced persons in Sudan. Undoubtedly annoyed by this intervention into Sudanese affairs, Sadiq sought to resolve his dilemma of not antagonizing the West without compromising Sudanese sovereignty by doing nothing; he left matters to his minister of defense, General Burma Nasr.

Despite Foreign Support,
Mass Starvation Continues in the South

By November nearly a score of PVOs were active in southern Kordofan, but serious problems remained in all of the major cities and towns in the South. Governor Lawrence Lual reported from Wau that in the period June through August, more than 100,000 displaced persons had crowded into the town. "Twenty to thirty people a day had died from hunger" before around 50,000 of the displaced persons had left at the end of the rainy season.[28] In October there were reports that once again the displaced were suffering in Malakal. The army had reacted to SPLA activity by "surrounding the town with barbed wire and mines," and the displaced people were stopped from "going out to plant or even forage for something to eat."[29] As the unfortunates starved, the inhabitants reported that "after nightfall army lorries regularly dump bodies in the Nile."[30] No one dared inquire who they were or dared to count them.

Supplies were also low in Juba. Since 1987 the UN World Food Program had provided food relief to 146,000 displaced Sudanese in the Juba and Yei areas—the only parts of the South it considered "accessible."[31] By September 1988, however, there was no food in the CART stores, citizens "stripped leaves from trees," and "many lives had already been lost through hunger."[32] The SPLA encircled the capital, and UNWFP was forced to halt transport between Yei and Juba. Although ten army trucks managed to sneak into Juba in October, they carried no relief food. After that, neither commercial nor military trucks would leave the city for weeks, and as the CART estimate of the needy soon surpassed 200,000 people, there was a growing sense of desperation. Aware that a disaster of incalculable proportions was imminent, UNWFP arranged an emergency airlift from Entebbe, Uganda, to Juba whose $3.1 million cost was paid by West Germany, Australia, France, Canada, and the United Kingdom. It was the first of many expensive airlifts.

UNWFP had contracted Southern Air Transport (SAT), a U.S. firm with a daredevil reputation, after seven other air carriers had evaluated and respected SPLA threats to shoot down planes landing at Juba. On 26 October the first food aid plane landed at Juba to a joyous reception from hungry inhabitants. Ironically, the plane was followed "within minutes by a state-owned Sudan Airways jet carrying weapons—a coincidence seized on by Southerners eager to point out the disparity between the behavior of their government and that of the international community."[33] The SAT planes and their U.S. pilots were instant heroes who had arrived just in time, because "up to the time the airlift began, officials in Juba had attributed fifty-five deaths to hunger and related complications"; in contrast, the private relief agencies "put the death toll in the hundreds."[34] By mid-November the airlift exceeded 100 tons a day, and although it slacked off in December, the two planes flew in at least sixty tons of food daily—barely enough to keep the city's displaced residents alive.

When the SAT airlift continued without incident, USAID-Sudan decided it was safe to resume an often-postponed airlift of 500 tons of sorghum and vegetable oil from Khartoum to Juba. USAID was finally in a position to provide more food aid when the 25,000 tons of U.S. sorghum ordered in spring 1988 began to arrive in Port Sudan in November. In addition to its donation, the European Community contributed 1,000 tons of food to the airlift. Next, the Lutheran World Federation, at the request of the Government of Kenya, sponsored a C-130 airlift that moved 1,200 tons of maize and beans the government had provided with the proviso that a substantial portion "would be made available for Juba's 150,000 permanent residents."[35] The shipments from Khartoum and Kenya were a godsend, because the town's embattled civilians received no help from either the government or an army garrison of 20,000 troops—"made up mostly by Arab and Muslim Northerners"—that was both unpredictable and corrupt.[36] The army was commanded by the inept Major General Allison Magaya, whose job seemed in jeopardy following a string of SPLA victories on the east bank of the Nile. With Magaya in command, Arab officers both fostered and protected a black market that was so blatant that it astonished Archbishop Paolino Lukudu. When purchasing food at the Juba market, Lukudu had discovered that commodities being sold at ruinous prices were actually "a gift of relief food from West Germany for last summer's flood victims in Khartoum." One southerner in the Ministry of Information could not disguise his bitterness: "Our people have sent memos to the Prime Minister, asking him to declare this a disaster area. But no food has arrived in the volume that the flood assistance arrived in Khartoum. It's a genocide. They are disappearing a whole people."[37]

In eastern Equatoria the situation was even worse in Torit than it was in Juba. A torrential downpour in September added to the miseries of the few civilians still left in the city, and Bishop Paride Taban informed Khartoum by radio on 28 November that hundreds of civilians had just arrived from Kiyala "hungry, naked and sick." Taban asked for UN intervention, claiming: "What we tell our people is, prepare your souls for a good death; what we have for you in Torit is our sweat, our blood and our tears."[38] In fact, Torit could not hold out much longer against the SPLA troops that ringed the city.

Using data accumulated from a number of sources, by December the OFDA in Washington estimated that 1.5 million displaced were "at risk of starvation in the southern provinces of Sudan." It was a very "rough estimate" since hundreds of thousands of southerners had made their way to the North and to Ethiopia and there was simply no idea of the numbers of displaced found within the SPLA-controlled areas. Neither USAID-Sudan nor AID-Washington had any notion of how many people had died or were in danger of starvation, but they were believed to number in the hundreds of thousands. More than 10,000 had died in each of a number of different sites including Meiram, Abyei, Aweil, Wau, Safaha, Akon, and Pibor. Thousands had died along the railway line between Aweil and Babanusa while tens of thousands lay dead on the trails leading from Aweil to Safaha, Abyei, and between Bahr al-Ghazal and Ethiopia. Various estimates have been given for the number of southerners who died of starvation in 1988. Relief officials offered a figure as high as 500,000 people.[39] One calculation made by a former member of the Refugee Policy Group of Washington, D.C., indicated 300,000 children alone had perished that year.[40] OXFAM and others quote the most frequently accepted figure of 260,000 dead, but OXFAM's executive director, Mark Duffield, thought it was a "conservative estimate."[41] It was likely that between 1983 and 1989 approximately eighty percent of the population of the South had been displaced at one time or another, and that nearly a million Southerners were lost in the same period.[42]

The United States Reevaluates
Its Sudan Policies

Ineluctably, Julia Taft, the U.S. Congress, and the international mass media forced the State Department to reverse its policy of silence in Sudan. From the day Sadiq took office, U.S. policy had been barren of initiatives and utterly lacking in imagination, whereas he had parried every diplomatic thrust with ease, remaining untouched by the West and doing nothing to settle the crushing burden of civil war in his country. According to Kenneth L. Brown, deputy assistant secretary of state for Africa, the State Department had indeed undertaken "intensive efforts" to end the war but had failed to bring Sadiq and Garang together in 1988. In fact, the contacts that had been made with the SPLA in Ethiopia and Kenya, including Brown's meeting with Garang in midyear, were only fact-finding missions. In the United States the SPLA representatives were studiously ignored by State Department officials, although they promised "to continue to seek an end to external interference in Sudan as well as progress with the Soviets in pursuit of negotiated solutions to the region's problems."[43]

Once the Department of State had been confronted with the issue of starvation in the South, the SPLA could no longer be isolated, and Garang and the SPLA had to be recognized for what they were—an inextricable part of the problem and its solution. In turn, the government of Sudan was warned that even though the United States was providing disaster relief funds, there was a law that governed USAID activity that would soon require the suspension of other foreign aid because Khartoum's debt repayments were so far in arrears. At a November 1988 meeting in Paris, the European nations pledged to support a $400 million UN Emergency Flood Reconstruction Program for Sudan, but AID-Washington balked. Its representative warned that the reconstruction of Sudan "while a ruinous civil war prevails is unimaginable."[44] OFDA then rejected UN efforts to seek $72.7 million for a "large scale humanitarian emergency" because it lacked regional specificity and included such questionable budget items as $6.1 million "for strengthening government capacity" and $13.3 million for "relief and survival items."[45]

That obvious reevaluation of foreign aid to Sudan occurring in the United States was soon reflected by other donors. In Khartoum, EC representatives and the British Embassy began to openly express their concern that the war and suffering had gone on too long. They began to badger the government and the SPLA to permit mercy flights throughout the South, and both urged the two sides to begin peace talks at once.[46] British Foreign Minister Geoffrey Howe visited Khartoum and Addis Ababa to express his government's disquiet, and in Addis Ababa French emissaries warned the SPLA in "secret" talks that France would ask the United Nations to denounce the rebel movement if it did not begin to work for peace. In Khartoum there was a slight shift in U.S. Embassy thinking. Garang was still the intransigent incorrigible whose political ideology was amorphous and thus untrustworthy, but for once the embassy's annual human rights report (published in November 1988) was relatively evenhanded. It gave cursory coverage to the massive violations in southern Kordofan and admonished both sides for using food as a weapon of war. The government, however, was blamed for impeding the movement of food by rail and barge to starving communities and for prohibiting the movement of southerners concentrated in the garrison towns. In contrast, the SPLA siege policy, although strongly deplored, was understood to be the only way the rebels could wage war with the promise of some success.

Although State Department officials generally avoid the press, television is actually feared by most officials. It is perceived as a superficial medium unable to present foreign policy issues with the in-depth reporting they require and deserve. Television is also a highly emotional medium, and when videotapes of the starving and dying Sudanese began to appear on U.S. television, there was considerable consternation in Washington. The Khartoum flood had whetted the appetite of the media, and when the Sudanese Ministry of Communications and Information eased internal travel restrictions, the Western press was able to reach locations unfamiliar to "chair-borne" embassy officials. BBC, Reuters, and Cable News Network camera crews visited Muglad and Meiram. Their footage provided a gruesome reminder that hunger had not been eliminated in Africa, and that in Sudan, as in Ethiopia, government policy was directly responsible for the deaths of thousands of its citizens.

The Sudanese famine also produced major coverage in U.S. newspapers. *The New York Times* highlighted the failure of Western donors to anticipate food needs in southern Kordofan, the venality and inhumane actions of local officials in places like Abyei, and government indifference in Khartoum. It had discerned that "underlying the practical difficulties" in the relationship between the donors and the Sudan administration was "the reluctance of Western governments to sacrifice friendship with the Sudan on the altar of humanitarian aid."[47] Readers who knew little or nothing about Sudan were informed of the myriad difficulties involved in working with a fractured government coalition that was heavily influenced by the National Islamic Front. Americans became angry when they were told that the Sudanese bureaucracy had grounded for weeks a USAID-funded relief plane scheduled to fly food from Khartoum to the camps in southern Kordofan. They tired of the excuses of Western diplomats who explained, "There is the fear that if you confronted the Government you wouldn't be allowed to do anything."[48] A great number of Americans who began to follow the Sudan story were left to wonder what kind of insensate officials governed in Khartoum and why the United States supported them.

A spokesperson for Interaction (a coalition of humanitarian and development agencies involved in Africa) put the situation squarely in focus: In Southern Sudan there was "a situation of genocide whether it's called that or not."[49] Its thesis that the U.S. government had defended the government of Sudan for too long was repeated in numerous articles, and by late 1988 congressional criticism of the Sudanese government and of U.S. assistance was increasing daily. Oral and written reports by Steve Morrison of the U.S. Senate's Africa Subcommittee were troubling. Morrison, who had visited Sudan on several occasions, offered the acid comment that the Congress "had two years to judge [Sadiq's] administration and in that time we've seen one of the worst outcomes." He noted, "We have unused influence, [including] $110 million a year in multilateral and bilateral development assistance that Sudan needs."[50] Morrison urged the State Department to use its political and economic leverage to withhold aid if the Sudan government was unwilling or unable to effect change. PVOs also joined the chorus of detractors, leading a congressional aide to state that U.S. relief agencies were "so frustrated by the deteriorating situation and the trouble they've had that they're demanding stronger protection from the U.S. government." PVOs wanted the Sadiq government to demonstrate an interest in the desperate situation in Khartoum, the South, and southern Kordofan. They refused to accept the State Department defense that the government was "trying to feed civilians on both sides of the line" but that the "technical and political obstacles [had] proven too large for the beleaguered government."[51]

In late November *The Washington Post* published a letter from Roger Winter of the U.S. Committee for Refugees: "When I visited Kapoeta and other towns in the Sudan's rebel-controlled south this summer, I thought the situation couldn't get worse. But the war has escalated since then, famine has worsened and more and more people have died in both government and rebel-held areas." Food was urgently needed, and Winter insisted that only "the United States has the credibility and the ability to launch such a humanitarian initiative, but it must make it clear to both sides that it will have no part in using food as a weapon."[52] In fact, Winter and Julia Taft were like minded—the United States would have to take the lead if a program of humanitarian assistance to both sides were to be sold. Their campaign gained momentum following the December distribution of a bipartisan congressional report that criticized the Department of State and claimed U.S. relations were "ineffectual and increasingly untenable on political and moral grounds." Among the critical problems congressional investigators had found in Sudan were "profound official malevolence, indifference," and—among aid donors and Sudanese bureaucrats alike—a pervasive "ineptitude."[53]

Silence from Washington

The State Department found solace in silence. It could not, however, overlook a telling rebuke by Representatives Wolpe, Leland, Ackerman and Solomon, who in a letter to Secretary of State Schutz on 9 December (with a copy to President-elect George Bush) expressed their concern that the food crisis was worsening in Sudan. They urged the administration to devote its attention to the terrible tragedy and made it abundantly clear that a continuation of the present policy would no longer be tolerated on Capitol Hill. As an example of these "extremist policies," the signatories cited the imposition of the Shari'a law and the government's tolerance, if not encouragement, of tribal militias. The representatives were "convinced" that the State Department had to make it clear to both the government and the SPLA that the United States was prepared "to mount a vigorous cross-border operation to reach those people who so desperately need our help."[54] They commended AID-OFDA's October airlift to southern Kordofan and Aweil, and the State Department was requested to protest in the future any action that might prevent food from reaching the needy in that area. The Sudan government could not ignore this criticism, and Ali Shibu, the government's minister for relief and refugee affairs, asserted at a news conference on 6 December that "the sensational media reports of famine in south Sudan are baseless" and used specious statistics to show "that necessary relief had been sent for the three southern regions in 1988." Commenting on the news conference, Minister for Information Abdullah Mohammed Ahmed proclaimed that Shibu's report "should silence the foreign media."[55] If anything, it only exacerbated the mistrust that existed between the international media and the Sudan government. Almost miraculously, but not so surprising given the extensive criticism the government was suffering, on 15 December a convoy finally left Babanusa for Aweil with thirty boxcars—900 tons—of USAID relief food assigned to the Aweil Relief Committee. Although the shipment was halted for some time at Meiram, where protesting police had not been paid for months, and at Malwal, where five boxcars of food aid were discharged and never found, the train finally arrived in Aweil on 16 January 1989. The cargo was received by the secretary of the Aweil Relief Committee, the respected Dinka leader Santino Deng, and a program was initiated to provide help to 50,500 registered displaced persons.

In December Representative Wolpe wrote directly to Sadiq al-Mahdi warning him that his government's disinterest in the delivery of relief food raised "serious problems in the relationship between our two countries." Wolpe (a democrat) warned that Americans would not permit him "to support aid to a government that does not keep its people from starving." He promised, "When the U.S. Congress returns to session in January, there will undoubtedly be hearings on the situation in Sudan."[56] Congressional ire was bipartisan, and Republican Silvio Conte admonished Sadiq in a separate letter included with that of Representative Wolpe.

> As a Republican Member of Congress, the party of the President and the President-elect [George Bush], and as one who has a major role in relation to funding of the foreign assistance programs of the United States Government, I must say that the relationship between America and Sudan is in danger unless the Government of Sudan, under your leadership, undertakes immediately to get food and shelter to all of the people of Sudan. There can be no excuse, no hesitation. Food must be provided to avoid more starvation and death. Beyond that a way must be found to end the ongoing civil war that underlies the disruption and famine in the South.[57]

Colin Campbell and Deborah Scroggins of *The Atlanta Journal and Constitution* quoted, with ill-disguised sarcasm, State Department officials who "said in interviews that they have been quiet about Sudan because they did not want to conduct diplomacy in public, [and] did not want to criticize a politically fragile ally and risk a backlash by the region's communists and Islamic fundamentalists."[58] They reported that whereas the State Department had condemned the SPLA for impeding relief flights—including an erroneous claim made on 25 September that the SPLA had fired on a USAID-chartered plane flying into Juba—the military and commercial flights were daily transporting supplies to government garrisons. Other journalists pointed out what was to them the unconscionably long time it had taken the State Department to declare the Sudan famine a disaster.

The Red Cross Plan of Action
for the Southern Sudan

As the pot began to boil in Washington, in Khartoum the International Red Cross went quietly about its business. In August 1988 it had completed famine surveys in the six sites approved by Sadiq and John Garang. The ICRC Plan of Action was stalled, however, as both sides studied it minutely, fearing the other side might benefit in some unexpected way. The donors wrote letters and *aide-memoire* and tried personal diplomacy to convince the government to accept the plan. African leaders, particularly President Museveni of Uganda, used their offices to extract a favorable response from the SPLA. Still, the government and the SPLA continued to argue over site selection and whether relief flights to SPLA-held villages could originate from airports located outside Sudan. The government opposed an extensive veterinarian assistance program in SPLA territory (where the scarcity of such services had caused losses of approximately 40% of the South's cattle population), and the SPLA argued that the plan unfairly allocated much more relief aid to government towns.[59]

During the frustrating impasse, the ICRC conducted surveys at Malakal and Juba, and an ICRC survey team spent a month visiting the SPLA villages of Kongor, Pochala, and Yirol. After months of tedious negotiations, in October the ICRC met with Sudanese Foreign Minister Hassan al-Turabi in Uganda and requested "more flexibility and understanding from the Sudan" to allow the survey of Akon and, eventually, the use of airlifts to SPLA sites from neighboring countries. When Turabi "asked for flight details the ICRC had them on hand."[60] When Turabi buried the issue, the United Nations, the donors, and the OFDA—assisted by the international media—excoriated Sadiq for his inaction, but the government continued to stall the ICRC's Plan of Action. Battered internally and internationally, as well as politically and economically, the government grudgingly granted the ICRC permission to fly from Kenya or Uganda to Akon to finish its last survey. When that survey was completed, the SPLA raised a final objection, arguing that it would approve the ICRC plan only if its SRRA controlled the receipt and distribution of relief supplies in SPLA territory. The ICRC would not accept such a condition, and the SPLA quickly relented.

In late November the Plan of Action's implementation phase began when planes loaded with relief supplies left Khartoum for Wau and Aweil and similar flights left Uganda for Leer and Akon, which the SPLA controlled. The ICRC airlift was virtually overlooked in Khartoum. The relief flights made headlines in *Al-Khartoum*, albeit with little in-depth reporting; *Al-Siyassa* reported the purpose of the program but mistakenly described it as a United Nations initiative. The independent *Al-Ayyam* was careful to report that supplies were going to both the government and the SPLA. Those papers that supported the Umma and the NIF were studiously silent. The Khartoum press reaction was characteristic of Northern Sudanese indifference to activities transpiring in the South. The international reaction was overwhelmingly favorable. Two days after the first plane touched down at Wau, Great Britain pledged $1 million to the Red Cross airlift, and other donors lined up with support.

These auspicious beginnings were followed by the expansion of the program at Malakal and Juba and in SPLA territory at Yirol and Kongor, where large cargo aircraft (particularly French Transalls) flew in from Entebbe. Donors and government officials used the ICRC flights to hitch-hike into garrison towns to investigate nutrition conditions. The State

Department, however, would still not permit U.S. government employees to accompany ICRC flights to SPLA towns. The first ICRC C-130 landed at Wau on 4 December, and within two weeks twenty-eight flights had delivered 500 tons of food. International Red Cross personnel were ecstatic, and Pierre Pont, the ICRC representative in Khartoum, remarked: "I think both sides finally decided it was politically futile to continue to stop and impede the relief."[61] In Washington U.S. Committee for Refugees chief Roger Winter applauded the ICRC program but expressed the concern that the ICRC airlift alone could not stave off yet another catastrophe in 1989. He warned: "The U.S. has held out for the ICRC option solely.... We all want that to work, but you really need to try all kinds of things, energetically and creatively."[62]

Peace with Suspicion

Politically, the ICRC Plan of Action was approved at a time when Khartoum was suddenly alive with rumors that peace was near. In Khartoum the Sudanese peace activists, whose activities had been stalled since the Kurmuk incident, had begun to show signs of life. In August the Democratic Unionist Party informed Sadiq that it planned to open direct talks with the SPLA regardless of whether he liked it or not; meanwhile, the army displayed unmistakable signs of discontent over the progress of the war and the dearth of military weapons and supplies. Days later a DUP delegation met with SPLA representatives in Ethiopia, after which the DUP leadership announced that talks had begun well and that future discussions would be based on the Koka Dam Declaration and its various provisions. Consequently, when Sadiq asked for consideration of the frequently postponed bill to officially legalize the September Laws, the DUP joined the opposition, which now had enough votes in the People's Assembly to send the bill back to committee where it would be pigeonholed indefinitely. It was reported in Khartoum that Sadiq and Garang would meet at an unnamed location on 25 October, but analysts discounted the rumor because Sadiq still seemed ill disposed to base peace talks on the Koka Dam agreement. Indeed, it was an open secret that a Sudanese delegation headed by members of the NIF Party had met with Libyan officials in Tripoli in October to sign an agreement that laid the groundwork for a Libya-Sudan union—which was anathema to the SPLA. In November rumors proliferated that the DUP and the SPLA were close to an agreement and that, despite unidentified gunmen firing automatic weapons at his home in Khartoum, DUP leader Muhammad Osman al-Mirghani had proceeded unperturbed to Addis Ababa. On 14 November the SPLA publicly announced that talks with the DUP and other Sudanese leaders had achieved their objective and that peace was possible if the government "endorsed an accord accepted by one of the country's ruling parties."[63] The agreement was different from Koka Dam in some respects: The SPLA did not demand the reinstitution of the 1956 constitution as amended in 1964; nor did it demand the abolition of the September Laws, agreeing rather to a freeze of the laws until a constitutional convention could meet to find a solution. The SPLA made it clear, however, that it would not offer or accept a cease-fire until "the government, with parliamentary approval, issues a decree committing itself to the agreement."[64]

In Khartoum the announcement was greeted with great rejoicing. To the surprise of some, the defense minister and respected military leader 'Abd al-Majid Khalil—who had helped sponsor Garang's academic training in the United States—endorsed the agreement. In contrast, *Al Raya*, the NIF Party newspaper, prophesied that the accord would lead "to the fall of the government, the dissolution of parliament and the destabilization of the army." NIF political affairs secretary and party ideologue Ali al-Haj Mohammed denounced the agreement and argued that "the only path to peace open to the SPLA was to enter unconditional talks with the Government."[65] The provisions of the agreement were published in a joint press communique and broadcast on Radio SPLA on 18 November and included most of the demands for which the SPLA had been fighting—lifting the state of emergency, freezing "all the provisions involving the *hudud* and related articles" contained in the 1983 September Laws, revoking the military agreements with other nations, and, when those actions had been taken, convening a constitutional convention to which the spectrum of Sudanese parties and interests would be invited.[66]

How the Umma Party would respond to the reports from Addis Ababa was something of a mystery. On the one hand, all aspects of the peace initiative were known by Sadiq prior to the agreement, and according to a diplomatic source Osman al-Mirghani and the foreign minister and DUP leader Hussayn Abu Salih "kept in close contact and consultation with the Prime Minister during the talks."[67] On the other, Sadiq would hardly be agreeable to freezing the Shari'a given the NIF presence in the governing coalition. Insofar as the DUP was concerned, its spokespersons claimed that its leadership acted out of conviction and was aware, as the *Sudan Times* pointed out, just "how hollow" Sadiq's other "highly publicized peace efforts" had been: "These efforts were always little more than public relations scams designed as much to cast the Prime Minister in favorable light among his embarrassed supporters in the West as to maintain his domestic credibility. It was only when the DUP's patience with the Prime Minister had run out that they took the highly unusual step for a government party of conducting their own negotiations with the SPLA."[68]

The response in Khartoum was electric. Ideologically and politically the DUP had seized the initiative, and Osman al-Mirghani had become the most popular man in Khartoum. Upon his return to the capital airport on 17 November, around 10,000 Sudanese gave him a hero's welcome, dubbing him "the man of peace."[69] In Addis Ababa John Garang told the press that the DUP "held dialogues with members of all sides of Sudanese life, the trade unions, farmers, politicians and the students before [the DUP and SPLA] took the initiative for peace." Garang cautioned, however: "All of them support the present initiative with the exception of the Islamic Front."[70] Most of the intransigents were indeed found within the NIF ranks, and Minister of Social Welfare Ahmad 'Abd al-Rahman expressed his party's mood: "It is not a peace agreement, it is a surrender."[71] The NIF made it clear that the party "bitterly opposed the peace talks" and argued that the pact was "part of a conspiracy aimed at blocking efforts to revive Islamic Shari'a laws in Sudan."[72] Al-Raya, the party's mouthpiece, accused the DUP and its leaders of treason.

The agreement had a tremendous impact in Khartoum. The Communist Party, the Ba'ath Party, the Sudanese African parties, and most trade unions and professional organizations supported the pact. In December a national front that favored peace and that called itself the National Committee in Support of the Peace Agreement composed of thirty-five political parties and thirty-nine associations and trade unions, issued a statement calling for Sadiq to formally endorse the peace agreement. Even the southern political parties set aside their disagreements and joined the movement. The day following Osman al-Mirgani's triumphant return to Khartoum, the Umma Party voted unanimously to welcome the DUP-SPLA agreement. According to its secretary general, Ali Hassan Taj al-Din, the agreement was "a step toward peace," to which the NIF leader Hassan al-Turabi prophesied that the pact would lead "to the fall of the government, the dissolution of parliament and destabilize the army."[73]

An attempt to destabilize the army did, in fact, occur a day later when a SAM-7 missile slammed into the C-130 carrying Sudan Defense Minister Abd al-Majid Khalil shortly after it took off from Wau. The plane was able to make an emergency landing, and within hours Radio Omdurman blamed the attack on the SPLA. The next day Sadiq declared that the incident proved the SPLA's insincerity, and an army spokesperson said that "the SPLA leadership must have approved the attack." Al-Turabi added, "Garang is harboring treachery and deceit and only understands the language of war."[74] Oddly, the person who seemed calmest in the midst of the storm was General Khalil, who reported that despite the incident, he was still committed to the peace process. John Garang was quick to deny that he had ordered the missile attack, and Radio SPLA broadcast that the attack was "aimed at wrecking the peace accord" and was, in fact, an "inside job."[75] Most politicians were willing to give Garang the benefit of the doubt—a telling indication of how the political climate had changed in Khartoum—and rogue officers in the army were generally blamed for the incident. As for Sadiq, he announced that despite the attack, both his coalition government and the General Assembly would agree to the pact.

The Peace Process Disintegrates

The prime minister was prepared, or so he said, to convene a constitutional conference and, in a new twist, to convene "another to supervise the peace accord."[76] He even began to refer to the SPLA as an "armed movement" rather than "terrorists." On 23 November the Umma party leaders again unanimously approved the peace pact, but *Al-Siyassa* reported the ominous sign that Secretary General Taj al-Din had indicated that some Umma leaders "had reservations about details of the pact which they would communicate to Democratic Unionists."[77] Nevertheless, a settlement appeared certain until Sadiq tried to commandeer the peace process. He began by creating two commissions, one to prepare for the conference and the other to investigate technical matters relating to a cease-fire. What followed was a succession of maneuvers that vitiated the momentum generated at Addis Ababa. On 5 December the government announced that Foreign Minister Hussayn Abu Salih would lead a delegation to Addis Ababa; it next reported that the delegation, which now included General Khalil, would commence discussions on 11 December. The first delegation never arrived, and talks were postponed indefinitely. This convinced both the DUP and the SPLA that Sadiq would bury the November agreement so as not "to risk his seven-months-old coalition by putting the pact to cabinet and parliamentary votes."[78] If he brought the agreement before the Constituent Assembly, there was little doubt that the NIF would walk out; to avoid that unpleasant prospect, Sadiq resorted to manipulation. On 20 December the government announced that it had foiled a plot by former officers of Numayri's state security apparatus to blow up Sadiq in his car. This clumsy attempt at assassination provided the perfect excuse for the government to declare a state of emergency and to cancel a peace march that involved a broad spectrum of interest groups that called themselves the National Alliance for the Salvation of the Sudan, which was to take place the following day. Hassan al-Turabi, who as attorney general had the authority to proclaim a state of emergency, was not about to approve a protest march by the same elements that had overthrown President Numayri.

With Khartoum in an uproar and the peace pact disintegrating, members of the Constituent Assembly openly complained that the prime minister was acting alone and detaching them from the peace process. Some members even suggested that Sadiq should dismiss Parliament to pave the way for elections to a constituent conference called for in the agreement. Sadiq had no intention of dissolving the assembly or consulting with its leaders, for, as one observer explained, "Mahdi wants peace too. But he wants to be its sole architect.... He is also a politician who has to protect his party's interests."[79] On 19 December he postponed the Constituent Assembly debate on the peace pact, offering instead to convene a constitutional conference on 31 December, but he refused to accept any of the other conditions set out in the November agreement. The DUP and the southern parties were furious, and they vehemently opposed this latest maneuver in a marathon six-hour debate on 22 December, at the end of which the assembly—dominated by the Umma Party and NIF— voted not only to approve Sadiq's plan to convene a constitutional conference on 31 December but also to give the prime minister a personal mandate to manage the peace process. *Al-Ittihad*, the DUP party newspaper, declared that Sadiq had quashed the DUP peace proposal, which indeed he had. Six DUP cabinet members submitted their resignations, and the party officially left the coalition government on 28 December. Sixty-three DUP representatives joined the Communist Party and the Union of Sudanese African parties in the political opposition. Seemingly unfazed by the political turmoil he had created, Sadiq disingenuously informed the press that he would personally contact the SPLA "on ways to convene the conference."[80] No one believed him. Peace seemed as remote as ever, and as 1989 approached and the SPLA began preparations for a major offensive, Garang made it clear that Sadiq had charted a policy that left "no option but to continue fighting."[81]

During an interview in November 1988 with Bona Malwal, the editor of the *Sudan Times*, Garang had declared that the SPLA movement "could not be indifferent to the plight of the people of Southern Sudan." The SPLA had closed off routes to halt the movement of arms and material to the Sudanese army, not because it wanted to starve the people. The SPLA's primary objective was "to make it as difficult as we can for the government to reinforce its army in the South"; Garang added, "no one can say that with the way the war has gone in the South in the past three years, that our strategy has been unsuccessful." Garang was particularly incensed that the government had discouraged assistance to the displaced southerners in the North. As for donor complaints directed against the SPLA, Garang asked, "What did the international agencies do to help the people in Abyei, Muglad, Meiram, Babanusa, Ed Daein, Nyala, El Obeid, Khartoum and all the other towns in the north?" He wondered why the agencies "went there months after these areas were riddled with the corpses of the starved Southerners." He asked rhetorically, "Was that due to the SPLA?" Garang would not eschew siege tactics, declaring, "In the end, the only guarantee for the survival of the people of the South, even after their numbers are reduced by the current famine and massacres by militia and government forces, is to return to the land and live on it as they have always done."[82] Like Bishop Taban of Torit, Garang was offering the southerners only more "blood, sweat and tears" in the coming year. The terrible famine had nearly run its course; in the year's final threnody UNICEF's Cole Dodge mourned, "whoever was vulnerable has died."[83]

Prime Minister Sadiq: Indecisive and Under Pressure

The chaos that characterized the last days of 1988 indicated just how unpopular Sadiq's policies had become. Strikes were widespread. Trains, buses, and planes operated infrequently or not at all. The airport was closed, and there were power and water shortages. On 29 December a protest in Khartoum attracted 10,000 chanting workers and students who denounced the government's politics of hunger. To calm passions the government raised the minimum daily wage; it then exacerbated the protests by issuing decrees increasing the price of sugar (by 600 percent) and other commodities. In the face of massive protests, which had been unseen since 1985, the government quickly rescinded the price increases and succumbed to the Sudanese Workers' Trade Union Federation demand to make salary increases retroactive to 1 July. On New Year's Day most of the crowd in downtown Khartoum appeared spent, and Sadiq responded with what was for him a lackluster speech to mark Sudanese Independence Day. Despite the swell of antigovernment sentiment, Sadiq alternated between petulance and belligerence. Although 31 December had come and gone and no constitutional convention had been convened, he chided the peacemakers, arguing that the fighting had been "imposed on Sudan" and that "if aggression continues, we must be prepared to stand up to it or we will become the joke of the world."[84] He rejected clauses in the November peace pact that required the abrogation of defense treaties with Egypt and Libya and the revocation of the state of emergency. The peace process seemed to be dead.

Shortly after the New Year, in its 3 January lead editorial *The Washington Post* conceded that maintaining an evenhanded policy was a challenge for U.S. officials in a place as difficult to govern as Sudan. It reported that the United States and other Western nations had "muted their public criticism of the food denial and concentrated on keeping the channels of quiet diplomacy open." The *Post* accepted, however, the judgment of critics who had suggested that such silence had contributed to the numbers of dead and dying in Sudan and that it was unconscionable for the United States to "stand by and be seen to acquiesce in a policy of starvation being conducted by the side it favors."[85] The *Post* editorial was a turning point; the newspaper, which was read by all U.S. elected and appointed representatives, had reevaluated the government of Sadiq al-Mahdi and found it wanting. It urged Sadiq to move toward a peace accord and then, in a bizarre non sequitur, suggested that Saudi Arabia, which could not publicly support the diminution of Shari'a, should play a role in the peace process. A few days later, *The New York Times*, addressing an allegation that poison gas was being used against the SPLA, warned that such an action "could be politically embarrassing to the United States" because the Reagan administration had "generally supported the Khartoum Government in its five-year struggle" with the SPLA.[86]

Even the State Department began to flow, however gently, with the shifting current. Deputy Assistant Secretary of State Kenneth L. Brown had failed in December 1988 to interest Sadiq in a U.S. mediation effort. After an oil deal appeared to have reignited the roller-coaster relationship between Sadiq and Qadhafi, the State Department issued a warning that Sudan was "playing a dangerous game by getting too closely involved with Libya."[87] In Khartoum a UN official warned that with or without a peace agreement, the United Nations anticipated the same disaster in 1989 as had occurred in 1988, and Representative Mickey Leland, for one, considered that specter impermissible. In a circular letter the chair of the House of Representatives Select Committee on Hunger advised his colleagues that the death toll from the 1988 famine could reach 500,000 people. He charged that "the militia, armed by the government [had] reportedly murdered many civilians, stolen cattle and other possessions and even abducted children who are sold into forced labor." Leland reminded his readers that although the United States had been the largest provider of relief aid to Sudan, U.S. policy was reluctant to pressure Sadiq "to alter policies which prevent food and medicine from reaching so many hungry people [and was loath] to take the steps necessary to get more food to where the affected population resides in the southern regions of the country." Leland promised that the Select Committee would address this issue at a hearing "early in the first session of the 101st Congress."[88]

The Impact of the Brooke Sanctions

Given the change of administrations and the succession of new officials, the Department of State was unable to change suddenly its policy toward Sudan. The department soon had even less influence because on 5 January Sudan became subject to the so-called Brooke Sanctions found in Section 518 of the Foreign Operations, Export Financing, and Related Programs Appropriations Act of 1989. Section 518 was a new prohibition that disallowed assistance to countries in default for more than one year on loans made under foreign assistance appropriations. Beginning in September 1988, USAID-Sudan had expressed to the Ministry of Finance its concern that Sudan was falling behind in its loan payments to the United States, especially with regard to loans that had been extended for military goods approved by the U.S. Department of Defense. It was also behind schedule in its payments for PL-480 Title I food commodities. To escape the penalties of Section 518, $12 million would have to be paid immediately, or both USAID and the Sudanese government would suffer the consequences. USAID could only hope that the government would respond because in 1987 and 1988, Sudan had met its obligations with great difficulty, and, as USAID conceded, the payments were made only "in order to sign PL-480 Title I agreements for those particular years."[89] USAID provided its annual sweetener when it informed the Ministry of Finance that if the government of Sudan were ready to meet its debt payments, the United States would ship $30 million in Title I U.S. wheat, which the government of Sudan wanted very badly.

When Sudan did not pay the arrears, a Brooke Sanction warning was invoked on 5 January 1989. When that failed to stimulate action, USAID prepared to invoke Section 620(q), the penalty sanction, on 16 March, which would require USAID to curtail drastically its program of activities. The restriction would not, however, prohibit funding *humanitarian* assistance if the AID administrator determined that its provision was in the national interest. There was no question that he would rule favorably on 123(e), a clause for humanitarian exceptions, because OFDA was already deeply involved in relief aid to the displaced southerners and was funding PVO activity in Sudan. With OFDA demanding that it move quickly, in January USAID-Sudan prepared a program to transport 20,000 tons of food to southern Kordofan and Aweil by the onset of the rainy season.

Before the Bush administration's State Department appointees had had time to warm their chairs, Julia Taft was busy. In the State Department Taft lobbied for more money, more food, and more disaster assistance for Sudan. In January she met with Mansour Khalid to discuss the problem of assistance in Southern Sudan. Khalid then told *The New York Times* "we need more involvement by the U.S. in relief efforts" and emphasized that the United States should "play a more active role in peacemaking between the north and south."[90] When the State Department was asked to comment on Khalid's activity in Washington, its spokesperson remarked that the department had "had contacts with SPLA representatives for a long time" (without mentioning the infrequency of those contacts) and blandly assured the journalists that "there's been no change in our policy toward Sudan."[91] State Department officials claimed that the United States wanted to move more food into Southern Sudan but were "concerned such an operation risked antagonizing the Sudanese Government."[92] The department was already concerned that an OFDA offer to lead a PVO team into SPLA territory might create problems for the U.S. Embassy in Khartoum. In Khartoum the U.S. Embassy and USAID-Sudan expressed their concern that food shipments to and through the SRRA "might be diverted to the guerrillas."[93] Paradoxically, neither was in the habit of protesting government transgressions, although at least in Juba it was common knowledge that "relief food has for a long time been the delicacy of those in positions of influence. Not only do the VIPs have unlimited and regular access to free relief food, such favors have also been extended to tribesmen, relatives, close friends and party loyalists.... This outright cheating, coupled with the fact that most of the local relief workers are seconded from government departments, may explain in part why it has been difficult to arrest these irregularities."[94]

In January Jane Perlez reported in *The New York Times* that the State Department had "recently improved channels" with mid-level SPLA officials through the U.S. charge d'affaires and his deputy in Ethiopia, which "conveyed a new attitude to the rebels," who felt that the United States was, at last "taking them more seriously."[95] Despite conciliatory remarks by Lam Akol, Garang's deputy, he firmly denied that there had been direct or indirect contacts involving the SPLA and U.S. authorities, but "if any third parties can bring their influence to bear on Khartoum, then we would welcome that."[96] Within a month after the change in administrations, the State Department produced what appeared to be a new and more balanced approach to the problem of the civil war in Sudan. A policy paper signed by Secretary James Baker and a longer document, "The U.S. and Sudan: Peace and Relief," indicated that a reevaluation was in process. The latter report noted that "as early as 1986, the United States opened discussions with the Sudanese Relief and Rehabilitation Association, the relief arm of the Sudanese People's Liberation Movement, to review the possibility of American PVOs providing assistance into the south. While the SRRA agreed in principle to such assistance, no established PVOs were willing to undertake relief operations in the circumstances which existed at that time."[97]

This obscured the department's fleeting interest in the SRRA, its unwillingness to meet with the SPLA, and its role in making such contacts and operations as difficult as possible, whether for AID or for PVOs. Nevertheless, Secretary Baker was generally commended for seeking a new approach to what was called the administration's "first plunge into African problems."[98] His support for an early cease-fire and the distribution of food aid to the needy found nearly universal acceptance outside the department. *The New York Times*, which was tracking the Sudan *affair*, applauded the secretary of state for breaking "an unbecoming silence on the Sudan." It added: "Mr. Baker rightly urges both the Khartoum Government and the insurgent [SPLA] to 'remove remaining obstacles' to emergency relief for victims caught in garrison towns and elsewhere in the war zone. It might have been fairer to place larger blame on the Sudanese Government for blocking relief shipments, but the Secretary's words represent an immense improvement on previous mumbling. Finally, a high official in Washington is saying out loud that thousands are dying for political reasons."[99]

Congressional response to the State Department policy paper was generally favorable. Representative Howard Wolpe, however, admonished the Department: "I hope this will be backed up with some straight talk, particularly with the government. This has been a very low priority, especially in light of the government's efforts to depopulate the south."[100] *The Washington Post* particularly commended the work of Virginia Representative Frank R. Wolfe, who had visited the SPLA at Kapoeta in January and had "investigated on the ground and got Secretary of State James Baker's ear."[101] A letter from Wolfe to Baker dated 25 January—two days before the two met privately—urged Baker to prod both sides to accept a cease-fire and to agree to an open-roads policy for food aid. Wolfe asserted that the secretary and the new administration had a unique opportunity to place a new emphasis—a Bush emphasis—on peace in Africa.

The response in Khartoum to the criticism in the media and in the U.S. Congress and the policy statements of the secretary of state were relatively mild. Regarding the change in U.S. government policy, the NIF's *Al-Ayyam*, which might have been expected to respond unfavorably, carried the secretary of state's various statements on Sudan as straight news with no embellishment; it thought the secretary's statements were positive but pointed out that it took two to make peace and regretted the fact that the U.S. appeal did not include a specific peace plan for Sudan.[102] *Al-Meidan*, the Communist Party organ, interpreted Baker's interest as an attempt to internationalize the conflict, and it mentioned without comment recent U.S. contacts with SPLA representatives, including Mansour Khalid.[103] Khalid had visited with members of the Bush administration, but he had not been officially received at the State Department. Nevertheless, because Khalid and President Bush had served together at the United Nations and had ostensibly become good friends, some Khartoum newspapers predicted that the United States would soon recognize the SPLA.

The new U.S. attitude toward Sudan also appeared to bring tangible economic benefits. In early January the Ministry of Finance was informed that despite Sudan's loan repayment problems, the United States would ship $40 million in wheat—a fourth of which would be swapped for Sudanese sorghum to be programmed by USAID-Sudan. A few days later Mubarak al-Fadl al-Mahdi, Sadiq's nephew and the minister of economy and external trade, announced that Sudan expected to export 1 million tons of sorghum, in 1989.[104] By swapping wheat for sorghum Washington hoped to force Sudan to provide some food for the aid effort and thus do more to assist displaced persons and other war-torn southerners. The USAID mission was told to "immediately enter formal discussions" with the government in order to gain its "maximum feasible support for relief operations, using the leverage provided by the wheat/sorghum swap."[105] Washington was ready to ship 40,000 tons of wheat in exchange for 50,000 tons of Sudanese sorghum to be programmed by USAID and to be employed as a strategic reserve.

Food Aid to the Southern Sudan

By January 1989 the ICRC airlift to the South was operating smoothly; an ICRC staff made up of twenty-one delegates and 225 local employees was at work in areas under government control, and twenty-one delegates were posted in Kenya or were working in areas controlled by the SPLA.[106] Nearly 200 tons of food had been airlifted into Wau, and small aircraft had dropped off medicines and supplementary food in Aweil. When Ibrahim Mohammed Osman of Sudan Red Crescent visited Malakal in January 1989 the city had been without relief food for a year. He found around 30,000 displaced persons in precarious health; about fifteen people a day were dying from starvation while the military openly offered to sell sorghum to NGOs at black market prices.[107] An ICRC team arrived, quickly registered 5,000 of the neediest people, and urged the donors to mobilize a barge convoy from Kosti. When the military refused to permit the barges to leave Kosti, the ICRC proposed an airlift, which was opposed by the SPLA on grounds of security. As far as the U.S. Embassy was concerned, the SPLA had again roadblocked the food relief effort, it urged Washington to contact the SPLA and to investigate its opposition to the proposed airlift. In Washington Assistant Secretary Kenneth Brown was forced to admit that even though the State Department had met with the SPLA, it had "little or no leverage with them."[108] The government of the Netherlands—which had traditionally provided a large grant-in-aid to Sudan—did, however, have leverage in Khartoum—which it used. Tug captains, crews, and military guards were quickly found, and a convoy of sixty-four barges carrying 23,000 tons of supplies reached Malakal on 13 February.

The convoy arrived just in time to prevent massive deaths from starvation. An estimated 150,000 people who had crowded into Malakal once again received a late Christmas present. Merchants received over 90,000 sacks—8,000 tons—of sorghum and threw sacks of rotting food they had hoarded into the Nile and restocked stores with new grain to await the next shortage. The bottom immediately dropped out of the price for cereals on the black market, and a ninety-kilogram bag that had sold a week earlier for £S1,500 could now be had for £S150. Donors and those with money could buy grain in Malakal for months to come at a relatively cheap price.[109] The convoy, which had been heavily guarded, met surprisingly little SPLA opposition since the insurgents had withdrawn many of their troops along the Nile north of Malakal for a major offensive in January.

In January 1989, the 1.5 million displaced Southern Sudanese comprised about one-fourth of the population of Southern Sudan. The UNWFP, working with other donors and PVOs, calculated that in 1989 the displaced persons would require 90,000 tons of food aid in the government-controlled areas alone—26,000 tons in Equatoria, 19,000 tons in Upper Nile, 31,000 tons for southern Kordofan and Bahr al-Ghazal, and the remainder for Southern Sudanese in Khartoum.[110] Given the government's plan to export at least a million tons of sorghum in its eternal quest for hard currency, the donors took it for granted that they alone would provide food aid to the displaced southerners, but at least the bumper crop of millet and sorghum in all parts of Sudan meant that another Western Relief Operation would not be required. Nearly a dozen PVOs were at work in the various camps, where they provided the logistical support and oversaw the distribution necessary to make the donor food plans work effectively. Much effort had been devoted to locating warehousing, providing camp services, and organizing camp administration.

During January 1989, representatives from USAID-Sudan and AID-OFDA visited Aweil and determined that over 5,000 tons of food aid would have to be shipped by summer in order to feed the existing displaced persons and an expected influx of 50,000 people who would arrive once the rains began.[111] The only way to get food to Aweil in the long term was by rail, but because the railroad was unreliable at best, a program was conceived to move 2,000 tons of sorghum, lentils, and vegetable oil by Air Serv planes until a somewhat reliable train service could be arranged. USAID-Sudan could program food quickly because it could draw from the 25,000 tons of Reagan dura that had arrived in late 1988; it was also collecting the sorghum ABS had owed it since mid-1988 and was finalizing a new round of wheat-sorghum swap negotiations with the government. As flights to Aweil proceeded, USAID-Sudan also worked through CARE to contract truckers to haul 4,000 tons of sorghum and 1,000 tons of lentils and vegetable oil to Abyei. It was estimated that at least 3,000 tons of food had to be on hand at the start of the rainy season to sustain a projected population of 30,000 displaced persons. Using LICROSS and Concern as key intermediaries in Babanusa and Muglad, the Abyei program began in February. In Abyei village water supplies were augmented by the efforts of the Sudanese Red Crescent, LICROSS volunteers, and MSF-Belgium. Temporary storage facilities capable of sheltering 4,000 tons of supplies were constructed.[112] USAID-Sudan next planned a shipment by air of 2,000 tons of sorghum to Juba from Khartoum, and USAID-Kenya pledged another 10,000 tons of grain for Equatoria. USAID-Sudan also consigned 600 tons of sorghum to Sudanaid in a brave attempt to try once again to truck food to Wau through Ed Daein and Raga. The feverish activity led Roger Winter to declare, "The Bush Administration had done more in three weeks for starving civilians in Sudan than the Reagan Administration had accomplished in the previous seven months."[113]

Despite Dispersement of Food Aid, Dissatisfaction Remains in Washington

Despite these activities there was still deep dissatisfaction in Washington with the policies of the U.S. government in Sudan. A report prepared by members of the congressional delegation and staff following the 1988 famine had urged the administration to adopt a tougher policy with the Sudanese government, whose response to the famine was labeled "incompetent" and in "disarray." After having studied conditions inside Sudan for more than six months, the authors wanted the Bush administration to "move quickly beyond existing diplomacy that appears to slant U.S. sympathies overwhelmingly in favor of the Sudanese government versus southern insurgents and that avoids overt challenges or pressures on the Sudanese government." It claimed that the army was diverting relief food for its own use and almost totally ignoring the plight of southerners. The militia attacked southerners moving north, and the "abduction of children, rape of women, theft of cattle and indiscriminate violence by these forces have become horrifyingly commonplace."[114] The congressional report represented tough talk from people who had personally witnessed the Sudanese holocaust. Although Congress championed the neutrality of food aid, the PVOs were hesitant to visit SPLA territory as long as the State Department disdained their doing so. Roger Winter, who visited Kapoeta in early February, found that Norwegian People's Aid and World Vision International were still the only PVOs working with the SRRA.[115]

At the end of February, the chair of the Senate Subcommittee on Africa and ten congressional leaders cabled Sadiq and Garang, imploring them both to declare a cease-fire and to support a program to supply food aid to the destitute. Once again the concern was bipartisan, and a voice close to the administration, Senator Gordon Humphrey, argued that the United States had not used the leverage derived from aid programs to get the attention of the Sudan government. "What kind of friends are friends that let kids die?" the senator asked.[116] The Bush administration, which had promised something new with the Baker policy statement, appeared to backtrack as the State Department's Africa Bureau maintained that the United States did not have "the leverage to force the Sudan's government to act" to save lives and said that the State Department could "promote the conditions for peace, not create them."[117] The Coalition for Peace in the Horn of Africa, a nascent association of sixty grassroots organizations, did not agree. The coalition argued that the United States—which provided substantial foreign aid and supported the hundreds of millions of dollars Sudan received through the World Bank, the International Monetary Fund, and the United Nations—should have ample leverage.

As the battle to provide food directly to SPLA villages was being fought in Washington, in New York the UN secretary-general had issued an appeal for $73 million in emergency funds for the Sudan displaced persons. In December the General Assembly welcomed the secretary-general's decision to organize a meeting of bilateral donors and nongovernmental organizations, but the request came so soon after the UN's call for $400 million in response to the Khartoum flood that it was dying a slow death until it was revived by UNICEF Director James Grant. Grant was convinced that an international response was needed. With the secretary-general's concurrence, he was able to obtain Sadiq al-Mahdi's approval for a March meeting in Khartoum to which he would invite donors "to prepare a crash delivery program of relief supplies to DP's in southern regions, South Kordofan and South Darfur."[118] As the State Department was busy sorting out the proper level of U.S. representation and the strategies to be employed at the meeting, Julia Taft knew precisely what she wanted—an agreement by both sides to allow safe passage of relief convoys to famine areas. She employed her considerable skills to warn the press and the public that the international community was locked in a race against time and that the Bush administration was quite concerned that other donors, such as the European Community, were not meeting their pledges with the required sense of urgency.[119]

SIX

■

Operation Lifeline Sudan

What distinguishes the Sudan situation is that the international community, out-raged by the suffering and by the use and access to food as political weapons, actively intervened. It has insisted that the protagonists adhere to minimum humanitarian norms of conduct, including the right of third parties to provide protection and assistance to civilian populations wherever they are located.
—UN Office, Khartoum, "Operation Lifeline Sudan: Proposal for a Case Study," 15 September 1989

By the New Year 1989, the lean years that had followed its founding were over, and the SPLA was better armed militarily and politically than it had ever been. Militarily, it deployed an arsenal that included SAM-7, ZSU 23-4, rocket-propelled grenades, mortars of various caliber and numerous small arms. Politically, Garang's New Year's Day message called on the Sudanese to demand a new peace pact, since "the first one was wrecked by Sadiq al-Mahdi and his clique."[1] His forces soon isolated Yei, driving the UN World Food Program to airlift food to 50,000 displaced Sudanese in the town as SPLA patrols began skirmishing with government defenders near Juba. The government then received a tremendous blow when Nasir fell to SPLA forces on 24 January. Several days later Nimule and Parajok, two important army garrisons in Equatoria east of the Nile, were captured. In mid-February the SPLA ambushed a heavily armed government column near Liria and frustrated its attempt to push through to Torit, where 6,000 army troops had been besieged since November and could only be supplied by airdrops. Having run out of food for the hungry, Bishop Paride Taban had sent word to Juba that Torit had become a "cemetery where people are living."[2] Within days, Torit—the most heavily armed garrison after Juba, Wau, and Malakal—fell to the SPLA, giving the organization its most important victory since Garang and the 105th had taken to the bush in 1983. Strategically, Torit dominated eastern Equatoria and the vital road link between Juba and Kenya. It was also a victory of tremendous psychological significance for southerners, because Torit had been the headquarters of the British-led Equatoria Corps and a symbol of that more beneficent era.

Sadiq al-Mahdi's Crumbling Government

Continuing a chain of political and military misalliances, on 1 February Sadiq announced a new government guaranteed to create enemies. Seven members of the NIF were included in a cabinet of twenty-four ministers, and the *Sudan Times*, an implacable antagonist of the NIF, argued that Sadiq had made it "the single most powerful party in the country, even stronger than its senior partner, the Umma party."[3] Well organized, well financed, and well led, the NIF was given powerful ministries as well. Hassan al-Turabi was made deputy prime minister and foreign minister. His protégé and fundamentalist hard-liner Hafiz al-Shaykh Zaki was appointed minister of justice and attorney general. Despite the humiliating loss of Nasir and the imminent fall of Torit, General 'Abd al-Majid Khalil continued as minister of defense.

Following the inclusion of the NIF in the ruling coalition, Sadiq found his government virtually isolated within and without Sudan. He was confronted at home by a group of influential intellectuals, professionals, and political opponents who had met with the SPLA at Ambo in Ethiopia for a workshop designed to keep the peace process from foundering. The reaction from abroad was even more dismal, both politically and militarily. General Khalil traveled to Jordan and Iraq in early February and received more moral support than weapons. Of course, the mercurial Colonel Qadhafi was pleased to fish in the troubled waters of the Nile in his eternal quest for Arab unification; so was Turabi who held secret discussions in Khartoum with Libya's minister of defense, Colonel Abou Yunis, that were designed to revive the Libya-Sudan brotherhood pact and obtain more military hardware. Qadhafi's ambivalence is nowhere better demonstrated than in his relationship with the Sudanese Muslim fundamentalists. On the one hand, the Muslim Brothers were anathema to him and were denounced in his Green Book; on the other he was on close personal terms with members of the NIF, who were frequent and welcome visitors to Tripoli.

Upon his return from his Middle East tour, a frustrated and angry General Khalil resigned as minister of defense. Khartoum's *Al-Adwa* reported that he had only taken the step because government policies had virtually eliminated Sudan's opportunity to obtain military and economic assistance on any terms. His resignation created an immediate crisis within the armed forces, and the following day Commander in

Chief General Fathi Ahmad Ali, with the support of 150 senior officers, issued a twenty-one-point ultimatum, giving Sadiq one week to increase defense spending or accept the DUP-SPLA peace plan.[4] The cabinet met in an extraordinary session, and a majority of its members demanded that Sadiq form a new broad-based government or lose their support. With a mutiny occurring in his government, Sadiq formally accepted the military's ultimatum "and agreed to draft a peace treaty to end the civil war."[5] He also responded to the army ultimatum with a memorandum in which he placed some of the blame for his situation upon Arab neighbors, who he charged had been stingy with military and economic aid.

Confronting the most difficult crisis to emerge since his election in 1986, the beleaguered Sadiq remained undaunted, claiming that he had obtained "hundreds of tanks, planes and other equipment for the Army."[6] With these mythical weapons, Sadiq counterattacked. In a speech to the Constituent Assembly he declared that he would resign on 5 March unless the army promised not to overthrow him and restive professional and trade unions pledged "not to strike."[7] The nation "would submit to discipline" or he would go.[8] It was an inspired *tour de force*, but the army remained unconvinced. The military command placed the army on full alert, and it insisted that all of the contents of its memorandum must be carried out. Still, the statement itself betrayed the military's hesitancy to seize power.[9] Its frustration was tempered by the fact that Sadiq might actually attempt to resolve the civil conflict through either war or peace. Undoubtedly, many professional military officers were sincerely disinclined to throw out a democratically elected government, and Chief of Staff General Mahdi Babu Nimr, who was both a relative of Sadiq and a stalwart Umma supporter, vowed that the military would "continue to protect democratic rule."[10] Indeed, most senior officers preferred to pin their hopes on the national elections scheduled for April 1990.

The political crisis continued into March, giving Sadiq time to carry out a series of audacious maneuvers to maintain power. Like a tightrope walker—blase one moment, feigning danger the next, but always in control and seemingly fearless—Sadiq put on a maddening display: "Who else in the world, when the military says you have a week to shape up, would come back and say you have a week to give me your full support or I'm going to resign, and get away with it?"[11] Political enemies and Western embassies were certain his days were numbered. U.S. Secretary of State James Baker was an exception. He understood that "the most telling sign of a compromise" was the nature of the army's ultimatum: "If the army wanted to take power it would not have given a seven-day warning."[12] Sadiq's first move was to travel to his old refuge in Tripoli in early March to conclude a $250 million arms agreement to deliver on his promise of new weaponry for the Sudan military. Qadhafi, however, drove a hard bargain. The weapons would hinge on "the continued participation and influence of conservative Islamic politicians in the Sudanese government," or, as a government official put it, the Libyans "would want to know who they're arming."[13] In Tripoli Qadhafi could demand NIF participation in the government, but upon his return from Libya, Sadiq was confronted by leaders of his own party who had reached an agreement with leaders of other political parties to dissolve the Constituent Assembly and exclude the NIF from the new governing coalition. Most important, the various party politicians indicated that the agreement "included a peace plan that meets the key SPLA demand for a suspension of Islamic Shari'a law."[14]

The government drifted, and the Sudanese economy did likewise. Sudan's foreign debt had ballooned to $13 million, or $600 for every Sudanese. The government's annual budget deficit surpassed a billion dollars at the official rate of exchange. Imports in 1988 had been almost four times the value of Sudanese exports, and government subsidies were ubiquitous. Ninety percent of the regional budgets were funded by the central government, which also supported a host of unprofitable parastatals. Wheat was subsidized at enormous cost, and the government price for sorghum rarely reflected true market conditions or the cost of production. In September 1988 Sudan was one of seven nations whose debts were so great and economic policies so egregious that the International Monetary Fund (IMF) cut off all loans and bank facilities. At that time Sudan was a billion dollars in arrears to the IMF; although the IMF scheduled two rounds of talks in February and April 1989, Sadiq was unwilling to accept its long-standing demands for structural economic reforms, including the reduction of subsidies, divestment of parastatals, devaluation of the Sudanese pound, and elimination of multiple foreign exchange rates. In October 1988 the government had introduced a parallel rate of 12.2 Sudanese pounds to the dollar that was designed "to lure remittances from Sudanese working abroad into the banking system."[15] These remittances were crucial to the Sudanese economy, because more than 500,000 Sudanese worked in oil-rich nations of the Gulf and remitted "about $400–500 million annually."[16] Most important, such returns were not handled by the banks, over which the government had some control, but by the infamous *tujjar al-shanta*—the "suitcase merchants"— who brought back cash to be exchanged at the black market rate.

By spring 1989 inflation was estimated at no less than 80 percent per annum, approximately double the rate when Sadiq had assumed office. Twenty million people living in the North faced shortages of wheat flour, sugar, citrus fruits, and eggs; at existing prices southerners had almost no opportunity to purchase these products. Among the most pressing issues was the availability of bread. In February 1989 Finance Minister Al-Tigani al-Tayib, an experienced economist, resigned when he could no longer accept the government's policies, particularly its management of wheat imports and the payment of debt arrearage to the United States. The market reacted predictably, and the black market rate for the Sudanese pound climbed until it reached twenty pounds to the dollar in April.[17] Following the finance minister's resignation, a severe bread shortage swept through Khartoum. In response, Sadiq proposed a national conference on the economy, but he held out little hope for its success since he was convinced that the economic downturn was a political problem that resulted from the massive demands of refugees and the displaced and the cost of their rehabilitation.[18] His government might have a conference and hold discussions with the IMF, but a country at war could not have a normal economy; he warned the IMF that his government would never come to an agreement "unless it is based on what the Sudanese economy can endure."[19] This was an anomalous situation, because as long as Sudan was at war, the economy could endure very little; even with the military practically at war with the government, Sadiq still seemed loath to end the conflict.

The United Nations Intervenes

During his struggle for political survival, Sadiq reduced the number of cabinet positions from twenty seven to twenty four, doing away with the Ministries for Relief, Rehabilitation, and Refugees. Thus, the Relief and Rehabilitation Commission almost assumed cabinet status, since it reported directly to the prime minister. The RRC's enhanced role occurred at a time when the donors in Khartoum were planning a major disaster relief program that was to build on the success of the Red Cross airlift and programs initiated in southern Kordofan and Bahr al-Ghazal. In January the donors, wanting no repeat of 1988, sensed that momentum was on their side and began to prod the RRC to confront squarely the myriad problems associated with the displaced southerners. Also in January the United Nations actively began to solicit pledges for its interim appeal, and James Grant, the executive director of UNICEF, was given responsibility for convoking an international conference on aid to the displaced in Sudan. Grant, like Prattley and de Mistura, was convinced that the delivery of humanitarian assistance transcended any other consideration, legal or military. He wanted a program that would offer relief aid to both sides in the Sudanese civil war, and he received direct support from AID-OFDA, whose personnel pushed the concept of a neutral relief program and indicated that significant OFDA funds would result.[20]

The European Community remained to be persuaded that a UN conference was needed. The existing donor-supported program to assist displaced southerners showed excellent promise, and the EC was not ready to commit funds to a UN program unless the government was willing to support it with deeds as well as words. The EC had a point, because USAID food was moving to Abyei and AID-OFDA was augmenting the Aweil airlift; a train convoy that included 900 tons of relief food left Muglad on 24 December and arrived in Aweil in mid-January (where it was greeted by 20,000 starving Dinka). At Wau a convoy of trucks from Raga had just transported food to local merchants, and the atmosphere in town had improved dramatically since the ICRC began an airlift in December. To the east, the Malakal Relief Committee had its prayers answered when a convoy composed of sixty-one barges, including thirteen loaded with 5,660 MT of relief supplies, arrived in February. Elsewhere in the south, the ICRC was flying into eight sites. In Equatoria a single ten-ton truck arriving at Kapoeta on 16 February was cause for celebration. The food from USAID-Kenya was delivered to World Vision and Norwegian People's Aid, which had created twenty-two sites to feed the 100,000 displaced people who had crowded into town. The shipment itself was, according to *The Washington Post*, "the first tangible result" of a change in U.S. policy toward the SPLA that had been "announced earlier this year."[21]

USAID-Sudan was convinced that if a UN conference were to succeed—even given the support of Julia Taft in Washington—a high-level delegation would have to attend. A Khartoum meeting could degenerate into a meaningless pledging session; thus, the more notable the participants, the more likely the government would be to approve proposals it had previously rejected. The issue of SPLA participation was potentially contentious, but Taft left no doubt that it would be a welcome partner. The State Department could not be seen as somehow disapproving of a conference with such lofty humanitarian motives, regardless of the financial cost or the inclusion of the SPLA.

Both the United Nations and the donors assumed that given Sadiq's tenuous political position, he badly needed the conference to bolster his sagging personal prestige. If the United Nations was bound to have a conference and the donors were bound to attend, he could not let it fail. He would find it difficult to deny the international community its plea for his government to recognize the neutrality of humanitarian aid; for both sides the conference could be seen simply as the natural progression of events once the ICRC had begun its program in the South. In March 1989 donor policy was fully conceptualized by the work of James Grant in New York, Julia Taft in Washington, and donors and PVO representatives in Khartoum and Nairobi. More than 1.6 million displaced southerners in Sudan would require assistance. (See Table 6.1.) The RRC would have to be strengthened. The government would have to agree to welcome and support expatriate PVOs and their role in the relief process, and it would have to establish local relief committees to cooperate with the donors and the RRC.

If the Sudan government was serious about assisting an international relief effort, among the most difficult problems to resolve was the foreign exchange rate. Either the government would grant the donors the most favorable dollar rate permitted by Sudanese banks (12.2:1) or there would be no program. In addition, the Ministry of Finance would have to release counterpart funds held by the EC and the Dutch and Canadian governments whose use had hitherto been blocked. The government would also have to ensure rapid customs clearance of relief commodities, issue visas and travel permits promptly, and allow participants to operate relief flights within Sudan and across international boundaries. Finally, PVOs operating in the field would be granted licenses to use radios. To ensure that the government would abide by its agreement, the donors wanted to have a High Ministerial Committee established. It would review complaints and resolve problems—especially with regard to military cooperation and to operations involving the Sudan Railways Corporation and the River Transport Authority. Eventually, Sadiq agreed to its creation and was named chair, with the RRC acting as the committee's secretariat.

The demands—in reality, they were little less—were designed largely to protect the private voluntary organizations. They had sent the United Nations a list of government constraints that required immediate resolution.[22] Their problems fell into three broad categories: recent legal decisions that hampered PVO registration, administrative obstruction, and logistical difficulties involving visas and travel permits and the clearance of commodities through ports of entry. Each had its own effect on field operations. For security's sake the PVOs wanted radios, but most important they wanted a clearly defined food aid policy that would be respected in Khartoum and in the regions. To that effect, AID-Washington wanted Sadiq to approve a Statement of Principles that would allow civilian noncombatants to travel freely throughout Sudan. OFDA wanted to force the government to respect the neutrality of humanitarian assistance, and, breaking with tradition, it had begun to sponsor PVO visits to SPLA territory. Julia Taft openly complimented the International Rescue Committee for an immunization program it had planned in SPLA territory, and OFDA gave its support to PVO activities under consideration at Kapoeta, Ikotos, Pochala, and Pibor. In New York, OFDA personnel working with James Grant developed a novel policy approach that involved the use of open roads and open skies. It would force the gov-

TABLE 6.1   Southern Sudanese Displaced, March 1989, Estimate

Site	Number Displaced	PVO Operations
South Kordofan		
Abyei	32,000	Sudanese Red Crescent, MSF-B
Babanusa	12,000	Concern
Meiram	11,000	MSF-France
Tibbun	3,000	Concern
Kadugli	5,000	AICF
Muglad	18,000	Concern
Total	81,000	
Bahr al-Ghazal		
Aweil	34,000	MSF-France, ICRC
Wau	40,000	ICRC, MSF-Holland
Raga	20,000	MSF-Belgium
Total	94,000	
Equatoria		
Juba	175,000	Sudanaid, SCC, Oxfam, NCA
Yei	50,000	Sudanaid, SCC
Total	225,000	
Upper Nile		
Malakal	50,000	SCC, Sudanaid
Renk	20,000	Concern
Total	70,000	
Central		
Kosti	60,000	Concern, MSF-Holland
Damazin	35,000	Sudanaid
Total	95,000	
Darfur		
Paired Villages	20,000	Oxfam, SCF-U.K.
Khartoum	1,015,000	
Khartoum North		SCC, SCF-U.K., Sudanaid
Khartoum		Concern, Goal, SCC
Omdurman		Goal, Interaid, MSF-F
Grand Total	1,600,000	

Source: USAID-Sudan, March 1989.

ernment and the SPLA to respect the neutrality of humanitarian assistance and the use of UN aircraft and UN-flagged convoys moving without military escort.

The donors asked a lot from the government, and within Sadiq's coalition the NIF argued that the government was being forced to recognize the SPLA and relinquish conditions of state sovereignty. Still, the government might be master in its southern garrison towns, but it was hardly the master of the South; if there were to be a UN program, it was impossible to exclude the SPLA. By late February the donor policy had coalesced, and invitations to attend a "High-Level Meeting on Emergency Relief Operations in Sudan, 8–9 March 1989" were issued to prospective participants on 26 February. Prime Minister Sadiq al-Mahdi had accepted the secretary-general's proposal that the government of Sudan and the United Nations jointly convene the conference, and a Draft Action Plan based on donor and PVO inputs and tailored by the UN New York Task Force (UN, UNICEF, UNDP, WFP) was sent on 1 March to the government and the Khartoum Inter-Agency Working Group made up of UN, donor, and PVO administrators. The conference was to consider the needs of the displaced and conflict-affected people in and from Southern Sudan and to determine how much food was needed from March to November 1989, how it was to get where it was needed, and who would pay for its movement. Sadiq al-Mahdi agreed to open the conference, and the UN secretary-general would be represented by James Grant, executive director of UNICEF, and James Ingram of the UNWFP. Some eighteen governments received invitations, as did seven UN agencies and sixteen Sudanese and international PVOs.

By the time the conference was convened in Khartoum, a secure foundation had been laid to ensure its success. The U.S. government and its conference representative, the Agency for International Development, was represented by Julia Taft, who favored a massive program of aid to the displaced persons. The EC also promised funding. Almost overlooked in the farrago of press coverage that preceded the conference was the fact that the donors had already planned and were moving substantial food commodities to displaced southerners. In a two-month period more food had been delivered to the needy in the South and in southernmost Kordofan—nearly 16,000 tons—than all of the food aid from 1983 through 1988. USAID-Sudan alone had trucked 4,000 tons of sorghum to Muglad, and an additional 10,000 tons for southern Kordofan was being loaded or was in transit from warehouses in Port Sudan and Kosti. Additionally, AID-Washington had promised 9,900 tons to Catholic Relief and Church World Service in Kenya for delivery to CART-Juba.

When the UN conference convened, Sadiq al-Mahdi had many problems, and the conference was just one of them. Indeed, the conference opened an hour late, and the high-level UN delegation and Sudanese government participants, which included Minister of Foreign Affairs Dr. Hassan Al-Turabi, wondered if Sadiq had changed his mind. The prime minister had left the day before for Libya where, according to military spokespersons, he was shopping for military weapons and had been unaccountably delayed. Sadiq arrived and opened the meeting with kind words for all, and attendees, who had initially worried that the meeting would prove difficult, were treated to the traditionally warm and convivial Sudanese hospitality. Sadiq was gracious host, and the only disagreement arose when Ministry of Finance personnel and the governor of the Bank of Sudan objected to the use of a preferential exchange rate for donor transactions. Donors and PVOs maintained that the black market rate was at least seventeen pounds to the dollar, and the official rate was 4.2:1; thus they should receive the government's restricted free-market rate of 12.1:1. The Bank of Sudan argued for a preferential export exchange rate of 7:1, and the donors balked. When they would not back down, Sadiq stepped in and with a statesmanlike flourish overruled his minister of finance and promised the £S12.1:1 exchange rate.

In the end the donors got virtually everything they wanted including James Grant's sobriquet—Operation Lifeline Sudan—which was adopted by the conference and dubbed OLS. About 71,000 tons of a total of 97,000 tons of food aid programmed for OLS was immediately pledged. The United States committed 35,600 tons of aid through USAID-Sudan and 16,000 tons of Kenya maize (swapped for U.S. wheat) through USAID-Kenya. In addition to food aid the United Nations received pledges of nearly $80 million of an estimated $132 million projected for OLS. AID-OFDA, which had provided over $60 million in emergency relief funds since the ambassador's February 1988 disaster declaration, stood ready to provide even more food and funding. OLS did not, however, include the million displaced southerners—many as needy as those further south—who were scattered in the camps around greater Khartoum.

The Difficulties of Implementing OLS

Following the conference Sadiq met with Julia Taft and Ambassador Norman Anderson in a friendly session. The conference itself received a sympathetic response from Khartoum and from an international press that had often been quick to criticize Sadiq, the war, the donors, and the SPLA. For Julia Taft, her expectations "had been fulfilled."[23] Grant, who had devoted his life to public health causes among the very poor, had every reason to be pleased. As for Sadiq, he promised that his government would respect a food aid truce in April and thanked the participants: "I have nothing but smiles and handshakes for you all. I thank you all and assure you that your recommendations will find necessary and proper response from my government."[24]

OLS was officially scheduled to commence on 1 April, and one of the most significant political aspects from the Khartoum conference was Grant's ability to sell Sadiq on the necessity of a food aid truce. Sadiq agreed to respect what Grant called a Month of Tranquility and accepted eight Corridors of Tranquility that were essential to the success of OLS. The corridors involved the use of truck, train, and barge from the North to the South and road and air from Uganda, Kenya, and Ethiopia. OLS would strengthen the right of voluntary agencies to provide relief aid to the needy as well as the government's obligation to permit the free and safe passage of relief supplies to noncombatants—precepts found in the 1949 Geneva Conventions, the 1977 Geneva Protocols, and the 1987 Charter on People's Rights of the Organization of African Unity.

The UN delegation still had to sell the plan to the SPLA, and Grant wanted to secure that approval in person. On 5 March the SPLA had announced that it supported OLS, and four days later its leadership declared that the free movement of relief supplies would be permitted anywhere within the area under its control. Ironically, Grant's path was smoothed by Mubarak al-Fadl al-Mahdi, who Sadiq had invited to open talks with the SPLA in Addis Ababa. Mubarak al-Fadl was just winding up discussions with Lam Akol when Grant and Julia Taft arrived at Addis Ababa, and rumors were already afloat that peace talks would be expanded "at the nearest possible time."[25] Following discussions with Ethiopian President Mengistu Haile Miriam, the visitors met with Akol. The SPLA spokesperson welcomed OLS and accepted the Corridors of Tranquility, but opposed a cease-fire to accompany the Month of Tranquility. The military balance had swung dramatically in favor of the SPLA, and it feared it might lose its advantage if the government used a cease-fire to resupply its beleaguered forces in Equatoria.

The SPLA still had no reason to trust Sadiq, especially since he had spent the day prior to the OLS conference shopping for arms in Tripoli; further, the secret $250 million arms deal he had signed with Libya reportedly hinged "on the continued participation and influence of conservative Islamic politicians in the Sudanese government."[26] Militarily, Sadiq was not dealing from a position of strength, because the SPLA's dry-season juggernaut seemed unstoppable. On 4 March the Nimule garrison located on the Sudan-Uganda border was overrun after only thirty minutes of fighting; with its capitulation the last major army outpost east of the Nile in Equatoria was lost, and a territory the size of Uganda was totally opened to the donors. Mongalla was captured on 17 March, the seventh garrison to fall in three weeks, and its loss tightened the siege

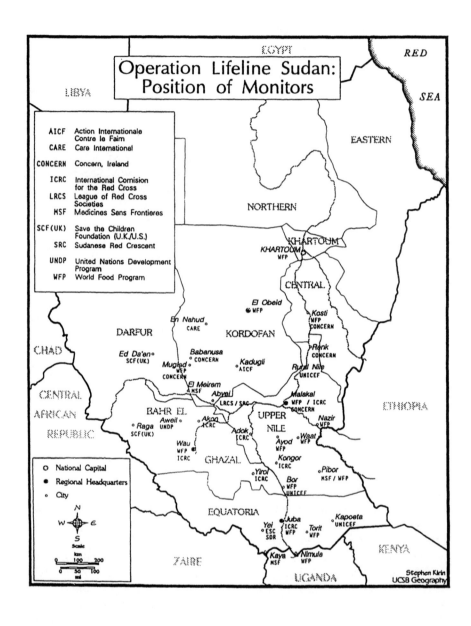

around Juba. It was just a matter of time before the SPLA attacked Terekeka and Bor, two garrisons down-river from Mongalla that could no longer be provisioned. Thus, if Grant wanted an Operation Lifeline Sudan, he was forced to accept the fact that it would commence without benefit of a cease-fire.

Privately, the SPLA thought the term *Operation Lifeline Sudan* was somewhat histrionic, and Grant seemed more unabashed huckster than an influential and respected official of the United Nations. Nevertheless, Garang approved the movement of UN-flagged food trains to Aweil, UN-flagged barges to Malakal, and UN-flagged truck convoys from Uganda to Yei and Juba and from Kenya to Kapoeta and Torit. He also agreed to support relief aid through Ethiopia to eastern Upper Nile and approved the continuation of relief flights from the North to Aweil. Grant met with Dr. Richard Mulla, director of the SRRA, in Nairobi and was given blanket approval to deliver commodities by road anywhere within the SPLA area for a six-week trial period. UN airlifts would require SRRA approval, but Mulla disingenuously anticipated few problems; in fact, the clearance process visualized was very awkward given the primitive communications network linking the SRRA in Nairobi with the SPLA in Addis Ababa and the complicated system the United Nations had worked out to pass clearances through its offices in Nairobi, Khartoum, and New York. The SRRA stipulated that the movement of relief aid barges to Malakal and other sites along the Upper Nile would have to be UN-flagged and could not be accompanied by commercial barges or moved under military convoy. It also approved the movement of trains to Aweil but only if en route they also delivered food to civilian populations located within SPLA territory. Finally, Mulla welcomed an expansion of the ICRC program in the south, and approved the posting of UN monitors in Kapoeta, Pibor Post, and Torit.

Grant and regional UNICEF officials then met with PVOs operating from Nairobi. They agreed that UNICEF should assume an umbrella role in OLS operations and that the World Food Program should assume the responsibility for logistics, planning, and reports on movements across the international frontier. In Nairobi the UNICEF representative would serve as the liaison with the SRRA, obtain operational clearances for food movements, and provide the donors, the PVOs, and the Sudanese charge d'affaires in Nairobi with monthly status reports.[27] With the United Nations in charge, numerous PVOs began to show an interest in taking part in programs in SPLA areas. This was welcome news to Egil Hagen, Norwegian People's Aid director, whose team had delivered 5,000 tons of food in SPLA-controlled areas since the start of the year.[28] AID-OFDA began by funding various proposals including a $535,000 water project for Kapoeta and Pibor, a food delivery project for Pibor and the Boma

Plateau, a $230,000 project to supply medicines to Kapoeta, and a Norwegian People's Aid food aid project in Torit.

While Grant was on a mission of personal diplomacy to Ethiopia and Kenya, his task of securing a Month of Tranquility was eased considerably when Sadiq fashioned a new cabinet. Following marathon meetings, ominous warnings from an impatient military, and a forceful memorandum from the opposition parties, unions, and associations, Sadiq formed his new United National Front government on 25 March. The NIF was excluded, which led its deputy secretary general Ali Osman Muhammad Taha to protest that the new government was unconstitutional and resulted from "pressures exerted by the armed forces, trade unions, donor organizations and embassies."[29] This was Sadiq's fifth government in less than three years, and for the first time the cabinet overwhelmingly favored a negotiated peace. It promptly endorsed the DUP-SPLA peace accord, and Sadiq announced that he expected a positive response from the SPLA.[30] Eight ministries went to Umma Party members, six to the DUP, four to Southern-based parties, and two to trade union organizations. DUP politicians assumed the portfolios of foreign affairs, attorney general, and social welfare, among others, and their appointments seemingly resolved a political crisis that had begun in December following the resignation of DUP ministers. The cabinet called for an immediate ceasefire, endorsed a tentative peace agreement, called for the suspension of Islamic laws, and formed a committee headed by Foreign Minister Sid Ahmad al-Hussayn to initiate direct contacts with the SPLA. Al-Hussayn expressed his complete confidence in the SPLA leadership and informed the ministry that henceforth it would deal with the SPLA from a "position of respect and confidence."[31]

The decision to move ahead with the peace process, which in effect secured the success of OLS, had in fact been forced upon a reluctant Sadiq. The crisis of February and March, for which the NIF was largely responsible, had shaken him. Moreover, his political life was complicated by religious and family problems: "In his three years at the head of the first democratic government in the Sudan in 16 years, he has been unable to bring himself to give up Islamic law, the mere threat of which perpetuates the civil war, now in its sixth year. Moreover, Mr. Mahdi is fighting a bitter battle within his own Ansar sect to become the sect's Imam, or religious leader. It has been widely reported that he took a third wife in 1987, a direct descendent of the last Imam, in an effort to strengthen his claims."[32]

His brother-in-law, Hassan al-Turabi, defiantly asserted that the NIF would "join the opposition where it would 'make Islam prevail with the power of the masses.'" He objected bitterly to Sadiq's offer to meet with Garang before the end of March.[33] Turabi called the government's policy "a submission [to the] rebels in Southern Sudan and to foreign designs [and] the forces of rebellion and evil."[34] NIF newspapers responded furiously when they learned that U.S. Senator Humphrey and Representatives Wolfe and Ackerman had met with Garang on 28 March without asking the government's permission, because the meeting proved to be a major propaganda coup for the SPLA.

The NIF was unhappy with the course of events, and so was Julia Taft. She complained that the United States had become the primary force behind OLS, and although AID was pumping money into the program, she added: "I don't see many other donor countries out there."[35] Ninety countries had provided disaster relief aid to the Soviet Union following the catastrophic earthquake in Armenia, but a much smaller number had shown an interest in the more serious tragedy occurring in Sudan. Nevertheless, thanks in large part to her badgering, the funding for all aspects of OLS was finally secured in April when the donors provided an additional $55 million for a program the United Nations called "the biggest emergency relief operation of its kind in the world."[36]

On 1 April Grant returned to Khartoum and listened at a news conference as Sadiq declared that the High Ministerial Committee for OLS had met for the first time the previous day and, thus, his government had fulfilled all of its promises to the donor community. Grant in turn expressed his pleasure that the Ministry of Finance had accepted the free-market exchange rate of 12.1:1. With that, Operation Lifeline Sudan was officially launched. Unfortunately, the program got off to a shaky start when Grant declared the United Nations' determination to deliver 100,000 tons of food aid *by 1 May.* The donors were aghast because the logistics system was already strained; barges would move at their own pace, as would the trains, and simply to get them moving would require more donor and UN energy than that needed for all other aspects of OLS combined. Mickey Leland, aware that Grant's target could not be reached, noted that "we're raising expectations beyond the ability to deliver" and added, "I would hope the United Nations would stop this public relations."[37] Much to the relief of donors and PVOs, Grant did so.

Meanwhile, the SPLA was politically cautious and publicly circumspect. Garang made no move to meet with Sadiq, but the prime minister and his new cabinet forged ahead and seemingly captured the initiative in the peace process. Despite the opposition of President Hosni Mubarak, Sadiq announced on 1 April that he would abrogate the 1976 Egypt-Sudan defense pact when the Sudanese Parliament had voted for its nullification. Of even greater significance, the Constituent Assembly voted (128 to twenty-three, with nearly 100 abstentions) to support the government's request to postpone the implementation of the September Laws until they could be reviewed by a national constitutional conference. When assembly members complained that the issue they had voted on was unclear, the subject was taken up again; a week later the members voted 206 to fifty-three specifically to postpone debate on the September Laws until after a constitutional conference was held. The NIF was outraged. The party theoretician, Ali al-Haj Amin Muhammad, vowed that the NIF would always "resist any move aimed at blocking ratification of the Islamic Bill." During the second debate, enraged NIF members stormed out of the Constituent Assembly, "chanting no God but Allah and no substitute for Allah's Shari'a."[38] Muhammed Yusuf Muhammed, NIF member and speaker of the assembly, resigned, and on 11 April the NIF militants took to the streets. At a rally at the University of Khartoum, Turabi admonished his followers to prepare for *jihad* (holy war) and claimed that "the Islamic revolution under the NIF leadership was the only force capable of breaking both the Ansari and Khatmiyya clutches on the Muslims of Sudan."[39] That same day Muslim Brothers incited a mob to attack the Catholic Church in En Nahud; the nuns' quarters and parish office were ransacked, and southern children who were attending a primary school nearby were threatened. It was an ominous portent of things to come.

Over NIF protests the assembly voted to approve talks with the SPLA, and a government delegation soon left for Addis Ababa. Sadiq also announced that his government was considering instituting a cease-fire, lifting the state of emergency, ending foreign military alliances, and freezing Shari'a. The prime minister also defused much of the criticism that had been directed at him for over a year by the international media. In April former U.S. President Jimmy Carter met with government officials, who expressed their appreciation for his support of "the ongoing peace steps."[40] Carter—whose Carter Center in Atlanta, Georgia, followed the activities in the Horn of Africa with great interest—was encouraging peace talks between the Ethiopian government and the Eritrean and Tigrean rebels involved in yet another (and older) civil war in the Horn of Africa. Carter, who often belabored the obvious during his trips to Africa, declared sententiously that OLS would only bring temporary benefits to the country and that Sudan would require peace in order to solve its problems. He promised, however, to return at a later date to take a more personal interest in the Sudan civil war. Sadiq also deflected State Department criticism, although Herman Cohen, nominated to replace Chester Crocker as assistant secretary of state for African affairs, was "known to have dwindling patience with Mr. Mahdi, the war and the consequent famine."[41]

In contrast, Sadiq's recent concessions impressed the usually impatient Mickey Leland. Accompanied by Representatives Bill Emerson,

Gary Ackerman, and Michael R. McNulty and nearly a dozen straphangers, including personal aides and the obligatory photographer, Leland arrived in Khartoum to kickoff Operation Lifeline Sudan's Month of Tranquility. Leland had been upstaged by Senator Humphrey and Representative Wolfe who, with a CBS camera crew in tow, had accepted an AmeriCares invitation to meet with John Garang in Southern Sudan. Garang gave the men his "unequivocal pledge" that food and medicine could travel through SPLA-administered territory "without any impediment whatever."[42] Garang then promised to dispatch Lam Akol to Nairobi to coordinate food deliveries from Kenya. Humphrey and Wolfe were duly impressed; at a subsequent press conference held in Nairobi, the two Democrats were careful not to take sides or, in what was fast becoming a ritual obligation, to blame both parties for using food as a weapon. Ackerman, who had joined the party and who could usually be counted upon to stir emotions, gave the media something new to cogitate when he asserted that U.S. military assistance to Sudan had been tantamount to the U.S. government "participating in genocide"—a point of view that generated little enthusiasm in Congress or the State Department and that was met with some amazement in the Pentagon.

The Politics of Operation Lifeline Sudan

Ackerman had first raised the charge of genocide at a March meeting called by OXFAM-America to press for a national day of concern for Sudan.[43] It had previously been leveled by such disparate critics as Archbishop Paolino Lukudo Loro of Juba and Aryeh Neier, Director of Human Rights Watch in the United States, but no one had ever accused the U.S. government of being an accomplice.[44] Although Neier was uncomfortable using such an emotion-laden word, he felt "the African and non-Muslim identity of the victims seems to be the cause of the victimization" and that it was "the one situation in the world today where the term might be appropriate."[45] Genocide had been implied by Bona Malwal when he argued, "How can this government tell you and me that the rebels are denying food to southerners when the army in these areas is being supplied by the same government?"[46] The situation became difficult to deny when Hassan al-Turabi, a government official, told Western visitors that "the more people die or flee the South, the weaker the SPLA becomes."[47]

When the Leland delegation arrived in Khartoum on 1 April, Sadiq's enemies used the visit to embarrass the government. NIF newspapers pointed out that the representatives and their entourage ("neo-Crusaders" and "neo-Colonialists" all) appeared in Khartoum without requesting government permission and without having an entry permit to

Sudan. Consequently, Leland and his colleagues refrained from directly criticizing the government and turned their attention to the UN administration of Operation Lifeline Sudan. Because Grant had raised such enormous expectations and the United Nations had been slow to deliver, Leland criticized the United Nations and warned that it needed "to get more to the substance as opposed to the PR [public relations] value of what this is all about."[48] Ackerman, who had rejoined Leland and who was aware that his New York City constituents enjoyed an occasional UN bashing, charged the United Nations with being "asleep at the switch," calling its operation "basically smoke and mirrors."[49] In contrast, Julia Taft, who had accompanied the group sensed that OLS would shortly be moving at top speed and was far more positive. The delegation met with Minister of Foreign Affairs Sid Ahmad al-Hussayn, who was effusive in his appreciation for the U.S. effort to assist starving peoples in the South. The delegation responded appropriately by confirming U.S. government concern for the displaced and underscored the importance Congress attached to Operation Lifeline Sudan. After a negative beginning, the delegation soon received favorable press coverage, and its meeting with the prime minister on 2 April was the feature story in most Khartoum newspapers. Sadiq pledged his government's total commitment to OLS, and claimed that a national constitutional conference would soon be convened. The members of congress, favorably impressed, promised that on their return to Washington they would urge the State Department to take a more active role in the peace process, and to use its influence to press the SPLA to move expeditiously to convene a constitutional conference.[50]

Throughout April, in its debates the Constituent Assembly exhorted the government to accelerate the pace of its peace discussions and expressed fears that the process was somehow diminishing. The Political Committee of the Ministry of Foreign Affairs continued the work it had begun at the first Addis Ababa meeting. A paper on the "Strategy, Tactics and Means of Achieving Peace" was prepared in late April, and the committee then began to assemble working papers for the proposed constitutional conference.[51] With enemies on the right and within the military, Sadiq's effort to remold his image as a grand peacemaker was tarnished, however, by an SPLA offensive that captured more than a dozen government towns in the South; Sadiq's enemies considered their loss a sign of the government's weakness rather than of SPLA strength. When Garang was slow to respond to Sadiq's personal letter to him, the prime minister expressed concern to James Grant of UNICEF that the SPLA offensive was disrupting both OLS and the peace process and characterized the fighting as "incompatible with efforts to end the civil war."[52] On 23 April Grant met with Garang and discussed the ambivalence that existed between the SPLA offensive and the concessions Sadiq had made and Garang's protestations for peace.[53] Garang agreed to support OLS whole-heartedly; on 29 April an SPLA press statement indicated that the organization would respect the movement of UN-flagged OLS trains and barges as long as they were not accompanied by a military escort.[54] There was no indication that the SPLA was about to declare a unilateral cease-fire.

Not surprisingly, both USAID-Sudan and the U.S. Embassy were startled when Representative Leland issued a number of questionable statements about OLS after he returned to the United States. Following his visit to Khartoum, he had met with John Garang in Nairobi, and he claimed the SPLA leader "would not tolerate a contemplated airlift of food by the United Nations from Khartoum to Juba." According to Leland, it was Garang's view that "such an airlift, intended to complement flights from Uganda and Kenya, could be too easily filled with goods for the Government army."[55] Leland, however, had been briefed in Khartoum that food flights from Khartoum to Juba were a daily occurrence and included flights sponsored by Norwegian Church Aid that moved USAID-Sudan food. The SPLA tolerated the flights, and even after the SPLA had shelled Juba on 13 April, Lam Akol explained that the target was the military base and that the SPLA had "no intention of bombing the airport or damaging the relief operation."[56] Leland also indicated that Garang would not even contemplate a cease-fire, shortly after which Garang declared a month-long truce to begin on 1 May. The move was not unexpected, because the SPLA offensive had nearly run its course, and Sadiq seemed definitely committed to the search for peace. Garang had, after all, pressed the government to avoid entanglements with the NIF, which he called the "lunatic fringe of Sudanese politics," and in a major concession Sadiq had done so. In response, the SPLA acknowledged that despite its irreversible commitment to the creation of a secular Sudan, "a temporary concession on the issue of Shari'a was inevitable if a breakthrough was to be made. After heated internal debate conducted at different levels, the Movement decided it would put up with a mere freeze on Shari'a rather than insist on an outright repeal of the abominable laws pending resolution of the thorny issue at the Constitutional Conference."[57]

As Leland was aware, to err was a common failing, and, to be sure, John Garang was a complex individual. Unfortunately, Leland was little better at reading Ethiopia's President Mengistu Haile Miriam, who reportedly told him that his government wanted to strengthen relations with the United States and agreed "to open his western border for relief aid bound for Sudan."[58] The UN World Food Program received approval to ship 10,000 tons of maize through Gambila to eastern Upper Nile, but after Leland had gone Mengistu changed his mind. The Ethiopian government would play no part in OLS, and the UNWFP was forced to resort to airlifts to supply the isolated Upper Nile region towns of Nasir, Akobo, and Pibor and the area along the Sobat River.

In Khartoum, Sadiq continued his diplomatic offensive. He prevailed upon Ali Al-Mirghani, the respected leader of the Khatmiyya, which had enjoyed a long and close association with Egypt, to enlist Egypt's support. This was a difficult request for Sadiq to make, given the historic enmity that existed between the Ansar and Egypt, but peace appeared not only obtainable but imminent when Radio SPLA announced its cease-fire on 1 May. Garang's offer was not only propitious but appeared to be a recognition of Sadiq's concessions to encourage the peace process. He responded, "For every one step taken by the SPLA, we will reciprocate by taking two steps."[59] A wary armed forces, however, was neither ready to match the cease-fire nor to lift the state of emergency. Nonetheless, Sadiq assured the United Nations that his government would continue to respect the Corridors of Tranquility and publicly proposed the creation of a joint committee consisting of representatives of the government and the insurgents to enforce the cease-fire. "Brother" John Garang seemed suitably impressed with Sadiq's announcements, but Major Deng Alor, the SPLA spokesperson, probably best expressed the feelings of the SPLA with his cool appraisal that the continuation of peace talks would succeed only when all of the conditions of the DUP-SPLA accord had been satisfied.

Garang Emerges from the Bush to Go West

As Sadiq and the army were reconciling themselves to peace, Garang prepared for what he hoped would be a triumphal tour of Europe and the United States. The SPLA was now an authentic indigenous Sudanese political movement, and Garang, who hitherto had been the leader of a little-known rebel army, discovered that politicians and statesmen were willing to receive him and to listen to him. In May the secretariat of the Arab Bar Association invited him to participate in its conference in Damascus in June, which he had to decline for the more important tour to the United States and Europe.[60] The SPLA declaration of a cease-fire would be to his advantage when he was abroad, but he was undoubtedly more pleased by the capture of Bor, his home district, on 17 April. The victory, which involved the eleventh government garrison and the third district capital to fall during the dry-season offensive, was cause for the SPLA's greatest celebration. In Torit, cigarettes—"a rare luxury"—were distributed, and there was cause for rejoicing and singing "in many different languages—Nuer, Latuka, Dinka, Madi."[61] Having captured Bor, the

SPLA now controlled the Nile from Malakal to Juba, and it had demonstrated that it was a dangerous fighting force. Garang had not been in the West since 1983, and he planned to visit former President Carter in Atlanta. Carter had again offered to act as mediator in the Sudan dispute and had received the tacit approval of the Bush administration, which considered negotiations to end the civil war in Sudan a priority item in its foreign policy for Africa.[62] Garang was to visit with economists and analysts at the Brookings Institution in Washington and with members of the House of Representatives Select Committee on Hunger.

The prospect that members of Congress would receive Garang on the steps of Capitol Hill, if not in their offices, was reason enough to move Assistant Secretary of State for Africa Herman Cohen to visit Khartoum to explain to Sadiq that the administration had not sponsored Garang's visit and that the visit was not an indication that the Bush administration was reevaluating its commitment to the democratically elected government of Sadiq al-Mahdi. Cohen, a soft-spoken yet incisive State Department official with extensive experience in West Africa, arrived in Khartoum on 24 May. He met with Sadiq, with Turabi of the NIF, and with Samuel Aru Bol, the government's southerner served up to him by the U.S. Embassy. Cohen rebuilt bridges the department felt had weakened through no fault of its own but, rather, from such issues as congressional trips to SPLA villages, the reduction of the aid package, problems with wheat imports, and Garang's visit to and treatment in the United States—all issues Cohen could not control. In an interview with the Khartoum newspaper *Al-Siyassa* he stressed the importance the United States gave to improving relations with Sudan. He praised the peace process yet implied that it was moving very slowly. He set his hosts' minds at rest by insisting that although the U.S. government was in contact with the SPLA, it did not officially recognize the movement and would object should the SPLA break off its self-imposed cease-fire. Cohen danced around the Shari'a issue, noting that he had no personal views on the subject and felt it was an internal matter. Turning to food aid, Cohen insisted that such aid was given for humanitarian rather than political aims and that the United States was pleased to support OLS.[63] As Cohen was well aware, the State Department and OLS donors had enemies in Sudan: The Muslim fundamentalists considered them neocrusaders, and for many students and union leaders they were the tentacles of a neocolonial octopus. Undaunted by his Sudanese critics on the right and the left, Cohen made it clear that if Sadiq and the SPLA wanted State Department assistance, he was ready to oblige.[64]

When Cohen departed for Europe on 26 May, it was said that the media and the Congress had finally flushed the State Department from the thicket of noninvolvement into open participation in the interminable tragic saga of Sudan. The State Department under Chester Crocker had hoped to engage the Soviet Union in a bipartisan strategy "to try to end Sudan's conflict," and it had bought the Fabian analysis that nothing could be done because Garang was forced to fight in order to solidify the centrifugal forces that existed within the ranks of the SPLA leadership.[65] Crocker's Africa Bureau, which had as much use for Sadiq as it had for the SPLA, thought a government-SPLA rapprochement was unlikely. Depending, upon the time and place, it had argued—always with sterile logic—that Sadiq was a closet Muslim Brother or a prisoner of both the NIF and his brother-in-law, Hassan al-Turabi, or a shrewd politician whose Ansar were threatened by the rising tide of Muslim fundamentalism. Privately, the Africa Bureau under both Crocker and Cohen considered peace unattainable unless the SPLA modified its stance against the September Laws. Thus, as events unfolded in Khartoum and Addis Ababa, the department was surprised at the fruitful efforts of the Ministerial Committee for Peace and astonished when, in late May the SPLA proposed and the government agreed to continue talks in Addis Ababa on 10 June. It was flabbergasted when both sides agreed to convene a constitutional conference in September for which yet another meeting would be held on 4 July to prepare its agenda.

With the peace process moving apace, Garang's trip to the West was shrewdly timed. Stopping first in Bonn on 1 June, he appeared before a West German parliamentary subcommittee on human rights and humanitarian assistance, during which he announced that the SPLA cease-fire had been extended for two weeks. He added, "I leave the other two weeks to the government" and said that if the SPLA noted "positive moves towards peace," it would be extended.[66] The following day, the Sudan government officially requested the cancellation of the Egypt-Sudan defense agreement and announced that the Ministerial Committee for Peace would resume talks with the SPLA at Addis Ababa on 10 June. Foreign Minister Al-Hussayn expressed his hope that the meeting would lead to "a long term ceasefire and an eventual peace settlement in Sudan."[67] All of this was just what the Germans wanted to hear.

Once in the United States, Garang sought to establish his revolutionary credentials yet also demonstrate to the Americans that he was not an African Fidel Castro: "I want to explain to the American people that SPLM is not the enemy of the people of the United States."[68] He also used the occasion to promote the book *John Garang Speaks*, which was something of a history of the SPLM and the SPLA, and to visit former President Jimmy Carter, who promptly offered to mediate. The peace process was moving along well without outside help, but he welcomed Carter's services. Garang continued on to Washington for three days of talks and speeches, where he was feted by members of Congress, academics, and the press. Thanks to the groundwork laid by Francis Deng, the former Sudanese ambassador to the United States, and Roger Winter of the U.S. Committee for Refugees, Garang was able to meet with numerous politicians and others seeking a resolution to the Sudanese civil war. In a lively discussion at the Brookings Institution, Garang argued that the civil war was not a war of North versus South or Christian versus Muslim or African versus Arab. Rather, it was a battle to ensure "Sudanism," or the coalescence of disparate ethnic identities into a single polity that would guarantee respect for all races and peoples and provide economic and political opportunity for all. When asked about Sadiq, he replied: "I don't [consider] Brother Sadiq Al-Mahdi has given me anything, because I don't expect to be given anything. I am part and parcel of the Sudanese body politic, and if there is a decision making, I have an equal right, like any other Sudanese, to participate in this process of decision making. So who gives and who takes does not arise."[69]

Garang was reluctant to name the "enemies" of the Southern Sudanese, but his insistence that the *hudud* must be abolished left little doubt that those proponents of the September Laws were his antagonists. He ridiculed his detractors for making him what he was not: "In 83 we were being accused of being anti-Arab, anti-Muslim, separatists and all that. I have a cartoon in Khartoum where I'm supposed to wear the flag of the United States written CIA, there is a Star of David, there is a Russian sickle and hammer, there's a big cross here on my tie. There is even a German swastika here.... I have been accused of being, in one sentence, an agent of international communism and a Church, all in one sentence!"[70] Speaking of himself, he added that his enemies claimed "that's a Communist, that's why he doesn't go to the United States. When I come to the United States, they'd say, 'Umm. He's a stooge of imperialism, that's why he goes to the United States.' Either way, I will be accused of something. And to tell you the truth, I don't give a damn. I know what my objectives are. I know what the objectives of the movement are. The objectives of the movement are to create a new Sudan."[71]

As Garang was aware, most analysts in the United States had stopped calling Garang a Communist and his movement Communist inspired. The conservative news magazine *Insight* informed its readers that he held a doctorate in agricultural economics from Iowa State University, was a graduate of the U.S. Army's infantry school at Fort Benning, Georgia, and based his Sudan People's Liberation Army in Addis Ababa, "the capital of Marxist-Leninist Ethiopia," but neither Garang "nor the SPLA is communist in orientation, despite Ethiopian largess."[72] For conservatives in the United States, Garang had passed the test.

Whether discussing philosophy at Brookings, politics with members of the U.S. Congress, SPLA aims with European intellectuals, or the "new Sudan" with African leaders, Garang steadfastly denied any secessionist tendencies. He had personally fought those in the SPLA who wanted to separate the South from Sudan. When asked privately about his early SPLA companion, Colonel Kerubino Kwanyin, who had become disillusioned with Garang's insistence upon a united Sudan, he admitted that Kerubino was under arrest and would not be freed because he knew too many of the SPLA's secrets, but he insisted that Kerubino would not be harmed. For Garang, the SPLA would remain a unionist movement and would attract soldiers from every region to fight for the cause of Sudanese rights for all ethnic minorities, tribes, or classes. His united Sudan involved political elements from Blue Nile, from Kordofan, from Red Sea; they included Beja, Fur, Nuba, southern tribal leaders, and the million or more displaced southerners in greater Khartoum. United, Garang argued, they created a political movement more powerful than the Umma or the DUP, and in the Sudanese assembly, which was composed of 272 members, his movement could win a minimum of 100 seats.

At Brookings Garang mused about the role of the South in a new Sudan. He saw that once peace had been achieved, the SPLM would be "part and parcel of the political power in Khartoum ... what will be given the South does not arise, because we will be in that political process.... Sudan is a big country, and you cannot administer it from the center." He explained to his U.S. audience that he visualized a new Sudan composed of federal states or local autonomous regions—a federal system akin to that in the United States—with Khartoum a unifying symbol for all Sudanese and not simply the seat of powerful political parties and religious forces. Khartoum would be neither Islamic nor African; rather, it would be autochthonous, a Sudanese amalgam. Fundamental to Garang's federalism was the separation of church and state. A federalism that permitted the *hudud* in one region and not another would be intolerable and unworkable: "The criminal law should be universal to all Sudanese." Garang concluded: "I'm confident that the Sudan is not a microcosm of Africa or a bridge between African and the Arab world. No we are not a bridge. We are not Arabs, per se, we are not Africans, per se. We are not Afro-Arab. This is a term I have been hearing nowadays being thrown around. Afro-Arab, of course, means Africans becoming Arabs. You can turn it around and say Arabo-Africans."[73] Why, then, should the South accept the term *Afro-Arab*? All such terms are demeaning, Garang argued, and would have to be sublimated for a greater good, a greater Sudan that had never existed previously.

Garang next visited Capitol Hill, where he was the invited guest of the House of Representatives Select Subcommittee on Hunger. He testified that Sudan had moved beyond "the simple stage of trying to talk about peace" and said the next step was "to work out a mechanism for peace."[74] He offered to extend the cease-fire indefinitely as long as the two sides could show progress and agree that "religion must be separated from the state." Mickey Leland responded: "Let me take this opportunity to publicly acknowledge Colonel Garang's help in providing safe passage in humanitarian relief in Sudan.... Colonel Garang and his organization recognizes the importance of international humanitarian law.... Without the active assistance of the SPLA under Colonel Garang, much of the 50,000 metric tons of food and medical supplies that have been delivered [under OLS] would not have arrived."[75] Ironically, despite the positive response by Congress to Garang personally and to his movement publicly, the Department of State remained adamant about giving no overt recognition to either him or his movement.

The Problems of Making Peace

Garang next met with James Grant in New York, and the two reviewed OLS accomplishments. Grant assured the SPLA leader that a recent bombing attack on Torit by an "unknown" plane was an isolated incident the government of Sudan deplored. Coming as it did just as the SPLA was ready to renew its cease-fire, the bombing was a grave reminder that there were elements within the Sudanese military willing to wreck the peace process.

Upon returning to Africa, Garang stopped in Addis Ababa for discussions with President Mengistu, who offered to hold the pending constitutional conference in his capital where he hoped to replicate the success of the 1972 meeting. In Khartoum the Ethiopians had been very active. Members were visiting African capitals to explain the government's position, and the SPLA was holding talks with the Egyptian government. Sadiq appeared to be riding a horse from which he could not dismount. According to *Africa Confidential* he had no more options: "The Premier's constant prevarications over the November peace initiative, which he accepted only under the duress of a military ultimatum and mass demonstrations in Khartoum, irreparably damaged his credibility. The events in Darfur and soaring prices only serve to reinforce the prevalent mood for peace. By accepting the peace initiative in March, the Prime Minister staved off his inevitable downfall."[76]

In Khartoum there was a sense of relief that the civil war might finally be ending. The atmosphere was captured in an article entitled "Peace at Last?" that appeared in the June issue of *New African*; optimism was tempered however, by a prescient forecast that "the next few months will be the most crucial in Sudan's modern history and will either usher in a new era of peace or will plunge the largest country in Africa into a process of disintegration."[77] Khartoum newspapers were brimming with news on the peace process and the Ministerial Peace Committee, headed by Professor Hamad Ali Bagadi of Khartoum University and retired general Yusuf Ahmed Yusuf, which had initiated a second round of talks with the SPLA's Lam Akol in Addis Ababa on 11 June. Talks began with a minimum of friction because the government had officially abrogated the Egypt-Sudan "fraternal" agreement of 1987, which had replaced the previous Integration Charter of Jaafar Numayri. The Egyptians helpfully agreed to the inevitable. The problem of the Libya-Sudan military proto- col of 1985 remained, and the SPLA was suspicious that it had not expired in December 1988 as the government claimed. Its fears were put to rest, however, when the cabinet secretariat publicly announced that the agreement had lapsed and would not be renewed. The two sides still could not agree on how to freeze the Shari'a laws, but their inability to resolve this concern did not derail the peace process. Certainly, the pre- paratory talks caused differences to surface that would have to be resolved before convening a constitutional conference, but the partici- pants had discovered that they agreed more than they disagreed. More important, their talks created a climate of mutual trust.[78]

When the government delegation returned to Khartoum even Sadiq was optimistic that the remaining differences could be resolved in advance of the national constitutional conference scheduled to open in September. Sudanese Foreign Minister Sid Ahmad al-Hussayn warned, however, that there were parties in Sudan that were very interested in destroying the peace process; nonetheless, he felt both sides were confi- dent that a "permanent ceasefire will take place and the constitutional conference will take place."[79] Ironically, only John Garang expressed doubt that all was not well. In an interview with the BBC in late June, he warned that the prime minister's promises were mostly noise and said that "an empty tin makes a louder noise, so we need action and not words." Regarding the future of negotiations, he grudgingly admitted some progress had been made: "Well, we did fix 18th September 1989 as a date for holding the national constitutional conference, only as a tenta- tive date that is obviously subject to change should the Khartoum gov- ernment fail to implement all the prerequisites or provisions of the SPLM/DUP peace initiative during this period."[80]

To allay Garang's concerns, a government envoy was sent to Libya on 16 June to erase all doubts in Tripoli that all military agreements with Sudan had been abrogated.[81] Three days later the Ministry of Foreign Affairs announced that a Ministerial Peace Committee was preparing position papers for the September constitutional conference. Yet, although there was a certain euphoria that peace was imminent, throughout Ramadan rumors circulated that a coup was imminent. The people wanted peace, but they were also tired of waiting for the economy to improve. The civil servants complained that they could not live on their salaries and were forced to take second jobs or resort to petty bribery to make ends meet. Outside Khartoum, the Farmer's Union and tenant farmer representatives asserted that the government was neglecting them. Despite a record sorghum harvest in 1988–1989, much had been hoarded because the government purchase price, which had risen from £S65 to £S75 a sack in February, barely covered production costs. In Khartoum, NIF protestors, including a small but vocal Popular Trade Union Alliance of workers and professional people, took to the streets to protest increases in the price of both superior quality and common loaves of bread. Khartoum politicians shook their heads; the government was courting trouble since the Sudanese, who were renowned for their patience, would suffer any indignity except bread shortages and government manipulation of bread prices. By June NIF protestors and student agitators were daily involved in demonstrations calling for a return to military rule.[82]

Concern that a popular revolt was imminent appeared to be warranted when the army announced on 18 June that it had unearthed a coup with the curious title of the National Movement for Rectification of the Situation (*Al-Harakah al-Qawmiyah Li Tashih al-Awda'*) designed to return Jaafar Numayri to power.[83] Numayri had given credence to these rumors at a press conference at his residence in Cairo during which he proclaimed his readiness to return to Khartoum where he had "overwhelming support."[84] Numayri's involvement seemed even more plausible when four senior army officers with close ties to the former military dictator were arrested along with fourteen senior army officers and twenty civilians. Sadiq claimed the plotters had intended to blow up the Constituent Assembly and assassinate political leaders, armed forces commanders, and selected members of the press, but the *modus operandi* seemed much too bloodthirsty to be Sudanese.

The Umma, DUP, trade unions, the Arab Bar Association, and other professional bodies all condemned the Numayri coup attempt, but within hours of its demise the capital was awash with rumors of other plots. Knowledgeable Sudanese politicians were alarmed that the recent air raid on Torit followed by the arrest of senior army officers was sufficient evidence that some elements opposed the peace talks. The military was obviously unhappy with the arrest of popular officers including Brigadier Muhammad Fadlallah of the parachute corps, who had reportedly confessed to taking part in the air raid.[85] It was also rumored that the parachute corps harbored many of the military's most disaffected junior officers, and on 27 June unnamed military officers issued an ultimatum that the government investigate and announce its findings on the Numayri coup within seventy-two hours. Sadiq responded with alacrity, and a meeting of senior military officers was soon convened, during which General Mahdi Babu Nimr explained to the assembled army commanders the coup leaders' objectives and warned that some groups were still attempting to divide the armed forces.[86]

Despite what had just occurred, as July approached the Khartoum press was filled with prospects for peace. The Ministerial Peace Committee was finishing the agenda for the 4 July meeting in Addis Ababa. Committee lawyers had studied the issue of the September Laws and planned to table proposals to eliminate the *hudud* provisions.[87] Professor Bagadi informed the press that the committee had received cables from many sources, including the U.S. State Department and the Canadian Ministry of Foreign Affairs, wishing it well and supporting GOS peace efforts.[88] As 4 July approached, for the first time in many years peace seemed about to descend upon a war-torn and famine-stricken land.

Food Continues to Move South
Despite Political Turmoil in the North

As the political protagonists maneuvered toward peace, OLS food aid was on the way south by train, truck, and barge. By mid-May 1989 USAID-Sudan had moved 23,000 tons of food to displaced camps scattered through southern Kordofan, and food aid targets in that area had nearly all been met. In the South, shipments into SPLA territory improved when bandit attacks by renegade Toposa on convoys hauling food aid from Lokichokio, Kenya, were halted. Elsewhere, the ICRC was delivering food throughout the South, and UN agencies were active in eastern Upper Nile. In contrast, Aweil never ceased to be a problem. The last train to haul food had arrived in January; when the Khartoum conference was convened in March the number of displaced persons in Aweil Town had risen to 33,000, and donors gave feeding them their highest priority. The UN's Bryan Wannop, who was responsible for managing the Operation Lifeline Sudan program from his office in Khartoum, regarded the train as the key instrument of the Sudan government's commitment to OLS. If food could reach Aweil on a regular basis, it would reduce the number of displaced Dinka who were arriving in Muglad and Abyei with harrowing tales of slavery, starvation, and death.[89] Wannop's plans were immediately frustrated when the train that reached Aweil in January did not return to Babanusa until April; James Grant announced that the train would leave for the South on 15 April, but that plan was frustrated by General Burma Nasr, now minister of transport, who insisted that all trains have a military escort.

The Nazir of the Missiriya, Ali Nimr, also objected to relief food passing south to the starving Dinka and retaliated against those in the Muglad camp by curtailing its supply of water.[90] To bypass this roadblock the United Nations and other donors were forced to fund well drilling in the camp and at a site in Muglad Town.

As Wannop struggled with the military about trains, the Aweil airlift continued. In March Air Serv began operations, and by April it had three light aircraft transporting an average of forty-two tons of sorghum a day from prepositioned storage sites at Meiram and Muglad.[91] The Reuters representative, Hemza Hendawi, reported from Aweil in March:

> For thousands facing starvation in famine-hit south Sudan, hope comes each day with a faint speck in northern skies. By the time the speck turns into the familiar outline of a four-engined DeHavilland Dash 7 or one of the smaller Twin Otter aircraft, the people of Aweil know they will live to see another day. Succour from the north is carried by a tiny squadron of relief planes flying a daily race against death, hopping from town to town above scorched bushland too dangerous to travel by road.[92]

Air Serv's frenetic activity continued throughout April; stevedores were paid a handsome bonus to load the planes in less than five minutes, from dawn to dusk six days a week. This idyllic picture of heroic relief flights was shattered, however, when USAID-Sudan received reports that illegal diversions had reduced the amount of food stored in the Aweil warehouse substantially. The RRC representative at Aweil was young and easily manipulated by the acting commissioner, who blatantly distributed more than 750 tons of relief food to military officers, merchants, and himself. The commissioner then restructured the Aweil Relief Committee to exclude Santino Deng, an Aweil resident and a veteran of Southern Sudanese politics, and two senior Dinka chiefs, Akot Deng Dut (father of minister of agriculture Aldo Adjo Deng) and Aher Ngoong Gau of nearby Wedweil village. This shocked both Julia Taft in Washington and Angelo Beda, chair of the government's Council for the South, who feared corruption in Aweil would compromise the entire OLS operation. Beda sent apologies to U.S. Ambassador Anderson and promised to take "immediate steps to redress the situation."[93] OFDA calculated that the chicanery in Aweil had cost the U.S. taxpayer's at least $1 million.[94] Prodded by Washington, Ambassador Anderson sent a letter to Sadiq asking the government to launch its own investigation to determine if willful wrongdoing occurred; in addition, he requested the assignment of a permanent commissioner to Aweil, the reactivation of the old Relief Committee, and the placement of a full-time UN monitor in the town.[95] The OFDA demanded that a train loaded exclusively with relief food move to Aweil immediately and that the government provide

USAID sorghum in the amount equal to that misappropriated in Aweil. Eventually, the government agreed to all of these requests, but in the end it never reimbursed USAID for the misappropriated sorghum nor moved expeditiously to rebuild the food aid inventory in Aweil.

In April it was still a race against time to save an estimated 100,000 lives considered at risk in Southern Sudan, yet although the planes took off, the trains stood still. Neither James Grant, who had had his photograph taken at Babanusa ostensibly boarding a train for Aweil, nor UNICEF representative Audrey Hepburn succeeded in moving the train. Fortunately, as the train languished in Babanusa and the first sprinkles in advance of the rainy season were reported in Aweil, the Aweil airlift continued. By May it had delivered nearly 2,000 tons of food in 1,500 flying hours at a cost to AID-OFDA of $2.7 million. When the train remained in Babanusa, the European Community added $750,000 to keep Air Serv in the skies. With the fall of heavy rains in mid-May, the operation was grounded, but by that time Air Serv had transported 2,750 tons of food aid to Aweil—an unbelievable performance for such a small operation.[96]

Despite SPLA assurances that the Corridors of Tranquility were intact, the regional manager of the Sudan Railways Corporation had received a mysterious message "not to allow the train to move from Muglad to Aweil."[97] After interminable negotiations, Wannop capitulated to government demands and reduced SPLA deliveries because the government objected to the 50–50 split.[98] A series of Byzantine maneuverings was concluded only after Wannop offered a handsome payoff of £S13,000 to each of the train's crew members and promised to insure them against bodily injury or loss of life. The crew was undoubtedly wise to look after its own interests, because Muglad was seething with discontent, and NIF party activists were distributing political leaflets that predicted the train would be destroyed before it reached Aweil. USAID-Sudan employees who were present in Muglad warned the UN party that Ali Nimr's promises of safe passage meant nothing because he had no control over NIF elements operating in the Muglad area. Wannop later reported that "the NIF had paid £S1,000,000 to stop the train."[99]

The UN-flagged train finally left Muglad in the dawn of 20 May loaded with nearly 1,500 tons of sorghum. It reached Meiram by noon, but beyond there the poorly maintained tracks and roadbed forced the convoy to a crawl. At the Bahr al-Arab Wannop learned that the Missiriya had suffered a serious defeat the week before in a major battle with the SPLA twenty miles to the southwest. The following day the train was stopped ten miles south of the river by about 200 *murahileen*, a "rag-tag band ... young and nervous and interested in looting."[100] They were well armed, ill disciplined, and looking for *khawajas*. Wannop and the UN monitors were marched to the bush, robbed, and stripped and would likely have been killed if the train crew had not intervened. The crew argued passionately for their release, and after collecting £S3,240 from their own pockets, ransomed them from the militia. The train continued to Malwal, where it left sixteen carloads of sorghum with the army commander who worried aloud that food might tempt the SPLA to attack his garrison. The train then entered SPLA territory, discharging sixteen wagons at Mabior, after which it continued to Aweil, where the train was met by thousands of cheering inhabitants. Wannop would later write: "There are lessons to be learned from our experience in mounting this first ever relief train into Southern Sudan. Had we left the arrangements entirely in the hands of any of the responsible agencies of the Government of Sudan, there is little doubt that they would not have been able to overcome the forces opposed to the train moving and thus it would probably never have left. It was thus necessary for the UN to become too interventionist in the affairs of Sudan, something that we should avoid wherever possible."[101]

In contrast, there was little cheering in Wau, where, despite an ICRC airlift, there was little change for the better. The Fertit militia was still active. It had attacked a displaced camp in January and the following month burned to the ground 300 huts in the Hay-Fallata quarter. Murder was a nightly pastime. Food relief trucks were habitually commandeered by the army, civil servants went unpaid, sugar was selling for the equivalent of $15 a pound, the hospital was low on medicines, and corruption was rampant. There was food available on the black market, which received military protection, but those who had money paid up to twenty-five times the Khartoum price for sugar, wheat, flour, and salt. Sorghum sold for £S1,500 a sack. In the midst of the misery some local merchants managed to run an occasional beer truck to Zaire.

In February the RRC had asked the donor agencies in Khartoum to fund a program to move food overland from Northern Sudan to Wau. USAID-Sudan employees who remembered the 1987 Raga nightmare strongly objected but were overruled by acting Mission Director Frederick Gilbert; consequently, the same donors—USAID and the European Community—agreed to transport 3,000 tons of sorghum to Wau despite the fact that the rains would surely begin in less than two months. The cost was an astronomical £S21 million (nearly $2 million at the OLS rate of exchange). Once again the operation began too late in the season, and trucking firms sponsored by the RRC would not perform satisfactorily. Of the 3,000 tons, a third disappeared; of the remainder, only 316 tons reached Wau. OFDA, which had been forewarned that the trucking scheme would fail, provided $3 million to support an ICRC emergency airlift that saved countless lives.

The Success of Operation Lifeline Sudan

By midyear OLS had met 80 percent of its overall food distribution goal, and more than 600,000 displaced persons had received some assistance. Despite the existence of a few pockets of need around Pochala in SPLA territory and in the government towns of Yei and Mundri, there were no reports of large numbers of Southern Sudanese on the move or dying in search of food.[102] In Bahr al-Ghazal two-thirds of all planned food aid to the government side had arrived, and the International Red Cross was airlifting food and other assistance to Akon and Yirol. Miraculously, a second UN-flagged train reached Aweil in June. ICRC cattle vaccination programs in SPLA-controlled territories were instrumental in keeping southerners at home, and in contrast to 1988 only thirty people a week were reported passing through the Safaha post on the Bahr al-Arab in June 1989. In southern Kordofan the delivery target had been exceeded. As heavy rains began to fall in May, the UNDP reported that "the Abyei food situation is good and the stocks sufficient [4,000 tons] to cover the needs till November 1989, provided the population does not grow extensively." The nutritional status of the Dinka had improved significantly, and the people were reported to be "healthy and in good spirits."[103]

In southern Kordofan and Darfur, the arrival of free food and PVO distributions had fed the starving; it had also exacerbated the historical ethnic tensions between the Baqqara and the Dinka. Open hostilities against the displaced Dinka in Muglad had only been avoided by the donors offer to drill badly needed water wells not only in the displaced camp but in the town as well. As camps at Abyei, Muglad, and Babanusa expanded, donors hoped to establish transitional camps in northern Kordofan to handle the spillover. The effort was hampered by a spate of violent incidents in En Nahud, Rashad, and El Fula districts, where Arab villagers fought relocation schemes and NIF elements circulated the vicious rumor that displaced Dinka were receiving arms smuggled to them in food aid shipments.

Although OLS was slightly behind schedule in the South, by July the food it had provided had markedly improved the physical condition of the displaced persons. In Juba only the recent arrivals required concerted assistance, and a nutritional survey of western Equatoria, where the rains had been good, indicated no serious dietary deficiencies except at Mundri and Yei. Elsewhere, the program in SPLA territory was gathering momentum. By May the SRRA had 2,200 tons of cereals in storage in Torit, and with a reduction in then number of bandit attacks, UN convoys were finally able to augment food convoys from Lokichogio to Kapoeta.[104]

By midyear it was apparent that OLS had succeeded, and even though many government officials despised what it stood for, few had actively attempted to sabotage the program. Even Sadiq, who had said "we shall do no more than what we defined in [the OLS] agreement," responded unexpectedly and extended indefinitely the unobstructed use of the Corridors of Tranquility beyond the month he had promised.[105] Appearing to champion OLS was not easy for the prime minister, because he was constantly badgered by NIF critics, who questioned his patriotism, and by the presence of arrogant Westerners involved in telling the Sudanese what they should do. Sadiq was not helped by donors and NGOs, who often publicly vented their unhappiness with the course of events, and on one occasion he reminded his Western critics: "It must be appreciated that Sudan is doing toward relief something that is unprecedented." He argued that through good and bad, the program "must be supported by all who are concerned about the humanitarian aspects."[106] Ironically, both Sadiq and Garang got along well with James Grant, and both tolerated Grant's performances for the international media—perhaps because he helped to improve their image. Neither Sadiq nor Grant cared much for the private agencies whose visibility came to dominate OLS, and Grant did not appreciate their criticism of both himself and UN operations for what they felt was a UN tendency to grab headlines and downplay the PVO role in Sudan. In contrast, John Garang was happy with everyone. OLS was for him "an historic agreement," a successful operation, and "a precedent that can be emulated in similar situations."[107]

By June 1989 media interest in OLS had dissipated, probably the finest testament to its success. The Khartoum dailies were preoccupied with the forthcoming peace talks, and in the United States much of the media interest in Sudan had waned. Assistant Secretary Cohen's visit to Khartoum in May had conveyed the impression that the United States welcomed the Sudan government's views on peace, relief programs, and refugees, leading *The New York Times* to complain that the State Department had not "abandoned the Reagan Administration attitude of saying nothing that might offend a regime regarded as a strategic ally."[108] As one administration official explained to *The Christian Science Monitor*, "We are looking at the Horn more in terms of settling its conflicts and meeting human needs rather than primarily as an area for securing Persian Gulf oil routes and seeking military base rights."[109] Thus, whereas AID-Washington would have been content to reduce the Sudan mission to a small staff to manage humanitarian assistance, the State Department fought the idea. If the United States wanted to secure its strategic and military interests in the region as well as influence the peace process, humanitarian foreign aid served as well as geopolitics to ensure the U.S. presence in Sudan. Ironically, the State Department still eschewed any direct links with the SPLA, and USAID employees chafed under the State Department restriction that "limited [USAID] capacity for conducting any sort of firsthand review" of PVO activities in SPLA villages.[110]

The State Department was embarrassed by the Sudan government's debt repayment problems, yet it still managed to prolong the Brooke Amendment process. Sudan's debt burden was huge, but it somehow managed to pay just enough to keep the United States from shutting off wheat imports and closing down its development program entirely. In April the Sudan government promised to remain current on future Title I repayments; it repaid $8 million and placed in escrow $6 million, which would be returned over the next three months. The government also deposited a long overdue £S42.5 million into USAID-Sudan's local currency account, which was badly needed to pay OLS internal transport costs. The government still owed £S102 million, which it promised to repay during its 1989–1990 (July to June) fiscal year. In the end, payments plus promises allowed Washington to complete arrangements for a 1989 PL-480 Title I wheat agreement, which was what Sudan had wanted initially. This allowed USAID-Sudan to move forward on a new swap that was to provide an additional 25,000 tons of sorghum in 1989. The government did not, however, move to resolve its difficulties with the IMF, and despite prodding by Cohen and Ambassador Anderson, Sudan's Ministry of Finance refused to institute the structural reforms the IMF had urged.

On 28 June James Grant returned to Khartoum in triumph. He planned to ask Sadiq for a three-month Period of Tranquility during which *all* Sudanese children would be vaccinated against preventable diseases. He also planned to ask Sadiq to give amnesty to all prisoners already tried and awaiting *hudud* punishments and to declare a cease-fire on 1 July to enhance the possibilities for peace talks to open in Addis Ababa on 4 July. In addition, he needed to investigate complaints made by the German and British embassies that military security offices were impeding the issuance of travel documents to expatriate aid employees. There were other pressing problems. The donors were concerned because Sadiq had called for a reduction in the number of displaced southerners in Khartoum, and the Council of Ministers had urged the government to force "able-bodied men" in displaced camps to relocate to places where they could be put to work. In southern Kordofan, local security and Missiriya leader Ali Nimr wanted to close down the displaced camps. Despite these challenges the irrepressible Grant remained optimistic. The United Nations had strengthened its "official presence in southern Sudan" by adding liaison offices in Kapoeta and Akon.[111] When costs mounted the donors had come up with $52 million, and it seemed not only possible but probable that 100,000 tons of food aid would be delivered by October.[112] Regionally, the early rains were generous and gave promise of a good harvest. As July approached the combatants continued to respect the Corridors of Tranquility, and even its critics concluded that OLS had contributed greatly to the ongoing peace process.

James Grant and Robert Reid of UNICEF await departure of UN-flagged train from Muglad to Aweil, 1989. Photo by Renee Bafalis.

AID/OFDA director Julia Taft and Prime Minister Sadiq al-Mahdi discuss Operation Lifeline Sudan, March 1989. Photo by Renee Bafalis.

Displaced Southern Sudanese living in unused boxcars, Babanusa, 1988. Photo by Renee Bafalis.

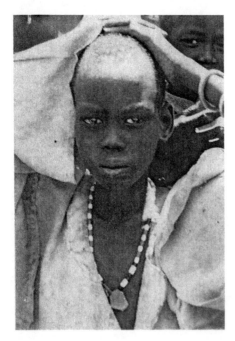

Southern Sudanese youth. Photo by Renee Bafalis.

Aweil Airlift and AirServ cargo plane, 1989. Photo by Renee Bafalis.

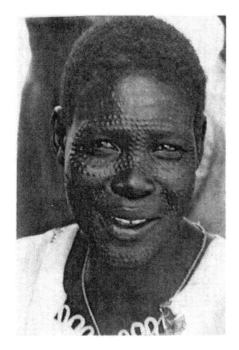

Displaced Southern Sudanese woman. Photo by Renee Bafalis.

Congressman Mickey Leland visiting a camp for displaced Southern Sudanese, Khartoum 1989. Photo by Renee Bafalis.

Refugee camp in the Equatoria province, 1990. Photo by Roger Winter.

Malnourished children in an Upper Nile refugee camp, 1990. Photo by Roger Winter.

Emaciated orphans awaiting Unimix in a refugee camp near Waat, 1990. Photo by Roger Winter.

John Garang de Mabior, leader of the Sudan People's Liberation Army, in the Equatoria province of Sudan, 1990. Photo by Roger Winter.

Roger Winter *(right)*, director of the U.S. Committee for Refugees, meeting with John Garang *(left)* and SPLA spokesperson Lam Akol *(center)*. Photo courtesy of U.S. Committee for Refugees.

An old Sudanese woman walking on the road between Bambouti and Bassiqbiri. She was aided by Red Cross workers. Photo courtesy of Jean Durand; UNHCR.

Refugees seek food in the bush of the Equatoria province, 1992. Photo by Roger Winter.

Unidentified bodies near the Ethiopian border.

Burned shell of a hut destroyed by civil war. Photo by Robert O. Collins.

Flooded village of the Nuer, Upper Nile province of Southern Sudan, 1992. Photo by Roger Winter.

SEVEN

— ∎ —

The Return of the Military

The June Revolution has come to restore to the Sudanese citizen his injured dignity and rebuild the Sudan of the Future.
—Radio Omdurman, 0900 Greenwich Mean (Meridian) Time,
30 June 1989

At 2:00 A.M. 30 June 1989, Radio Omdurman fell ominously silent, only to return to the air at 8:00 A.M. blaring martial music. At 9:00 A.M. an unannounced speaker proclaimed that the government of Sadiq al-Mahdi had been overthrown by a military junta. The coup leader was Umar Hassan Ahmad al-Bashir, an unknown forty-four-year-old brigadier and the third-ranking officer in the paratroops corps. Bashir broadcast that his was a "revolution of the people against injustice, corruption, partisanship and factionalism" and one "not tilted to the right or left."[1] He claimed that the political parties had failed to provide the Sudanese with a decent standard of living and would therefore have no role in the Sudan of the future. The coup was both efficient and bloodless. A military junta composed of fifteen junior officers and calling itself the National Salvation Revolution Command Council (NSRCC or RCC) made it clear that it had acted to eliminate an irresolute government. General Fathi Ahmad Ali and officers identified with the peace movement were arrested, and twenty-eight senior officers were retired immediately.

Although there were many indications that most NSRCC members had close ties to Muslim fundamentalists, in an early interview Bashir seemed to exclude the NIF from having any role in the revolution. He reasserted that the revolution was "basically launched to end the corruption of political parties" and that there was "absolutely no plan" for their resurrection.[2] Indeed, many of Bashir's statements condemning the political parties for failing the people were taken directly from the military's February 1989 ultimatum, which Bashir had reportedly signed. On 3 July

205

the NSRCC published the "National Salvation Revolution Program," a document more pragmatic than ideological, deploring the absence of an effective security apparatus and blaming The Sudan People's Armed Forces (SPAF) defeats on an impecunious government.

Umar Hassan Ahmad al-Bashir, born in 1944 at Al-Matmah village near Shendi, was a Ja'aliyyin Arab from a poor family. His extended family was said to have belonged to the Khatmiyya religious sect that formed the political base of the Democratic Unionist Party (DUP), but Bashir soon made it clear that he was not a DUP sympathizer. One brother lived in Abu Dhabi, and another was a former editor of *Al-Sudani* which supported the NIF.[3] Bashir graduated from the Sudan military academy at Wadi Sayyidna in 1966, and his early political leanings, or what could be learned of them, indicated he was neither Umma nor DUP, Ansar nor Khatmiyya. Bashir himself claimed "I do not belong to a religious party or to any non-religious party. We, as officers, belong to the armed forces. Religious piety is a mercy from God; one likes to achieve it and one would hope that this attribute which is given to us is real. Belonging to parties is not in our character; we have not worked inside parties."[4]

What was certain was that Bashir was a soldier with political ambitions. He was second in command of a Sudanese paratroops detachment posted along Egypt's Suez Canal during the October 1973 war with Israel, for which he was awarded an Egyptian military decoration. He received counterinsurgency instruction in Malaysia—where he revealed that he wanted to become the chief of the government of Sudan. Bashir had spent his last tour of duty in Southern Sudan and was described as the hero of a victory over the SPLA at Mayom in 1988. Other reports called him "one of the best 'professional soldiers' with a long record of success in southern Sudan."[5] Ironically, the 30 June coup occurred only hours before Bashir was scheduled to depart for Egypt to attend a long training course at the Nasser Academy—a sure sign that he was not trusted by the senior officers of the General Command. Bashir admitted that the army "had old suspicions" of him, and as he finalized his travel arrangements a colleague joked, "it seems your coup will be postponed another year and a half."[6] Egypt's *Al-Ahram* claimed he was a leader with "tremendous popularity," but few Sudanese had heard of him. The SPLA Radio refused comment on Bashir for some time. In August 1989 it reported that the previous year, Bashir's forces had wiped out a nest of black marketers and Anya-Nya II bandits operating out of Bab Tong Island. A month later it unleashed a barrage of epithets calling Bashir the "thief of Bentiu," "looter of people's cattle, sheep, goats, money and even children," and "chief slave trader."[7]

In an interview with Egyptian journalist Makram Muhammad Ahmad, Bashir explained that his friendships with his NSRCC colleagues were forged during the regime of Jaafar Numayri: "We began to group ourselves in total secrecy on the basis that we should be ready if and when there was a need to make our move to save the homeland."[8] The movement expanded slowly around a small nucleus of military officers and used a series of cells to maintain secrecy. Conspirators were soon known to senior officers who, although distrustful, tended to discount any potential danger. In October 1985 *Al-Dustur*, which was published in London, had described Bashir as a "Muslim Brother who will probably be entrusted with preparing a coup d'état with the assistance of officers loyal to former president [Numayri] on behalf of Hassan al-Turabi."[9] According to Bashir, the revolutionaries were led by Air Colonel Mukhtar Muhammadayn Ahmad, who died when his MIG fighter was shot down over Nasir on 21 January 1989. The movement's guide then became Brigadier Osman Ahmad Hassan, who under Bashir would be named chair of the NSRCC's powerful Political Committee.

Bashir was reported to be a "close friend of Muslim fundamentalist and retired General Abdel Rahman Swar Al-Dahab" and retired Major General Muhammad al-Hadi al-Mamoun al-Mardi.[10] The latter was eventually name NSRCC political councilor. General Mardi, also from Shendi, was the foster father of another conspirator and Muslim Brother, Brigadier Faisal Ali Abu Salih, who was named minister of interior and chair of the NSRCC's Security and Operations Committee. Of the various NSRCC committees (security, information, political, economic), security became the most feared and became as purposeful an organization of state suppression as Sudan had ever known.

Three NSRCC members involved in plotting the coup—Brigadier Muhammad Salih al-Zubayr, Yusuf Abd al-Fatah, and Brigadier Osman Ahmad Hassan—had known ties to the NIF. Zubayr, deputy chairman of the Revolutionary Command Council, had attended the Islamic African Center south of Khartoum where he studied Muslim fundamentalism and acquired the nickname "the Imam." Given his mediocre military record, some officers were convinced he had been named the NSRCC's second in command only because of his close ties to the Muslim Brothers, of which he was undoubtedly one. Major Ibrahim Shams al-Din of the 7th Armored Brigade, an outsider who respected few social conventions, was another plotter fanatically devoted to the NIF and the Muslim Brotherhood. Bashir contacted Shams al-Din at the armored division headquarters on the night of the coup, and he frustrated the orders of Chief of Staff Mahdi Babu Nimr to be alert for an attempted coup.

NIF leaders were alleged to have known of the impending coup and, if not apprised of its details, appear to have been in contact with the conspirators. Ali Osman Muhammad Taha, a young lawyer who was called the "new Turabi," was reputed to be the chair of an amorphous Council of 40, presumably based on the Council of 40 sanctioned by the NIF Party constitution, which was to advise the NSRCC. This shadowy body of Muslim fundamentalists included Mahdi Ibrahim, former army officer, member of the Constituent Assembly, and editor of the NIF newspaper *Al-Raya*; Osman Khalid Mudhawi of the Feisal Bank; Dr. Ibrahim Abdallah, professor of economics and adviser to Islamic banks in Sudan; Ahmed Abd al-Rahman, perhaps the most influential member of the NIF hierarchy other than Turabi; Hafaz al-Shaykh Zaki, former attorney general and champion of the September Laws; and other NIF stalwarts including Ali Osman Taha, Swad al-Fatih, Dr. Ali Al-Haj Muhammad, and Ibrahim al-Sanusi. When the junta named a twenty-one member cabinet to implement NSRCC policies, twelve of its sixteen civilians were openly sympathetic to the NIF. They included Ali Muhammad Shummo, minister of information and the NSRCC spokesperson; Minister of Justice and Attorney General Hassan Ismail al-Bieli, a former adviser to the powerful Faisal Islamic Bank; the Minister of Agriculture Ali Ahmad Genief; Industry Minister Dr. Muhammad Omar Abdalla; and Farouk al-Bushara, the minister of commerce and construction minister. Included in the cabinet were four ministers from the South, none of whom was popular with southerners.

A New Regime, a New Era, and an Ideological Revolution for Sudan

The NSRCC was not, however, a solid phalanx of Muslim fundamentalists. To some members friendship with Bashir seemed more important than ideology. Brigadier Pio Yukwan Deng, a Shilluk, had been the commander in Kapoeta in 1976. Under both Swar al-Dahab and Sadiq he had served as commissioner of western Equatoria. Southern opinion was divided—some thought him a political and some simply did not trust him. A less savory southern member of the NSRCC was Martin Malwal Arap, a Dinka from Akot in Lakes District. During a flamboyant career, Malwal had come to the attention of USAID-Sudan in early 1989 when the agency discerned that he would have to be paid off so it could obtain an army cargo aircraft to move food aid to Malakal. Colonels Malwal and Yukwan were joined in the NSRCC by Brigadier Dominic Kassiano. Kassiano, from western Equatoria, had led an army column against the Bor mutineers in May 1983. He was removed as military commander of western Equatoria after he assisted the Islamic Dawaa in building a mosque near Tambura. There were virtually no Muslims in the area; thus, his fellow Zande were outraged and obtained his dismissal. Although these three men constituted the southern membership of the NSRCC, the most powerful southerners in a position to influence the council were Ali Tamim Fartak from Raga and Ahmad al-Radi Jabar. Jabbar represented the NIF in the prorogued Constituent Assembly and had been involved in all aspects of civil administration in the South.

Using a state of emergency, the NSRCC incarcerated cabinet officers and scores of political figures in Kober prison in Khartoum North. DUP leader Muhammad Osman al-Mirghani, the NIF's Hassan al-Turabi, and Communist Party chief Muhammad Ibrahim Nugud were detained. Sadiq al-Mahdi went into hiding but was soon discovered and jailed. Mubarak al-Fadl al-Mahdi, who was under investigation for peculation during his tenure as minister of external trade and economics, was an experienced fugitive and used his many contacts to flee Sudan. It was soon learned that Hassan al-Turabi was given special treatment and, unlike other detainees, was allowed "to go home to pack a suitcase."[11] This consideration led analysts to speculate that Bashir had to be a Muslim Brother, and, indeed, Bashir's pro-Arab and pan-Arab sympathies soon emerged. In an early interview in Kuwait's *Al-Anba*, Bashir stated: "We believe that the Gulf Cooperation Council, which I consider a major step on the path of Arab unity, has scored a tangible success. I also believe that the Arab Cooperation Council and the Arab Maghreb Union represent steps in the same direction. Therefore, we believe that Egypt, Libya and Sudan represent the flanks for the Arab East and Arab Maghreb. We have proposed this plan in principle, and when we put Sudanese house in order, we will make this plan a reality, God willing."[12]

There was also an early interest in building bridges with the Muslim world at large. The NIF was said to have arranged a secret meeting between Bashir and Iranian leaders in Teheran in August, during which Bashir was accompanied by Shams al-Din and two members of the NIF executive committee, Ali Osman Muhammad Taha and Mahdi Ibrahim. The latter was reported to have visited Teheran shortly after the coup and, in a meeting with Hashimi Rafsanjani and the ministers of interior, oil, and trade, warned of "the dangers Islam faces in Sudan" from both communism and the West.[13]

Certainly, the NSRCC demonstrated no interest in a return to democracy. The 1986 constitution was suspended and the Constituent Assembly dissolved. Political parties, nonreligious organizations, and trade unions were dissolved; political meetings were banned; and only the armed forces newspaper was published. In effect, the NSRCC became "responsible for sovereignty and legislative tasks," and a civilian cabinet responsible for "executive work" was selected from "honest and compe-

tent" civilians.[14] Nevertheless, the coup evoked little popular enthusiasm, and there were no spontaneous street celebrations in support of it.
An organized march on 1 July attracted no more than 2,000 people, most
of whom were of NIF students from the University of Khartoum. Two
weeks later at another pro-government demonstration Sadiq was
burned in effigy, and a small crowd led by NIF agitators intoned
unenthusiastically, "One Army, One Nation." Bashir got the message and
informed his followers, "This is the first [demonstration] and the last."[15]

Egypt was the first country to recognize the NSRCC. Egyptian-
Sudanese relations had been lukewarm at best, and official statements
did little to disguise the fact that Egypt welcomed the demise of Sadiq al-
Mahdi. The Egyptian military attaché had been the first foreigner contacted by the junta in the early morning of 30 June, and the Egyptian
ambassador was the first member of the diplomatic corps to meet with
Bashir. Egypt's Middle East News Agency introduced Bashir as a moder-
ate and pro-Egyptian; and given such signs, other embassies were quick
to assume that the NSRCC would work closely with Egypt and the West.
Despite President Hosni Mubarak's vociferous denial, many Sudanese
suspected that Egypt was behind the coup, and it was some time before
the embassies and Sudanese were disabused of that notion. In the U.S.
Embassy the sudden ascendance of Bashir and his colleagues came as a
surprise and virtually nothing was known of the NSRCC's members.
Nonetheless, in Khartoum the NSRCC seemed an anodyne to Sadiq's
policies of drift and delay.

Among non-Arab dignitaries, James Grant met first with Bashir the
day following the coup. The president promised that OLS would continue but added an ominous warning that he was disturbed by the
actions of some NGOs. Bashir indicated the NSRCC would be investigating their operations, and, unknown to Grant, he had already received a
dossier on every expatriate operation from NSRCC Commissioner Al-
Hag al-Tayeb. The next day Ambassador Anderson met with Bashir, and
the NSRCC leader reiterated his interest in OLS but provided another
ominous warning that the NSRCC wanted Sudanese military attaches to
approve all food shipments entering Sudan from Uganda and Kenya.
Anderson followed up his meeting with a personal message commending Bashir's interest in OLS; the message contained the mystifying
assessment: "It is providential, I feel, that Sudan's government is one
headed by one who has himself struggled to relieve the plight of innocent civilians affected by the war."[16] USAID-Sudan staff was aware that
in January 1989, when Bashir was the army commander in the Bentiu
area, he had written to the Council for the South urging food and medicines for the "needy" in Bentiu and Mayom. The reality was that both
towns were inhabited by Anya-Nya II members, and Bentiu was practi-

cally devoid of civilians. When the donors asked to survey needs in the area, the request was retracted, and Bashir never again demonstrated concern for "innocent civilians" in the vast area that stretched from Bentiu to Muglad. Despite Bashir's professed interest in OLS, within the week the NSRCC suspended for one month all permits for travel inside Sudan.[17] This nearly suspended Operation Lifeline Sudan, and it was an unmistakable signal to Grant, USAID-Sudan, and other members of the diplomatic and foreign assistance community that OLS was not as sacrosanct as they had thought. Through 1989 the U.S. Embassy would only grudgingly admit that the junta had a Muslim fundamentalist orientation; confusing cause and effect, it assumed that the junta was using so many NIF people because other political forces would not cooperate with the NSRCC.

The NSRCC was determined not to repeat the traditional Sudanese benevolence toward those it had replaced. One of the first objectives of the National Salvation Revolution Program was to establish "an able security apparatus."[18] The organization was now headed by Colonel Ibrahim Shams al-Din and Colonel Bakri Hassan Salih, neither of whom had much regard for human rights. Hundreds were arrested and taken by members of vigilante squads to "ghost houses," where torture was employed. To enhance security the junta began the form of Popular Committees based on a Libyan model created by Colonel Qadhafi. Yassin Omar al-Imam was placed in charge of the movement, and committees were soon formed throughout Sudan and were used to warn the government about dissenters and subversives.[19]

Despite imprisoning many of those associated with the peace process, the regime publicly proclaimed in the government-controlled press its intention to seek a settlement with the SPLA: "The whole world is now awaiting the result of the Revolution's active effort to solve the problem, and it expects that the Revolution's determination and earnestness ...will be positively received by the [SPLA].... Optimism prevails. The good intentions will finally bear fruit for this country and the war will end forever."[20] Bashir implied that the NSRCC would soon proffer new peace proposals because those of Sadiq were only "political machinations and not serious."[21] The NSRCC declared a unilateral cease-fire on 4 July and offered amnesty to rebels who had fought the government for political reasons and who were willing to surrender their weapons.[22] Such statements appeared auspicious, but Bashir's comments, including the possibility of unification with Egypt and Libya, were hardly calculated to reassure Garang or the SPLA. Nor were matters helped when Bashir declared that if the issue of the Shari'a could not be resolved through peaceful negotiations, it would be decided by a national referendum. This was impossible because even those Muslims who agreed that

Shari'a should not dominate the legal system in a secular state would be placed in the untenable situation of appearing to vote against their religion.

Nevertheless, MENA reported that Bashir planned to invite Garang to Khartoum to begin peace talks, something Sadiq had tried and failed, and that a delegation headed by NSRCC members Lieutenant Colonel Muhammad al-Amin Khalifa and Colonel Martin Malwal would begin talks with Ethiopian government officials and the SPLA in Addis Ababa on 11 July. An NSRCC spokesperson then announced that the delegation would only deliver a letter to Ethiopian President Mengistu Haile Miriam but would not meet with the SPLA. Next, Sudan's only television station reported that the junta had just invalidated the November 1988 DUP-SPLA peace agreement. On 11 July Colonel Khalifa met with President Mengistu in Addis Ababa to express the NSRCC's desire to negotiate an end to the civil war and asked Mengistu to act as mediator.[23] A separate message for John Garang was left with the Ethiopian president, and Khalifa returned to Khartoum. By mid-July the NSRCC had still not made "any direct, formal contact with the SPLA."[24]

A New and Pernicious Government in Khartoum

Perhaps the most surprising event in the first two weeks of the junta's rule resulted from an interview published in *al-Khaleej*, a Sharjah, United Arab Emirates, newspaper. Bashir was quoted as saying that the junta "would accept any rebel demand, including secession, that would end the nation's six year-old war" and that the various southern political factions should decide their own destiny.[25] The interview was a revelation. For years the NIF had argued that if national conscription had been tried and had failed and that if the war was unwinnable and continued to bleed the country dry, as a last resort the South should be permitted to secede—a proposal that was anathema to John Garang. The development was picked up immediately by the international media; just as quickly the NSRCC spokesperson denied that Bashir had ever suggested secession as one alternative in the peace process. Bashir, however, would not let the matter die. In an interview with *Reuters* in September, he suggested that secession could end the civil war.[26]

Within hours of taking power, the junta began to outline its foreign policy. It would abide by the UN Charter, support the Palestinian cause, assist black South Africans in their struggle against apartheid, and play a larger role in the nonaligned movement. Bashir could count on the initial goodwill of a number of Arab states, most notably Egypt and Iraq, and it was reported that Iraqi arms were being loaded in Aqaba, Jordan, "as a token of Iraqi gratitude for the support [Sudan] gave Baghdad during the eight-year gulf war."[27] Egypt was the first country to recognize the new government, and it was the first to be visited by a member of the NSRCC; on 4 July Minister of Interior Brigadier Faisal Ali Abu Salih met with Hosni Mubarak in Alexandria. Bashir visited Cairo on 12 July, and Mubarak, who had had his fill of Arab unification schemes, rejected the tentative feelers from the NSRCC for a united Egypt, Libya, and Sudan while stressing the importance of regional cooperation. Following Egypt's lead, Saudi Arabia recognized the NSRCC; it announced on 2 July that it considered the change of government in Sudan an "internal affair" and emphasized "its keenness on continuing its brotherly economic and political ties with Sudan."[28]

Bashir's first appearance at an international event occurred shortly after he took power when he attended the annual meeting of the Organization of African Unity (OAU) at Addis Ababa, the highlight of which was the inauguration of Mubarak as OAU chairperson. Optimists had hoped Mubarak would launch an OAU- or Egyptian-sponsored peace initiative in Sudan, but in his inaugural address he did not address the role the OAU might play in resolving conflict or civil war in Africa. Still, Mubarak did confer with John Garang and urged the SPLA leader to cooperate with the NSRCC to end the civil war.[29] In addition, both President Museveni of Uganda and Kenya's President Daniel Arap Moi offered Mubarak their assistance in moving the peace process forward. Bashir used his inaugural speech before the conference to call for the resumption of peace negotiations in Sudan, making the questionable point that his government was composed of "no party, no tribe and no grouping."[30] He proclaimed: "In your presence and in front of the international media, I would like to assure you of our commitment to peace in Sudan by extending the cease-fire already declared by another month."[31] During the conference Bashir seemed to be mending fences with the government of Ethiopia and was openly sanguine that relations would improve since both sides had influence over dissidents in each other's countries. In response, Ethiopian Vice President Desta claimed that his country stood ready to act as mediator for the NSRCC and the SPLA.

Bashir's relationship with the Western nations was less demonstrative than those with nearby African and Middle Eastern states. His bearing toward the U.S. Embassy was proper but cool. In Washington the spokesperson for the State Department diffidently told reporters "we regret the military action to overthrow Sudan's democratically elected government, and we urge an early return to democracy."[32] It was then business as usual, and the State Department bid good riddance to Sadiq al-Mahdi and to the peace process, about the success of which it had always been skeptical.

Ironically, the Egyptian foreign ministry was the first to realize that the NSRCC was at heart a totalitarian regime with a very limited following. Few realized, however, that the young colonels had studied the past carefully. With unflinching determination they immobilized the popular forces—students, unions, professional associations, political parties— whose demonstrations had been crucial to the overthrow of General Abboud in October 1964 and President Numayri in April 1985. This time there would be no manifestation of the popular will. The leaders of these groups were swept into the ghost houses and prisons, and overnight the military was either purged of or made to pension its senior officers and those soldiers and police whose loyalty was suspect. Sympathetic officers were promoted, made regional governors, or given other perquisites to ensure their loyalty.

Despite Its Political Success, Bashir's Government Could Not Escape the Debt

Although Sadiq's government had been placed under the sanctions of the Brooke Amendment on 5 January 1989, the NSRCC was granted a respite and retained its eligibility to obtain low-cost wheat. In June Sudanese Ministry of Finance had paid off $8 million of the country's debt, which then allowed the delivery in $30 million of PL-480 Title I wheat in 1989.[33] Although the government still owed $26 million, the junta was given time to resuscitate an economy with an external debt of $14 billion and a cost of $1 million a day to fund the war. An effort to repay at least a portion of the debt could be used by the State Department to demonstrate to the U.S. Congress and the administration that Sudan was making some attempt to initiate economic reforms.

At his first meeting with Bashir on 2 July, Ambassador Norman Anderson had tried to explain the importance the United States attached to the repayment of at least some of the Brooke averages if Sudan hoped to escape the punitive provisions of Section 620(q) of the 1989 Foreign Assistance Act. Anderson had the even more onerous task of explaining that Section 513 of the same act prohibited foreign aid funds to governments that had seized power by deposing a democratically elected government. Unless the new government was granted a waiver, eight months from the date of the coup USAID could neither authorize new funds for projects nor approve the use of unexpended project funds authorized since 1986. Title I wheat would be stopped, although Title II wheat shipments would continue, and only disaster relief and the mission's operating budget could be funded. Operation Lifeline Sudan funding could continue as long as a disaster declaration had been issued by the U.S. ambassador. USAID-Sudan could expend development funds for a maximum of eight months, during which time the embassy would have to prove the NSRCC was working to restore democracy. If the case could not be made, most foreign aid (as opposed to disaster relief) would be terminated in February 1990, and the USAID mission would be reduced to only those persons necessary to administer disaster relief.

After informing Bashir of these dire consequences, Ambassador Anderson suggested that if the government paid off some of its debt to the United States and demonstrated a credible effort to make peace, it would strengthen the argument for a presidential waiver. Bashir was taken aback at first but recovered to argue that Sadiq's coalition "was not related in any way to a genuinely democratic system."[34] Still, the prospect of a waiver was the carrot by which U.S. foreign assistance need not be terminated but also the stick by which the State Department and the ambassador could beat the new regime. The USAID program was, in the view of the State Department, the only means at its disposal to influence policy in Khartoum.

Unfortunately for the U.S. Embassy, Bashir had no use for democracy. Although he occasionally claimed that neither he nor the army intended to rule forever, his statements became less credible each day. In an interview with *Al-Ittihad* he stated: "Partisan practices perpetrated during and after the elections made us believe that the democracy practiced in Sudan is not at all good for Sudan and that any attempt to restore liberal democracy will be a repetition of this experience.... I am sure that liberal democracy will be worse than it has recently been if we attempt to revive it once again."[35] Minister of the Interior, Faisal Ali Abu Salih was more direct. In a 26 July statement to a MENA correspondent, he stated, "The Army will never think of handing over power to civilians again."[36] Such statements and others like them alerted some Western embassies in Khartoum, but most preferred to listen to Brigadier General Osman Ahmed Hassan, chair of the NSRCC Political Committee, who did not foresee a hostile "attitude of all the West toward us." He found the United States "very understanding and what it has said is satisfactory to us, at least for the time being."[37]

When Bashir returned to Khartoum from the OAU meeting, many were hopeful that some breakthrough in the peace process had occurred. During a 28 July press conference he announced that peace talks would be held with the SPLA at Addis Ababa during the first week of August. Shortly thereafter, Bashir rejected former President Jimmy Carter's standing offer to mediate the dispute, acknowledging that a "homemade solution" was preferred. Surprisingly, he added that the junta representatives at the August talks would "not insist that Sudan's Islamic Shari'a law be maintained," but he also repeated his previous proposal that "the Shari'a issue is open for negotiations and if we fail to reach a solution, the other options, including holding a national referendum on the issue, will be considered."[38] The first week of August 1989 came and went with no talks and no signs that any would occur.

The first public indication that the SPLA was formulating its policy toward the NSRCC occurred in July when Garang indicated that the SPLA and SPLM would not meet with the NSRCC until the junta's goals had been clarified. Of specific interest were the status of previous peace accords and historic agreements with Egypt and Libya.[39] On 1 August Radio SPLA indicated that a meeting with the NSRCC was imminent and that the SPLA had approached both Mengistu and Mubarak to ask them to play a role in the peace process.[40] When nothing happened Garang spoke on SPLA Radio on 14 August and left little doubt that the breech between North and South was as wide as ever, if not wider. He attacked the junta for its "fundamentalist Islamic inclinations, and its violations of human rights." He accused the government of having "a hidden agenda to impose a theocratic state on Sudan and to partition the country." Garang reviewed the history of the religious issue in Sudan and contrasted the SPLA's desire for peace with the junta's dictatorial activities. He reviewed the history of modern Sudan and praised the religious tolerance of Sayyid Ali and Sayyid Abd al-Rahman, two Muslim leaders of the late colonial Condominium, who Garang argued at the time of independence could have imposed an Islamic constitution on Sudan but had the wisdom not to do so. He demeaned Numayri, who he felt had been abetted by the Muslim Brothers in enacting the September Laws; the laws were an indication, if one were needed, of Numayri's conversion to Islamic fundamentalism. Garang then denounced General Swar al-Dahab for pursuing a policy of religious intolerance little different from that of his predecessor, insisting that "as things stand today, there is no greater danger to our country's unity and stability than that posed by [Muslim] fundamentalism."[41] Assuring his listeners that the SPLM was not anti-Islam, Garang asked Bashir to reject the fundamentalist's platform, which Garang had previously called "dangerous, unhistorical and alien to Sudan and to Africa."[42] Garang characterized the junta as a disaster and a "retrogression" to the peace process, asked the members of the NSRCC to explain to the people why they had abandoned the DUP-SPLA peace agreement and questioned if in fact Bashir actually had a peace program. He concluded by condemning the NSRCC for its "very shallow and distorted" perspective of the Southern Sudan issue, and he called Bashir "just as much a rebel as is the SPLA and a junior one for that matter."[43]

The following day Garang again used Radio SPLA to declare that to achieve peace, the junta would have to resign and democracy would have to be restored. He reminded his listeners that the SPLA was not a separatist movement and that it had remained constant since routing the southern separatists. He asked Bashir not to take the path of the NIF, the one group that had expressed interest in the partition of North and South. Peace could only come when the NSRCC agreed to hold free elections and freed all political prisoners for the junta's record in regard to human rights was "already very dirty."[44] Nothing was said about an SPLA cease-fire.

Despite Garang's tough words, it was soon announced that the two sides had agreed to begin talks at Addis Ababa on 19 August. The SPLA delegation was led by Major Deng Alor Deng, who had previously indicated that he expected little from the meeting. The government delegation was composed of eleven people led by Colonel Muhammad al-Amin al-Khalifa, a confidante of Bashir. Khalifa, a Berti from Darfur, had formed a close relationship with Bashir when both headed units of the last army convoy to travel between Kosti and Juba. Like other NSRCC members, Khalifa was strongly influenced by Muslim fundamentalism.

The teams met behind closed doors for two days, but the meeting was compromised almost immediately when Khalifa neither provided nor agreed to an agenda.[45] Rather, Khalifa urged a general cease-fire; Lam Akol countered with demands that negotiations should be based on agreements the SPLA had already reached in a process that had begun with the Koka Dam Declaration of 1986 and that had continued in the months following the November 1988 DUP-SPLA agreement. The SPLA insisted that the junta lift the state of emergency, freeze the September Laws, and agree to the abrogation of Sudan's defense agreements with Libya and Egypt. After four sessions, with no headway being made on the quintessential points—Shari'a and the abrogation of military treaties—the talks were broken off. The two sides did agree, however, on tangential issues; according to UNICEF's James Grant, who was following the situation closely, the two sides agreed only that "OLS should continue and that they would meet again" at some unspecified date.[46]

Both sides claimed that peace was the grand objective, but Lam Akol insisted, "at this stage [the NSRCC has] no clear view of what they want to discuss with us."[47] Colonel Khalifa characterized the talks as "frank" (always a bad sign) and "earnest" (even worse). He admitted that the Shari'a issue engendered significant disagreement, but he declined to call the meeting a failure.[48] Rather, he considered it a preliminary effort that was needed to create trust between the two sides. He called the meeting the first phase of what would be an extended diplomatic effort and then announced that the NSRCC would soon convene its own national peace conference.

The second phase began almost immediately with the convocation of a national conference that was chaired by Colonel Khalifa. "Neutral and patriotic citizens" as well as the SPLA were invited to "set aside all points of difference and review the real causes behind the surge of the rebellion."[49] The conference was to be the essential stepping stone required for peace; when it was concluded all that would remain would be for the former belligerents to clear the South of land mines and rehabilitate the region. The scenario envisioned was a curious way to come to grips with the problem of peace in Sudan. It implied that peace could be realized by expending little effort and that it could occur despite NSRCC policies and actions that made peace impossible. As Colonel Khalifa persevered in Khartoum, leaving the door open for a second meeting with the SPLA, the national peace conference agenda introduced a new element—the imposition of a federal system of government as a solution to the southern problem. In counterpoint, Lam Akol responded that the subject of federalism had not been raised in the Addis Ababa talks and that its implementation would be a substitute for the elimination of the September Laws. As Khalifa prepared for his conference, the verbal sparring continued, and any hope for a quick end to the war slowly evaporated.

The Price of War, Drought, and Famine
on Sudan's Economy

If the NSRCC could not ignore the war, it certainly could not forget the economy that sustained it. The junta's program for the economy promised to "provide essential and basic necessities, control market prices, combat smuggling, [and] punish monopolizers, black marketers and middlemen."[50] All convertible currency was to be exchanged immediately for Sudanese pounds at the official rate. Price regulations were introduced, and there were immediate shortages of bread, meat, and dairy products. In July the government raised the price of bread from 15 to 20 piasters per 140-gram loaf; in October it increased the price to 25 piasters and decreased the weight to 120 grams. Inflation soared to over 100 percent per annum, black market activity increased and was stimulated by "unofficial" remittances brought back from the Gulf by the suitcase merchants. By August queues at Khartoum gas stations were longer than ever, and when supplies dwindled the Saudis were pressed for an emergency delivery to save the nation from grinding to a halt. The power supply was intermittent, air conditioning failed, and government and business offices sweltered. Forced to reduce their prices on meat, eggs, poultry, and other commodities, most of Khartoum's shopkeepers waged silent war on the NSRCC. When the city began to suffer shortages of fuel, bread, sugar, soap, and cigarettes, the NSRCC blamed the problem on hoarders and black marketeers and promised to prosecute them with great vigor.[51] Shops closed, buses stalled, tap water turned brown, and tempers became short. The Khartoum airport was reopened, but the early crush to escape the country was checked momentarily by Sudanese customs agents, who meticulously searched departing wealthy travelers for currency violations.

When the junta seized power, only $4 million in hard currency remained in the Bank of Sudan—barely enough to cover the cost of imports for one day. Sudan had experienced negative economic growth since 1982, and the governments were accustomed to running up huge budget deficits; by summer 1989 Sudan no longer even tried to service its estimated $14 billion foreign debt. However, whether the issue was of foreign debt, inflation, or foreign exchange, the junta seemed to have taken power with no long-range economic plan. One Khartoum banker remarked two months after the coup, "Most of the ministers and officials I meet seem not to have a clear idea of what to do next."[52] The locus of economic policy was the NSRCC Economic Committee, chaired by Navy Colonel Salaheddin Muhammad Karrar, who had a degree in public administration and little knowledge of economics. In September the NSRCC and the Council of Ministers held an extraordinary session to discuss what the Khartoum press called the "deteriorating economic situation." Not surprisingly, Minister of Finance Sayyid Ali Zaki blamed "the reliance on the banking system" rather than government policies for a decline in the value of the Sudanese pound and an increase in prices, and all that came of the meeting was a slight increase in the price of bread, which was followed in November by increases in the cost of sugar, vegetable oil, and soap.[53]

The government was, however, determined to increase domestic crop production. Summer rains were close to normal, and preliminary indications were that cereal output in the 1989–1990 crop year would be better than average but well below the 5 million tons harvested in 1988–1989. Despite the good news, the government still seemed bound to a treadmill: It planned to import an estimated 771,000 tons of wheat to meet domestic demand, and the U.S. Department of Agriculture estimated it would probably not export more than 700,000 tons of sorghum from the 1989–1990 crop season.[54] Still, no one, especially no one in government, could be sure of precisely how much sorghum was actually held by traders in Sudan. In October 1989 USAID estimated that the Agricultural Bank of Sudan held 400,000 tons and that unofficially there might be as much as 2 million tons of 1988–1989 production in private storage, much of which was in the process of being exported under licenses issued by the previous regime.[55] Faced with a hard-currency shortage, the NSRCC eventually permitted the massive draw down of Agricultural Bank of Sudan stocks and the unlimited export of domestic sorghum and edible oils, thus stripping national grain reserves following the tremendous 1988–1989 harvest year.

Government Opposition Growing Against Operation Lifeline Sudan

Following the coup, Bashir made it a point to allay expatriate concerns with regard to Operation Lifeline Sudan. During his meeting with James Grant on 1 July, Bashir approved the continuation of ICRC flights, promised to resolve the tug-barge slowdown on the Upper Nile, and extended the OLS Period of Tranquillity. Grant was immensely gratified that Bashir had given him "a positive response and firm commitment to Operation Lifeline."[56] Bashir did, however, insist that all expatriate agencies would have to reregister, making it clear that the role of PVOs had been discussed well before the junta seized power. True to his word, Bashir publicly endorsed OLS in a speech on 5 July. He justified the decision to "allow relief operations to continue in the South" because the "beneficiaries were Sudanese who should not be permitted to die of hunger."[57] Then, inexplicably, within hours of the speech the United Nations, embassies, and relief agencies were informed that only military air flights would be permitted within Sudan for at least a month. Grant put the best face possible on this unforeseen development and forecast that the situation was impermanent and that UN air operations would soon be resumed. They were not.

All expatriate travel permits were nullified, and diplomatic and UN personnel could only travel in an emergency and after receiving approval from military security. USAID personnel were grounded, but after a short hiatus the International Red Cross airlift of USAID food to Wau was allowed to continue until a contracted 3,000 tons was completed on 11 August. The Red Cross flights carried no passengers and accepted no expatriate travel in and out of Wau. The government activated a Commandeering Committee in Port Sudan that forced truckers to move government commodities at low tonnage rates. Existing contracts were nullified and trucks previously contracted by USAID to haul food from Port Sudan were commandeered. For a period of three weeks, trucks were forced to move wheat and other commodities to Khartoum.

The army then began to sequester donor fuel supplies. In southern Kordofan and Darfur, PVOs reported that their fuel stocks were "frozen" by the local military and that it had become nearly impossible to purchase fuel, even on the black market. Within two weeks of the coup, the army confiscated 11,000 gallons of USAID fuel in Kosti and 8,500 gallons at Wad Medani, effectively halting the shipment of relief food from Port Sudan to Kosti and from Kosti to southern Kordofan. When Ambassador

Anderson protested directly to President Bashir, he was informed that in the future, embassy messages addressed to Bashir "should be channeled through the Ministry of Foreign Affairs."[58] The embassy was dealt a second blow when it learned that RRC Commissioner Al-Hag al-Tayeb had been dismissed. Al-Hag al-Tayeb had thought he had Bashir's complete support, but while Bashir was attending the OAU meetings at Addis Ababa in July, al-Tayeb was removed and subsequently imprisoned for alleged theft of relief commodities. He was eventually found innocent, but Bashir did nothing to resurrect him. Al-Tayeb's replacement was, ironically, the old RRC war-horse Kamal Shawki. Despite rumors that Shawki had close ties to Muslim Brothers, by August NSRCC had lost its virtual autonomy and was buried in the newly created Ministry of Relief and Displaced Persons Affairs. Minister Peter Orat Ador, a former chief of Port Sudan customs who had a reputation as an honest if somewhat sleepy administrator, moved into the RRC building.

Through July and most of August, expatriates involved with OLS fretted as they endured a period of enforced sedentariness. A train of fifty freight cars loaded with 1,500 tons of food that should have left for Aweil on 17 July remained on a siding in Muglad for more than a month. Barges loaded and prepared to leave Kosti languished at their moorings. The SPLA approved and the donors agreed to send a mission to Bentiu to investigate food needs and a kala-azar outbreak in Anya-Nya II territory, but the NSRCC never asked the donors to proceed. In July the number of displaced persons in Abyei increased from 21,000 to 39,000 but no expatriates were permitted in the town. In early August the number of new arrivals reached 500 a day, and the LICROSS team and USAID-Sudan could only pray that there was enough food to last through the rainy season. Rainfall, which had been generally good in the South, had been very sparse in villages around Mayen Abun, and it was expected that tens of thousands of Dinka from that region might soon move to Aweil or to Abyei in search of food. Still, the donors were unable to obtain a train to discharge sorghum to Mayen Abun or Aweil.

The Death of Mickey Leland
and Its Consequences

There was much expatriate gnashing of teeth in Khartoum. Meanwhile, on 13 August a U.S. Air Force helicopter located the wreckage of a plane that was flying Representative Mickey Leland and fifteen others from Addis Ababa to the Fugnido refugee camp near the Sudanese border. All aboard had perished. A huge search-and-rescue operation had finally located Leland who more than any other person had compelled Americans to focus on African drought and starvation. African issues were his special interest, and it was said that the transcendent moment of his congressional career occurred in 1984 during a visit to Sudan when a starving child died "before his eyes," and "what had been a commitment became a crusade."[59] After that, Leland was "one of the few Americans who was prepared to invest his time and energy in inspecting the conditions" of unfortunate refugees in Ethiopia and displaced persons in Sudan. He argued for and eventually founded the Congressional Select Committee on Hunger, which alerted Congress and the American public to the plight of starving people around the world.[60]

Leland had been flying to the Fugnido camp, which housed nearly 60,000 Sudanese refugees, nearly half of whom were unaccompanied minors. "Generally recognized as the most vulnerable of refugee children," this was perhaps the largest such group the UNHCR had ever assisted.[61] It was to have been Leland's seventh trip to the Sudanese camps, and one could expect that just when it was needed most, his reporting would have been both prescient and thought provoking. Ironically, Leland's death refocused attention on Ethiopia, Sudan, and Operation Lifeline Sudan at a time when interest in the United States had been waning. The MacNeil-Lehrer news report reviewed the recent history of Sudan, and a Canadian Broadcasting Corporation video on Fugnido featured the flight of young Dinka from Bahr al-Ghazal to Ethiopia: "The flood of boys warns that a special terror is taking place back in the bush. They huddle together, weak, confused.... The surviving members of their families instead head north, crowding into refugee camps there."[62]

The report touched on the sensitive subject of slavery and the fear of becoming slaves, which had caused children to march hundreds of miles to the east rather than follow their grandparents and mothers to the north through the lands dominated by the Baqqara militia. In the great Dinka exodus, thousands of young males had been ordered away by families anxious to save their lives, for they knew that when a village was attacked by *murahileen* or militia, the men were killed and the women and children were taken as slaves. Thus, it was left to the boys to escape with the family animals. Relief workers estimated that of every ten young boys who began the trek to Ethiopia, four perished along the way; of those who made it, 15 percent died after their arrival.[63] By the time the camera team arrived to capture the scenes presented in the MacNeil-Lehrer report, there were few adults in Fugnido to supervise the tens of thousands of children. The broadcasters found that "you can sometimes find a few of them in corners weeping because they miss their mother or their father.... They search for words, songs of brave bulls or cattle they once had."[64]

Had Leland survived he would have found that the situation in the four refugee camps had improved greatly since his previous visits. In February 1989 the UNHCR reported that the number of Sudanese refugees exceeded 400,000, with 200 arriving daily. Most were fleeing from the fighting in Upper Nile, but in contrast to 1988 fewer than 5 percent required therapeutic feeding.[65] Despite heavy rains in the southwest and another drought in Tigre and Eritrea, food stocks were sufficient in all camps except Asosa, where transport was hampered by poor roads. Leland would also have recognized that tensions had been growing for months as tens of thousands of refugees competed with Ethiopians for increasingly scarce space, land, and resources. The NSRCC would eventually used these antagonisms to its own purpose and assist the Oromo Liberation Front to attack and force the closing of Sudanese refugee camps.

The NSRCC's month-long flight restrictions were ended in August only to be replaced by security procedures that drastically reduced PVO opportunities to fly from field sites to Khartoum and vice versa. In Wau—where more than 70,000 displaced persons were counted in September—the head of military intelligence refused any visits by the *khawaja*, including replacement personnel, unless clearance was granted by military intelligence at the General Command, Khartoum.[66] Expatriates working in Wau soon found themselves trapped in a situation not unlike the one that had occurred in late 1987. An uneasy truce had existed for months between the Dinka and Fertit and between the Dinka and the military. On 18 July the tenuous peace was shattered when army soldiers ran amok after one of their comrades was badly injured by an antipersonnel mine planted two kilometers north of the Wau military base. According to one witness, the slaughter was carried out by elements of the 311th Field Artillery Battalion who rushed to town and began an indiscriminate attack on Dinka in the Zagalona sector.[67] The violence was initiated as military units and civilian officials were attending a farewell ceremony for the regional commander, Major General Awadallah Muhammad al-Fatih, who was leaving Wau to become governor of Kordofan. The displaced, including women and children living in the International Red Cross camps, seemed to be particular targets. Once the slaughter had started, the police—who were mainly Dinka—tried to intervene only to be halted by armed military. Outgunned, they were forced to retreat. When the soldiers had finished venting their fury, more than 100 Dinka were dead and scores were badly injured. When the frenzy abated, the soldiers collected the dead and the mortally wounded and dumped them down a well located northwest of the military post.

Details of the massacre circulated freely in Wau, and some of the survivors were taken to the Wau hospital where their wounds were treated by expatriates. Neither the military nor the local government investigated the affair; General Awadallah's replacement, Brigadier Muhammad Omar Idris, could not find the time given his duties as military governor, area commander, and chief of the ubiquitous regional security committee. The brigadier was more interested in readying his troops for battle and in turning the Fertit militia from a rabble into a disciplined auxiliary. Tangentially, the Wau incident placed the International Red Cross in an unfortunate situation. Operating the only relief flights to the South, the ICRC was daily receiving closer scrutiny from members of the NSRCC, who questioned its activities and could terminate flights to Wau at will. The ICRC was well aware that the junta doubted its neutrality; should the news of the Wau atrocity leak to the Western media, as the Red Cross was sure it would, the aid agency would likely be blamed for spreading the news and thus for committing an unfriendly act. Accounts of the Wau massacre were, in fact, brought to Khartoum by army personnel and by southerners who sent their reports out through Raga. Despite rumors circulating in Khartoum, the junta remained silent. The NSRCC buried the story and instead devoted extensive publicity to the investigation of the former governor of Bahr al-Ghazal, Lawrence Lual, and 16 aides and 150 senior officers arrested on charges of corruption.[68] The new military governor reorganized the Wau relief committee and installed the brother of Ali Tamim Fartak, who detested the Dinka, as the head of the RRC office in Wau. The committee was soon completely ineffectual.

Operation Lifeline Sudan Begins to Unravel

In August 1989 Bryan Wannop, UN resident representative in Khartoum, resigned from the United Nations, and Michael Priestley, the UN secretary-general's special representative in Ethiopia, was named to replace both Wannop and UNICEF's James Grant. Priestley, who was given special representative status in Sudan—something Wannop had coveted but never received—was not scheduled to arrive until October. Before he left Sudan Wannop provided the media with an arresting story as he blasted UNICEF for having turned Operation Lifeline Sudan into "a turf war for leadership" and treating it "as a public relations exercise." The fates, however, allowed Wannop a final triumph when the junta finally permitted a relief train standing by in Muglad to leave for Aweil on 12 August. Then, with a well-placed pat on his own back, Wannop retired: "The operation is over. We have done the impossible."[69]

Unlike previous adventures, the UN-flagged train dropped off food to SPLA villages and arrived in Aweil without incident on 20 August. It unloaded and returned to Muglad by 28 August, the quickest turnaround since 1983. It loaded another 1,500 tons of sorghum and was ready to leave for Aweil when the shipment was blocked. Arguing that the SPLA had received a disproportionate share of the donor food, the NSRCC refused to release the train unless two-thirds of the food went to government towns and villages. The SPLA refused, the government remained adamant, and for weeks the loaded boxcars baked on a siding at Muglad. Commissioner Shawki quietly warned donors that they should move whatever they could by truck, because the military would soon take charge of all train movements to Aweil. Future food aid might have to accompany military supplies if it were to move at all.

The impasse in southern Kordofan was matched in Upper Nile. A convoy with 1,750 tons of relief food arrived in Malakal on 21 August, and on 29 August a second convoy left Kosti transporting 5,700 tons of food aid. Commodities destined for SPLA villages were discharged en route almost without incident. In Malakal, however, the sequestering of donor food by the government became a very real problem that was blamed on the military governor, Lieutenant Colonel Gatluak Deng, who took control of the distribution of food aid in September and appointed his personal representative as chair of the Malakal Relief Committee.[70] Colonel Deng eventually sacked the entire committee, created a pliable alternative, seized the donor warehouses, and required prior approval for all NGO and UN radio messages between Malakal and Khartoum.

The success of August barge and train convoys ended OLS for 1989. By September most of the food aid was in place or on the way. The OLS objective had been met in Equatoria, although the oversubscription in Juba masked the fact that Yei and some SPLA towns were as yet under-supplied. OLS had had its successes and its disappointments, and donor food had sometimes been carelessly bagged or distributed. There were also occasional cruel reminders that people were hungry and that food was scarce in some districts; in southern Kordofan the food targets had been exceeded, but the number of displaced persons crowding into Abyei neared 50,000, and there was still cause for concern. Nonetheless, the donors, despite their many detractors, had proven that even with the fragile transportation system in Sudan it was possible to move nearly 100,000 tons of food to the needy in a very short time. (See Table 7.1.) Thanks in large part to the shipment of U.S. sorghum, USAID had con-tributed half of the food subscribed, and it loaned thousands of tons of food to expand their participation to other donors. The total U.S. emer-gency assistance to Sudan since the first civil strife disaster was declared in February 1988 had exceeded $120 million, of which more than $100 million was spent in support of Operation Lifeline Sudan.

Although OLS would not officially end until 31 October, the donors began to discuss what should follow. Some expatriates were almost pleased that OLS was ending; in late August the NSRCC reissued travel permits, but the interminable delays in obtaining them was driving a

TABLE 7.1   Operation Lifeline Sudan Food Aid Deliveries, 1 March–30 September 1989

	Metric Tons	UN Target	Percentage Delivered
Government Areas			
Equatoria	26,934	16,050	167
Upper Nile	3,995	9,910	40
Bahr al-Ghazal	10,665	12,525	85
South Kordofan	16,000	18,815	85
Darfur	1,921	4,000	48
Central	456	3,000	15
Khartoum	424	1,165	36
Total	60,395	65,465	98
SPLA Areas			
Equatoria	12,309	12,500	98
Upper Nile	6,517	12,925	50
Bahr al-Ghazal	5,736	9,380	61
Total	24,562	34,805	71
Grand Total	84,957	100,270	88

Source: Government of Sudan, Relief and Rehabilitation Commission, Food Aid Deliveries 1 March to 30 September 1989, 9 October 1989.

wedge between the RRC and the embassies, NGOs, and visiting consultants. NGOs were required to obtain approval from both the Ministry of Defense and military security, and four separate security checks from four separate agencies caused long and frustrating delays. Throughout August only military flights transporting arms and military materiel to Malakal, Wau, and Juba moved regularly from Khartoum. The ICRC reported that shortages of fuel had reduced its flights from Khartoum to the South, and the United Nations had great difficulty maintaining its weekly flight schedules. British Ambassador James Beavan had been one of the first to welcome the change of government, but he was also one of the first to perceive that with regard to disaster relief, the NSRCC was even more perplexing than Sadiq had been. Beavan was especially peeved when the NSRCC continued to deny the British Embassy travel permits, particularly when Sudan-ODA agreements included provisions for the unhindered movement of U.K. representatives.

James Grant, who could barely disguise his delight over the success of OLS and his relief at turning it over to someone else, had returned to Khartoum in August to discuss with Bashir the future of the program. Bashir told Grant that he "foresaw the need for a second phase" and nominated the United Nations to coordinate a program that "would include elaboration on non-food assistance, as well as priority emphasis" on a program for the Khartoum displaced persons.[71] In New York the Sudanese representative to the United Nations officially thanked OLS participants and affirmed the NSRCC commitment to continue the program. Foreign Minister Ali Sahloul, who attended the opening of the General Assembly, returned to Khartoum and announced that the United Nations had agreed to increase its funding from $140 million for OLS I to $250 million for OLS II. The demoralized donors received the information with little enthusiasm. Nonetheless, the UN-Khartoum staff began to draft position papers for Michael Priestley, who had been "charged with preparing for Phase II and submitting a program to the UN–New York in mid-November."[72] For some Western embassies the nagging preoccupation remained that there was no getting off the Sudanese merry-go-round because Sudan, like Ethiopia next door, had become another "theme park for the Four Horsemen of the Apocalypse."[73] Most important, donor fatigue had become contagious, and in Khartoum it was most noticeable within the European Community.

Government Embarrassment
of Southern Sudanese in Khartoum

For USAID-Sudan September was a time to contemplate disaster relief assistance in light of the realities of a new fiscal year beginning 1 October and the changing circumstances within Sudan. In May 1989 there had been an estimated 2.7 million displaced southerners in Sudan; four months later there were 2.8 million, and the vast majority were located in Khartoum, which had no OLS support. The Khartoum displaced persons were a persistent problem, and many analysts—including the new AID-OFDA Director Andrew Natsios, who had just replaced Julia Taft—felt it was time to reduce the emphasis on the food aid programs and substitute reconstruction and rehabilitation projects. This, ironically, meshed perfectly with NSRCC plans to relocate the Khartoum displaced persons into so-called production areas well south of the capital.

The NSRCC policy toward the displaced southerners was to be even more sinister than the *kasha* campaigns of Jaafar Numayri and Sadiq al-Mahdi. By 1989 more than a million southerners had moved into the Khartoum area. For most, home was a patchwork shack. Water was costly, latrines were practically nonexistent, educational opportunities were scarce, and vaccination and public health campaigns were rare. In general, northerners despised the flotsam of war and famine in their midst; the aid that was distributed to forty-eight major settlements found in Khartoum, Khartoum North, and Omdurman was provided by Sudanaid, SCC, and a score of expatriate aid organizations. Whereas the NIF had previously complained that the influx of southerners was altering the Arab character of the capital and its suburbs, the NSRCC reversed the trend.

Although the junta assured the expatriate community that there would be no forcible evictions of displaced southerners, , it began to consider a number of relocation schemes. On 19 August 1989 it announced that ten agricultural projects would be established in the central region to "accommodate the displaced people" of that region; simultaneously, the junta began to circulate word that displaced persons living within planned areas of greater Khartoum would have to move.[74] Deputy Commissioner for the National Capital Lieutenant Colonel Yusuf "Rambo" Abd al-Fatah then ordered "inhabitants of the slums in the Capital to remove their makeshift dwellings in a ten-day period." The displaced persons were warned to avoid areas "allocated for planned housing" because a plan was in effect to "accommodate the displaced citizens in big camps and provide them with basic services."[75] Such camps seemed, however, to be located on wasteland near Jabal Auliya south of the Khartoum city limits and west of Omdurman.

The announcements alerted the United Nations and the aid agencies that the NSRCC was in fact determined to move the displaced persons from Khartoum. The consequences of such a move were debated, but the Relief and Rehabilitation Commission offered little support. After years of providing funds to build a competent counterpart agency, the donors found the junta had vitiated its effectiveness. In less than two months the RRC had been staffed by inexperienced Muslim fundamentalists, and the organization was relegated to an insignificant bureau. The donors finally sent an *aide-memoire* to Bashir expressing their concern that the 19 August announcement could affect over 200,000 displaced persons living in planned areas.[76] They requested a suspension of the program and offered to help prepare a suitable plan to move the displaced people, one that "would attract help rather than criticism from the international community." The president did not respond directly. Instead he informed NSRRC Commissioner Shawki that the RCC considered the situation of the Khartoum displaced persons a very important domestic issue and expected as little expatriate interference in its policies as possible.[77]

This calculated snub was followed by a government draft memorandum circulated by Shawki that delineated the basic principles involved in the relocation of the displaced persons. There would be no compulsory repatriation or expulsions "except where temporary settlements are a threat to health." Health was not a useful criterion because the junta considered all settlements a menace to public health. The government warned that it would "actively discourage any dependence on food aid" and migration to urban areas. In September a draft memorandum entitled "The Government's Policy Towards International Organizations and the NGOs" was disseminated within government circles but soon came to the attention of the donors. It offered a sure indication that the junta would soon take charge of activities dealing with the displaced persons and thus reduce the expatriate presence and was officially revised and distributed to the donors on 29 September, the essential parts of which were that the government was:

1. To provide for the basic needs of the displaced wherever they are throughout the country.
2. To establish reception centers at interregional boundaries to help stem unchecked migration and to [keep] people as close as possible to their original homes, and
3. To resettle the displaced in a participatory and voluntary fashion as close to their homes as possible.

The first two parts of the policy were to be implemented immediately in order "to satisfy urgent basic needs and to check migration."[78]

The National Dialogue Conference

When the August Addis Ababa talks proved inconclusive, the NSRCC issued a decree creating a National Committee of "academicians, public figures and distinguished personalities [to produce] a new power-sharing formula between Sudan's Arabized Moslem majority and its ethnic and religious minorities."[79] On 4 September the National Dialogue Conference on Peace was convened, consisting of seventy-seven members, including twenty-three southerners chosen with great care. Although its agenda included discussion of a series of topics (the history of North-South relations, the civil war, and the southern economy), its raison d'être was to rubber-stamp government solutions to the southern problem. The NSRCC began ominously by announcing that conference resolutions would "be binding on any future [peace] settlement."[80] Colonel Khalifa, the conference chair, announced that Garang had been sent a personal invitation and was offered full protection in Khartoum. In what must have come as a rude surprise to the SPLA, Khalifa added that the conference would be "a substitute to the long-proposed Constitutional Conference" wherein conferees would discuss issues including the system of rule best suited for Sudan, the distribution of wealth, power sharing, and the relationship between religion and the state.[81] The NSRCC insisted that the conference would convene and would proceed regardless of whether the SPLA appeared, and few were surprised when the SPLA failed to do so. Instead, in addition to its historic preconditions to peace talks, it issued new demands including "the release from detention of politicians and trade unionists, the lifting of the ban on political parties and trade unions and restoration of freedom of the press."[82] In the end, the SPLA was unwilling to attend a conference whose agenda was preceded by dogmatic pronouncements and whose participants were disposed to draft "appropriate solutions" with or without the SPLA.[83]

Other dissenters were also excluded, including a group of fifty-seven southern "chiefs, academics, clergymen and others" who delivered a signed petition that was intended to be read at the conference. In it they declared that "Moslem Khartoum discriminates against the South's mainly Christian and animist inhabitants," regards Sudan "as an Arab country," and plans "to spread Arab culture and Islam to the South."[84] The petition, although circulated throughout Khartoum, was neither read nor published, although its harsh conclusions were reported by Reuters.[85] Although the Khartoum press gave extensive coverage to speeches blasting Garang, it hardly noticed a speech by Major General Peter Cirillo—the former governor of Equatoria and no friend of the SPLA—in which he blamed past governments for "using religion as a means of obtaining and holding political power, which they then used to subjugate non-Muslims."[86] The government neither published the speech nor commented on any part of it including its most important section, which belittled the government's proposal to hold a referendum on Shari'a.

The conference, which was to have lasted a month, actually concluded after forty-four days. The final conference report and recommendations were prepared in October 1989 and approved at a joint session of the NSRCC and the Council of Ministers held on 1 November. The report recorded that the second civil war had cost the lives of around 4,600 army officers and enlisted men (an obvious understatement) and of 27,000 SPLA members (perhaps closer to the mark) and the deaths of 262,000 civilians because of the war and the related causes of starvation and disease (certainly an undercounting).[87] The conference also concluded that about two of every three southerners had either fled the South or been killed since the war started. Seven million cattle had been destroyed.

Few doubted that the war had inflicted terrible suffering, but most southerners protested the conclusion that among the root causes of the civil war was the lack of regional development, the result of which was "economic instability, which gave room for foreign capital, which promoted its own gain."[88] To overcome years of inertia, the conference advised: "The government should reform the economy, rehabilitate development projects, encourage external investment and attract foreign aid," a curious and seemingly contradictory remedy given the report's conclusion.[89]

The conference participants unanimously agreed that a federal system would be most appropriate to Sudan. The federal government would control the armed forces, the defense budget, national security, foreign affairs, customs, national economic planning, currency, higher education, telecommunications, land, natural resources, and policies for the protection of the environment. They also recommended that the NSRCC should move expeditiously to adopt presidential elections by direct vote and a unicameral legislature based on proportional representation. Buried deep within the conference report was the recommendation that the Koka Dam and November 1988 DUP-SPLA agreements be rejected as bases upon which to hold peace talks. No unanimity existed with regard to the implementation of Shari'a, but the final report did guarantee freedom of worship and recommended that "states shall have power to pass legislation within the jurisdictions allocated to them."[90] Despite conference efforts to fudge the issue, the NSRCC insisted that because Islam was the religion of the majority, the application of Shari'a was correctly national in scope and application.

There Can Be No Peace
Without Total Victory or Compromise

On 1 October Bashir extended the cease-fire and admitted that negotiations with the SPLA would take much more time. The NSRCC was particularly furious and vigorously protested the formal welcome accorded to John Garang by Zimbabwe and Zambia, which it felt was "unjust and harmed Sudanese dignity."[91] In a visit to Tanzania in October Garang told a friendly audience that Bashir was not eager to negotiate in good faith and said the SPLA would fight until the NSRCC accepted the DUP-SPLA agreement as the basis for talks. Several months of mudslinging followed. Brigadier Ibrahim Nail Eidam asserted that the Communists in the SPLA had inflamed the movement, that Garang was being manipulated by the Communist trend within the SPLA, and that the conflict had indeed become "a war of ideological nature."[92] It was not unusual for the junta to claim that serious disagreements existed within SPLA ranks and that a "substantial element [wanted] to advance the peace process."[93] Repeating reports that had initially appeared in the *Sudan Times* in 1988, the government media claimed that of five field commanders who had been with the SPLA, only Garang and William Nyuan Bany remained, whereas Kerubino Kwanyin Bol and Arok Thon Arok were in the movement's prisons; further, although the SPLA complained about human rights violations in the North, Garang had imprisoned at least twenty-nine SPLA officers.[94] The SPLA had often cracked down hard on dissent within the ranks, expelling or jailing those who chose separatism over a united Sudan or those such as Joseph Oduho, who was expelled in 1987, and Arok, expelled in 1988, who sought a negotiated peace at the expense of SPLA policy. Radio SPLA could give as well as take, and a continual stream of propaganda denounced the junta and Bashir as running dogs of Islamic fundamentalism and stated that the army command was nothing more than the National Islamic Front in uniform.

Whereas the junta had ordered a cease-fire but then began to search for new arms suppliers, the SPLA reduced but did not cease fighting. In July army units in southern Kordofan were under attack by the SPLA's New Kush Brigade, commanded by Yusuf Kuwah Makki, a Nuba, and composed mostly of Nuba soldiers. The army garrison at Talodi was surrounded, and Kadugli, which had been swollen by the arrival of 30,000 displaced persons, was threatened. The SPLA then began to move east of Kadugli in a wide arc to the north and threatened to interdict the main road leading north to El Obeid. By September the army Central Command at El Obeid patrolled the road on a daily basis, and the hills stretching between Kadugli and Talodi became the scene of extensive skirmishing. Elsewhere, in Equatoria the UN World Food Program was unable to move trucks from Kenya to Yei because of fighting between SPLA units and Ugandans who were armed and supported by the Sudanese army.[95] The SPLA actively patrolled the area around Juba. In the Blue Nile region the SPLA probed army positions on 22 August and followed with an attack that began on 26 September and lasted six days. With peace no closer at hand, SPLA activity indicated that the group might try to replicate its successful 1988–1989 offensive.

EIGHT

———————— ■ ————————

The Junta Is Challenged

Whatever is being said up until now that we are preparing for war in southern Sudan is incorrect. There is this risk of our national space being penetrated and therefore because we care for the people who serve in the relief agencies and such people, we are going to stop this [OLS] until we are sure these citizens are not in danger.
——Interview with General Bashir, BBC World Service,
9 September 1989

In August 1989 former President Jimmy Carter passed through Khartoum and like many other visitors was beguiled by Bashir, who spoke effectively of peace and democracy. Carter was followed by the Department of State's Herman Cohen, who assured the NSRCC leader that the State Department would support a waiver of the Brooke Amendment and promised to continue disaster relief funding. When Cohen tried to raise the problems the donors were experiencing in their relief programs Bashir turned to politics. He indicated that there were no immediate plans to reinstitute political parties; he skirted the issue of the Shari'a and downplayed the importance of Sadiq's past peace efforts. Cohen indicated that he would share his discussions with the U.S. Congress in September and promised U.S. support as long as the NSRCC made reasonable efforts toward peace, supported a return to democracy, and made an effort to reverse the economy's precipitous decline.[1] Cohen, like Carter, left Khartoum favorably impressed by Bashir. Nevertheless, although Bashir talked of peace, there seemed no end to war.

Despite Talks of Peace,
the NSRCC Was Preparing for War

When Bashir broadcast the NSRCC's political principles to the nation on 3 July, he left no doubt that the junta was determined to rebuild Sudan People's Armed Forces. Two days later in a speech at the Jabal

Auliya military base and later at Atbara, Bashir appeared more eager to make war than peace. The junta immediately resuscitated the moribund military agreement with Libya, and within hours Libyan armaments arrived in Sudan. These were soon deployed, as fighting occurred throughout much of August in southern Kordofan. SPLA forces operated near Kadugli, and at Talodi an incipient PVO effort to airlift food to the displaced persons was halted when the military helicopter was abruptly transferred to the Blue Nile region where the SPLA was also active.[2]

Despite the skirmishing in Blue Nile, the NSRCC made light of "isolated incidents," including a mid-September clash on "the Kurmuk road."[3] Also by mid-September, the Muglad garrison was swarming with troops as two army battalions were being readied to move by train to Aweil in what Muglad *suq-talk* predicted would be the first step in a major attack near Rumbek. In October Chinese munitions and military vehicles appeared on flatcars in the heart of Khartoum, and in Port Sudan selected piers were placed off limits as weapons arrived from secret destinations. John Garang, who had just completed a tour of seven African countries, informed journalists at a Nairobi news conference that the NSRCC had launched a massive rearmament operation and was positioning its forces to threaten the SPLA on a number of fronts.

It was rumored in Khartoum that the army commander in Kurmuk, Blue Nile region, had celebrated the conclusion of the National Dialogue Conference on Peace on 16 October by firing on SPLA troops. According to the SPLA, the army's 14th Brigade had left Damazin on 9 October and had initiated an "unprovoked offensive" code-named *aman al-Kurmuk* ("Safety of Kurmuk") on three SPLA positions at Surkum (see map). The SPLA reportedly repulsed the attack, and the government force retreated to Kurmuk. When the brigade attempted another attack, it was badly mauled.[4] In London SPLA spokesperson Mansour Khalid acknowledged on 21 October that fierce fighting had erupted in both the Nuba Mountains and at Kurmuk. Two days later the army went on the attack in Equatoria when government forces crossed the Juba bridge and moved toward Torit; the army was ambushed, beat a hasty retreat, was fired on by friendly forces, and suffered heavy casualties as it sought to recross the Nile.

The government's arms buildup and trips to Iran and Iraq had worried SPLA field commanders, and they had reportedly urged "their leaders to press home the military advantage they had seized."[5] Troops commanded by William Nyuan Bany did just that and took Kurmuk on 28 October. Kurmuk was a special case, because it was one of four districts that despite terms of the 1972 Addis Ababa Agreement were never permitted a plebiscite to determine if they should be incorporated into the South. Radio SPLA celebrated the victory, condemned the National

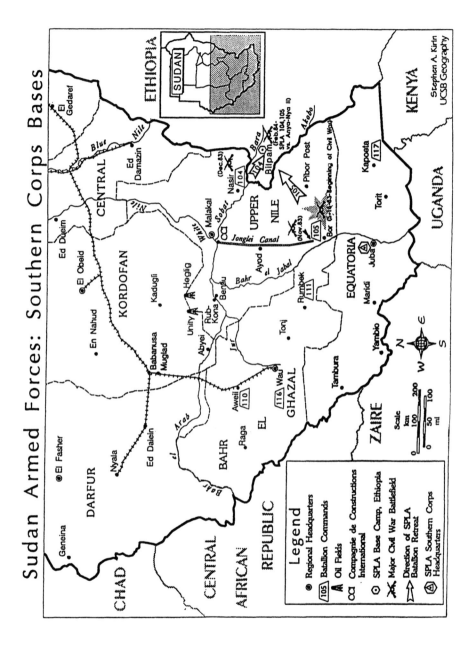

Sudan Armed Forces: Southern Corps Bases

Legend

- ◉ Regional Headquarters
- [105] Battalion Commands
- ⚓ Oil Fields
- CCI Compagnie de Constructions International
- ⊙ SPLA Base Camp, Ethiopia
- ✗ Major Civil War Battlefield
- ⟹ Direction of SPLA Battalion Retreat
- Ⓐ SPLA Southern Corps Headquarters

Stephen A. Kirin
UCSB Geography

Dialogue Conference on Peace, and urged Bashir "to go back to his desk or wastepaper basket, where he might find the SPLM/SPLA's peace program. He should read it properly and repeatedly. Perhaps with luck it will help him to understand and then he might realize that the peace upon which all sections of Sudanese people are agreed is embraced by the four points of the program."[6]

For the second time, the SPLA had captured Kurmuk. The NSRCC complained, as had Sadiq al-Mahdi, that its loss could be attributed to Ethiopian perfidy, and its protests that Ethiopian artillery and tanks had supported the SPLA attack resulted in the rupture of diplomatic relations with the Mengistu government.[7] For the NSRCC Kurmuk appertained to the North; the army vowed "not to give up one inch of the soil of this homeland," and the government radio signed off its broadcasts with Muslim invocations and vows to retake Kurmuk.[8] The NSRCC then orchestrated a hysterical campaign, characterized by racism and religious bigotry, that appeared to tolerate attacks on Southern Sudanese found in Khartoum. Junta officials rushed to Arab nations to request funds to win back an "Arab" town captured by Africans and infidels.

In the wake of the Kurmuk debacle, the bloodiest fighting in Bahr al-Ghazal for more than a year occurred near Rumbek. In southern Kordofan there were reports of a major SPLA attack on the outskirts of Kadugli. On 3 November the International Red Cross reported that two unmarked planes, a jet fighter, and a turboprop bomber dropped around twenty-five bombs on Yirol, killing four people and wounding ten. Several bombs exploded near the Red Cross hospital. When the ICRC protested the apparent targeting of a neutral site, the NSRCC denied knowledge of the attack and announced that it had formed a committee to investigate the incident. The junta was, however, in no mood to tolerate ICRC complaints and used the protest as an excuse to halt *all* donor food aid flights and to subject the ICRC operation to a rigid "evaluation."[9] The junta insisted the ICRC had favored the enemy, even though the agency could prove that overall it had delivered almost twice as much food to government sites as to SPLA-controlled locations. (See Table 8.1.) When Kamal Shawki attempted to persuade the NSRCC to allow flights into the South to replace or relieve UN monitors, the junta's political committee warned that he was "not being Sudanese enough."

In Blue Nile the SPLA "New Funj" forces under William Nyuan Bany continued their offensive along the Ethiopian border and on 9 November captured Chali el-Fil, once the administrative center of the Uduk tribe. Khawr Yabus fell on 12 November, leaving the SPLA in control of the Yabus River region. The NSRCC again blamed the loss on the support the SPLA had received from foreign elements, including fifteen Israeli military advisers.[10] Despite the series of reverses, the army continued its

TABLE 8.1 International Committee of the Red Cross, Southern Sudan Relief Operations (in metric tons)

	SPLA Deliveries		GOS Deliveries		
	Food	Nonfood	Food	Nonfood	Total
From inception to Operation Lifeline Sudan 26 December 1988– 11 March 1989	1,280	50	1,340	120	2,790
Operation Lifeline Sudan to Military Coup 12 March 1989– 1 July 1989	5,570	420	5,740	590	12,320
Military Coup to Blue Nile Battle 2 July 1989– 14 October 1989	5,740	580	9,790	1,190	17,300
Blue Nile Battle to Suspension of Flights 15 October 1989– 11 November 1989	5,740	590	10,010	1,650	17,990

Source: International Committee of the Refugees, Khartoum, Situation Reports for South Sudan, SPLA, GOS.

extensive military buildup, and in Malakal it prepared to attack Bor. The attack was foreshadowed by the activity of grain traders—including army officers—who formed a cartel that controlled the grain market from Malakal to the junction of the Nile and Sobat rivers. When the *jallaba* ceased trading, it was concluded that the army would need all the food it could get. The army then sequestered the UN World Food Program's commodities.[11]

Dilemmas of the International Community Concerning Sudan

The State Department voiced concern over the outbreak of fighting and acknowledged, "We are particularly distressed by the breakdown at this time because of earlier indications that both sides were thinking positively about the peace process" and a new disaster relief program.[12] Ambassador Norman Anderson, in the last major act of his tour in Sudan, had issued a disaster declaration that permitted AID-OFDA to support OLS through 1990. Anderson was replaced by James Cheek, a career diplomat, who had been formally nominated ambassador to Sudan on 1 August but was not confirmed by Secretary of State James Baker until 16 October. During the interim his search for a history of U.S. policy in Sudan led ineluctably to a single document—an outdated 1981 national security memorandum. Following Numayri's demise, State Department policy had been ad hoc, as were Cheek's instructions. He was to push for peace, democratization, and OLS.[13] As for the SPLA, Assistant Secretary Cohen felt Garang had ignored his July warning that the SPLA should respect the NSRCC's cease-fire, and U.S. Embassy analysts were convinced that the SPLA had little to gain by peace whereas the junta had nothing to gain by continuing the war.

Cheek was forced to wait to present his credentials as Bashir and his colleagues dealt with the Kurmuk crisis. In the meantime, Cheek openly voiced the opinion that the SPLA was responsible for wrecking the putative cease-fire and, in a move that surprised USAID-Sudan employees directly involved in Operation Lifeline Sudan, argued that its SRRA could not be trusted to distribute food aid. This argument was unjust, because under the OLS aegis the SRRA had received 30,000 tons of food and other aid; and although it lacked trained personnel, the ICRC in Bahr al-Ghazal, the UN World Food Program monitors in Upper Nile, and the Norwegian and Catholic aid agencies in Equatoria had reported favorably on SRRA operations.

The cumulative importance of reports commending SRRA efforts was, however, significantly diminished by a single cable sent to Washington following a 29 September–14 October meeting of USAID's OLS personnel. A "wrap-up" cable prepared by USAID-Sudan used a World Vision complaint to tar the SRRA operation in Equatoria with a very broad brush. USAID reported that PVOs had charged that the SRRA had diverted relief food to nonrelief activities and perhaps even to the SPLA. USAID-Kenya, which had not cleared the cable, later disagreed with USAID-Sudan's conclusions, but it was too late. In Washington the cable persuaded Cheek, and he used it to justify his suspicion of the SRRA—NGO, PVO, USAID-Sudan and USAID-Kenya arguments to the contrary. During his introductory meeting with USAID personnel, both U.S. and Sudanese, Cheek left no doubt that he distrusted the SPLA. To attack the SRRA, however, seemed curiously premature since USAID had no actual working arrangement with the SRRA—just as the embassy had no satisfactory working arrangement with the SPLA—and State Department strictures precluded USAID personnel from visiting SPLA territory. Both USAID and the embassy depended on the United Nations and PVOs for reports. The SRRA was, in fact, increasingly able to make decisions in the field rather than seeking guidance from Addis Ababa or Nairobi. Still, despite reports that the SRRA's performance had greatly improved,

Cheek remained stubbornly suspicious of the SPLA, the SRRA, and the OLS program in SPLA territory.

Cheek was mercurial and often incautiously undiplomatic. He was openly bitter because his career had been sidetracked by conservative politicians who had objected to his performance as chief of the political section in Nicaragua and later as a deputy assistant secretary of state. He had been the charge d'affaires in Ethiopia during the 1980s and had made friends with Michael Priestley, the UN representative in Ethiopia. He apparently developed a profound distaste for the SPLA and its leaders. Thus, Cheek gave the appearance of being sympathetic to NSRCC aims—despite the growing number of human rights violations and the warnings from southerners that it was a mistake to think that foreign aid would influence the NSRCC "for positive policy change."[14] Cheek favored without reservation a presidential waiver of Section 513 of the Foreign Assistance Act and the continued infusion of development and military aid, disaster assistance, and the PL-480 program. Cheek did not believe Kurmuk was a complete setback for the peace process, because a military evaluation had indicated that the SPLA could not hold the town for long. Further, despite Kurmuk, the NSRCC had not renounced the peace process that both sides had vaguely agreed in August should be continued.

In contrast to the thinking that dominated the U.S. Embassy, by November the Egyptian Embassy had few illusions that the NSRCC was committed to peace. The most powerful NSRCC members were NIF sympathizers, the junta's foreign policy was an NIF creation, and government administration was directed by NIF ideologues. Egyptian Foreign Minister Boutros Boutros-Ghali was convinced that the junta posed a greater threat to regional stability than had Sadiq al-Mahdi. British Foreign and Commonwealth Minister William Waldegrave expressed similar concerns. After talks with President Arap Moi, Waldegrave "rejected a call by Sudan's military junta... to put pressure on the SPLA to come to the negotiating table"; claiming that both sides required pressuring, Waldegrave added: "I think our view is that there is no question of Garang being defeated militarily and there is no question but that the issue of Shari'a law and the rights of citizens of South Sudan... must be directly addressed if there is to be permanent peace."[15] Waldegrave's expostulation was precise, to the point, and guaranteed to infuriate.

The Revolutionary Command Council's
Determination to Control

The NSRCC continued methodically to arrest, disperse, and confound its enemies. It extended its control throughout the civil service and purged the military and security forces with ruthless efficiency. It revamped the judiciary and created Revolution Security Courts, which operated little differently than star chambers. Price Courts were created to try merchants for price gouging and to "punish those who jeopardize the State's security and economy."[16] When Sudanese judiciary refused to recognize the legality of extra-judicial tribunals, scores of judges were dismissed. The Executive Committee of Sudan Bar Association and over forty trade unionists were held, as were hundreds of politicians, educators, and civil servants. Most languished in jail for months, and many were tortured.[17] Among those jailed was the former prime minister, whose inhumane treatment included a mock execution. The military tribunals were replaced in October by Revolution Security Courts with civilian judges who were loyal to the NSRCC. They received the imprimatur of Minister for Justice and Attorney General Hassan Ismail al-Beili and Chief Justice Galal Ali Lufti, both militant members of the NIF. Civilians would no longer be tried by military officers, but defense lawyers were given almost no opportunity to represent their clients. Legal appeals had little chance of success. Thus the courts and the independent judiciary, of which Sudanese were justly proud and that every regime had respected to some degree, were summarily buried.

Shortly after the loss of Kurmuk, the NSRCC set in motion one of the most sinister schemes attempted to control the Sudanese since independence. On 6 November the Popular Defense Forces Law was promulgated, creating a Popular Defense Force (PDF). In effect, it legalized the existence of the tribal militias that had brought such destruction and death to the South. Direction was provided by a PDF Council composed of the Army chief of staff, the directors of the police, prisons, and the fire brigade, plus at least one representative of Sudan Security Organization headed by Brigadier Muhammad Al-Sanousi Ahmad but actually controlled by the sinister Major Ibrahim Shams al-Din. Enlistment was "voluntary," and although open to all Sudanese age sixteen or older, the Dinka were not welcome. From district to region a special PDF register was maintained. In Khartoum the PDF would receive three months of training, and Khartoum University students were expected to volunteer or jeopardize the loss of their stipends. PDFs were also to be created in the South, but in Equatoria Governor Allison Magaya later admitted that the PDF law had not been applied because the army "already have militias that work and cooperate with the armed forces."[18] Ironically, what the NSRCC imposed by fiat, Sadiq had failed on numerous occasions to legalize. The creation of a PDF had been rejected by a large number of Umma politicians and by every political party except the NIF. Hassan al-Turabi, who had consistently argued in favor of the moribund People's

Defense Law authorizing a PDF to defend the "homeland and religion," had finally won.[19]

Among the first militia elements to be received by Bashir following the law's enactment were the Fertit of Bahr al-Ghazal, who pledged "their readiness to stand against the rebellion"; they were followed by a Missiriya delegation "representing the PDF leadership in South Kordofan."[20] As the junta began to arm the PDF, it also vetted the old militia. In Muglad and Abyei, where the militia had owed allegiance to Ali Nimr who, in turn, supported Sadiq and the Umma Party, the militias either pledged allegiance to the NSRCC or hid their weapons and assumed a low profile. Brigadier Babikir Abd al-Mahmoud Husayn, commander of the Popular Defense Forces, soon disclosed that PDF units had been formed in many towns throughout southern Kordofan. Recruits received military training and were to represent the second line of defense after the armed forces. Consequently, when the army returned to Kurmuk, the PDF included units from southern Kordofan, whose commander claimed that 2,000 of his men took part in the operation.[21] Indeed, the PDF was expected to take part in any mission "delegated by the Armed Forces Commander," but as far as most observers were concerned, the Popular Defense Forces Law "expanded the violence rather than controlled it."[22] SPLA Radio advised, "Anyone interested in Sudan politics will note that this so-called PDF was the direct creation of the National Islamic Front before Omar al-Bashir took over."[23] Garang called the PDF the offspring of Swar al-Dahab and Hassan al-Turabi and contended that its members would become co-religionists in the NIF's jihad against the SPLA.

Along with the special courts and a Popular Defense Force, the administration of the new Sudan was to be built from the ground up and imposed from the top down. National People's Salvation Committees, or simply Popular Committees (PCs) based on a system employed in Libya by Muammar Qadhafi, would take the place of political parties. The system, which Bashir admired greatly, involved the control of every neighborhood and village by a committee whose membership was based on loyalty to the nation's leadership. The committees did not pretend to be democratic. In Darfur the Fur leadership was excluded from the El Fasher PC; in Equatoria, where a PC made up of 114 members under the leadership of Bernaba Domo began functioning in December, and in Bahr al-Ghazal, where a PC was formed in January 1990, the leadership had a very small political following. By 1990 the NSRCC had a block-by-block spy system at work in Khartoum and Omdurman. PCs were used to effect a January 1990 census of the national capital area during which all citizens were forced to remain at home. Thereafter, throughout Sudan the customarily voluble Sudanese relearned what it meant to live without asking a question or offering an opinion.

Will Operation Lifeline Sudan Continue?

When Operation Lifeline Sudan officially concluded on 31 October, James Grant boasted that the program was both a signal success and a historic breakthrough. The victory declaration was not, however, a threnody for Operation Lifeline Sudan. The program had already gained new life, because the NSRCC and the United Nations agreed that "large scale emergency and rehabilitation assistance would have to be provided to Sudan for some time to come, on a priority basis."[24] In New York Grant had pushed for an OLS II accompanied by a three-month cease-fire to begin in January 1990. The arrangement would permit the realization of Grant's dream—an extensive immunization campaign involving all Sudanese children. In Khartoum the UNDP and UN World Food Program offices had begun to plan for OLS well in advance of Michael Priestley's arrival. The program they devised was quite different from OLS I, since Commissioner Shawki insisted on the inclusion of the Khartoum displaced persons in the calculations.[25] A similar planning exercise occurred in the UN office in Nairobi; when the two plans were matched, the OLS II food aid requirement was only slightly less than the amount delivered in 1989. Significantly, more food was to be delivered from Kenya and Uganda to SPLA-controlled villages in the South (27,000 tons) than to the government garrison towns (20,000 tons).[26] Countrywide the plan called for the delivery of 89,500 tons of cereals in 1990, and a principal component was to discourage the displaced persons from becoming permanent recipients of food aid or, as experienced UNWFP adviser Peter Jobber put it, to "move DP's off the dole." It would be Michael Priestley's task to obtain NSRCC approval and submit the program to the donors by December 1989.

A UN draft proposal was sent to the government on 30 September, but the NSRCC found the proposal unacceptable. The government wanted to increase the food aid delivered to Equatoria and reduce the distribution in SPLA territory. The United Nations complied with this demand, and an effort to advance the principle of parity was written out of the program. OLS II would be difficult to sell, given adequate rains that had led to a good 1989–1990 harvest. The donors were reluctant to fund emergency airlifts, which had been extraordinarily expensive and often entailed a dollar spent for every pound of food delivered. Priestley had already found that the donors were skeptical and he failed to convince them of the need for an interim $20 to $25 million program to transport 20,000 tons of food to large numbers of needy at Yei, Mundri, and Bentiu (controlled by the government) and Abwong (held by the SPLA).

The need remained, however, for a disaster relief program. After the

NSRCC halted food aid flights in November, Radio SPLA asked: "Since the junta has banned the relief flights to the South, with what is it going to feed these people since everybody in Juba depends on food relief? Where is the junta going to get food for these people?"[27] The number of displaced persons receiving a bimonthly distribution through CART auspices had increased from 100,000 in January 1989 to 185,000 in November that same year. Relief agency airlifts rather than government charity had saved Juba as the number of displaced spiraled "out of control."[28] When Brigadier Dominic Kassiano confidently announced that the South had sufficient relief supplies to last three months, the donors knew better. Less than a month later CART warned that its next distribution would exhaust its supplies, and it urged the resumption of airlifts. The junta still refused to allow relief flights other than to government towns, and only Lutheran World Federation accepted this condition and resumed food aid flights to Juba.

In contradistinction, Norwegian People's Aid (NPA) continued its rogue flights of small unregistered and uninsured Relief Transport Services planes into SPLA villages. NPA was providing aid for 100,000 southerners, and the donors found that in Kapoeta, Pibor, Narus, and Torit, where the NPA had been active, there were no indications of widespread starvation or deaths from starvation-related diseases. Egil Hagen and the NPA were the NSRCC's favorite target, but it could do nothing to stop a man some considered a modern reincarnation of "Chinese" Gordon and Dr. David Livingstone, both of whom had marched to the beat of their own drum in support of the needy. The flamboyant Hagen had supplied SPLA villages long before OLS and was the conduit through which Garang's supporters in Kenya had funneled food aid to the rebels. He was also charged with being an instrument of Kenya President Daniel Arap Moi, who in November 1990 categorically denied that Kenya was providing military assistance to the SPLA and, NSRCC claims to the contrary, that he had an interest in "destabilizing the situation in Sudan."[29] Hagen's detractors disliked his contempt for regulations, and he disdained PVOs that would not provide assistance to people in SPLA territory. He despised the lethargic UN bureaucracy that he knew well from tours in Khartoum and Lebanon.

When UN officials began to work on an OLS II program, they faced an uphill battle. Emergency assistance was needed elsewhere in the world, including Ethiopia, where the threat of another famine existed. There was also a pronounced sense of donor burnout, which was exacerbated by the difficulty of working with the NSRCC and the sense that the political, economic, and human rights situations would not soon improve. OFDA had spent more for Sudan—$115 million in food and disaster assistance since January 1988—than it had in any other country in the office's history, but for 1990 it projected only $16 to $18 million to support Sudan's disaster assistance programs.[30] The OFDA funding level was, however, hypothetical because the NSRCC was quickly running out of friends in the United States. Changes in security procedures at the Khartoum airport had severely curtailed the efficiency of OLS operations; travel requests were turned down without reason, as were requests to clear commodities through customs. Security agencies used surveillance on expatriate PVOs, and in September Brigadier Nail Eidam of the NSRCC Security Committee approved a government report designed to restrict their activities. PVOs were required to reregister and to submit forms that included salary data for both indigenous and expatriate employees. The report was especially critical of house rentals, for which PVOs usually paid in hard currency.

As the NSRCC investigations intensified, two employees of Concern were expelled from Sudan for "national security reasons" that were never satisfactorily explained. An MSF-France nurse working in Meiram was picked up because she had a magazine that contained a picture of John Garang. She was held under house arrest for weeks, and no explanation was provided, not even to the French Ambassador. Her confinement was the final insult in MSF-France's interminable battle with Meiram authorities, and the French team discontinued its health program, which had been in place since 1988. An Air Serv helicopter pilot was roughed up and placed under house arrest after he found an army officer rifling through the Air Serv office in Babanusa.

Not surprisingly, the PVOs began to reevaluate their programs and played a cautious rather than their usual aggressive role in meetings held with donors and the NSRRC. They did, however, help to prepare the most extensive nutritional study ever undertaken in Equatoria east of the Nile. UNWFP, PVO, and SRRA personnel collaborated to carry out surveys in sixteen SPLA sites. Field teams found that fish, meat, milk, and wild plants were available in most locations and that serious nutritional deficiencies existed only in Chukundum.[31] The result was surprising insofar as the effort was undertaken just prior to harvest when hunger was traditionally the most severe. West of the Nile nutrition was also generally good. In Yei, where in March 1989 a PVO team had found that 40 percent of the children under age five were severely malnourished, there was "an improvement in the nutrition situation with a malnutrition level of 15 percent" even though the number of registered displaced persons had increased from 50,000 to over 70,000.[32]

By October it was clear that the NSRCC wanted the donors to devote more energy to the Khartoum displaced persons. Surprising the donors, the Commission for the Displaced publicly announced that a survey had located 1.8 million displaced persons in the national capital. The number had enormous significance. It had taken three-quarters of a century for Khartoum-Omdurman to grow from an overgrown village of 50,000 people in 1900 to a conurbation of 1 million residents in 1975. By 1989, over a million children of Southern Sudanese were residing in the capital area. The commission located forty-eight settlements, the largest of which, Zagalona, had 377,000 people—which under normal circumstances would have made it the second largest city in Sudan.[33] The commission's figures generally coincided with data the donors had collected and were the largest ever accepted by the government. Thus, the displaced persons probably accounted for at least 40 and perhaps 50 percent of the population of greater Khartoum.

A UN General Assembly Resolution on 24 October urged the continuation of Operation Lifeline Sudan and required UN officials in Khartoum to submit a draft OLS II proposal to the NSRCC by 31 October. When that day arrived, Priestley had barely had time to organize his staff. He did have a perfunctory interview with Bashir in early October but then spent weeks trying to arrange another meeting. Despite his office, Priestley received only slightly better treatment than Sadiq al-Mahdi; he had not helped his cause when he announced that he would take a month's vacation in December and would hold the UN job for only a year. The activities of OLS I were terminated by a decree from President Bashir, and the junta appeared ready to push an entirely new approach to foreign aid. Although Information Minister Ali Shummo denied vehemently that the government had terminated Operation Lifeline Sudan outright, within hours the government halted all aid airlifts and insisted that the attack by two "unknown" planes on Yirol that had so exercised the ICRC had "created a security situation" that required government measures to protect the expatriates. The NSRCC was resolved to restrict PVO operations and their relief flights to SPLA territory, especially given the arrival of new weaponry including 130 mm artillery pieces and "Stalin Organs" from Libya and the first appearance of white phosphorous and 500-pound bombs. On 2 November Priestley informed the donors that the NSRCC had at last agreed to participate in an OLS II conference, but it would either be held in Khartoum or not at all. The SPLA would not be invited, a condition to which the United Nations acquiesced. Priestley was promised that a senior UN official, but not the Secretary-General, would attend. A conference date was tentatively fixed for 28–29 November.

In New York planning for OLS II was compromised by the fighting that had erupted in Sudan in October, and a November conference date was considered out of the question. UN Secretary-General Perez de Cuellar publicly expressed his concern and personally asked for a cease-fire and the resumption of food movements to the South.[34] The United

Nations was already strapped for cash to continue OLS, and the task of obtaining donor pledges was made just that much more difficult by the warfare. Even worse, Michael Priestley had been unable to form a productive relationship with Bashir or anyone else among the NSRCC leadership. Even though he seemed willing to try anything to ingratiate himself to his Khartoum hosts, the NSRCC never warmed to the UN representative—a fact Priestley admitted during a visit with the SPLA in Nairobi months later.[35] The NSRCC committee created to review OLS II was in no real hurry, and as the army prepared to clear the SPLA from Kurmuk, it began a campaign to clear Khartoum of the displaced southerners.

The issue of the Khartoum displaced persons had preoccupied the junta leadership from the first days of the coup. In November 1989 the government's Commission for the Displaced announced that it had already begun transporting displaced persons in Khartoum to "production sites" at Al-Genaid, Al-Gedida, and Sennar where the government had reported labor shortages. Commissioner Shawki warned the donors (shortly before being fired) that the NSRCC would expect the donors to fund this relocation, a proposition to which USAID-Sudan and the European Community representatives were not adverse so long as the transfer occurred voluntarily and with proper respect for property and human rights. The donors feared they might fund the forced movement of displaced persons and find out about human rights violations after the fact. They soon had more reason to worry. At a 6 November meeting of the NSRCC's powerful Political Committee, which was attended by about fifty government officials, it was decided that a Steering Committee would be created to prepare a National Dialogue Conference on the Displaced, a conference that seemed destined to decide the parameters of an OLS II program.

A worried Michael Priestley was finally granted an interview with Bashir on 16 November. It was an unhappy encounter. Bashir argued that it was illogical to believe that the SPLA had become so strong in Bahr al-Ghazal without donor help through Operation Lifeline Sudan. He added that if OLS II were launched, there would have to be much greater coordination between the government and the donors. Bashir did not think the OLS II conference could possibly be held before January and emphasized that OLS II had to be accompanied by a cease-fire respected by both sides. He then raised a new issue about drought in Kordofan and Darfur and wanted to know what the donors intended to do if an emergency arose in those regions. The interview ended with Bashir and Priestley disagreeing over whether the government had ever approved airdrops over Waat—although the United Nations had received government approval and reported OLS airdrops into Waat, Pibor, and Pochala beginning in mid-June 1989.[36]

The meeting was hardly a success, but the men had much in common. For each the displaced persons were a numerical abstraction rather than suffering human beings made of flesh and blood. Each was more interested in rehabilitation than in food aid, and neither had much use for NGOs or the SPLA. In Khartoum Priestley had the backing of Ambassador Cheek, USAID Director Frederick Gilbert, and virtually no one else. In Washington he had an ally in OFDA Director Andrew Natsios who wanted the displaced persons off relief and into productive activities. Priestley had little rapport with the European Community ambassadors and their aid representatives. The Netherlands, which traditionally had allocated much of its annual development budget to Sudan, had become increasingly disenchanted with the RRC performance and the UN's extravagant financial demands.

Following the Bashir-Priestley meeting, government newspapers reported that OLS II would not only provide food aid but would also rehabilitate educational institutions and upgrade undisclosed water systems.[37] This was news to the donors, but Minister of Information Ali Shummo argued that the Sudan government had fulfilled its promises with regard to Operation Lifeline Sudan and that in the future the donors would have to play under NSRCC rules or leave.[38] The government also pressed the donors (but they would not agree) to place army officers at donor loading points in Kenya and Uganda, and Bashir complained privately that the SPLA did not need donor food because it was receiving supplies from a nearby "friendly" nation. The NSRCC soon made it clear that it would remove the displaced persons from Khartoum and that it wanted food for the drought-affected districts of northernmost Kordofan and Darfur.[39] In the latter case, draconian fuel rationing had reduced to a trickle the movement of food aid to the drought-stricken west, and Darfur families who bought grain at the Omdurman sorghum market spent weeks finding a truck with sufficient fuel to return them and their food to their villages. In response, USAID pledged 5,000 tons of sorghum for Kordofan, and it was expected that the European Community would take the lead in Darfur.

The National Dialogue Conference and Its Failure

As the donors were refocusing on the West, the Steering Committee for the National Dialogue Conference on the Displaced called a meeting of Sudanese experts on 28–30 November to prepare a conference agenda. Of the expatriate aid organizations, only the United Nations was invited

to attend. From the start the meeting was dominated by Islamic fundamentalists, the Islamic Da'wa and the Islamic African Relief Agency. The
committee recommended that Western PVOs be prohibited from implementing projects that directly assisted the Khartoum displaced persons.
The donors, however, would be asked to fund twenty-three projects
costing 232 million Sudanese pounds for the benefit of the Khartoum residents who, the commissioner of Khartoum claimed, "have had to suffer
for too long the presence of the displaced persons in their midst."[40]
Finally, the Steering Committee recommended that the government
begin at once to relocate the Khartoum displaced persons and proposed
the construction of five major camps for the displaced on the outskirts of
the capital well beyond the city limits. As word of the committee recommendations spread through Khartoum, the donors had even more reason
to question if there was a role for them in Sudan.

Both the State Department and Egypt urged the belligerents to continue peace talks when former President Carter appeared in Khartoum in
mid-November en route to Addis Ababa, where he hoped to effect peace
among Ethiopia's warring factions. As a lone dove of peace representing
the International Negotiation Network of the Carter Center in Atlanta,
Carter offered to mediate the dispute in Sudan; to his surprise, Bashir
accepted. Indeed, Bashir had already undertaken a peace offensive of
sorts, which began at a press conference in the Yemen Arab Republic
where Bashir praised the work of the National Dialogue Conference for
Peace and indicated that he had personally approached Egypt to "help
persuade the rebel forces to agree to peace talks."[41] On the southern
front, Brigadier Osman Hassan Ahmad had solicited the good offices of
Kenya's Arap Moi.[42] Carter was convinced that Bashir was honestly
willing to meet with the SPLA "anytime, anyplace" in the search for
peace. Although the junta leader did inform Priestley on 16 November
that there would be a delay in initiating OLS II, Bashir also told Carter he
was ready to continue relief operations to the South—only to contradict
himself a few moments later, indicating he would not continue without
an end to the conflict. Nevertheless, Carter had achieved a success of
sorts. In Khartoum Sudanese media praised the former president's
efforts, and even the military newspaper *Al-Qwat Al-Musalaha* reported
that the government had accepted "in good faith" Carter's intention to
chair a meeting between the belligerents.

On 20 November President Carter met with the SPLA in Nairobi. The
peace effort had stalled, and the SPLA claimed it had been waiting for
nearly three months for an NSRCC response to its four-point program or
for the NSRCC to offer its own program. If nothing else, Carter was a
means by which to communicate with Khartoum.[43] Although the State
Department was somewhat skeptical that Carter might succeed in resus-

citating the peace process, *The New York Times* gushed: "Suddenly, after nearly a decade in the political wilderness, Carter was back and seemingly everywhere, running a kind of shadow State Department with the advice, consent and even encouragement of the Bush White House."[44] The SPLA, already under considerable pressure and considered culpable of reigniting the war by both Cheek and the State Department, agreed to join Carter and NSRCC representatives in Nairobi on 1 December. For reasons that were never made clear, the junta then announced that the SPLA had agreed to a "dialogue without preconditions," which was untrue.[45] The SPLA had not deviated from its proposals that had been tabled in the August 1989 Addis Ababa talks. It had never agreed to an agenda based on the National Dialogue for Peace; thus, each side was operating under completely different assumptions.

On 26 November Carter met with Lam Akol, Major Deng Alor, and Elijah Maluk in Addis Ababa at which time Akol, the SPLA spokesperson, repeated the demands made the previous August: The September Laws had to be frozen, the military pacts canceled, and the state of emergency terminated before a cease-fire could be undertaken by the SPLA. Once a cease-fire was declared, the SPLA wanted to form a broad-based government of national unity, convene a national constitutional conference to debate and resolve Sudan's fundamental problems, and draft a permanent constitution for a united and democratic Sudan. As far as both parties were concerned, Carter would play only a minor role; he would chair the first day of the discussions, and the meeting would continue "without a mediator at the delegations' request."[46]

When negotiations opened in Nairobi, the NSRCC was in an ebullient mood, having just recaptured Kurmuk after a "swift and fierce" battle that was a figment of the government's imagination. Colonel Khalifa reassured Carter that his government had come to undertake serious negotiations, and Carter's trust in the NSRCC seemed vindicated when he received a telephone message from Ambassador Cheek in Khartoum informing him that his efforts to free Sadiq al-Mahdi, Muhammad Osman al-Mirghani, and Hassan al-Turabi had succeeded. Unfortunately, the embassy had failed to verify the news item, which had appeared in *Al-Ingaz Al-Watani*, and only Mirghani (who had suffered two heart attacks while in prison) and Turabi had been transferred to house arrest. Sadiq was only released into house arrest five weeks later.

On 1 December President Arap Moi and Carter addressed the conference participants. Carter reminded the delegations that in 1988 more people perished in Southern Sudan as a result of the civil war than had died in all other world conflicts combined. For Carter, the "basic purpose [of the meeting] was to reach a cease-fire."[47] Colonel Khalifa and Lam Akol then spoke, the latter making it clear that the SPLA would not renounce the Shari'a issue: "We remain committed… to the creation of a united Sudan of peace, justice and equality…. A Sudan in which religion is the individual's moral and personal law and a matter between him and his God…. We believe that religion cannot play a positive role in any state legislation. Besides we trust that, being almighty, God is more than able to enforce his own laws without assistance of human agencies like the police and the courts."[48]

Akol reminded listeners that the peace process had begun with the Koka Dam Declaration, which had served as a base for the November 1988 DUP-SPLA agreement, and argued that if it had not been for the coup d'état of 30 June, Sudan would have entered a period of peace and stability. He openly admitted that the SPLA lacked enthusiasm for the meeting and acknowledged that the two sides would not be meeting had it not been for President Carter.

The participants then met behind closed doors at the Serena Hotel. The agenda was prepared by Carter, and it began with a discussions of the Shari'a. Carter felt certain that if this sticking point could be dealt with successfully, the other pieces of the agenda would fall into place. Discussions would follow on the National Dialogue Conference on Peace, military agreements, the state of emergency, expanding the base of a future government, creating a permanent constitution for Sudan, the role and composition of a national army, the pending constitutional conference, and arrangements for a cease-fire.[49]

From the outset, the issue of the Shari'a proved intractable, and no agreement was reached. No agreement could be found on the future of existing military pacts; the point was "quickly passed over," and the junta "refused to give the movement's delegation a chance to debate it."[50] No agreement was reached on the amalgamation of the SPLA and Sudan army or on the inclusion of democracy in the political process. The constitutional conference and the constitution itself were brought up in passing, and the joint agreement to respect a mutual cease-fire was not even discussed.[51] Both sides did agree, however, that the National Dialogue Conference had provided a number of proposals that they could support. The peace talks adjourned; to put the best possible face on the worst possible outcome, President Carter announced to the press that the government had agreed to the resumption of relief operations in the Southern Sudan and that flights could begin following a conference of the government and donors in Khartoum.[52] Otherwise, he did not bother to hide his disappointment over the failure of the talks. He seemed taken aback when he learned that the government delegation had no authority from the NSRCC to deal with the issue of the September Laws and remained convinced that if the junta had agreed to freeze Shari'a, a cease-fire would have been possible. In a statement delivered to the

press, Carter claimed: "In my opinion, neither side came to Nairobi prepared to take the difficult steps necessary for peace. Sudan government
team was eager for me to help with mediation, but did not have full
authority to make decisions on the key issue, the Shari'a laws. The
SPLM/SPLA delegation had authority, but were not willing to accept
necessary mediation services. Both sides, at the end, seemed ready to
emphasize their differences, postpone further action, and let the war continue."[53]

The SPLA's Lam Akol acknowledged that the talks had collapsed and
felt the differences were so great that it would take a miracle to bridge
the gap. Carter, who at first had received praise from the NSRCC conference spokesperson for handling the Shari'a issue "with profound efficiency and diplomacy" did not remain sacrosanct for long; a week after
the conference concluded, Colonel Khalifa began the process to denigrate
Carter's effort. With no further prospects for peace talks the U.S. State
Department could only hope that the two sides would not stop speaking
to one another. Assistant Secretary Cohen planned to devote more time
to the peace process and to press Mubarak to host a round of talks in
Cairo. All of this appeared a formidable task, for the Khartoum media
had become more strident, declaring the SPLA to be "outlaws" and their
leader "Communist Garang." In return, the SPLA denounced the junta
for portraying it as "anti-Islam" in what it called "a cheap attempt to
arouse Muslim sentiments against the SPLA." Calling Omdurman TV to
account, the SPLA condemned the station for showing themes whereby
"the SPLA had turned the Kurmuk mosque into a stable, and worse still,
they showed the Quran ... being torn and its pages used as toilet tissues.
People who can go that low," the SPLA argued, would go to any lengths
in their propaganda.[54] When neither side demonstrated any interest in
reviving negotiations, diplomats who wanted to move the process
forward found very little room to maneuver. As 1990 approached, the
chances for peace seemed slim.

The Increase of Islamic Militancy in Sudan

When the peace talks concluded unsuccessfully, the NSRCC reacted
by calling for the national mobilization of all able-bodied forces to fight
the SPLA. In Nairobi Colonel Muhammad al-Amin Khalifa was defiant
and announced that Sudan would not "follow the dictates of the West
and the insurgents which oppose the implementation of the Shari'a."[55]
The NSRCC did not even wait for its delegation to leave Nairobi and on
the afternoon of 5 December began an air attack on Waat. At a Conference on Foreign Policy, Bashir advised Sudanese diplomats that the
nation would go its own way and choose its own friends. The friends

were found almost totally within the Arab world and there only among the radical states, Libya and Iraq. The NSRCC became increasingly infatuated with pan-Arabism, the promotion of which began to appear prominently in the Khartoum newspapers with headlines reporting that the government "aspired to set up an Arab State from Morocco to Bahrain."[56] Bashir reiterated pan-Arab themes, emphasizing that "Sudan is an Arab country which supports Arab national unity" and advocating a "preferred" economic association that would include Egypt and Libya.[57]

The junta relentlessly demonstrated its commitment to the political right. It accepted the NIF contention that because "Muslims are the majority," the Shari'a was "the expression of the will of the democratic majority."[58] "The Muslims are Unitarian in their religious approach to life. As a matter of faith, they do not espouse secularism. Neither do they accept it politically. They see it as a doctrine that is neither neutral nor fair, being prejudicial to them in particular: it deprives them of the full expression of their legal and other values in the area of public life, without such detriment to those non-Muslim believers whose creed is exclusively relevant to private and moral life."[59]

The NSRCC totally embraced the precepts of the NIF's Islamic Revolution, especially that which Turabi had called "breaking the Ansari and Khatmiyya clutches on the Muslims of Sudan."[60] By 1990 more than 6,000 government civil servants and nearly 1,000 journalists had been fired and been replaced by Muslim fundamentalists or persons who claimed to be. "Lists were drawn up by fundamentalists spying on colleagues," and in one case a dozen directors of the giant Gezira agricultural complex were discharged because they were known to drink alcoholic beverages.[61] Women in government were singled out and discharged en masse. Sudanese women were no longer free to travel, and a single woman could not travel by air either in Sudan or outside the country unless accompanied by an adult male relative. The NSRCC eliminated all vestiges of Communist Party influence, and it circumscribed trade and professional union activity. Western, or "neo-Crusader," cultural influences were extirpated, and English as a medium of instruction was replaced by Arabic—much to the distress of southerners seeking to attend the University of Khartoum. The media reinforced the policies of the NSRCC and gathered into its fold "what it could among the remnants of *Alwan* and *Al-Raya*," newspapers that had previously been NIF mouthpieces.[62] When asked to comment specifically on the NIF involvement in his government, Bashir claimed he paid no attention to such accusations.[63] When asked about his apparent sympathy for the Shari'a law in Sudan, he avoided the question: "As for my closeness to the Islamic tendency, religious affiliation is a natural phenomenon among the Sudanese, whether Muslims or Christians. Most of Sudan has always been Muslim, even before the arrival of the Muslim Brotherhood. So why these classifications? The main thing is for the Sudanese ruler to be religious and clean, irrespective of his religion, so that he can be an example to his people."[64]

The media was quick to note that following the failure of the Nairobi peace talks, the NSRCC's "relations with Egypt and the West had cooled, mainly over fears that most of the junta's 15 members subscribed to a militant Islamic ideology."[65] Even the Vatican, which had issued a document in February 1989 condemning the imposition of Shari'a on non-Muslims, expressed its concern about the spread of Muslim fundamentalism in Sudan.[66] Although the West remained relatively mute on the issue of Islamic fundamentalism, Radio Moscow warned that peace was losing ground in Sudan and said it was essential that the NSRCC "cool the tension in the southern regions of the country." It was thought that federalism as proposed by the NSRCC could split the country in two, but at least this would permit the South to handle its own affairs, whereas the North could "declare itself an Islamic Republic." Radio Moscow concluded that economic disintegration could "put Sudan in the hands of right-wing Muslims [and] if that happened, the dismemberment of Sudan will be imminent."[67]

In contrast to Moscow, the U.S. State Department seemed unconcerned with the NSRCC's swing to the right, and in its annual review of embassy reporting, it suggested that officers were devoting too much time to providing information on the Muslim fundamentalist proclivities of the NSRCC and other top government officials and were tending to reduce speculation on who was actually running the NSRCC. The SPLA claimed that "a 40-man *shurah*" (Islamic Parliament) composed of Muslim Brothers and conservative NIF and Umma members was orchestrating junta activities "and implementing the program of the [NIF]."[68] The NSRCC also appeared to have close ties with the forty-member *shurah* of the National Islamic Front that under the NIR's constitution directed the operation of the party. At the least there was a group of influential leaders who met daily in a Khartoum mosque after the evening curfew, and many felt the *shurah* was to be more powerful than the NSRCC, which ostensibly controlled military affairs.

By 1990 there were other reports that many of the "shadowy group of 40" civilians belonged to the younger generation of the NIF. Ahmad al-Radi was among those civilians who reportedly played a key role in the *shurah*. A Muslim Brother and secretary for southern affairs in the NIF, he was a Nuba who had worked his way up through the NIF hierarchy to an influential position in the Constituent Assembly in Khartoum. He was known to report directly to Vice President Zubayr and was considered one of the most powerful southerners in the NSRCC. In November 1989 *Africa Confidential* reported that the NIF's Muhammad Osman Mahjoub had become a security adviser to the NSRCC; Mahdi Ibrahim advised the Ministry of Information, and Muhammad Taha was a consultant on international affairs. All were reported to be members of the *shurah*.[69]

The NSRCC approved a law governing charitable donations *(zakat)*, and it created institutions to supervise *zakat* collection and stipulated punishments for persons who refused to pay.[70] The government also began to use the payment of "blood money" *(diyya)* to resolve issues involving crimes between Arabs and other tribes, which avoided the necessity of calling to account the leaders of the Baqqara militia. The *diyya* was even applied as compensation to the relatives of British citizens killed in the terrorist attack on the Acropole Hotel and the Sudan Club in May 1988, which would permit the Palestinians involved to go free. The family of the deceased refused this offer, and the NSRCC postponed the trial until 1990 when, after numerous intercessions by Palestinian Liberation Organization (PLO) leader Yassir Arafat, the subjects received a light sentence. The NSRCC also removed the restraints that had been placed on the use of the *hudud* and permitted the courts to continue the punishments allowed under the September Laws. The ubiquitous Colonel Khalifa informed the Khartoum press that judges were now free to impose the Shari'a punishments as they saw fit because "Sudan is a sovereign country. The era of weakness and humiliation is over. Sudan must apply the Shari'a wanted by the people."[71] According to Minister of Justice and Attorney General Hassan Al-Biali, breathing life into the dormant September Laws was perfectly just because their cancellation would "contradict the demand of the Muslim majority."[72] The application of the laws was "inevitable," and amendments would only rectify "defects" that might have occurred in the drafting of the law.[73]

A lecturer at the University of Khartoum summed up what many believed was happening in Sudan: "It is not any more a question of whether the junta is one of Moslem fundamentalists"; it was only the "question of whether they are entertaining the idea of announcing an Islamic republic."[74] At both Khartoum University and Cairo University in Omdurman, the student union elections were won by Islamic fundamentalists. Not surprisingly, the chair of the Political Committee, Brigadier Osman Ahmad Al-Hassan, while addressing the inaugural session of the National Students' Dialogue Conference on 26 December, had only the highest praise for the students and their support of the revolution.[75] Arab values and virtues were constantly extolled as part of the government's propaganda which included such events as the first Sudanese Arab Day for Illiteracy held on 9 January 1990—although it is doubtful that many Arabs actually favored illiteracy. In Sudanese prisons the Islamic Da'wa was active among prisoners seeking converts to Islam—particularly southerners—and, according to a Sudanese government report, "donating" £S500 to each convert.[76] The Ministry of Education worked closely with the Islamic Da'wa to enhance the importance of the Islamic African Center and its other schools and used the Ministry of Orientation and Guidance to ensure that imams praised NSRCC policies and practices.

The U.S. Embassy in Khartoum discovered that many of the serious human rights violations that had affected southerners during Sadiq's regime continued under Bashir with the refinement of arbitrary arrest.[77] Military authorities in the South and in Darfur continued to detain people who were thought to be SPLA sympathizers without a charge. Perhaps the most vocal critic of the new regime was the International Arab Bar Association, whose secretariat visited Khartoum in October and left convinced that the NSRCC leadership "gave priorities to the regime's security at the expense of Sudanese human rights."[78] Among violations cited were the elimination of trade unions, the massive arrest of trade union leaders, and extra-legal coercion to dominate the judiciary. In response, Minister for Information and Culture Ali Shummo argued that the Arab Bar Association had not observed "its moral responsibility as an association that represents an Arab Nation" and indicated that its report encouraged sedition and anti-Arab feeling.[79] He demanded a retraction, which the association refused to give.

Likewise, the Catholic Church urged the NSRCC to change its policy toward the church, and on 23 November Radio Omdurman broadcast the text of a speech given at a meeting of the Catholic Conference in Khartoum formally asking the NSRCC to respect the activity of Christians in general and of the church in particular. The church protested that "certain areas of Sudan are out of bounds for Christians" and that in some villages Christians were not allowed to pray together. The Catholic Conference also formally objected to the "offensive language" the government media used against it and expressed concern for "the Church personnel who are trapped in the war zones, particularly the case of one of us, Bishop Taban, who had to stay in Torit with the people out of a sense of duty. The captain of the ship must sink with his ship. Their position [could be] misunderstood, and we want to explain that the Church and her services to people know no boundaries. Wherever people are in need, there the Church has to be."[80] The NSRCC was especially unhappy with Taban, who, along with other Christian leaders located in SPLA territory, had created his own regional Council of Churches independent of Khartoum or Juba. The church's plea fell on deaf ears, and the NSRCC was soon denying residence permits to priests and pastors working in southern Kordofan and reducing their freedom of movement elsewhere in Sudan.

Authoritarianism Soon Leads to
Human Rights Violations

When students agitated against the government, harsh reprisals were taken. When about 70 percent of Sudan's doctors went on strike in late November to protest government actions, the government moved swiftly to incarcerate the leaders, insisting that the profession was infiltrated by Communists. Within days a trial was held, with the accused being permitted no legal counsel. Two doctors were acquitted, one was given a sentence of fifteen years for carrying out an illegal strike during the state of emergency, and a fourth was sentenced to hang by a Special Military Court. The fact that the NSRCC was determined to carry out the death sentence galvanized the small community of Sudanese who were concerned with human rights. The United States was quick to protest the trial of the doctors, and a letter from President Bush was delivered through the Secretary-General of the United Nations to Bashir requesting a review of the death sentence given to Doctor Mamoun Muhammad Hussein and informing Bashir that if the sentence were carried out, it would "severely jeopardize" U.S.-Sudan relations.[81] The International Labor Organization contested the sentence, as did the UN Secretary-General, who cabled on 12 December requesting clemency for the doctor. Eventually, his life was saved after Egypt's Hosni Mubarak strongly protested the death sentence during a visit to Khartoum.

On 6 December the clandestine Human Rights Committee for Sudan distributed its first publication in Khartoum in commemoration of the UN Human Rights Day to be celebrated on 10 December. The committee reported that the government was controlling the trade unions by means of a Steering Committee dominated by NIF members. Its reports were circulated throughout the capital, along with a list of 215 politicians, bureaucrats, labor organizers, and southerners who had been arrested.[82] The stories of torture were so numerous and the individuals were so well-known that the atrocities could not be kept secret. Information Minister Ali Shummo denied that torture was employed and said that if it were, he would personally "denounce it."[83] Perhaps the minister's squeamishness was the cause for his replacement a few months later by Muhammad Khojali Salihayn, best known for his defense of the September Laws as Numayri's minister of information.

The NSRCC next arrested many of its enemies in the commercial sector, making a dramatic example of Magdi Mahgoub, a respected businessman and relative of former Prime Minister Muhammad Ahmad Mahgoub, for currency violations that occurred when he distributed to legatees funds bequeathed by a deceased family member. Mahgoub was arrested for illegal trade in foreign currency, tried by a Special Military

Court, and hung on 17 December. The NSRCC next turned to smugglers. Girgis Butrous, a Sudan Airline pilot and son of the Coptic bishop of Khartoum, was charged by a Special Military Court with carrying currency out of the country. Convicted of economic sabotage, he was hung on 16 December. The Coptic community of Khartoum held a silent funeral march through Khartoum to protest the judgment. The NSRCC made no move to disrupt the march, but it did take note of its participants.

Human rights violations were not limited to the more sophisticated environment of Khartoum. Nothing was done to reduce the trade in Dinka slaves in southern Kordofan, although long lists of Dinka children held in captivity in towns and villages circulated in Khartoum and were known to government officials.[84] Southerners had been assiduous in gathering names and calculated that at least 75,000 Dinka children had been sold into slavery in the North. The precision of this number was not as important as the large numbers. When the SPLA moved closer to Kadugli and Talodi, the local Baqqara became even more hostile. When the New Kush Brigade attacked Kadugli in April 1989, more than 250 Nuba were detained without trial. Southerners and Nuba were "perpetual suspects," routinely accused by government security authorities "of being sympathizers of the SPLA."[85] The Nuba, the preeminent warriors of every government of historical Sudan, had throw in their lot with the SPLA and were to suffer for it.

Requiem—the Lagowa Massacre

Although the NSRCC had managed to reduce tensions surrounding the Muglad, Babanusa, and Kadugli displaced persons' camps, the Missiriya still wanted to force the Dinka to leave. In October thousands of displaced persons poured into the camps; west of Kadugli as many as 20,000 displaced persons moved into Lagowa, where the tension between the southerners—Nuba, Nuer, Dinka, and Luo—and the Missiriya was nearing a flash point. It was customary for the transhumant Baqqara and the sedentary Daju to prepare crops on the plains below the Nuba Mountains just prior to the onset of the rainy season in the spring. The Baqqara then moved to northern Kordofan to take advantage of rainy-season pasturage. When the grasslands were depleted, the Baqqara would return to the south to harvest the fields they had planted earlier and to search for available pasturage at the same time the Daju were harvesting their cultivations. In 1989, however, the drought in northern Kordofan caused many Baqqara to arrive near Lagowa earlier than usual, to the consternation of the Daju cultivators. A courageous, professional, and impartial army lieutenant convened a highly charged but traditional conference between Daju and Missiriya leaders from 20–27 October. The conference was adjourned only when the army commander believed the Missiriya would respect the Daju farmland.

The army left on 28 October, leaving behind a sullen Missiriya militia whose commander "had a force of 3,500 strong with which he could wipe out Lagowa town and district in a matter of one day."[86] Two days later a band of Missiriya in Lagowa started an argument with a Nuba woman, killed her father, and sprayed Lagowa with their automatic weapons. Thirty Nuba were killed, and a Camba Nuba quarter was burned. The Missiriya militia, now a mob, swept through the nearby Daju villages, leaving behind their trademark—dead, dying, and burned *tukuls*. When the day was done at least 125 Nuba and Daju had been killed, four Daju and eight Nuba villages were destroyed, crops had been burned, and more than 500 head of cattle had been rustled. A small army reconnaissance unit that stumbled on the atrocities was ready to intervene to assist the Africans but was warned off by the local police. Inevitably, news of the massacre spread, and on 5 November the Khartoum press published a cryptic report that a conciliation conference would soon be held in Dilling in order to ensure the peaceful coexistence of peoples in the area.[87] A week later the press reported accounts of SPLA "provocations" in Lagowa District, but the governor of Kordofan and the Regional Security Committee were there to "contain" the situation.

Radio SPLA thundered: "Criminal elements in El Lagowa took it into their heads that the Government's call for popular defense meant to kill Nubas."[88] When the pillage had run its course, at least 20,000 people were displaced, and Save the Children Foundation–U.K. was asked to help. It requested food through the Relief and Rehabilitation Commission, but when an RRC donor team tried to visit Lagowa District, it was stopped by the commissioner for South Kordofan, Abd al-Wahab—also known as the putative father of the Missiriya militia of Dilling. Abd al-Wahab stripped the doors off the Kadugli Relief Committee warehouse, made off with USAID-Sudan food, and distributed 500 sacks of sorghum to "needy" Missiriya in Lagowa. In December the NSRCC Political Supervisor for Kordofan Brigadier Faisal Medani and General Awadallah Muhammad al-Fatih, the governor of Kordofan, visited Lagowa to investigate and organize a reconciliation conference in El Obeid in January, which provided only rhetoric rather than results.

When the Lagowa massacre was reported in December 1989 by Amnesty International, the London-based group concerned with human rights violations, the organization left no doubt that the deaths of tens of thousands of southerners were the direct responsibility of the Arab militias. Its investigations were meticulous and proved that "mass executions and burning [were among] the methods used to punish and terrorize suspected supporters of the SPLA." The Baqqara militias, were also used to seize pasture and steal women, children, crops, and cattle from the Dinka, and "far from acting against these killings the authorities have deliberately stifled criticism."[89] When representatives of Amnesty International met with members from the NSRCC in Khartoum in December, they were informed that the various killings in Wau had been investigated, but the NSRCC "declined to release the results of the inquiry."[90] Amnesty International did not forget the human rights abuses by the SPLA. Among the charges was that the SPLA "shot possibly hundreds of government soldiers" after capturing Bor in 1989.[91] Surprisingly, the NSRCC never raised the issue of SPLA atrocities, and the SPLA did not respond to the charges made by Amnesty International.

The NSRCC may have been able to ignore Amnesty International, but it was not about to permit the activities of Operation Lifeline Sudan to go unchallenged, particularly when numerous Muslim Brothers and NIF members resented its presence and operations in Sudan. In March 1989 Hassan al-Turabi had introduced legislation that would "control contacts" with the SPLA, whether "undertaken by the Sudanese side or any other organization."[92] After the inauguration of OLS, the National Islamic Front "condemned the government's procedures to safeguard carrying of relief supplies" and objected to cross-border movements of food aid, which the party said, "contradicts [the] presence of a legitimate government."[93] There was constant suspicion in a suspicious land that Operation Lifeline Sudan brought not only food to the rebels but also information and supplies to further their cause. The first official to criticize OLS publicly was Dr. Gassim al-Sid Abu Ghozeiza, the adviser for relief to the NSRCC Political Committee. Abu Ghozeiza used his position to intimidate the Relief and Rehabilitation Commission and to accuse the donors of providing illegal aid to the SPLA. He was primarily responsible for reducing the amount of food relief designated for the SPLA in the UN draft prepared for Operation Lifeline Sudan II.

The Government of Sudan
Seeks to Rid Itself of OLS II

The question of whether donors had been used as cover to move military supplies to the SPLA was alluded to by Bashir shortly after the recapture of Kurmuk, but he had dropped the subject, and it was not raised when Bashir met with Priestley on 4 December. Thus, it was something of a surprise to donors when almost immediately after the meeting the NSRCC began a campaign to discredit OLS. On 7 December Bashir indicated that the continuation of OLS would depend on security considerations and on donor guarantees that relief aid would "actually be delivered to the afflicted." The next day he told Sudanese diplomats that with regard to OLS, his government had "ignored some malpractices," and Colonel Khalifa, who had just returned from Nairobi, claimed that "many irregularities characterized Operation Lifeline."[94] Khalifa added that when the army occupied an area in need of food aid, the relief did not arrive; when the same area was occupied by the SPLA, relief materials reached it in large quantities. He added, "Not only food reaches that area but also arms."[95]

As a symbol of the government's dissatisfaction, on 8 December Kamal Shawki was dismissed as the commissioner of the Relief and Rehabilitation Commission. Although he had frequently infuriated the donors, Kamal Shawki was an honest broker trying to placate two masters—the Westerners, who had both food and compassion for the displaced persons, and his Sudanese superiors, who had neither. Unlike the unsophisticated and xenophobic leaders of the NSRCC, Commissioner Shawki realized how important the United Nations and the donors could be to Sudan, and his arguments that criticism of their efforts would be counterproductive fell on the deaf ears of those who already questioned his political orthodoxy. The first secretary of the Ministry of Relief and a very correct Muslim, Dr. Ibrahim Abu Awf, became the new commissioner of the RRC. In what had become standard operating procedure, Shawki was permitted some weeks of freedom, after which he was picked up in January by security forces when they checked the commission's books for any misuse of commodities or funds.

The United Nations was especially disturbed that NSRCC allegations had surfaced in the wake of a General Assembly hearing that had praised the conduct of OLS participants. When the allegations continued, Priestley lodged a complaint with NSRCC Vice Present Zubayr; when that did not work, the UN headquarters in New York ordered Priestley to deliver a strong letter of protest to Bashir. The letter was prepared and delivered, but UN outrage was tempered by its offer to resume food aid flights and by a pledge to cooperate with the NSRCC to achieve the successful outcome of OLS II. The UN protest, if such it could be called, did not impress the NSRCC. On 17 December Colonel Khalifa reiterated, but never supplied proof, that the junta had uncovered irregularities practiced during OLS; he indicated that the NSRCC had evidence that arms and ammunition sent with relief supplies to SPLA-held areas were later used in SPLA operations.[96]

The next blow to strike the expatriate aid community occurred when an MSF-France plane was shot down by government forces shortly after taking off from Aweil on 21 December. When the NSRCC had prohibited all food aid flights from Khartoum on 5 November, the MSF-France "technical flights" were virtually the only exception to the restriction, and the aircraft was near the end of a flight plan to move personnel and medical supplies from Khartoum to Aweil. The program was funded in part by the AID Office of Foreign Disaster Assistance and only serviced government-controlled towns; the flight itself had received SPLA and junta approval. MSF-France lost three French and one UN Sudanese employee in the crash. It was a great tragedy, because MSF-France was an elite unit made up of highly qualified personnel who had been active in some of Sudan's most politically and socially troubled villages and towns—Aweil, Meiram, Yei. They frequently encountered the hostility of the local and central authorities, but they were quintessential humanitarians. The head of military security in Aweil argued that the plane had crashed on the outskirts of town after being struck by a SAM-7 missile fired by the SPLA; in truth, the 82 Islander aircraft was hit by a missile fired from a location not more than 200 meters from the houses of the MSF personnel. The plane dove out of control and crashed within sight of the Aweil airstrip. All aboard were killed. Since its return to Aweil in December 1988, the MSF-France team had transformed Aweil hospital, vaccinating 57,000 persons against meningitis and establishing a feeding program for more than 5,000 severely malnourished children.[97]

Ironically, it was an incident at the Aweil rice project, which was functioning better than it had in years, that was undoubtedly responsible for creating problems between the expatriates and the local military command. On 11 November a truck packed with rice-field workers exploded a land mine that *the army was aware had been planted under the roadbed*. When a radio report of the mining incident reached Khartoum, the ICRC offered to fly five badly wounded survivors to a hospital in Khartoum, and a flight plan was approved by Khartoum military operations. The flight was then delayed by the chief of military security, who stalled the request for a day. As he explained to his officers—within hearing of donor employees—the critically injured were "only Dinka." MSF-France, which had a flight plan already approved for the following day that would make an intermediate stop in Aweil, was allowed to move the injured (a policeman, two men, two women) from Aweil to El Obeid.

When reports of the mining incident began to circulate in Khartoum, MSF-France was blamed for spreading false information. During Priestley's meeting with Bashir on 16 November, the NSRCC chief stated that a Ministerial Committee chaired by Brigadier Nail Eidam of the NSRCC Security Committee was looking into OLS I and investigating the "suspicious" activities of expatriate donors in Bahr al-Ghazal. The ICRC and MSF-France were the only expatriate operations active in Bahr al-Ghazal; thus both felt they had been unfairly targeted. The fear that the MSF-France team was becoming increasingly isolated worried the MSF-France director, and employees were contacted and asked if they wanted to leave Aweil. None did. Their very success made them believe that their lifeline, the Islander airplane, was inviolable. After all, Colonel Daniel Awet Akot, the SPLA commander for northern Bahr al-Ghazal, had repeatedly promised that his troops would never shoot down a light plane marked with relief insignia.

The destruction of the MSF-France plane was immediately condemned by the UN Secretary-General Perez de Cuellar. The SPLA was not blamed, and it argued: "There is no way that the missile which shot the plane could have been the SPLA's unless the ruling junta wants to tell the world the two warring forces are co-existing in Aweil town."[98] It recalled the November 1988 attack on the plane carrying Defense Minister Khalil from Wau to Khartoum and how military forces inimical to the ongoing peace process had blamed the rebels. The SPLA counted that the junta had shot down the plane "in an attempt to wreck relief work and to justify the Junta's continued ban on relief activities in southern Sudan." The SPLA urged the international community to "demand an impartial investigation into this tragic incident."[99] The SPLA then offered its condolences and expressed the hope that MSF-France would continue its humanitarian work.

The death of MSF personnel was a tremendous blow to PVO operations. So was the government response. On 28 December the Sudanese mission to the United Nations issued a press release regretting the deaths of the three MSF-France personnel and blaming the SPLA for firing "a SAM-type missile [from] their camp within Ariath-Aweil." That same day, a shocked and disturbed diplomatic community and group of donors turned out in force at Khartoum's St. Matthew Cathedral for the funeral of the MSF personnel. As hundreds waited, a coffin being transported by an MSF-France light truck from Khartoum airport exploded en route to the church. The explosion occurred only minutes after the bodies had been transferred from a Red Cross airplane that had flown the bodies from Aweil. The government promptly claimed that the explosion was caused by "a buildup of natural gasses" inside one of the coffins. Dr. Issa Bushra—a practicing chemist, Muslim brother, and Popular Defense Force official—had reportedly utilized the potentially dangerous calcium hypochlorate rather than the innocuous sodium hypochlorate for embalming. Additionally, no one could explain the yellow fireball that "engulfed the rear of the truck in flames."[100] Had the explosion occurred inside the ICRC Beechcraft, it would have been destroyed in flight. The French Embassy stated that a "dry explosive" had been placed inside the coffin or had been attached to it.[101] Nevertheless, its efforts to investigate what occurred in Aweil and at Khartoum airport were at best pro forma, and it did not request an official investigation for more than two weeks. The NSRRC eventually replied that the plane "was downed at Aweil area ... by a Sam 6 missile fired from the Rebel Movement camp at BARIAK."[102] The French Embassy seemed satisfied with the response.

Given the sinister circumstances surrounding the Aweil episode the various MSF withdrew: MSF-Belgium from Darfur, Raga, and Malakal; MSF-France from Aweil, Yei, Tambura, Yambio, Kassala, and Omdurman; MSF-Holland from Darfur, Wau, and Abyei. In addition, AICF prepared to leave northern Sudan. The MSF-France incident was another roadblock to the OLS II process, which was making little headway. The NSRCC seemed in no hurry to move the program forward. As it undertook one maddening review after another, the United Nations was forced to evacuate its monitors from villages in Upper Nile and the Air Serv operation ground to a halt in southern Kordofan.[103] The International Red Cross, which had no friends in the NSRCC, was also forced to retrench because its formal agreement with the Republic of Sudan was nearly over. The frigid atmosphere at RRC-donor meetings disconcerted RRC Commissioner Abu Awf, but President Bashir and Colonel Khalifa continued to claim that "certain individuals" had supplied the rebels with weapons.[104] When the United Nations urged the junta to produce what Khalifa called "irrefutable evidence that arms were being smuggled to the rebels through Operation Lifeline," Bashir responded by reiterating charges that "weapons were reaching rebels in Southern Sudan through a famine relief operation led by the United Nations."[105]

The spurious claims infuriated EC representatives and enhanced their mistrust of the NSRCC. Having spent $55 million on OLS, they concluded that junta policies made the success of an OLS II most unlikely, and the representatives soon became irregular attendees at RRC meetings. In contrast, Ambassador Cheek was less concerned with NSRCC policies; he assured Bashir that the United States did not support any organization that violated donor aid guidelines and promised that if one did so, it would be excluded from aid programs.[106] OLS II, however, was already in serious jeopardy, and in addition to the prevarications, postponements, and rhetoric that enveloped the program, it received an additional shock following the tragic incidents at Jebelein.

More Massacres—Jebelein

Jebelein (Jabalayn), a town on the White Nile 224 miles south of Khartoum, sits amid a fertile region contested throughout the centuries by Shilluk and Dinka from the south and the Arabs from the north. Following 1983, thousands of Shilluk fled to Jebelein from villages along the White Nile and integrated with kin who had lived in the area for many generations. In December 1989 alone, an estimated 40,000 southerners were registered as they settled in or prepared to move northward toward

Renk in search of food and work. Ironically, the NSRCC considered Jebelein an ideal site for the resettlement of Khartoum's displaced persons.

The Jebelein incident was initiated by an Arab landowner who demanded that his Shilluk field hands return to work on the last day of their Christmas celebrations. In the ensuing altercation the *omda* was killed; before the bloodletting was done, over a thousand Shilluk had been slaughtered by Sabaha Arabs. (The Sabaha were an insignificant segment of the Ta'aisha Baqqara who had generally lived on amicable terms with the Shilluk.) The local Sabaha militia arrived in vehicles supplied by local authorities and armed with automatic weapons and even a truck-mounted machine gun. Huts were torched, and panicked Shilluk were mowed down or picked off as they tried to swim across the Nile. The local police permitted the Sabaha to enter their station, and at least 100 Shilluk seeking sanctuary were slaughtered. Within hours a Shilluk settlement of around 10,000 people was deserted. Survivors were "coerced and made to return to their burnt out huts to be hastily thatched by towns people and local authorities. Those huts where bodies had been burnt inside leaving behind indelible fat marks were leveled to the ground by a bulldozer."[107] The dead were buried in mass graves scraped out by the same bulldozer.

Over 1,000 people died at Jebelein, and scores of women and children with severe burns and gunshot wounds were later treated at the Kosti hospital. On 3 January the NSRCC asked USAID-Sudan to provide 3,000 sacks of sorghum ostensibly for 500 families made homeless by the raid; USAID countered that a donor team would have to investigate, and Concern, which was working in Renk, received RRC approval to do so. When Vice President Zubayr arrived by helicopter to inspect the damage in Jebelein, he was enraged to find foreigners in the town and refused to include them in meetings with the local authorities. Zubayr's team concluded that 49 people—eighteen Shilluk and thirty-one Arabs—were culpable of criminal acts and that there was no need for donor food.[108] Eventually, the UN World Food Program provided 300 tons of food aid, but the organization never received an adequate accounting of how or where the food was used because most of it was diverted to the military garrisons in Upper Nile.

The Neo-Crusaders, As So Many Before Them, Are Weary

USAID remained the largest donor of food aid. In December 1989 it had 24,000 tons of sorghum at Kosti and El Obeid and was negotiating a new wheat-sorghum swap with the Agriculture Bank of Sudan. Elsewhere, neither the EC nor the UNWFP had much food. Additional shipments of food to Abyei, Meiram, and Muglad were required; by mid-December USAID sorghum was being shipped to Muglad, where, despite vigorous opposition by Muslim Brothers and South Kordofan administrators, LICROSS had contracted with Fakki Nowatny to move 7,000 tons of food to Abyei.

In Southern Sudan, Juba remained critical because of the sheer number of displaced persons. Market prices for food commodities were very high, and nearly everyone had been made a pauper. Once a displaced person entered the city, escape was difficult because the army controlled the movement across the Nile River bridge into eastern Equatoria and by boat up and down the Nile. Escape to the west was equally difficult because the city was ringed by minefields. Life had ground to a standstill because there was no diesel to run the waterworks.[109] Little firewood arrived from Yambio and Maridi, and the famous tree-shaded streets of Juba were rapidly being denuded. In October CART's food inventory dropped below 4,000 tons, and the seventy cooperatives serving about 38,000 families and even the *jallaba*, were almost out of cereals. No one was starving, but almost 190,000 displaced persons were competing with 150,000 residents for survival. Town residents disappeared, only to emerge in displaced camps, and families began to construct huts inside camps so they could benefit from CART food distributions. Around Juba, agriculture, animal husbandry, and forestry were neglected. In what was a blow to regional pride, the government closed Juba University in October, and only 700 of its 1,500 students transferred to Khartoum.

The UNWFP had succeeded in moving a cross-border convoy of food aid into Yei in October, but there were no plans to continue that dangerous task. When the NSRCC halted airlifts to the South following the fall of Kurmuk, the donors were soon faced with a difficult dilemma because the population in Juba was close to panic. They stopped food aid flights as demanded, but when the NSRCC reopened the South only to garrison towns on 17 November, the donors refused to reinitiate OLS activity unless some form of parity between NSRCC and the SPLA were introduced. Only Lutheran World Federation continued to fly food into the South, and although the State Department did not object to other PVOs flying food to Juba, the United States would not fund the effort. On 20 November CART advised the RRC in Khartoum that it was down to a six-weeks' supply of food.

In December the NSRCC asked USAID-Sudan to fund half the cost of purchasing 1,000 tons of government sorghum from the ABS in Kosti (Canada had promised to provide the other half), which would be flown to Juba. The RRC next approached the donors and, disregarding its own rule that internal freight had to be paid for in hard currency, requested

£S6.5 million to cover internal transport costs. The donors balked on two accounts. First, the purchase price of the grain was too high; second, the air freight cost was half again as high as that paid by Norwegian Church Aid to airlift food from Khartoum to Juba. For once the U.S. Embassy did not aspire to NSRCC approval, and the minister was informed that "a positive decision would be dependent upon a lifting of the ban on relief flights to the south."[110] When the NSRCC received no support, it decided to assume the task itself. It took more than two months to deliver the food; half was given to cooperatives for sale to the public, and much of the rest was delivered to the Equatoria Relief Committee, founded by Military Governor General Allison Magaya; there was never an accounting.[111]

With OLS II in jeopardy, the UNWFP for once held fast and informed the government in January 1990 that it would continue Juba operations only if the government lifted the ban on flights to SPLA territory. The daily ration of cereal per person per day had dropped from 400 to 200 grams, but the WFP had supplies ready in Entebbe, Uganda, that it could commit within a week if the government responded positively.[112] There were only 350 tons of food aid in CART's inventory, and merchants were charging up to 600 pounds a *kilo* (a local measure of about 14 kilograms) for sorghum. Once again, "starving people attempting to leave to forage for food in the countryside [were] turned back by the Army."[113]

NINE

—— ∎ ——

Escalating the War
and Reducing Relief

We will eat what we grow and wear what we make.
—President Bashir at Hasahisa, Sudan, 4 February 1990

With the end of the Nairobi peace talks came the escalation of the war. In Upper Nile bombings began only minutes after the termination of the peace talks in Nairobi, and Bashir promised that the army would soon liberate "every inch of [Sudan] sullied by the traitors and renegades."[1] In December 1989 the government claimed several victories at specious locations, but the army's phantom triumphs were soon overshadowed by an SPLA offensive launched on 31 December. Operation Bright Star under the command of James Wani Igga began with the capture of Kajo Kaji. Kaya was overrun on 14 January 1990, and two border posts, including the infamous trading center at Talata-Telateen (Post 33), fell shortly thereafter. On 17 January SPLA ambushed a convoy moving from Yei to Maridi, and the following day Kaya was captured. When SPLA forces occupying the civilian sector of Yei were unable to dislodge the army garrison across the river, its forces continued west without opposition. Other SPLA units converged on Juba from three sides, but despite the military advantage, Garang declined to storm the city. Instead, the SPLA's notoriously inaccurate artillery opened fire, and seventeen civilians died in two afternoon barrages. Civilians had been advised to keep away from military targets, but there was no escape for thousands of displaced persons whose camps were located near army bases.[2] The bombardment caused consternation among NGOs operating in Juba, although expatriates had been warned to leave the city at the start of the Bright Star campaign and the warning had been repeated by Wani Igga on 27 January.[3] As military aircraft and civilian charters evacuated thousands of military dependents—or anyone who had the £S1,300 or more

267

that it cost to buy a ticket to Khartoum—the NGOs were trapped inside the city. The SPLA approved but the NSRCC stalled a U.S.-U.K. request for a momentary cease-fire. When negotiations dawdled in Khartoum, the expatriates retired to Nairobi on a flight arranged by Lutheran World Federation. Within hours of their evacuation, the army had commandeered food located in CART warehouses.

The SPLA on the Offensive

In December, army forces finally took the offensive when about 3,000 troops supported by tanks and armored personnel carriers moved south from Malakal. Shadowed by SPLA units and ambushed along the way, the column soon ran short of fuel. It lost a major battle at Ayod, then fought an inconclusive engagement near Mongalla. After losing most of its materiel and suffering heavy casualties, it straggled into Juba in late February 1990. In the meantime, the SPLA was active in Bahr al-Ghazal, where commander Daniel Awet Akot's units penetrated Aweil Town on at least four occasions in February and frustrated an army drive toward Akon. In southeastern Kordofan the SPLA's New Kush brigade attacked the army's garrison at Umm Dorein and moved freely through the region. By March, however, both the government offensive and Operation Bright Star had guttered out. SPLA forces surrounded a mechanized infantry division in Yei and both Maridi and Yambio were besieged. In Khartoum, defeat sowed dissension, and Chief of Staff Lieutenant General Ishaq Ibrahim Omar reportedly tendered his resignation following a quarrel with Major Ibrahim Shams al-Din who blamed the general for the losses incurred. General Omar stayed on, but the army replaced General Allison Magaya as military commander for Equatoria. Despite the numerous reverses, Omar bravely announced that 1990 would witness the end of the rebellion in the South. Given the growing SPLA threat, Bashir visited Iraq in late January and returned with the promise that the armed forces would receive military materiel that would "please Sudan's friends and frighten its enemies."[4]

As bullets killed and maimed combatants in Southern Sudan, the National Security Conference on the Displaced, which had been postponed on numerous occasions, was finally convened on 3 February 1990. Conference Chair, Brigadier Osman Ahmad Hassan stated that the government's principal goal was to provide the displaced person with the "basic factors of production," trusting in their ability "to rely on themselves and to contribute to the building of a new Sudan."[5] The displaced would be moved to "production areas," which cynics regarded as the deployment of slave labor on government projects. Brigadier Hassan met with UN officials but did little to clarify the policy. He said nothing regarding the numbers to be moved although the junta had begun a widespread *kasha* campaign and had deliberately, but without fanfare, begun to shift thousands of displaced persons from spontaneous settlements to wastelands south of the Khartoum city limit and west of Omdurman.[6] When the donors refused to fund relocation projects unless they were involved in the planning, the government proceeded without them. USAID-Sudan was especially leery, because it had already encountered problems with a $1 million project involving new relocation sites in northern Kordofan and had been roadblocked by military officials who opposed their construction. In early March, the NSRCC announced the rehabilitation of 770 families in Upper Nile, and the Khartoum media reported that displaced persons willing to return to their villages had left Khartoum railway station on 26 February for the Bahr al-Ghazal.[7] The process of emptying displaced camps was to continue—quietly but ineluctably.

Undoubtedly the most foreboding government policy to be implemented in the capital area was the arming of a Khartoum militia. In February 1990 the junta began to enroll eligible males—excluding all Dinka—in a "Capital Popular Defense Force" designed to provide security in the displaced camps. Inductees were expected to "help in maintaining security in the National Capital," and about 5,000 men and women age sixteen and older were given three months' indoctrination and training.[8] Who was to be made safe from whom was unclear, and southerners residing in Khartoum warned that having an armed urban militia was playing with fire. Predictably, an element of the capital militia was soon involved in a bloody incident. Following an argument over water use at the crowded Souk Markazi displaced persons' settlement, an armed Nuer "militia" killed more than a score of Dinka, and neither the police nor the military intervened. The junta promised that the incident would be investigated, but the UN World Food Program found that the Commission for the Displaced and the Khartoum commissioner were "continuing to place people in the [Souk Markazi] camp, with plans to remove all displaced to sites outside of Khartoum at some later date."[9] Meanwhile, the PDF continued to grow. When 2,000 students from Khartoum University were sent for training in April, the University of Khartoum was adjourned. By summer the NSRCC had formed a militia that, the SPLA argued, would soon be "pushed to the front to form a human shield intended to absorb initial SPLA fire."[10]

Operation Lifeline Sudan II in the Line of Fire

In October 1989 satellite imagery confirmed predictions of a sharp decline in cereal production in Darfur and Kordofan. Pasturage was scarce, and the Baqqara were moving their herds south. Minister of Finance Zaki commanded donors to "take all necessary steps" to meet the government demand for 100,000 tons of food aid. The EC rejected the demand outright, and an NSRCC-Donor-UN team that visited the West in December estimated that Darfur would need only 3,750 tons of food aid and Kordofan 11,500 tons.[11] The team found that even though the harvest was below average, the regional price for cereals remained stable. Thus USAID-Sudan pledged 5,000 tons of sorghum for northern Kordofan, and the EC offered the food it had stored in Darfur as a strategic reserve. The tepid response was a sure indication that the donors were tiring of emergency relief programs and were unhappy because PVOs had been straightjacketed. Military security had impeded their travel in Kordofan, jeopardizing MSF, Concern, and LICROSS projects. In Kadugli District, projects had been halted after the commissioner for South Kordofan expelled PVOs from Kadugli, Anglicans from the Nuba Mountains, and Catholic priests from Dilling, Kadugli, and Babanusa. Although the NSRCC had once used its good offices to obtain visas, travel permits, and other needs, the Commissioner for Khartoum, the commission for the Displaced, and Sudan Security were rarely helpful. Security officials were deeply suspicious that the expatriates were in Sudan to spy, subvert, or proselytize. It was clear that rather than force the expatriates out by fiat, the junta would strangle them with red tape and harassment.

When the junta spurned a proposal to move 4,500 tons of food aid to Aweil by train—a commitment to which EC participants attached great importance—the EC reconsidered its funding levels and demonstrated lukewarm interest in both Western relief and OLS II. USAID continued to ship food to southern Kordofan, and in a district short of fuel and a region where promises were often broken, Fakki Nowatny moved sorghum from Muglad to Abyei as long as USAID funded the operation and provided the diesel fuel. The program was, however, one of the few bright spots in Sudan. In the South relief workers warned in January 1990 that "tens of thousands of people could starve" because the NSRCC was "delaying a relief program with near-impossible conditions." Grain production in Equatoria had been only 20–40 percent of the normal amount in 1989, and agricultural activity was termed either "impossible or very insignificant."[12] Inside Juba, fuel shortages drove relief aid costs ever higher, and the CART budget was severely strained just at the time its principal funding agent, the European Community, was reducing its budget for Sudan.

As the NSRCC procrastinated in its review of Operation Lifeline Sudan II, the AID Office of Foreign Disaster Assistance became daily more frustrated with Sudan government. Like the EC, AID-OFDA had begun to earmark funds to support a relief operation in Ethiopia, where drought had caused an estimated 90 percent shortfall in food production in Eritrea, Tigray, and Wollo provinces. Given conditions in Khartoum, USAID-Sudan itself was unsure whether it would reduce its staff to the bare minimum or continue to fund the half dozen personnel involved in the OLS relief effort. After having provided $325 million for disaster relief since 1984 and more than $250 million in development and human-itarian assistance since 1987, AID had reason to expect that USAID-Sudan representatives would be treated with common courtesy; instead, they were largely shunned in the OLS II process. By the time military intelligence, the NSRCC Technical Committee, and the NSRCC itself had approved the draft for OLS II, it had undergone substantial changes—none of which had been discussed with the donor community.

In Washington, the U.S. Congress was becoming increasingly suspi-cious of NSRCC intentions. In January 1990 Steve Morrison, an experi-enced U.S. Senate staff member, visited Khartoum to prepare for congressional hearings on Sudan scheduled for March. He found that Ambassador Cheek had already informed members of the NSRCC Politi-cal Committee that the United States would not sit back and watch people starve and that it was prepared to provide food aid to besieged government garrison towns regardless of what the other donors did. Despite the best arguments of the International Red Cross and some U.S. NGOs for a strong diplomatic effort to allow the displaced persons in the government garrisons to return to their villages, the State Department refused to criticize NSRCC policy that held hundreds of thousands of dis-placed persons captive. Unlike the West German Foreign Ministry, which complained that the NSRCC had failed "to produce a strategy for peace" and had begun to reduce its aid contribution, the State Department still wanted an OLS II program on any terms.[13] USAID-Kenya reported in January that only Norwegian People's Aid and World Vision were trans-porting food to SPLA areas, but the State Department was not interested in locating other agencies to work with the SRRA. Thus, Morrison left Sudan aware that OLS II was suspect, but he worried that a catastrophe similar to that which had occurred in 1988 was building in Aweil and other southern garrison towns. The State Department suggested and the U.S. Embassy agreed that a letter from President Bush to Bashir demon-strating U.S. concern might move OLS II along more rapidly. The letter was prepared, but despite Cheek's request for a meeting with Bashir, several weeks passed before he was granted an audience on 16 February. Bashir appeared open-minded yet noncommittal.

Ironically, *The New York Times* had claimed only days before that "the United States, the chief financial backer of last year's United Nations relief effort, appears virtually impotent."[14] When all U.S. foreign aid except for humanitarian assistance was cut off to Sudan on 28 February 1990, the NSRCC responded with fury. The media was uniformly critical and rejected what was called a U.S. attempt to impose on Sudan a "policy of humiliation." The European Community received similar treatment after France, the United Kingdom, the Netherlands, and West Germany all reduced aid because of the NSRCC's failure to end the civil war, its alleged human rights violations, and its inability "to resolve long-standing problems with the IMF."[15] Human rights organizations mistrusted the NSRCC; at a March 1990 hearing held by the Select Committee on Hunger many PVOs agreed with Roger Winter of the U.S. Committee for Refugees that the future of international relief for Southern Sudan was doubtful.

Despite the growing antipathy toward NSRCC policies, in New York the pressure built within the UN system to move forward with OLS II. In Washington Andrew Natsios, the new director of AID's Office of Foreign Disaster Assistance was consumed by neither Sudan nor OLS. AID-OFDA had numerous demands on its limited budget, and as Natsios was aware, with or without an OLS II the USAID-Sudan mission had 40,000 tons of food aid stored to meet emergency needs. USAID-Sudan's requirement for local currency to pay transportation costs was surmounted when AID-Washington shipped 100,000 tons of wheat to Sudan and in exchange received its cash value ($20 million) in Sudanese pounds—albeit at the unrealistic official exchange rate of £S4.5 to the dollar. In February USAID-Sudan's 1990 program to transport 20,000 tons of food aid to displaced persons' camps in northern Bahr al-Ghazal and South Kordofan was nearing its goal. In Nairobi USAID-Kenya had swapped U.S. wheat for 17,000 tons of local maize and beans for delivery to southern Sudan, and that program was underway. Like U.S. Ambassador to Sudan James Cheek and USAID-Sudan Director Frederick Gilbert, Natsios held little sympathy for the SPLA; after a visit to Khartoum in early March 1990, he developed a visceral dislike for the NSRCC as well.

Natsios, most USAID personnel, and PVOs all believed an OLS II program would fail given the NSRCC's repressive political agenda, and PVOs were convinced that the NSRCC wanted an OLS II only for its propaganda value. The junta continued to contest the neutrality of both Western food aid and PVO activity, and it appeared unwilling to reopen the neutral Corridors of Tranquility, which had been the outstanding characteristic of OLS. In Kordofan, where PVOs provided food aid to more than 70,000 displaced southerners, an NSRCC-sponsored regional "dialogue" held in January 1990 urged greater state control of PVO operations and the expulsion of all foreign Catholic missionaries.[16] The PVOs were squeezed out of South Kordofan, and Sudanese military blocked PVO efforts to create new and improved displaced persons' camps in

North Kordofan. Cheek, whose knowledge of Ethiopian politics was much greater than his understanding of Sudanese realities and NSRCC aims, was convinced the PVOs were overreacting. He met with leaders of the international aid community on 12 March, and after absorbing a litany of complaints, he was never again as optimistic that an OLS II program would succeed. Nevertheless, Washington supported the continuance of OLS, and even though Natsios appeared ready to reduce substantially OFDA activity in Sudan, after discussions with Cheek he bowed to State Department policy and proclaimed his support for OLS II.

The Sudan Government Proclaims
Self-Sufficiency in Food as Its Highest Priority

Among the myriad "national campaigns" the NSRCC would initiate in 1989 and 1990, the drive to achieve self-sufficiency in food production was undoubtedly the most important. Wheat imports had increased dramatically in response to domestic demand, and Sudan had used the United States and Saudi Arabia to supply its annual deficit of the more expensive grain. This situation galled the NSRCC. In July it reduced the subsidy on wheat bread and increased its price from fifteen to twenty piasters per 140-gram loaf; in October the loaf was reduced to 120 grams and the price raised to twenty-five piasters. When the 1989–1990 grain harvest promised to be less than expected, on 31 October, the government suspended sorghum exports. Exceptions were made, however, and sorghum and edible oils located in Port Sudan and inventories held by brokers possessing valid export permits were allowed to deliver outside the Sudan. As the economy continued to deteriorate and the NSRCC scrambled to obtain hard currency, it issued export permits for more sorghum than existed in Sudan. Exporters, anticipating that the junta would one day nationalize the grain trade, shipped all the grain they could obtain.

To combat a habitual food grain deficit, in January 1990 the NSRCC made the near-term elimination of wheat imports a national goal. "Self-reliance and the liberation of the national will" would be of fundamental importance, and cereal self-sufficiency and growth in the amount of exports were considered essential components of national well-being.[17] The NSRCC Economic Committee ordered an increase in wheat cultivation (to 630,000 acres), and the president kicked off a national self-sufficiency campaign. Bashir informed cotton and cereal farmers that the government would execute the slogan "to eat what we grow and wear what we make" and, in a speech abounding in xenophobia, called for increased productivity to "preserve the honor and dignity" of Sudan.[18] Rallies were then held in Darfur where Bashir reiterated the themes of self-sufficiency and national salvation. The people were told, "Because we do not want to beg for our food, and we do not want the relief agencies to humiliate our dignity; through you the homeland, and through your production, we will rid ourselves of this bitter humiliation."[19] In speeches at El Fasher, Geneina, and Nyala, Bashir derided the need for *igatha*—a local term that referred directly to donor-derived food—and left no doubt that the NSRCC wanted to dispense with expatriate food aid. With Bashir insisting that the NSRCC would practice what he preached, Darfur was thrown into a panic. Residents remembered and were thankful for the foreign aid they had received, especially during the 1984–1985 famine, and Bashir raised concern at a time when North Darfur had just suffered a calamitous 1989–1990 harvest. He promised to deliver 50,000 tons of grain to make up Darfur's existing food deficit, but when February turned to March and no government food arrived, village officials were convinced the NSRCC would do nothing. When concern became too vocal, the NSRCC warned Darfur (and the rest of Sudan) that it would not tolerate the complaints of "defeatist voices."[20] Ironically, sorghum still moved from Gedaref to Port Sudan, and 1990 food shortages were caused by the export of huge stocks of grain while precious foreign exchange was spent on weaponry from China.[21]

Operation Lifeline Sudan II
in a Different Environment

An OLS II conclave was finally convened in Khartoum on 26 March 1990. It received none of the fanfare that had characterized the OLS conference in March 1989, and as one journal remarked: "It is striking how little noise has been made about the second phase of a program whose first part the UN loudly trumpeted as the salvation of hundreds of thousands of starving Southerners."[22] The meeting was a pro forma exercise to which the SPLA was not invited. A handful of donors, with varying degrees of apathy, agreed to support a program that would cost a hefty $118 million and entail the delivery of 103,000 tons of emergency relief food. OLS II would include a Western Relief Operation and would fund projects to assist the Khartoum displaced persons. The Ministry of Relief requested funds for pilot projects whose vague "relocation and income-generation schemes" smelled of forced reallocations. Ideally, OLS II would assist at least 4.5 million people—2.2 million people in the South, 400,000 southerners in the North, 1.6 million Khartoum displaced persons, and an undetermined number of people in northern Darfur and Kordofan. To ensure that the program got off to a fast start, the United Nations included all food aid distributed *since 1 November 1989*, in its calculations for OLS II. Thus, of the 103,000 tons of food programmed, *well over half* had been distributed or consigned.

Following the OLS II conference in Khartoum, Michael Priestley met with the SPLA in Addis Ababa. His reception was frigid, because the United Nations had been very slow to respond to Garang's requests for food aid for the 150,000 displaced persons generated as a result of the rebel's Bright Star campaign, which had begun in November 1989. More important, the SRRA was incensed that its 1990 food aid forecast had been halved; OLS II had programmed 73,000 tons for NSRCC programs while apportioning only 19,000 tons for SPLA sites. Nonetheless, the SPLA swallowed its disappointment and rescinded its threat to boycott OLS II as long as it was "coupled simultaneously" with a UN assessment of the South's "actual needs."[23] The nutritional situation in SPLA territory had improved significantly, and the 1989–1990 harvest in the South had been good. The SPLA speculated that its emergency food needs would be met and asked donors to earmark more funds for development projects.

OLS II began on 2 April when a UNICEF plane carrying seeds, tools, medicines, and UN personnel left Lokichoggio, Kenya, for Bor. Simultaneously, a UN World Food Program aircraft took off for Juba, where 300,000 people remained almost totally dependent on airlifts. The flights were an unhappy reminder that during OLS I, the donors had transported 40 percent of all food aid by air at an average cost of $700 a ton. They did not want to continue expensive airlifts when more efficient means of transport were available—but Juba was always the exception. In the North, where transport was hampered by frequent fuel shortages, the OLS II–Western Relief Operation for Darfur and North Kordofan were very slow off the mark. Despite exorbitant transport costs per ton, USAID-Sudan continued to support the Kordofan program, even though one witness found that some food aid had gone "to the relatively well-off who fed the grain to animals while others, the truly needy, received far too little, and continued to starve."[24]

Ironically, although the OLS II program began very slowly, a UN program to provide food aid to drought-ridden Ethiopia received substantial international support. Both the European Community and the United States diverted personnel in Khartoum to help create relief corridors and coordinate the movement of food aid from Sudan into Eritrea. For months thereafter, the U.S. Embassy in Khartoum considered the Ethiopian relief effort as important as, if not more important than, OLS II, and representatives of a variety of Ethiopian rebel forces friendly to the NSRCC (and not so friendly to the SPLA) were welcomed by Ambassador Cheek at the U.S. Embassy.

Elsewhere, the UN's Michael Priestley, who was already a pariah in the eyes of much of the NSRCC and SPLA hierarchy, continued to blunder. He obtained SPLA approval to *airlift* 400 tons of food to the growing number of displaced persons in Yambio, only to find that the NSRCC would not go along with the plan. When Priestley then decided to move the commodities from Uganda along the Yei-Maridi road without first obtaining SPLA clearance, the rebels found out what was afoot and warned that they would attack any overland convoy that might relieve the government garrison at Yei.

Despite UN pleas, OLS II was born underfunded and continued that way. Donors did not immediately step forward to fund the $31 million UNICEF component of OLS II, a large part of which was spent in Khartoum. In May UNICEF director James Grant "went public" at a press briefing at UN headquarters in an effort to move the OLS II program along. He beseeched donors for funds to assist 4.5 million people, mostly women and children. Grant pointed to studies of the Khartoum displaced persons, whose horrific data indicated that nearly a quarter of the children under age three were severely malnourished, two-thirds of Khartoum families lived in unsanitary conditions, and almost 90 percent of the displaced children did not attend school.[25] Khartoum was indeed a horror, but Grant neglected to state that Western PVOs who attempted to work in Khartoum were shunned by government agencies (Ministry of Health, National Urban Water Corporation, Commission for Khartoum, Sudan Council for Voluntary Agencies) and indigenous aid agencies (Islamic Da'wa, Islamic African Relief Association). In fact, only twenty-three international relief agencies had been registered by the government—a decided diminution from OLS I, when the Ministry of Social Welfare had quickly registered eighty-two voluntary agencies that were avid to work in Sudan. And despite NSRCC promises, by June only one PVO had succeeded in exchanging money at the favorable rate (12:1) the government had promised all OLS II participants.

Human Rights Violations in Sudan
and the International Response

Although the State Department tended to powder over the NSRCC's many blemishes, the junta was branded by an Africa Watch report that claimed it had "embarked upon the repression of political opposition in Khartoum on a scale never before seen in Sudan." The human rights organization added that "the outside world has yet to realize that it is not dealing with pragmatic soldiers, but with a ruthless and intolerant regime following an ideology of Islamic fundamentalism."[26] The NSRCC junta had forced the resignation of Sudanese Red Crescent Society lead-

ership; the society itself—a nonpolitical institution that had been officially recognized by the government of Sudan in 1956—was thoroughly
cowed, and its board of directors was captured by Muslim fundamentalists. On a national level, the Ministry of Orientation and Guidance and
the proselytizing Islamic Da'wa worked hand in hand, and the enhance-
ment of the latter's work in Kordofan was termed an essential task to be
supported by regional officials.

Despite Bashir's claim that the junta was not composed of "crazy
people" and that NSRCC officials were responding to "a war situation"
involving "people who seek to undermine the government," the junta
became daily more repressive.[27] An April coup attempt was put down
with unexampled savagery. People's Committees intruded into affairs of
ordinary Sudanese citizens, and the junta began to increase the number
of People's Defense Forces that were under arms, forecasting that by
mid-1991 it would be able to call on more than 150,000 armed Muslim
vigilantes. As violations mounted, in June the European Parliament
issued a resolution urging members to suspend all program aid to Sudan
and to freeze all discussions of economic development programs.[28] It also
called for the release of all political prisoners and a return to democracy.
The European Community response was a major blow to the minister of
finance and Sudanese economy. The impact was lessened only slightly in
July when the IMF granted Sudan an additional three-month grace
period to institute economic changes before a high-level IMF delegation
visited Khartoum in September. Meanwhile, the NSRCC was working on
a three-year economic plan and a 1990–1991 budget that the government
promised would move Sudan out of its "state of deterioration" and
would gain IMF approbation.[29] Despite a change of ministers of the
economy, this was a forlorn hope.

In late spring 1990, the United Nations and PVOs began to receive
reports from a variety of sources that thousands of Khartoum displaced
persons were making an effort to return home. AID-OFDA investigated
the reports and found that the government had initiated a controversial
program designed to move 50,000 Khartoum displaced persons to the
South. (Southern leaders reported that it was in fact 50,000 families, or
about 300,000 people.) According to an AID-OFDA report, "The military
reportedly used intimidation tactics to force many of the displaced out of
Khartoum. Furthermore, the GOS attempted to lure displaced southerners by promising them assistance from the international community once
they returned to the south; such promises had not been agreed to by the
international community."[30]

One plan advocated by NSRCC member Brigadier Pio Yukwan
entailed the return of 35,000 displaced persons to Bentiu and 30,000 to
Mayom. As potential returnees were being rounded up (including indi-

gents in jail), Khartoum received a new report that Dinka were returning to the south through Abyei, South Kordofan. Displaced persons who passed through military checkpoints at Abyei village were stripped of their belongings and charged a fee of thirty pounds. Jane Perlez of *The New York Times* (who, unlike USAID-Sudan officials, could not be prevented by the U.S. Embassy from visiting SPLA sites), visited SPLA-controlled Akon in Aweil District and reported in early July that UNICEF had determined that about 60,000 Dinka had already returned to northern Bahr al-Ghazal. Perlez reported that the government "was forcing tens of thousands who fled to Khartoum from the south to return home." Consequently, in Akon food supplies were greatly reduced by their unexpected arrival.[31] The fact that such a large movement of people had gone unremarked resulted in part from the severe reduction in the number of relief workers in South Kordofan and northern Bahr al-Ghazal.

After a good start, the spring rains failed in much of Sudan. The SRRA reported that a "mass population movement" of displaced southerners had resulted after the government spread rumors that the United Nations was delivering food "to all war-affected areas of south Sudan."[32] Thousands appeared at Leer, in SPLA-held western Upper Nile, where the SPLA reported that their numbers included "some of the 40,000–60,000 families" who had returned from the north to the Akon-Mayen Abun area of Bahr al-Ghazal between December 1989 and April 1990.[33] The NSRCC eventually admitted that it "was helping" about 190,000 displaced persons to return to the South, but Pio Yukwan denied the claims of human rights violations and statements that coercion was being used to force the return to Bahr al-Ghazal.[34] Nevertheless, by mid-1990 a stream of southerners was again on the move, and thousands of displaced persons from Upper Nile and Bahr al-Ghazal arrived at the Itang refugee camp in Ethiopia.

With an economy that few thought could get worse deteriorating, with the loss of freedoms and human rights suffered under the NSRCC, with OLS II in a muddle, with the reoccurrence of food shortages in the South, and with indications that the early rains had failed in the West and hunger had begun to stalk that region, *The New York Times* asked in June 1990: "What does it take to get the United States Government to express revulsion and horror?" It argued that Washington had "expressed only perfunctory concern about Sudan ... where a wave of political terror has claimed doctors, lawyers, journalists, poets, and trade unionists." It also argued that with Qadhafi's connivance, "an Islamic fundamentalist regime now foments civil war and tribal massacres."[35] The State Department did indeed leave the impression that it was coddling a repressive regime but justified its silence as the price to be paid for saving lives that might otherwise be lost. As the State Department became more defensive, a department source commented that its critics "have their opinions, but often it's pretty contradictory, like telling us to make sure the food moves and to get the government in Sudan to help, but at the same time telling us to condemn the government publicly as a bunch of brutal fundamentalist thugs."[36] Still, for more than nine months the embassy downplayed the role of Muslim fundamentalists who fed upon the NSRCC corpus, and well after such leanings were made pellucidly clear and human rights violations had been pyramided, the embassy muted its criticism of what nearly everyone outside the NSRCC agreed was indeed a government of brutal fundamentalist thugs.

The State Department would have been forgiven if a peace agreement could have been brokered to end the civil war. Despite the failure of the December 1989 Nairobi peace talks, there was substantial international interest in continuing the process. Thus, very quietly and nearly simultaneous with the OLS II initiative, the State Department commenced a two-track initiative: Politically, it supported the efforts exerted by Egypt's President Hosni Mubarak, in his capacity as chair of the OAU, to initiate peace talks in Sudan; economically, Ambassador Cheek informed Sudanese press that the United States was ready to help solve Sudan's economic problems if Sudan reached agreement with the IMF or the World Bank to initiate long-overdue economic reforms. The NSRCC was offered a new $20 million wheat deal on very favorable terms. The West was, however, unable to wean Bashir from his fundamentalist advisers, and a Western diplomat foretold correctly that Mubarak did "not want to be dragged into active mediation in a Sudanese civil war.... He knows that if he does he runs the risk of monumental failure."[37]

To escape the dilemma, Mubarak enlisted Zaire's Mobutu Sese Seko to take charge of negotiations. Mobutu met separately with Bashir and Garang in March, and in April a personal representative of the Zairian president indicated that a conference of Sudanese would soon be convened. Mobutu had in fact been a key player in March 1990 when Assistant Secretary of State for Africa Herman Cohen tabled a new Sudan peace plan that called for a cease-fire, following which a multinational force was to be interposed between the belligerents. Next, a conference with no set agenda would be convened, and the two sides could take as long as necessary to negotiate their differences. The United States left little doubt that it supported the re-creation of a federal Sudan and that it would provide generous support to rebuild Sudan once the civil war was over.

Neither side rejected the Cohen initiative outright, but there was significant disagreement with regard to the Agreement on a Framework for the Peaceful Settlement of Sudan's Conflict that he had tabled. Although it agreed to consider a federal system of government, the SPLA insisted:

"Sudan will remain united in a multi-national and multi-religious state. There shall be no discrimination among the citizens on the basis of race, religion, sex or area of origin."[38] The NSRCC, which returned its comments to the State Department in early April, accepted four fundamental principles but rejected one outright—the multiparty democracy the SPLA wanted. With regard to the Modalities for Disengagement of Forces in Sudan, the NSRCC objected to the use of international monitors to ensure a disengagement of military forces. In May Ambassador Cheek met with Bashir to discuss NSRCC objections and, most important, NSRCC opposition to the interposition of a multinational force to keep the peace. The NSRCC argued that it did not want to internationalize the problem and that if it thought it necessary to do so, it would only accept forces from a neighboring country or those provided by the OAU.[39]

Cohen then met with John Garang in Nairobi and found that the SPLA would accept a supervised cease-fire and the use of a multinational force as long as all government troops were "pulled north of the 13th parallel." The NSRCC rejected the condition and in turn demanded that the SPLA "consolidate below the Bahr al-Ghazal, Bahr al-Arab, Sobat River Line" and demilitarize parts of Kordofan and Blue Nile "contested by SPLA forces."[40] The SPLA rejected the demand, particularly because its hand had been strengthened following a major victory at Melut, Upper Nile, which threatened barge traffic on the Nile and sorghum production near Renk.

In June Bashir finally rejected outright the State Department's mediation, and a plan that Colonel Khalifa once described as commendable was now termed "this strange proposal calling for withdrawal of Sudanese government forces from [their] own territory." The NSRCC discontinued discussion of what it called a furtive effort "to internationalize the south Sudan question."[41] Within hours two government planes bombed Torit killing twenty civilians in a crowded marketplace. Bor, Yirol, Akon, and Waat were bombed repeatedly by TU-22 bombers, causing scores of civilian casualties. The SRRA claimed, and, ironically, the Khartoum media agreed, that the bombing had a simple objective—"to stop the ongoing relief effort" in the South.[42] To express its indignation the U.S. Embassy sent no representative to gatherings celebrating the NSRCC's first anniversary. In return, no NSRCC member attended the embassy's Fourth of July celebration.

As the political climate darkened, by June 1990 Western private voluntary organizations were on the defensive, and their presence in western Sudan was greatly reduced. Regional insecurity, brought about by battles between the forces of Chad President Hissene Habre and Chadian rebels operating from Darfur and supported by the NSRCC and between the Fur and their Arab attackers, was an important aspect of the problem. In the latter case, representatives of Africa Amnesty International and Africa Watch warned that "two particular ethnic groups, the Dinka and the Fur, have been targeted by General Bashir's junta for extinction. Though the circumstances for the two groups are different, the common themes between the two are that they are both non-Arab and large enough groups to be considered a threat to reactionaries like Bashir to what he would consider 'his people'—fundamentalist Moslem Arabs."[43]

Without aid agency presence in the field, reporting on incipient famine conditions in Sudan's far West was greatly restricted, and travel permits to and from Darfur were almost impossible to obtain. By May the scarcity of grain forced the price of sorghum upward until it surpassed £S300 a sack in El Fasher; the price spiral spared neither Darfur nor any other region. To ensure the availability of bread in Khartoum, the junta contracted for 155,000 tons of Saudi Arabian wheat at a cost of $25 million—payment in advance. The arrangement was kept quiet, but Khartoum did not suffer from bread shortages, and the NSRCC continued to trumpet the virtues of self-sufficiency.

The End of Operation Lifeline Sudan II

In May 1990 the AID-financed Famine Early Warning System (FEWS) reviewed remote sensing data for Africa and alerted Washington that farmers in western Sudan would be particularly vulnerable in the coming months. It had calculated that there had been an unexpectedly large—1.2 million ton—cereal shortfall in the 1989–1990 harvest year, and reserve stocks from the previous and more productive years of 1987–1988 and 1988–1989 had been seriously depleted. USAID-Sudan once again offered a swap of wheat for sorghum, but Agricultural Bank of Sudan stocks were minimal and no exchange could be made. FEWS warned of a budding catastrophe, but the only NSRCC response was to alert Sudanese that "they might well have to sacrifice food and health [to assure the] fight to the finish" with the SPLA.[44] People's Committees and their "salvation" subcommittees were "imposed on villages from outside to supplant local leadership," and they took charge of the distribution of food aid.[45] In North Kordofan, where USAID-Sudan was in the process of trucking 2,000 tons of emergency food aid, the military governor ordered CARE—one of the last of the major PVOs to operate from Khartoum—to turn over USAID commodities to "his agents," after which it was allowed "to conduct un-targeted general distributions."[46]

In June 1990 the prospect of a satisfactory harvest appeared so unlikely that the NSRCC strategy of domestic self-sufficiency in food grains was badly damaged. In the major production areas of northern Sudan, the rains arrived fifty to sixty days late, and insufficient rainfall in eastern and central Sudan necessitated massive replanting. OLS II also limped along in the South, where the government had roadblocked UNWFP attempts to move food overland from Kenya and Uganda. In June the United Nations was forced to resume its on-again, off-again food airlift from Entebbe, Uganda, using prohibitively expensive aircraft chartered from the Sudan government. By midyear, not one OLS II food target had been met, even though the UN office in Khartoum claimed that "60 percent of relief food requirements for government areas and 50 percent of relief food needed for SPLA-held areas [were] either in stock or delivered."[47] More to the point, nearly half of the percentages claimed were in stock and were *yet to be delivered*. By August OLS II was moribund.

Sparse August rains were followed by searing heat in the Sahilian belt from Darfur to the Red Sea hills, and FEWS reported that in the mechanized farm sector—the crucial breadbasket of Sudan—the harvest would be less than normal. The Sennar and Gedaref mechanized farming areas were unusually dry, as was the Gezira scheme, where only 2 million of 2.7 million acres were expected to produce a crop.[48] In Khartoum a new tide of displaced persons appeared, and for the first time since an NSRCC crackdown in July 1989 cleared Khartoum's streets, beggars appeared in the capital. During August the market price of sorghum rose by 30 percent per week at Gedaref, and the number of traders active in the local suq doubled from 150 to 300. Khartoum middlemen, many of whom were fronting for Feisal Bank and Baraka Bank, were active purchasers; indeed, both banks seemed poised to use the drought to achieve huge windfall profits—just as they had in the disastrous 1984–1985 harvest year when Khartoum's Faisal Bank cornered the critical sorghum market at Gedaref. With grain prices moving sharply upward, the NSRCC intervened in September and forced traders to register their sorghum stocks with the market authorities and then to sell their sorghum to the government.[49]

The cycle of drought and famine was about to be repeated in Sudan, but the government collected only 65,000 tons of grain from traders and owned little more than 125,000 tons as an emergency reserve. NSRCC intervention was unable to slow the price spiral, and the price of sorghum rose to unprecedented heights in the capital's wholesale markets and on the black market. The NSRCC sought foreign aid from reluctant Arab states, refined its nascent three-year development plan, and mortgaged its cotton crop for the next two years. Meanwhile, FEWS warned: "We may be seeing the initial stages of a major, nation-wide food crisis of 1984 proportions in Sudan."[50] At midyear the food supply situation in the Sahilian belt was so precarious that the civil war and the possibility of drought in the South were largely forgotten. In mid-August

AID-OFDA reported that with the exception of western Equatoria rains were inadequate throughout the South. Hundreds of thousands of displaced persons were already seriously at risk, and food aid inventories in Juba and Wau were dangerously low. In Malakal about 100,000 displaced persons were in desperate need of food, and the UN's Michael Priestley sought unsuccessfully to gain NSRCC approval to move barges loaded with food aid that were standing by at Kosti. Although the SPLA had long agreed not to attack barges on humanitarian missions (a promise reiterated during Priestley's visit to Nairobi in July 1990), Malakal had not received a single food aid barge in nearly a year. The army, which had suffered a series of defeats in battles between Renk and Malakal, continued to use regional security conditions to block the movement of food aid. As fighting spread through Upper Nile, military officials wanted no expatriates to report on the large numbers of displaced persons who had begun to flood into Renk from Malakal and Upper Nile villages, and they forced the departure of the last of the expatriate PVOs working in government towns south of Kosti.

In SPLA-held Kapoeta crops were desiccated, and seed distributed under OLS II was destroyed when sparse rainfall was followed by very high temperatures. When the rains completely failed in northern Bahr al-Ghazal, the donors worried that crop and cattle losses could result in a repetition of the massive loss of life that had occurred in 1988. The issue that perfectly limned the deterioration of aid donor–NSRCC relations involved the International Commission of the Red Cross, the most scrupulous of all aid agencies, and centered on the *Red Cross II*, a million-dollar barge the ICRC had shipped to Bor. The barge could haul sixty tons of cargo and was programmed to move along the Upper Nile and through the Sudd and to provide food and other aid to civilians found in villages under SPLA control. The NSRCC, however, claimed its actual purpose was to transport supplies to the SPLA and absolutely refused to permit its use in Sudan. The ICRC had already used a smaller barge operating from Bor and thought there was no need for NSRCC clearance.[51] The junta thought otherwise and ordered it to move to Juba or Malakal where the army could sequester the vessel. The SPLA wanted the barge to remain at Bor, and it pressed the ICRC to begin operations because the onset of summer rains, infrequent as they were, had closed the truck path between Torit and Bor.

The ICRC decision to dry-dock the barge at Bor until it received NSRCC approval for its work pleased no one. When the possibility of famine in the South grew, the ICRC sought to escape the impasse by donating the barge to the UNWFP—which wanted nothing to do with what was proving to be an expensive misadventure. As the SPLA became progressively more angry, the NSRCC decided to settle the issue by sinking the barge. In September repeated air strikes failed to destroy the vessel but managed to kill and wound civilians. For the ICRC, which had gained NSRCC approval to begin an airlift in what would be a desperate race to provide food to the 100,000 displaced persons in Malakal, it was painfully clear that it could neither work with nor continue to suffer the junta's indignities. It had attempted to revive the concept of food aid neutrality; it had failed, and it prepared to leave Sudan. When neither USAID-Sudan nor the European Community would touch the airlift unless it was matched by one that would benefit the needy in SPLA-controlled territory, the UNWFP was forced to take over the Malakal operation.

Elsewhere in the South, warfare added yet another dimension to the problem of food shortages. Thousands of families had chosen exile rather than return to Yei, Maridi, Yambio, and other villages under siege by the SPLA. As siege warfare and skirmishing continued in Equatoria, thousands of displaced persons streamed toward Zaire. The aid agencies that continued to work in the South were nearly overwhelmed by the dimension of the displaced persons problem yet Lutheran World Federation continued to fly food to Juba, and east of the Nile, World Vision and Norwegian People's Aid persisted in their work with the SRRA. By September more hundreds of thousands of Sudanese were on the march. In Ethiopia the UNHCR counted more than 430,000 refugees in its four Sudanese camps, and new arrivals claimed thousands were on the way. In the North the number of displaced persons in Kosti reached 100,000, and a large percentage of those arriving were malnourished. There were reports of starvation deaths in the Red Sea hills, and the scarcity of food in northern Darfur and Kordofan was daily more apparent. Yet even as the drought worsened, the government continued to ignore the situation—just as Sudanese President Jaafar Numayri had in 1984 and President Sadiq al-Mahdi had in 1988.

In October 1990 OLS II was officially terminated. Although UN agencies had begun to consider an OLS III, donor petulance ensured that such a structured program would be unlikely. Only half of the OLS II budget had been pledged by a donor community that was increasingly skeptical of NSRCC humanitarian and political aims. The United States provided $10.4 million in disaster relief aid and $24 million in food aid, but the AID-OFDA program soured when the relationships between the NSRCC and Western PVOs became openly antagonistic. Aid workers (now virtually *personae non gratae*) and diplomats (including U.S. Ambassador James Cheek) were denied travel permits to visit drought-stricken areas. Unappreciated and unwanted, expatriate aid organizations were forced to confront the moral dilemma of whether to remain in Sudan or to leave. Only the possibility of yet another massive famine in 1991 restrained them from leaving. Indeed, Western experts were postulating that Sudan would require more food aid in 1991 than the amounts provided through OLS I and OLS II combined. FEWS analysts even suggested that Sudan might require more food aid than the total amount delivered during the gigantic Sudan Western Relief Operation of 1984 and 1985.

The Ambiguities of the Gulf War for Sudan

Any U.S. participation in an OLS III seemed moot once the NSRCC gave its support to Iraq following the August 1990 invasion, conquest, and assimilation of Kuwait. Nevertheless, as the U.S. State Department sought to quarantine Iraq and its allies, USAID-Sudan continued its disaster relief program. Meanwhile, Sudan was isolated politically when, as a member of the Islamic Conference Organization, it abstained on a vote supported by forty-five Islamic states that called for an immediate Iraqi withdrawal from Kuwait. In supporting Iraq, the junta virtually ended any hope of maintaining cordial relations with Saudi Arabia, the Gulf Coast states, and Britain—all of which "washed their hands of Sudan." Egypt officially suspended its support for mediation efforts to end Sudanese civil war and for a time closed its airspace to Sudan Airways. Sudan economy was buffeted when Saudi banks demanded "iron-clad guarantees for loans and concessionary funding" from their own government before they would consider loans to Sudan.[52] Most important, with up to 750,000 Sudanese expatriates working in the Gulf states—including 15,000 Sudanese in Kuwait alone—as tens of thousands returned to Sudan the crisis cost the NSRCC as much as $1 billion a year in lost hard-currency remittances.

The decision to ally itself with Iraq created a deep fissure within the NSRCC, and council hard-liners berated their southern colleagues for their lack of enthusiasm for Iraqi leader Saddam Hussein. In September there were reports of a stormy NSRCC meeting during which some members sought "the reversal of the junta's support for Baghdad."[53] The hard-liners won out, and subsequent reports regarding divisions within the NSRCC were more smoke than fire. Sudan was not ready to dump Iraq, an ally that along with China and Libya, had been the NSRCC's principal source of arms and financial support. A grateful Iraq sent ten planeloads of arms to Sudan, after which Bashir undertook a "secret" trip to Baghdad, ostensibly to thank Saddam Hussein for the donation to the Sudanese war effort. Most important, because Sudan's support of Iraq created a rift with Libya—Qadhafi had opposed the Iraqi invasion—the NSRCC began to seek out a more dependable source of military hardware. In December 1990 Bashir visited Iran, praised its Islamic revolution, and admitted "we have, in practice, started the islamisation of the life of Sudanese people"; when Iran agreed to provide arms and to support the NSRCC in its war against the SPLA, the budding relationship was seen as "the most important new foreign factor in Khartoum," and one that ruled out any chance of negotiations with the SPLA.[54]

The NSRCC support of Iraq's brutal occupation worsened an already unhappy relationship that existed between donor nations and aid organizations. The U.S. Embassy eschewed its customary timidity in the face of NSRCC provocations, which in turn led critics to note that "the State Department, exhibiting no shame for its past position, has done an about-face and has become harshly critical of the Khartoum regime."[55] It was only a matter of time before the embassy's relations with the NSRCC turned frigid. When drought and war produced a dramatic increase in the price of cereals in Khartoum, a determined minister of commerce ordered the sequestration of all food stocks held outside government warehouses—including those of USAID-Sudan. In September USAID food being shipped to the West had been halted, and some of its sorghum had been forcibly seized in Kosti. To protest, Ambassador Cheek met with Minister of Commerce Farouk al-Bushara Gadeir, but their meeting concluded in an undiplomatic shouting match. Within hours Cheek and the UN's Michael Priestley met with Bashir to protest the government's seizure of USAID food and, tangentially, the NSRCC's tepid support for OLS II. The meeting proved unsatisfactory on a number of counts: Priestley had been instructed by UN Secretary-General Perez de Cuellar to ask Bashir to explain the attempted bombing of *Red Cross II* carried out between 20 and 24 September, which had killed numerous southerners and endangered UN personnel and aircraft. Priestley added that if the junta wanted to relieve the pending massive food deficit, the NSRCC would have to acknowledge publicly that the possibility of a famine existed in Sudan. Bashir responded that the United Nations had misinterpreted the situation in Bor and the West. Ambassador Cheek then protested government actions to seize USAID relief food. The president brushed aside the complaint, terminated the discussion, and suggested that Priestley and the ambassador discuss their problem with Sudanese Relief Commissioner Abu Awf, who had been present at the interview.

Immediately following their meeting with Bashir, Cheek and Priestley met with Awf. Cheek insisted that the government had seized USAID food and that if it was not immediately returned, the United States would freeze all food shipments to Sudan and suspend consideration of any further relief for 1991, including emergency programs.[56] Priestley, whose assignment in Sudan was nearing an end, and who was still fuming because Bashir had brushed aside the UN protest, discarded the cloak of ultra civility and the policy of appeasement he had used since his arrival in Sudan. He openly berated the NSRCC (and, thus, Bashir) for claiming Bor was off-limits to OLS II. Priestley argued that the air force bombings had introduced "a new and very dangerous element" and added that "even John Garang warns us to stay away from an area which [is] unsafe for security reasons."[57] Awf, like Bashir, gave Priestley no satisfaction, and the unlucky bureaucrat left Sudan aware that he had been frustrated whereas his predecessor, James Grant of UNICEF, had enjoyed success with OLS I.

After his meetings with Bashir and Awf, Cheek urged Washington to halt all food shipments to Sudan until there was "complete restoration" of USAID control of 40,000 tons of food the junta had "seized."[58] On 28 September Cheek left for Washington to brief the State Department, which issued a statement condemning the wave of bombing attacks on southern villages; it noted: "Our Ambassador in Sudan has raised these bombings with Sudan's President al-Bashir, but has received no assurances they will stop."[59] At State Department insistence AID-Washington diverted 45,000 tons of wheat already bound for Port Sudan; at Kenya about 25,000 tons were diverted for Ethiopian famine relief, and 20,000 tons were swapped for Kenya maize to be transported cross-border to the needy in Southern Sudan. Bashir denounced the United States, and the diversion was termed a form of "silent political pressure" and an "economic blockade."[60] Sudanese minister of finance argued that USAID-Sudan had received Sudanese currency in payment for the wheat diverted from Sudan and that the United States had thus expropriated Sudanese property.

Much legal haggling followed, and anti-American demonstrations orchestrated by the NSRCC led the British ambassador to recommend that the dependents of British families leave Sudan. It was difficult for British or other expatriates to imagine that relations would soon improve as long as the government-controlled media published headlines such as "Death to America Should Be the Motto for Every Muslim," which preceded one article about the Gulf crisis.[61] In the end the NSRCC emerged victorious, because it had actually deposited £S110 million in the USAID trust fund in expectation of the future delivery of 90,000 tons of wheat. The United States was faced with the embarrassing choice of providing the wheat or repaying the cash, and since Sudanese pounds were badly needed to pay local expenses and food aid transportation costs, a new shipment of wheat was entransit. Ironically, it was barely noted in Washington that despite the furor over food aid, neither the State Department nor AID was willing to shut off aid to Sudan: On 1 October soon Cheek issued another official declaration, this time authorizing the continuance of disaster assistance in fiscal year 1991. Given its problems with the

NSRCC, this apparent non sequitur was dictated by USAID fears of an imminent and widespread famine in Darfur and Kordofan.

Famine, Starvation, and Government Indifference

A FEWS evaluation produced in October 1990 indicated that crops had failed in Umm Keddada, El Fasher, En Nahud, Umm Ruwaba, and Bara districts and that extensive crop losses were expected in Nyala, Mellit, and Soderi. A UN-FAO field survey, also carried out in October, predicted that without multinational assistance, 5 to 6 million Sudanese could starve in 1991. In Washington the reports were taken very seriously, as was the possibility of at least a 1-million-ton shortfall in Sudan's 1990–1991 grain harvest.

Internally, the small USAID-Sudan food stock, which the government had finally relinquished, was committed to northern Kordofan, and the other donors had virtually no food supplies. "The responsibility and burden of food aid" had been handed over to USAID "by default," and in response, AID indicated that it would consider favorably a formal NSRCC request for $150 million in food aid that, given the reluctance of other donor agencies, would provide the "kick start" for a 1991 relief program.[62] To get the ball rolling, AID-Washington offered to provide immediately "up to one third (not to exceed 100,000 metric tons)" of emergency food aid. So the United States could avoid being the donor of "first and last resort," AID-Washington began the "long and complicated task of getting other donors on board."[63] For a change, Ethiopia had just harvested a good crop of sorghum, and although there was some need in Eritrea and Tigre, the UNWFP attempted to purchase some food in Ethiopia for rapid shipment to Sudan.

In the South, a pocket of drought was located in the area surrounding Mayen Abun, Bahr al-Ghazal. To the east, drought in Upper Nile had been followed by flooding in Nasir, Akobo, Waat, and Kongor, and displaced southerners who tried to escape the drought by walking to refugee camps in Ethiopia found themselves trapped by rising rivers flowing out of the Ethiopian highlands. By November, UN analysts felt that in a worst-case scenario, drought could have a direct impact on as many as 11 million people—or about 40 percent of the population of Sudan—three-quarters of whom lived in the North. The UN predicted that in 1991, Sudan would need at least 1 million tons of relief food—most of which should be delivered before the spring rains. Such a prospect was, however, pure fantasy because the Sudanese transportation system was incapable of handling that amount of tonnage even if the NSRCC agreed to such a mammoth food aid program. For USAID the reduced PVO presence made distribution even more problematic, particularly because the government's own Relief and Rehabilitation Commission had been relegated to bureaucratic irrelevancy.

Despite its warnings, AID-OFDA was baffled by the NSRCC's blasé response to a late October FEWS report that warned that as many as 8.9 million Sudanese could be at risk in 1991. The junta seemed utterly unconcerned with either the shrinking number of friends it had in the international community or the impending famine in the South and the West.[64] Satellite data and the UN-FAO harvest assessment were ignored, and Abu Ghozeiza, NSRCC adviser on relief aid, predicted in November that Sudan would produce a grain surplus. Minister of Agriculture Ahmad Ali Geneif declared that there was no famine in Sudan, and Minister of Finance Abd al-Rahim Hamdi asserted that the harvest was normal and that the government had never requested assistance to confront the famine, as "antagonistic Zionist circles claimed."[65] On 3 November the government's nascent English language newspaper, *New Horizon*, proclaimed that there was "No Famine in Sudan," and international relief agencies were blamed for causing Sudan's food shortage. The agencies were unjustly accused of making large purchases of domestic sorghum.[66] The editor of *Al-Sudan Al-Hadith*, Al-Naguib Qamr al-Din, summed up the junta's attitude toward the *khawaja*: "Sudanese people are smart enough to understand that most of the relief agencies have religious objectives and many of the Western agencies understand relief as offering assistance to the rebels in southern Sudan. It is not beyond the Sudanese people's intelligence to know that the problem of the South would not have been so aggravated if the Western agencies had not supplied [the SPLA] with the means of subsistence and added fuel to the fire in the form of arms, ammunition and food."[67]

On 5 November President Bashir denied the possibility of famine in Sudan and accused the Western media of tarnishing Sudan's image.[68] Regardless, and NSRCC rhetoric aside, the prospect of widespread famine, starvation, and death was inescapable; in November the NSRCC's representative at the United Nations quietly appealed for the urgent delivery of 75,000 tons of food to drought-stricken areas.[69] The State Department acknowledged that there were "conflicting views from Sudanese officials" but said it was making its own plans to deal with the drought. The department concluded: "We continue to believe that prompt action by Sudanese Government is needed in order to avoid another major human tragedy."[70] In sum, the NSRCC might obtain food aid, but it could not secure the donors' trust, which, like sorghum in Sudan, was in very short supply.

In November the government trumpeted its self-sufficiency campaign and announced that more than a million acres of wheat would be cultivated in Sudan in 1991. Still, there was virtually no sorghum to be had on the open market, and its price at the important Omdurman *suq* had soared to unheard-of heights, which prompted the NSRCC to seize grain from farmers. When the NSRCC found that such measures were counter-productive, particularly when the shortage of sorghum became apparent in Khartoum, the Ministry of Commerce announced that it would not interfere with the marketing of the 1990–1991 crop. The movement of grain between regions was permitted, but a total ban on sorghum exports remained in effect. Meanwhile, the numbers of destitute increased dra-matically, and the flux of dispossessed continued. In November it was reported that "even the birds have moved south" from northern Kord-ofan, and Soderi, a town of 20,000, was nearly deserted.[71] Carcasses of dead cattle littered the road from Soderi to El Obeid, and at El Obeid itself the arrival of thousands of displaced persons had drastically reduced the city's water supply. When reservoirs and wells ran dry, water had to be trucked from the Nile. Where the displaced persons congregated, severe malnutrition was found. When Kordofan Governor and NSRCC member Colonel Faisal Medani Mukhtar openly objected to NSRCC policies in the face of an impending crisis, he was placed under a form of house arrest until he was judged to have regained his composure.

The Destruction of Hillat Shook

In the midst of famine, and despite the number of accusations holding it responsible for human rights violations, the government decided in November to level the notorious displaced camp for dis-placed Southern Sudanese at Hillat Shook. Located a few kilometers south of Khartoum's international airport, the camp had been built by waves of Shilluk and Dinka who with patience, perseverance, and adapt-ability had spent years constructing a small city atop a garbage dump. It took a joint army-police crew just three days to tear it down. Bulldozers cleared the area of *tukuls*, and fires were set to the mounds of rubble. A clinic, schools, a church, and a chapel were leveled, and the 35,000 inhab-itants were forced at gun point to pack their belongings or have them destroyed on the spot. Some displaced persons managed to settle in other displaced camps that ringed the city. Hundreds of mothers who escaped the roundup became indigent beggars throughout the capital, seeking food and collecting scraps of material for a new shelter. At least 5,000 people, mostly women and children, were piled into vehicles and driven to the Jabal Auliya "resettlement site" thirty miles south of Khar-toum, where they were dumped in a desert wasteland with no shade and little ground cover and only a single small tank to hold water. They were soon joined by another 5,000 displaced persons who had been forcibly removed from settlements in Khartoum. The United Nations called the

Jabal Auliya site unsuitable for settlement, but Brigadier Pio Yukwan assured the donors that NSRCC motives were "purely humanitarian" and, despite complaints, that water was "abundant."[72] In fact, it was a very long walk to the Nile bank. In addition, there was no fuel, food, housing material, or administrative support, and the NSRCC left the provision of such services to the Western relief agencies.

Hillat Shook's destruction was hardly surprising, because the NSRCC had advertised its determination to rid the capital of as many displaced southerners as it possibly could. It was the prelude to a campaign to raze similar sites. In the end, hundreds of thousands of displaced southerners were forced onto wasteland camps located well beyond the capital's city limits or to ephemeral "peace villages" in Upper Nile and Kordofan. The NSRCC assumed that Western aid agencies would take up the responsibilities for feeding and resettling the displaced persons in locations miles from any work and where the cost of a bus ride to work was beyond the means of nearly everyone. Left without hope, the displaced people deserted government camps by the thousands, some returning to Khartoum and some returning to the South (which was what the NSRCC hoped would happen).

As the NSRCC was losing friends at home and abroad and actively sponsored the mistreatment of its Southern Sudanese citizens, SPLA leader John Garang went on the offensive, both diplomatically and militarily. He reaffirmed the SPLA's commitment to the principles of Operation Lifeline Sudan and the peace process and strongly supported a three-month Period of Tranquility in Sudan during which UNICEF would be allowed to vaccinate Sudanese children against childhood diseases. Radio SPLA flayed the NSRCC for rejecting the peace initiative and offered to disengage for a long enough period to provide time to negotiate a cease-fire. The NSRCC responded by blaming the war on the SPLA, and both sides continued to fire verbal blasts. Neither side was ready for peace, and in November the SPLA began its third successive dry-season campaign. Daym Zubayr, Bahr al-Ghazal, was captured, as were posts along the Central African Republic border. In a surprising development that was probably more an issue of greed than of political conversion, the government-armed Fertit militia in Bahr al-Ghazal joined the SPLA to capture Raga and Kafia Kingi in southern Darfur. In December Bazjia located fifty miles south of Wau, was overrun, and the SPLA even penetrated the predominantly Dinka ward of Nazareth on the southern outskirts of Wau. By 1991 all of Bahr al-Ghazal except Aweil, Wau, Rumbek, and Tonj was in SPLA hands. Donor food for the displaced persons who had congregated in Aweil continued to rot on the railroad siding at Muglad, where the local militia and the regional military commander opposed its departure.

In Equatoria, Yambio and Nzara were captured in late December and Source Yubu, a garrison town on the Zaire-Sudan border and the geographical center of Africa, was taken on 2 December. Tambura fell five days later and Maridi shortly thereafter. The army was left with only Juba and Yei and both were besieged. In effect, the SPLA had reached its apogee after more than seven years of civil war. In response, the NSRCC resumed its tactic of bombing SPLA towns, particularly Torit. Food aid flights continued to land in Juba, where the indomitable Lutheran World Federation provided food for the 250,000 displaced persons packed into the city's camps. The ICRC had finally given up its effort in the South after it was informed that all flights to SPLA-held villages had to land at the Juba airport and be cleared after NSRCC inspection. It was the last insult the institution was prepared to take, and it reduced its staff and prepared to leave Sudan. Unlike Equatoria, Upper Nile was relatively quiescent. In just a few months, famine had driven more than 100,000 southerners north to Kosti, where military security had made life so difficult for MSF-Holland that the relief agency was forced to leave the displaced persons camps it had served faithfully since 1988. By December the Malakal displaced persons, who numbered more than 100,000, had run out of food, and there were reports that thousands more were walking toward Renk.

The Frustrations of the Humanitarians

Even given the plethora of human rights violations, limitations on personal freedoms, and Sudanese willingness to support Iraq in the face of a number of UN Security Council resolutions condemning the invasion of Kuwait, the United States was still unwilling to make a clean break with the NSRCC. Although it was ready to attack Saddam Hussein and was preparing to attack Iraqi troops in Kuwait and Iraq, the State Department handled the Sudan situation very gingerly. It had no intention of giving any Muslim nation cause to say that U.S. policy toward Sudan was symptomatic of a pervasive anti-Arabism. In late November AID-OFDA reevaluated requirements in Sudan and estimated that the country would require a minimum of 500,000 tons of food aid in 1991. In New York the Sudan mission to the United Nations announced that the government's food strategy for 1991 was to import as little food as possible and to increase the wheat harvest on mechanized farms. It was wishful thinking, but at least the Sudanese pledged before UN agencies that donor supplies would be delivered in a "just and equitable manner."[73]

Despite the foreboding that existed in the West and in military reverses in the South, on New Year's Eve 1990, Bashir announced the creation of a federal system of government. The new Sudan would be composed of nine states (including Khartoum State), and Shari'a was imposed as the law of the land—albeit with every state given the right to exclude itself from the unwanted consequences of "any religious laws."[74] The NSRCC thus ensured the dominance of Shari'a in the nation's capital and made all Sudanese residents subject to Islamic law regardless of their wishes. The junta retained the three political units in the South—Bahr al-Ghazal, Upper Nile, and Equatoria—but the SPLA complained that they were "in effect Islamic federal states" because political power in each resided in the "hands of Muslims" who were NIF members or affiliates.[75] In southern states the governor was a figurehead; the real power resided in Muslim appointees to the posts of a deputy governor in charge of fiscal and economic affairs, the minister for state government, and the minister for education. The NSRCC aim was clear: It would impose upon the South the will of the Muslim North. In so doing it exploited tribalism and made it difficult for southerners to re-create a single political unit. As a result, southern separatists were more certain than ever that the South should seek a destiny independent of Khartoum.

The new year also began with a FEWS prediction that a shortfall of 1.2 million tons of cereal grains would allow the NSRCC to "satisfy only 63% of its food needs in 1991."[76] Still, despite foreign policy differences and the harassment of Western aid personnel and their Sudanese employees, the international donors had pledged 313,000 tons of food aid. Unfortunately for the needy, pledges were one thing but the commencement of the UN's Operation Desert Storm and the battle for Kuwait was another. On 16 January USAID personnel were evacuated from Khartoum, and nearly forty expatriate UN employees were sent on furlough; the following day a UN force began its attack on Iraqi forces. With the Gulf War raging, the NSRCC could no longer depend on the West to make up its cereal deficit. It doubled the price of a 120-gram loaf of bread, and sorghum merchants and farmers were given a week to report their holdings. Stockpiling was prohibited, grain movements within the private market were restricted, and farmers were required to sell the government three sacks of grain per acre cultivated. Consequently, the sorghum trade was driven underground, and within days the price of sorghum doubled on the black market, soaring to £S3,200 per sack—as opposed to £S300 in May 1990 and the official price of £S700 fixed on 1 January 1991. Fuel was severely rationed, and in late January a fifty-four-gallon drum of diesel fetched £S10,000 on the black market. Tangentially, the black market price for the dollar jumped to £S55:1 and then to £S70:1.

As Operation Desert Storm raged, in Kuwait, the food supply situation deteriorated in Sudan virtually without foreign witnesses. There were also few witnesses to the continuing human rights violations carried out against the Khartoum displaced persons. In February about 10,000 displaced southerners located in Khartoum North were forced from their settlements. Others were moved from Khartoum, and on 20 April the NSRCC approved a program to move an additional 215,000 displaced persons out of Khartoum in 1991. Ironically, despite the Gulf War, Operation Lifeline Sudan maintained a life of its own, and in February James Jonah, UN Secretary-General Perez de Cuellar's personal representative, visited Sudan to discuss the continuation of the UN program and the increased assistance for the Khartoum displaced persons. Although this was dubbed the ground breaker for OLS III, there was no likelihood of the program's success until the Gulf War ended. Indeed, it was doubtful that there would ever be an OLS III, because as one senior Western official put it: "We don't trust them, and they don't trust us."[77]

Although predictions of a major shortfall in grain production were five months old, in February 1991 the NSRCC reversed a policy of grudging openness and once again began to denigrate Western concern with the prefamine conditions in Darfur and Kordofan. Nevertheless, reports leaked to the West that thousands of starving displaced persons, whom *The Washington Post* called "victims of a famine created by misrule and economic collapse," were straggling into Omdurman.[78] Such reports led Bashir to accuse aid organizations of "defaming Sudan by begging on behalf of Sudanese people," and he promised that self-sufficiency would be achieved "in a year or two."[79] The NSRCC imposed currency restrictions requiring the exchange of high-denomination bills, only to find it had insufficient currency in the Bank of Sudan to implement the program; the policy stimulated a rush to obtain hard currency, driving the pound to 100:1 against the dollar on the black market. Although it had no representative in Khartoum, the United Nations continued to estimate a 1.2-million-ton cereal shortfall and predicted that 7 million people would be at risk, especially from July through October 1991.

When the Gulf War ended in May 1991, a dozen USAID officials returned to Khartoum, where they joined with a handful of UN advisers and Western private aid organizations who had preceded them to try to breathe life into the relief operation in western Sudan. It was, however, late in the year to begin such efforts. The food supply situation was critical in Darfur, and, in a frantic search for food, thousands of Sudanese had fled to Chad. Without significant expatriate and indigenous PVO input from the field, relief agencies that returned to Sudan soon "found themselves struggling to deliver hundreds of thousands of tons of grain to stave off starvation ... against what have been almost insuperable barriers placed by [the NSRCC]."[80] Travel restrictions remained onerous, and the donors found that government reporting on famine conditions and food availability in specific locations in both Kordofan and Darfur was virtually nonexistent.

In addition, conditions throughout the South were virtually unknown. When the Gulf War began, the SPLA and the SRRA urged donor nations to ignore the NSRCC, and they offered "protection for any agencies seeking to initiate a relief operation outside of official Sudanese channels."[81] The effort in the South had continued with some cross-border trucking of food aid from Lokichoggio, Kenya, but in early 1991 the SPLA and SRRA had become increasingly hostile toward Western relief officials. The SPLA, which on occasion seemed to enjoy shooting itself in the foot, was reported to have expelled UN monitors who "asked too many questions" and had made life difficult for at least one agency, Aide Medicale Internationale.

With the Gulf War's conclusion, for the first time since the civil war had begun in 1983, the State Department allowed a USAID team to make a grand *tour d' horizon* in the SPLA-controlled South. On 27 April a trio of USAID officials departed from Nairobi and spent nearly a month traveling in SPLA territory. They reported that at Kapoeta local inhabitants seemed healthy, the hospital was operational, and PVOs were very busy. At Chukundum an agricultural center was operational and provided assistance to more than 6,000 displaced persons, including between 500 and 800 unaccompanied boys reportedly being trained by SPLA military. At Torit, food was plentiful. As the team drove north to Bor, at Tibari near the Juba-Bor road junction it encountered 10,000 Bari and Mundari displaced persons who had succeeded in fleeing NSRCC-controlled Juba in March 1990; their nutritional status was generally good. At Bor and surrounding villages, International Assistance for International Development (INTERAID) provided food supplements to malnourished children, and German doctors were at work at the local hospital—which had been slightly damaged by a 9 March air raid that killed nine patients. In nearby villages the populace was quietly farming, fishing, and tending cattle. Near Kongor a UNICEF team was vaccinating cattle; at Yirol the former ICRC hospital had no medicines, but the supply of food and the nutritional status of the population were better than expected, given reports of large population movements from northern Bahr al-Ghazal. At Adok, a former Chevron Oil base camp, the team found mounds of fish for sale. At Leer MSF-Holland was operating a primitive hospital, and it was operating a Kala Azar clinic at Duar. At Waat the local clinic had received basic drug kits from UNICEF, and although malnutrition was present, cases of marasmus or kwashiorkor were few.[82]

The USAID team found conditions in no way comparable to those in autumn of 1988 when starvation had been rampant throughout the region. It verified that there were signs of real progress in the South, although pockets of drought existed north and east of Yirol, north of Tonj, and around Akot that affected an estimated 250,000 southerners. The team then flew from Waat to Nasir on the Upper Sobat River where it witnessed not only the aftereffect of a political implosion within Ethiopia but also without realizing it, the birth of an implosion of historic consequence within the SPLA. In May 1991 a succession of military defeats at the hands of Tigrean and Eritrean rebels drove dictator Mengistu Haile Miriam from Ethiopia and reconfigured the shards of East Africa's political kaleidoscope. Mengistu had allowed the SPLA to operate from Addis Ababa and also from inside four huge Sudanese refugee camps. In contrast, the Ethiopian People's Revolutionary Democratic Front, which took charge of the government, was not disposed to assist Sudanese rebels. In the ensuing chaos, which affected all Ethiopian regions, the political vacuum in western Ethiopia was filled by soldiers who were inimical to the Sudanese in general and to the SPLA in particular.

On 14 and 15 May, Sudan air force planes bombed Sudanese refugee concentrations and a hospital near Nasir, "claiming they were part of the SPLA."[83] Thus, when the USAID team arrived at Nasir on 18 May, it encountered a number of wounded women and children. The team met with SPLA commander Riak Machar and local commander Gordon Kong. Machar explained that Operation Lifeline Sudan II had delivered no food beyond Ayod and was told to expect little immediate help given the enormity of the logistical problems. Riak reviewed other battlefields—Angola, Iraq, Afghanistan, and Central America—and wondered aloud why some rebel movements had received U.S. military assistance whereas others, like the SPLA, had not. With a handful of Stinger missiles, he asserted, the SPLA could bring the Sudan conflict to an early end. Although he asked what the SPLA could do to improve its image within the international community and with the U.S. government in particular, Riak must have known that the State Department had long ago rejected any military assistance and only in 1989, after the huge loss of life the previous year, approved direct U.S. participation in the delivery of humanitarian assistance in areas controlled by the SPLA. The USAID trip report and other reports on conditions astride the Ethiopian border spurred AID efforts to airdrop and airlift food to the hundreds of thousands of former Sudanese refugees who were being chased from Ethiopian camps into the wilds of central-eastern Sudan.

The Impact on the Southern Sudanese
of the Ethiopian Debacle

By June the huge mass of Sudanese who had sought sanctuary in Ethiopia from drought and war were fleeing for Sudan. Nasir, a town of 3,000 people, was soon surrounded by an estimated 240,000 displaced persons. In Addis Ababa the "clandestine" Radio SPLA closed down, and the SPLA hierarchy fled to the bush or to neighboring nations. Oromo Liberation Front (OLF) forces, composed primarily of Muslim soldiers, roamed the Ethiopia–Upper Nile frontier and pillaged Sudanese refugees. The OLF, which had first attacked Sudanese refugees at the Asosa camp in January 1990, received both financial and military support from Sudan's NSRCC. On 26 May, OLF forces overran the Sudanese refugee camp at Gambila, and almost immediately Sudan air force cargo planes began to use its airstrip. When Itang was threatened, Sudanese refugees, including some SPLA, made off with fifty UN relief trucks and sprinted out of Ethiopia.[84] Throughout June Sudanese air force continued its bombing at Jokau, Nasir, and Akobo, where about 200,000 displaced Sudanese remained. In the United States, AID-OFDA Director Andrew Natsios publicly admonished Sudan government for its attacks on congregations of unarmed civilians. Thanks to Natsios, many European protests, and UN appeals "not to bomb Sudanese refugees returning from Ethiopia," in June Khartoum agreed "to safeguard relief operations"; still, as one Middle East journal evaluated the NSRCC's probity, regaining international respectability would be "an uphill struggle."[85]

In mid-June John Garang made a surprise trip to the United States to seek State Department backing at a time when the SPLA had lost Ethiopia, its greatest benefactor. His supporters had little more than twelve hours' notice of his arrival and were thus unable to use the occasion to repeat a triumphant 1989 tour during which Garang had taken Washington by storm. Indeed, Garang seemed unable or unwilling to seek center stage precisely at a time when the NSRCC was highly unpopular in Washington and when his appearance could have provided the SPLA with a propaganda windfall. The SPLA leader met with Assistant Secretary Cohen, but the meeting did little to further the peace process and ended inconclusively. In a discussion with AID-OFDA's Natsios, Garang promised to upgrade the SRRA and appointed a trusted aide, Elijah Maluk, to cut through the red tape and the bad blood that existed between some aid agencies and the SRRA. He met with PVOs and thanked them for the transport of nearly 6,000 tons of food aid to civilians in SPLA territory since 1989. No effort was made to meet with the press, and thus Garang's visit went practically unnoticed. It ended on a low note when British Airways security guards were forced to disarm Garang's bodyguards before he could enter the plane that would take him to London for what was to be another inconclusive meeting with supporters and allies before he returned to the bush.

While Garang was in Washington, the NSRCC was busy uncovering coup plots, quashing student protests, and destroying settlements of

Khartoum displaced persons. In May the *Guardian* reported that dwellings housing 10,000 displaced persons had been flattened and that the re-displaced had been forcibly removed to a camp located in a desert wasteland ten miles west of Omdurman where a UN adviser had once claimed that "not even a locust could survive."[86] The point was proved when the children and the feeble began to perish. Soon, the number of graves that had been dug outnumbered the ramshackle *tukuls* that were still occupied. In June at least 35,000 displaced persons were uprooted from the site at Souk Markazi and moved to the desert site at Jabal Auliya. The displaced persons suffered everywhere, as did most Sudanese. The price for sorghum continued its upward spiral; by July it was selling for £S1,500–2,000 a bag at Rahad, a major production and marketing center. Public servants found it increasingly difficult to make ends meet even though their salaries had increased between 40 and 100 percent.

In Khartoum the second anniversary of the 30 June coup arrived with only Libya's Muammar Qadhafi and Chad's Idriss Deby on hand to celebrate the event. As one diplomat noted: "That sums up the extent of success achieved by the junta in two years—just Qadhafi and Deby... I think the West had largely given up on the junta, and Khartoum has given up trying to win friends there."[87] The UN effort to elicit financial support for an OLS III was going nowhere; Trevor Page, the UN director of operations, was detested by the few PVOs that had returned to Khartoum. A number of Western diplomats, including the U.S. ambassador, urged their governments to seek his removal. Page was also despised by the SPLA, because he openly professed that Priestley's lack of success resulted from the NSRCC perception that he enjoyed too close a relationship with the SPLA. Page had little interest in cultivating a relationship with the rebels; thus, any UN plan to continue the legacy of food aid impartiality founded in Operation Lifeline Sudan I was doomed.

The NSRCC began its third year in power with famine in the West, food shortages in Khartoum, and no sign of peace in the South. Although sorghum was in short supply in Khartoum, stories of terrible privation in the West began to circulate. Thousands of helpless flocked to El Fasher and Geneina in search of food. In June the United Nations warned that unless food aid was soon made available in the West, "the rate of starvation could escalate rapidly"; it predicted that the situation there "could be as bad as 1984–85."[88] Not until July, however, were food aid donors finally granted permission to carry out an extensive regional evaluation. A report prepared in July by USAID's Brian D'Silva found: "We are now witnessing the onset of a major famine in both North and South Darfur. There is no doubt that people are dying from hunger and that hunger exists in widespread areas of Darfur. Furthermore, the relief effort in Darfur is stalled. A major rethinking and redirection of the relief effort needs to take place in the next week to ten days so as to stem large-scale loss of life and mass migration into towns."[89] Tragically, famine conditions were very similar to those D'Silva had encountered during his trip to Darfur in January 1984, after which a similar report had alerted the donors to the potential for a terrible famine.

By mid-1991 in the West the strong had moved or were on the move to the cities, and "only the weak and the young had stayed behind."[90] Starvation was widespread near Geneina, and the donors immediately funded an emergency airlift. Startled by reports of extensive famine, donors increased their pledges to 650,000 tons of food. About 350,000 tons arrived by September 1991, but again there were myriad problems trying to force food aid through the archaic and inefficient transportation system. Everything went wrong. There were serious fuel shortages and problems with truck contractors. The welcome summer rains, which had been good in much of southern Kordofan and Darfur, played a part in closing roads and hampering deliveries. Thus, by October only 14,500 tons of aid had found their way to Darfur, and UN employees returning from the West reported that the famine must have killed many tens of thousands—certainly more than 100,000. There were, however, no eyewitness accounts of massive deaths similar to 1988 reports from Abyei, Aweil, and Meiram. This time the tragic mosaic of death was composed of hundreds of tessera (mourning) occurring outside the field of vision of Western donors. When finally forced to confront the reality of a massive famine, the NSRCC responded in predictable fashion by criticizing the tardy response of the international relief agencies. The criticism was not appreciated in Washington, because by October 1991 the United States had pledged 320,000 tons of relief food and $113 million to cover transportation costs.[91] UNICEF, which had taken charge of the OLS office in Khartoum, found that the United States and other Western donors simply were not interested in another campaign.

The SPLA Divides into Disaster

As drought stalked the North, the southern regions that were similarly affected generally benefited from heavy summer rains. Although the besieged government garrison towns were short of food and there were reports of localized food shortages, for once conditions in the South actually seemed better than those in the North. Then, on 30 August 1991, the South's worst nightmare came true as differences within the SPLA ranks that had been papered over for years reached crisis proportions. Riak Machar, Nuer tribal and zonal commander for western Upper Nile; Lam Akol, Shilluk leader and deputy to John Garang; and Gordon Kong Chol, former Anya-Nya II leader and Nuer, joined forces and broke with

Garang. Garang was blamed for excessive authoritarianism (which even his critics had claimed was one reason the SPLA had managed to stick together) and human rights violations. He was also accused of press-ganging adolescents into the SPLA. According to the so-called SPLA-Nasir group, Garang's "obsession with the military aspect of the civil war" led him to downplay the development of a civilian administration or the creation of community organizations capable of providing health and education services or leadership development in the region under SPLA control.[92] Even more important, however, was the conviction that the racial and religious intolerance practiced by a succession of Khartoum governments was a phenomenon without end. After nearly a decade of civil war, during which Khartoum governments had approved policies and practiced warfare that verged on the genocidal, there was no reason to believe that the Arab two-thirds of the population of Sudan would ever guarantee the rights and privileges of the non-Arab population. Thus, the secular character of a Republic of Sudan—Garang's and the SPLA-SPLM's *raison d'être*—was a political and a logical impossibility.

At SPLA headquarters in Torit, Garang denied the charges, especially the SPLA-Nasir claim that he had both sponsored and approved human rights abuses. He did admit, however, that the Nasir faction could "turn the movement toward democracy."[93] After reviewing the separatist issue at SPLA headquarters on 12 September, ten SPLA commanders declared their loyalty to Garang while committing themselves to an ambiguous course of action—"resolving the war through a united democratic Sudan, confederation, association of sovereign states or self-determination."[94]

Although SPLA-Nasir insisted on southern Sudanese secession, few of its followers (in exile or in Sudan) foresaw that its creation would soon spark a civil war within a civil war or that the Nasir faction would be as ruthless as the army in exterminating its enemies. The split engendered a shock wave of seismic proportions, particularly because it was followed almost immediately by the eruption of an internecine conflict along tribal lines. Riak's Nuer attacked and pillaged Dinka villages in Kongor, carrying out atrocity after atrocity. In November they attacked Dinka communities located within the traditional Nuer districts of Akobo, Waat, Bentiu, and Leer. They then carried out a second deadly attack in Kongor, forcing the evacuation of most expatriate aid workers from Upper Nile. The attacks shattered any State Department hopes for reigniting interest in the on-again, off-again peace process or in its new peace plan—this time focusing on an arrangement involving "confederal states."[95] With the split in the SPLA ranks, the United States was forced to conclude that its efforts would likely be in vain, and the issue of a cease-fire and peace talks was left to the OAU to resolve. Then, on 1

October, USAID-Sudan eschewed the role of primary implementing agency for food aid in Sudan, "transferring that function to the UN World Food Program." USAID staff was soon reduced to one official and five local staff.[96] With the United States out of the picture attempts to bring all factions of the SPLA and the NSRCC together in peace talks passed to the OAU and to Nigeria's General Ibrahim Babangida.

Peace talks could not come too soon, because Bor District, which in antebellum Sudan had been home to about 350,000 Dinka, had become the nexus of a horrible tragedy. The district, which had already endured a series of shocks—including an early drought followed by extensive flooding and then the inundation of tens of thousands of Sudanese refugees fleeing Ethiopia—was literally devastated. An estimated 30,000 Nuer rampaged through the area, burning and killing, leveling hospitals and clinics, destroying crops and stores, killing cattle, and creating chaos. In December 1991 the United Nations reported that "more than 200,000 residents of the Bor and Kongor districts—in an exodus unlike anything seen before in Sudan—fled south in search of food, shelter and security."[97] Tens of thousands crossed the Nile to the west or moved south toward Mongalla and Torit. Norwegian People's Aid, which had lost its celebrated director Egil Hagen to cancer, reported that by "the end of November up to 5,000 Dinka—mainly civilians," had been killed by Riak's faction in what was "an outright massacre between Bor and Mongalla."[98] An NPA videotape made the rounds of the United States and captured on film the terrible atrocities carried out by Riak's forces in the Gemmiza region north of Bor.

In November Sudanese and Kenyan church officials offered their good offices to effect a cease-fire, and, thanks to their exertions, peace talks were opened in Nairobi on 22 November. They were broken off four days later, after which the SPLA-Nasir forces continued their depredations. There were reports from Nairobi in mid-December that the two sides had patched up their quarrel, but the announcement was premature and the antagonists broke contact. When Garang's forces counterattacked, the rebels fled toward their bases in Ayod and Waat, stopping at Kongor to continue the fight.

The Years of Sorrow

For southerners 1991 was another terrible year. The OAU-sponsored peace talks scheduled for December 1991 in Abuja, Nigeria, were postponed indefinitely. The NSRCC moved swiftly to widen the cleavage between SPLA factions. Birgit tribesman and Darfur-born Ali al-Haj Muhammad, long an NIF ideologue and a self-described expert on Southern Sudan, met with Lam Akol in secret talks in Frankfurt,

Germany, in February 1992 and thereafter was employed to widen the rift between Lam Akol and John Garang. Even worse for Garang, the NSRCC signed a treaty of friendship with a reconstituted government of Ethiopia, thus placing eastern Equatoria in grave danger of a Sudanese army attack through western Ethiopia.

Equally in grave danger were the Khartoum displaced persons. A Commission for the Displaced statistical report circulated in September 1991 indicated that nearly a million displaced persons had disappeared from the capital area since July 1989. A *kasha* campaign instituted in late 1990 had dismantled and destroyed a score of built-up settlements. When the displaced persons had settled on land the government wanted cleared, residences were bulldozed and the displaced were forcibly removed. The huge Souk Markazi site was flattened in June 1991. The sprawling Hillat Kusha settlement was next, followed by Zagalona. There was method in the NSRCC madness; two temporary transition camps were created for Southern Sudanese who had arrived in Khartoum *after* 1983, and three "resettlement areas" were constructed for those who could prove they had arrived before 1984. However, by 1992 the Commission for the Displaced—the NSRCC's leading agency—had restricted access to the official settlements, and a UN request to hold a census at thirty-six sites in the Khartoum area was rejected. When the United Nations persisted, the effort was stonewalled by Minister for Peace and Development Abou Ghozeiza, the PVO *bête noire*, who instead demanded $10 million from Western donors for a model housing program for 2,000 Khartoum displaced persons.

As the displaced persons went hungry, in the northern cities most bureaucrats were alarmed by their unrelenting impoverishment. A government salary of £S600 a month did not go far when sorghum was selling for as much as £S2,000–4,000 a sack. Sudanese were not only impoverished, but in what was to have been the "Arab breadbasket" they were malnourished as well. Nearly a third of the inhabitants of Darfur and Red Sea were reported to suffer either severe or significant malnutrition, as did a quarter of Kordofan and Upper Nile residents. A FEWS preharvest assessment published in October 1991 was a precursor of possibly worse news to come. FEWS advised that the 1991–1992 crop would likely be less than average because a late-season drought had greatly reduced the harvest in the Sahilian tier. Still, an estimated grain harvest of 2.6 million tons, combined with 400,000 tons of food remaining from 1991 commercial import and the large store of donor relief food, would allow Sudan to meet its domestic needs. Food aid would be needed in Darfur, Kordofan, and northern Bahr al-Ghazal as well as for tens of thousands of desperately hungry people located in parts of the South that could be reached despite the warfare within the SPLA. These included the 150,000 Sudanese crowded into and around Nasir and another 35,000 refugees, formerly at Itang camp, who were located at Pakok, the Ethiopia-Sudan border. Juba suffered its usual shortages. For the PVOs that continued their work in Sudan, the situation in the South was all too familiar and, overall, was as bad as it had ever been since the outbreak of civil war in 1983.

■

Conclusion:
A Decade of Despair

A whole culture, a whole civilization is disappearing.
— UN World Food Program official, reported in
The Washington Times, 26 January 1993

In 1992 the Sudan National Salvation Revolution Command Council was widely condemned because of the callous disregard it had demonstrated for the rights of its citizens in the North and the almost total lack of respect shown to citizens of Southern Sudan. The U.S. Senate, the European Parliament, the Vatican, various Arab organizations, and the UN General Assembly all passed resolutions strongly condemning NSRCC human rights violations. Nevertheless, despite international censure, the military junta did virtually nothing to improve political circumstances inside Sudan or to enhance the conditions for peace. Indeed, the deaths were to continue until more than a million southerners were casualties of the terrible civil war.[1] Thus, by 1992, Sudan, a nation rich in human and natural resources, was nearly impoverished, and the new year promised no great change.

The split within SPLA ranks had led the NSRCC to move quickly to widen the cleavage between the factions, and it successfully played on the egos of Machar and Lam Akol to do so. It also continued its military buildup thanks to the beneficence of another arms supplier. The Islamic Republic of Iran had followed the progress of events in Sudan since the NSRCC took power in 1989, and it reacted quickly when the NSRCC's ties to Libya began to deteriorate. By December 1991 there were reports of a conspicuous influx of Iranians into Khartoum, many of whom were "believed to be working in Islamist military training camps" in Sudan.[2] Iranian President Ali Akbar Hashimi Rafsanjani, who had already declared the Sudanese civil war a *jihad,* visited Khartoum for three days

305

in December 1991 and offered his complete support for the NSRCC.[3] In what was the first visit by an Iranian head of state to Sudan since the 1979 Iranian revolution, Rafsanjani signed a number of protocols, including one promising $300 million in Chinese military materiel paid for by Teheran. Iran was also reported to have agreed to provide the NSRCC with a million tons of oil a year until the civil war ended.[4] As the NSRCC created ties to Iran's Islamic *jihad*, to Hamas (composed of fundamentalist Palestinians), and to Muslim fundamentalist political movements in Egypt, Yemen, Algeria, and Tunisia, it seemed determined to chart a collision course with its neighbors and, eventually, with the United States.

The New Offensive by the
Sudanese People's Armed Forces

The SPAF, armed with $300 million in modern weaponry, used the split within the SPLA to begin a major offensive in February 1992. The government was able to concentrate its military activity on four fronts at once. A government column moving south from Malakal overran Duk Fadiet and prepared to attack Bor, and for the first time there were reports that the government had used helicopter gunships. When the SPAF succeeded in taking Bor on 3 April, Garang accused the Nasir faction of "allowing the government free passage" in the territory under its control.[5] The SPAF, also attacking through Ethiopia and assisted by Oromo militia forces, took Pochala on 8 March; as a result, tens of thousands of southerners—including more than 15,000 orphans ("unaccompanied minors") who had fled the Ethiopian UNHCR camps in May 1991—moved southward toward Kapoeta and the Kenya-Sudan frontier. Continuing its attack, the SPAF captured Pibor on 23 April, where the forces of Riak Machar melted into the bush with no resistance. In Bahr al-Ghazal government troops from the Wau garrison began to move toward Tonj and then toward the SPLA stronghold at Yirol. Another column headed north in a campaign that was designed to open the railroad and road routes that had been closed between Wau and Aweil since 1986. The SPAF took Yirol on 11 April. Indeed, the Nasir force offered no resistance anywhere in the South, and only Garang's elements put up resistance. Finally, at Juba, Southern Command forces began to move toward the besieged Yei and crossed the Nile in an effort to take Torit.

Chaos in the South was attended by the spread of hunger and disease. Malaria was on the increase, and of an estimated 1 million cases, at least two-thirds went untreated. Four million doses of meningitis vaccine were needed. In April Norwegian People's Aid, which continued to be active east of the Nile, reported that conditions of the civilian population in the South were the worst they had been since the civil war began in 1983.[6] Famine conditions worsened; in May the UN Operation Lifeline Sudan office offered to initiate relief flights to fourteen famine-affected sites in Southern Sudan, but the NSRCC rejected the plan.[7] Eventually, the government gave the UN-OLS office permission to deliver food and other assistance to Pibor and Pochala. USAID-Sudan later reported that this was done "to maintain an image of balance between UN assistance for SPLA and GOS controlled area."[8]

Flushed with victory in the South, in April 1992 the RCC announced the creation of a Transitional National Assembly of 300 appointees that would "rule" Sudan until elections for a Parliament were held in 1995. The Parliament, the ubiquitous Colonel Khalifa stated, was "a purely Sudanese invention," and the NSRCC would wither away and be "confined to matters of sovereignty and national unity." There was no possibility of a return to a multiparty system;[9] NSRCC critics argued that the group would not soon relinquish power and that the Parliament would be the home of its toadies and NIF party members.

Although he maintained a very low profile during the first six months of NSRCC rule, NIF leader and Muslim ideologue Hassan al-Turabi had played an increasingly vocal role in Sudan's political life. Disclaiming any direct role in politics, Turabi served as a globe-trotting NSRCC emissary until he was assaulted by a Sudanese dissident in a Toronto airport. Turabi survived the incident, but the attack reduced his effectiveness for some time. It did not, however, put a halt to the interviews he granted to nearly everyone. As he explained in an interview with the *Middle East Times* in May 1992, Sudan was "now becoming one of the leading models because it is a complete movement with political, economic, social, cultural dimensions, very well-organized."[10] Because he preached a form of laissez-faire economics and insisted that "the state is the guardian of social justice, rather than the proprietor of the economy," it was little wonder that so many Arab capitalists found Turabi's Islamic fundamentalism beguiling and that conservative Saudi bankers were willing to bankroll his movement. Southern Sudanese and Arabs fighting for a secular Sudan found no comfort in Turabi's credo—promoted by the NSRCC—that "the difference between a democracy and an Islamic state would only be that there is a higher system of law on top of all institutions of government, which is the Shari'a."[11]

As Turabi and the NIF were completing their infiltration of the government, the SPLA factions fought another murderous engagement at Kongor, and Dinka clans from the Dukridge and Nuer clans from Ayod engaged in a battle that lasted through August. Nuer forces continued to pillage, rape, destroy crops, kill cattle, and poison wells. They destroyed scores of Dinka settlements and murdered untold thousands of Dinka, virtually depopulating one of the most dynamic centers of Southern

Sudan. In effect, the SPLA-Nasir carried out a murderous campaign directed almost entirely against civilian targets, and it was launched by Nuer leaders who themselves had only recently complained of human rights violations authorized by John Garang. A USAID-Sudan report later noted that observers flying over a vast area in which about 300,000 head of cattle had been enumerated in the early 1980s sighted "not one single cow."[12] For the Dinka, there could be no greater tragedy.

Although battling in the field, from 28 May through 3 June the Sudanese antagonists finally met at Abuja, Nigeria, in what were termed preliminary peace talks. The NSRCC was represented by Colonel Muhammad al-Amin Khalifa, who had just been named speaker of the Transitional National Assembly; chair of the assembly's Peace Committee Ahmad al-Radi Jabar, long the NIF's *éminence grise* for Southern Sudan issues; and NSRCC delegate and NIF ideologue Ali al-Haj Muhammad, who claimed he would not discuss "self-determination or the separation of Sudan."[13] The NSRCC had made it clear that the war in the South was no longer a civil war but a *jihad*, and that it was not about to countenance the secular demands of the Garang faction or the demands for secession the Nasir faction employed. Nor would it approve a referendum permitting southerners (or Sudanese, for that matter) to vote on the issue of self-determination. Consequently, Nigeria's General Ibrahim Babangida was only able to secure agreement that a committee would be created to consider "interim arrangements, including some form of power-sharing in Sudan."[14] The meeting ended inconclusively, with both sides agreeing only to meet again.[15]

As talks were progressing at Abuja, it was reported that the SPLA stronghold at Kapoeta had fallen to government troops. In response, nearly 25,000 refugees fled to Kenya, about half of whom were orphans who had fled from Ethiopia in 1991. Given this insecurity, all PVO operations were halted. Nothing could be done for about 250,000 drought-affected southerners the United Nations reported were making their way to the North. In the South, only NPA resumed full operations in April 1992. For PVOs willing to work in the South, the NSRCC granted permission for food aid flights to Akobo, Waat, and Nasir—sites controlled by SPLA's Nasir faction; no permission was given to assist the needy in the area under Garang's control. Nevertheless, NPA continued to move 500 tons of food a month, along with 100 truckloads of other material to civilians under SPLA control. Its program was drastically reduced, however, when Kapoeta fell on 28 May. Also in May NPA reported that of the 3 million inhabitants of eastern Equatoria, Upper Nile, and Bahr al-Ghazal, more than 1.2 million were seriously affected by warfare. With the fall of Kapoeta, the SPLA stronghold at Torit was threatened from three directions, and as many as 150,000 southerners ("a conservative figure") began to make their way toward the border with Uganda.[16] SPLA supporters received a tremendous shock, what was even perceived by some as a mortal blow, when Garang's headquarters at Torit fell on 13 July to a force of 10,000 army and militia. It was too early to bury the SPLA, but Garang was forced to move his headquarters to Kajo Kaji, west of the Nile and just north of the Uganda border.

At midyear nearly all SPLA units throughout the South (and in the North in southern South Kordofan and South Darfur) were on the defensive. As the government's military offensive wound down, in July the UNICEF-OLS office in Nairobi wrote that military activity combined with crop failure had "affected 668,000 people in accessible parts of southern Sudan." It admitted that the "plight of hundreds of thousands of others, residing in areas inaccessible to UN/Non-Government Organization assessment teams but affected by crop failure, factional fighting and military activities, remains unknown."[17] For the first time in the civil war, Garang's artillery began to pound at Juba on a regular basis. In one of the civil war's most ironic moments, the U.S. Embassy in Nairobi was demanding that Garang permit the unhindered movement of humanitarian assistance to Juba just as the United Nation ceased all aid flights to the city. As Agence France Press later reported, the United Nation had discovered that the NSRCC had been using Ilyushin-76 chartered aircraft with UN markings to move soldiers and materiel through the Juba airport.[18] Despite SPLA shelling and the discontinuance of airlifts, the people survived on short rations and hate. Well in advance of the SPLA attacks, the military had begun to destroy displaced persons' camps and neighborhoods and to pack the population into an area one-quarter its previous size. About 300,000 people were literally held hostage by the Sudanese army, the rains made living conditions absolute hell. When the SPLA attacked the Southern Command inside the city, the army—an occupying force in the first place—was used as an instrument of terror to cow the populace.

The Humanitarian Agencies Overwhelmed by War

Few foreigners were allowed to live in or even visit Sudan following the Gulf War, and representatives of the Western media were treated like typhoid carriers. Thus, it was easy for indigenous Islamic agencies (Islamic Da'wa, Islamic African Relief Agency, a government-reorganized Sudanese Red Crescent organization, and the Nidda al-Jihad organization that supported the Popular Defense Forces) to supersede PVOs and foreign aid agencies. In July 1992 the United Nations, which maintained an Operation Lifeline Sudan office in Khartoum, prepared a Comprehensive Plan for Access, but the attempt to revive OLS and its Corridors of

Tranquility went nowhere. Indeed, given the diminished PVO presence in both the North and the South and the factional infighting that was shredding the SPLA in the south, the NSRCC had no reason to support the UN plan.

Donor interest in Sudan reached a low point in mid-1992, when the military continued the extirpation of villages settled by ethnic Nuba in the Nuba Hills regions of southern Kordofan; by August 1992 the government had created more than 50,000 displaced persons, and a diabolical program was undertaken to forcibly relocate tens of thousands of Nuba in the drought-stricken districts of North Kordofan. Although most Nuba were eventually allowed to return to South Kordofan, families that traveled from Khartoum to the camps of South Kordofan to collect their relatives and move them to the capital were not permitted to do so. Instead, the regional government began to implement a plan to congregate 160,000 displaced persons (Nuba and Southern Sudanese) in 100 "peace villages"; UN officials who were allowed to visit selected sites found that they were little more than prisons guarded by NSRCC Popular Defense Force recruits.

U.S. relations with the NSRCC reached their nadir when NSRCC security forces arrested UN European Community, German, and USAID personnel employed in Juba. The U.S. Embassy response to the arrests of USAID personnel was both tardy and ineffectual, and a trusted and well-loved Sudanese USAID employee with many years of service was executed as an SPLA spy. The United States did, however, initiate efforts at the United Nations that eventually led to the passage of a resolution demonstrating widespread discontent with the condition of human rights in Sudan. The resolution was supported by 102 nations, whereas Sudan received the backing of only Iraq, Iran, Libya, and Syria.

In December 1992 the NSRCC announced that it had reached an agreement with the SPLA on a UN-brokered plan to supervise the delivery of food aid in Southern Sudan. The plan, similar to that used in the first Operation Lifeline Sudan program, proposed the use of the Nile River corridor to supply food from Kosti to Juba. However, no sooner was the plan presented to the PVOs than the NSRCC imposed a number of strictures within the country agreements that permitted foreign aid agencies to operate in Sudan. Realistically, by 1993 Western agencies had worn out their welcome in northern Sudan. The 1991 rains had been generally good, and when the irrigated croplands provided a record harvest, the North counted a small grain surplus. In 1992 the rains were again good, and the drought in Darfur was broken. There were still, however, more than 2.5 million displaced southerners located in areas under the control of the Khartoum government, nearly all of whom were in great need, but for Western agencies that had returned to Sudan, the NSRCC provided virtually no opportunity to work either in the regions or among the Khartoum displaced persons. In the capital area and the countryside, the distribution of humanitarian assistance had been politicized through the instrument of Islamic organizations that coupled proselytizing with providing services.

No Longer Were the *Khawaja*
Wanted by the Government

Renowned for their courage in a harsh land, by spring 1993 the Sudanese had endured a decade of terrible suffering. Most of their principal leaders were still alive; whether in exile or in Sudan, in the government or out, their actions had done little to contradict the principle of the English political philosopher Thomas Hobbes, who concluded that the "war of each against all was the normal state of existence" and the fate of mankind. Still, Allah had looked kindly on the Northern Sudan and provided it with a bumper grain crop in 1991–1992 (more than 3 million tons); the 1992–1993 harvest was also bountiful. In January 1993 the NSRCC acknowledged that it had exported sorghum to Somalia and Kenya but claimed there was "no shortage of food in other parts of the country."[19]

Grain in the fields did not, however, produce peace, and in 1993 the Sudanese protagonists seemed no closer to accommodation than they had been in 1983. The junta was still ensnared in an unwinnable conflict at a time when the southerners were divided and fighting among themselves. This division had greatly impeded agricultural activity in the South, and in April 1993 the UN World Food Program reported that food shortages there were at a "crisis point" and that malnutrition rates were "among the highest in the world."[20] The United Nations, in what had become an annual peregrination, approached the international donor community for additional funding for a new OLS program in Sudan. The United Nation wanted $130 million for Southern Sudan, where it claimed starvation was "rampant" and about 2.8 million people were at risk.[21] Cynics wondered why Western donors would provide funds to a nation that restricted access to areas in need that were under its own control and that the UN's OLS information officer had scored for its relentless and indiscriminate bombing of civilian population centers, usually with "old Soviet-made cargo planes flying at 12,000 feet or higher over rebel-held areas," and for randomly dropping 500-pound bombs.[22] Still, Assistant Secretary of State Herman J. Cohen warned the U.S. House of Representatives Foreign Affairs Committee, Subcommittee on Africa that "several hundred thousand face starvation [in Southern Sudan] if they do not receive assistance in the coming months. In at least some areas, people are already dying in large numbers, at rates comparable to the worst [famine conditions then existing] in Somalia."[23] When the UN and international response to the impending disaster was tardy, and as heavy rains inundated much of Southern Sudan, making airlifts impossible and airdrops questionable, the Southern Sudanese began a second decade that promised to be as bad as, if not worse than, the decade that began with the Bor mutiny in May 1983.

Tragically, the political destiny of Sudan was no nearer resolution than it had been when Garang vanished into the bush in 1983. For John Garang the trek from Bor to the bush has been long and replete with many contradictions. Despite his intellect and military talents, Garang had failed as a politician. He preferred the company of his troops to that of politicians, which may have been rewarding but was not necessarily wise. In an age when anyone committed to a cause learns to exploit the media or perishes from its neglect, Garang has been singularly inept. Concerned to save Sudan from itself, he has presided over an insurgency that has caused the deaths of hundreds of thousands and the dislocation of millions of Sudanese. The SPLA had won numerous battles, but by 1994 it was losing the war. It had been unwilling to shed the blood or was incapable of mounting the attack required to capture a southern capital and create a recognizable seat of government inside Sudan. Simply put, commanding the countryside is not the same as commanding the country, and the insurgents required a recognizable base inside Sudan from which to continue their military operations not only for the propaganda value but also to demonstrate to their sympathizers in Muslim Northern Sudan as well as in the West that their cause was not only ideologically but also politically realistic. Instead, the second Sudanese civil war, like the first, has dissolved into an interminable guerrilla war with no defeats and no victories, only casualties. Consequently, Sudan remains a state but is not yet a nation; the South is a region but has yet to become a state.

Whether the government in Khartoum, whatever its political philosophy, will ever accept Southern Sudan as a partner in the Sudanese nation remains to be resolved. For that matter, can southerners forget that 1.3 million southerners have died and millions have been displaced by war and its devastation? Can they forgive the Arab governments for using food as a weapon of war, water as a means of coercion, the *murahileen* and the PDF as means to sow terror, and the army as an instrument of revenge?[24] Governments in the North have broadcast the seeds of bigotry and racial prejudice, and their efflorescence has been witnessed in places like Ed Daein, Wau, Jebelein, Lagowa, and hundreds of villages and scores of displaced persons' camps in both the North and the South where Sudanese have perished.

With the exception of Operation Lifeline Sudan I, no relief operation could be termed a success despite the millions of dollars spent. The Western Relief Operation of 1984 was activated well after an extensive drought had ravaged the region, and it—like the 1991–1992 operation—was frustrated by geography, history, and infrastructure. Operation Rainbow was a propaganda success and a program failure. Operation Lifeline Sudan II was dominated by a repressive Sudanese government that was capable of ignoring basic human needs; it was bound to fail, and it did. Nevertheless, the individuals who created Operation Lifeline and propelled it forward were able to dominate the media and in doing so generated a worldwide interest in Sudan and its peoples that exists to this day.

In 1993, as Western agencies began to program aid to myriad southern Sudanese still snared in a cycle of war, dislocation, drought, flood, and famine, they had little to be ashamed of after years of service in Sudan. As they go about the business of saving lives, the Sudanese wait, as they have for many millennia, for the rains to water the fields and for the grass to spring forth and spread across the pasturelands. They anticipate those great thunderclouds, which rise out of the South Atlantic to cross the great tropical rainforests of Zaire, cool the land, fill the Nile and its tributaries, and bring with their water the gift of life. It is the thunder on the Nile that drowns the sounds of battle and the sorrows of dislocation and brings hope once again to the Sudanese and to all those who love Sudan.

Notes

Chapter 1

1. U.S. Agency for International Development, "Case Report, Sudan Civil Strife, 1973," Washington, D.C., 1973.

2. Musaddag A. El Haj Ali, "The Redivision of the Southern Sudan," in *Decentralization in Sudan*, Graduate College Publications no. 20, University of Khartoum, 1987, p. 230.

3. U.S. House Committee on Foreign Affairs, *Hearing Before the Subcommittee on Africa, Committee on Foreign Affairs*, 28 March 1984.

4. *The Times* (London), May 1983.

5. SPLM, *Manifesto*, 31 July 1983, p. 15. See also "We Want a New Sudan," Africa, no. 177, May 1986; *SPLA/SPLM Newsletter*, no. 1, 10 July 1986.

6. House Committee, *Subcommittee on Africa*.

7. "African Rebel Actions Threaten Peace in Sudan," *Gulf Daily News* (Bahrein), 29 March 1983; "Khartoum Outflanks Its Hungry Rebels," *The Times*, 1 May 1985.

8. "La longue marche du Che Africaine," 23 September 1988, *L'Express*.

9. J. Garang de Mabior, *John Garang Speaks* (London: KPI, 1987), p. 58.

10. "40,000 from Sudan Cross into Ethiopia," *The New York Times*, 6 May 1984.

11. J. Burr, "A Working Document: Quantifying Genocide in the Southern Sudan, 1983–1993" (Washington, D.C.: October 1993), U.S. Committee for Refugees.

12. Noel J. Coulson, *Conflicts and Tensions in Islamic Jurisprudence* (Chicago: University of Chicago, 1969), p. 86, provides useful insights regarding the implementation of Shari'a.

13. *An-Nahar Arab Report and Memo*, 10 September 1983.

14. *Al-Majallah* (London), 15–21 October 1983.

15. R. K. Badal, "The Addis Ababa Agreement Ten Years After: An Assessment," in *North-South Relations in the Sudan Since the Addis Ababa Agreement* (Khartoum: Khartoum University Press, 1988), p. 32.

16. House Committee, *Subcommittee on Africa*.

17. *Al-Tadamun*, 6 December 1986.

18. *Al-Raya*, July-September 1989, p. 47.

19. Radio Omdurman (in English), 1530 GMT, 25 September 1989.

20. "Quarterly Economic Review of Sudan," *Economist Intelligence Unit*, no. 2, 1985, p. 11.

21. "Allah and the Rains," *Economist Development Report*, December 1984.

22. "End of the Line for Hungry Children of Nyala Station," *The Observer*, 30 June 1985.

23. OXFAM/UNICEF/Kordofan Regional Government, "A Report on the Nutritional Status of 4,896 Children in Kordofan Region, May/June 1985," Khartoum, October 1985.

24. *Al-Dustur*, 26 September 1983.

25. U.S. General Accounting Office, National Security and International Affairs Division, Letter B-211263, 2 June 1986.

26. USAID-Sudan, "Concepts Paper, Country Development Strategy Statement," Khartoum, March 1984.

27. "We Want a New Sudan," *Africa*, no. 177, May 1986.

28. USAID-Sudan, Inspector General, "Predication" Report of USAID Investigation, RIG/II/N, Case no. N8660031, 31 October 1986.

29. "Sudan Chaos Paves the Way for Another Strongman," *The Observer*, 7 July 1985.

30. *Al-Ayyam*, 8 July 1985.

31. Sudan News Agency Radio, 1730 GMT, 21 July 1985; Foreign Broadcast Information Service, "Daily Report, Middle East and Africa," 23 July 1985.

32. Lakes Drought Committee Report, SSU/LP/1.c.c/3, Rumbek, 9 November 1984.

33. P. Anade O., "Famine and Drought in Upper Nile Administrative Area," Malakal Famine Relief Committee, Malakal, 10 July 1985.

34. U.S. Department of State, *Country Reports on Human Rights Practices for 1984* (Washington, D.C., February 1985), p. 328.

35. S. Lukudu and P. O. Bulu, *Report on Drought and Hunger Threatened Areas of Equatoria Region* (Juba: Ministry of Agriculture and Natural Resources, Equatoria Region, Juba, December 1984).

36. Radio Message, Aldo Adjo Deng to Dr. Lawrence Wol, Khartoum, Wau, 4 January 1985.

37. "Relief and Rehabilitation for Drought and War Affected Areas in Lakes Province," Commissioner for Lakes Province, Rumbek, 27 April 1985.

38. E. Hagen and B. Kurup, "Trip Report to Southern Region from 28 May to 1 June 1985," UNICEF, Khartoum, 5 June 1985.

39. Bahr al-Ghazal Administrative Area, Governor's Office, "Emergency Food Estimates," Memorandum C8GAA/K/19.A.1, 11 November 1985.

40. Ibid.

41. Catholic Relief Services—USCC, Nairobi, "Emergency Relief for Southern Sudan," 25 November 1985.

42. Anon., "Report on Relief Dura Brought to Malakal by Sudanaid," Malakal, September 1985.

43. Reuters Library Report, "Western Volunteers in Sudan Brave Dangers," 5 September 1989.

Chapter 2

1. U.S. Agency for International Development, Khartoum, "Sudan, PL-480, Title III, PAAD Review," 5 February 1986.

2. USAID, Khartoum, "Sudan—Contingency Plan for Southern Sudan," 15 December 1988.

3. USAID, Khartoum, Memorandum (Farnsworth to Martella), "Food Supply in Malakal," 18 December 1985.

4. USAID, Khartoum, Inspector General, "Predication," Report of USAID Investigation, RIG/II/N, Case no. N8660031, 31 October 1986.

5. USAID, Khartoum, Memorandum (Martella to Brown), General Development Office, PIO/C 650-9010, 24 February 1986.

6. Sudan Council of Churches, "Especial Report on South Sudan," Khartoum, 3 February 1986.

7. Agencies involved in Southern Sudan, "Minutes," Khartoum, 19 July 1986.

8. B. Ammann, "Sudan: An African Tinderbox," *Swiss Review of World Affairs*, January 1988. *Khawaja* was originally a pejorative term used in the Medieval Muslim world for a Christian merchant. In the Sudan it has become a generic slang expression for foreigners from the West or the East.

9. John Garang de Mabior, *John Garang Speaks* (London: Kegan Paul International, 1987), pp. 145–147.

10. R. D. Kaplan, "Sudan, a Microcosm of Africa's Ills," *Atlantic*, April 1986.

11. "War, Peace and the Generals," *Africa*, May 1986.

12. "Walkout Hits Sudan Parliament," *The Washington Times*, 7 May 1986.

13. "Dangerous Days in the Sudan," *Collin Legum's Third World Reports*, 2 September 1986.

14. Kaplan, "Sudan," p. 15.

15. SPLA/SPLM Representative Dominic Mohamed to James K. Bishop, U.S. Department of State, letter dated 18 July 1985. For the London meeting, note "Islamic Zeal Plunges Sudan into New Turmoil," *The Observer* (London), 20 May 1984.

16. "Portrait of an Exploiting Class," *SPLA/SPLM Newsletter*, no. 10/86, 21 November 1986, p. 43.

17. Economist Intelligence Unit, *Sudan in Transition: A Political Risk Analysis*, January 1986, p. 43.

18. *Africa Report*, July–August 1989, p. 45, no title.

19. Resource Management and Research, *Sudan's National Livestock Census and Resource Inventory*, vol. 31 (Khartoum: Department of Agriculture,1977).

20. Institute of Environmental Studies, *Sudan's Southern Stock Route* (Khartoum: University of Khartoum, 1985).

21. M. Burr, *Khartoum's Displaced Persons: A Decade of Despair* (Washington, D.C.: U.S. Committee for Refugees, August 1990).

22. Episcopal Church of the Sudan, "Progress Report: September 1986," Juba, September 1986.

23. M. McLean and C. Williams, "Economic War Against the Dinka," OXFAM, July 1986.

24. "Sudan's Hidden War Escalates as Ugandans Join the Fray," *The Guardian*, 13 June 1986.

25. "Uganda: UPDA-SPLA," *Africa Confidential*, 31 March 1989.

26. Norwegian Church Aid, *Sudan Programme, Annual Report, No. 17*, Oslo, 1986, 1987.

27. "Mundari Chiefs Support SPLA/SPLM," *SPLA/SPLM Newsletter*, no. 9/86, 5 September 1986.

28. USAID-Juba (Fields to Van Doren), "My View on Events Which Took Place During the Week," Juba, 7 February 1986.

29. U.S. Embassy—Khartoum, Cable 8445, 24 June 1986.

30. Agencies involved in Southern Sudan, "Minutes," Khartoum, 19 July 1986.

31. U.S. Embassy—Khartoum, Cable 8915, 4 July 1986.

32. African Medical Relief, Nairobi, "Displaced People's Health Support Project," Juba, 1987.

33. UN/RRC—Southern Sudan Emergency Operation, Technical Coordination Committee, "Minutes," 11 August 1986, Khartoum.

34. Ibid., 2 July and 17 November 1986.

35. Ibid., 11 August 1986.

36. Sudanaid, South Desk, "Release of 150 MT of Dura at Kosti to Fill a Barge at Kosti," 16 January 1986; USAID-Sudan Memorandum, "Dura for Barge at Kosti," 22 January 1986.

37. USAID-Sudan, Memorandum to WFP/MALT, 14 May 1986, Khartoum.

38. UNICEF-Khartoum, "UNICEF Sudan Recommended Press Release, Operation Hope 1986," 24105-sco-sd, 12 February 1986.

39. K. O'Rourke, "Sudanaid Relief to the South—Upper Nile Administrative Area, January, February, and March 1986," 5 March 1986. Also, K. O'Rourke, "Report on the Transport and Distribution of 1100 MT Dura in Upper Nile, July, August, and September 1985," Sudanaid, Malakal, October 1985.

40. Ibid.

41. H. Baya et al., "Sudanaid—Sudan Council of Churches Nutritional Survey," Malakal, 11 August–14 August," Khartoum, 20 August 1986, p. 9.

42. U.S. Embassy—Khartoum, Cable 9623, 22 July 1986. Also, Agencies involved in the Southern Sudan, "Minutes," Khartoum, 19 July 1986.

43. United Nations—UNEOS, "Brief for Donors, Southern Sudan Emergency Operation," Khartoum, 7 July 1986.

44. A. Mackie and J. Sarn, "Juba Food and Nutrition Status Trip Report," USAID-Sudan, Khartoum, 24 June 1986.

45. UN/RRC—Southern Sudan Emergency Operation, Technical Coordination Committee, "Minutes," 17 November 1986, Khartoum.

46. "Stranded Amid the Gunfire," *The Times*, 1 September 1986.

47. "Alarm Bells," *Middle East International*, 22 August 1986.

48. Radio SPLA, 1300 GMT, 18 August 1986.

49. *Al-Majallah*, 2 September 1986, p. 14, Joint Publications Research Service, Translation NEA-86-136, 28 October 1986.

50. *SPLA/SPLM Newsletter*, no. 10/86, 12 September 1986.

51. "U.S. Urging 'Food Truce' for Besieged Sudan," *The Washington Post*, 12 June 1986. Also, "'Food Truce' Urged in Sudan," *Arab News*, 12 June 1986.

52. Radio SPLA, 1300 GMT, 16 September 1986.

53. "The Sudan Relief and Rehabilitation Association (SRRA)," *Sudan Times*, 18 March 1987.

54. "Urging 'Food Truce' for Besieged Sudanese," *The Washington Post*, 28 August 1986.

55. U.S. Embassy—Khartoum, Cable 11529, 3 September 1986.

56. Government of Sudan—RCC, "The Future Role and Structure of the Commission for Relief and Rehabilitation," 7 July 1986.

57. D. Boyles, *African Lives* (New York: Weidenfeld and Nicolson, 1988), p. 130.

58. "Italian U.N. Aide Runs Risks to Deliver Food in Sudan," *The Washington Post*, 29 September 1986.

59. "Sudan Blocks U.N. Famine Aircraft," *The Washington Post*, 26 September 1986; "Politics in the Sudan Is Delaying Relief," *The New York Times*, 28 September 1986.

60. U.S. Embassy—Khartoum, Cable 11613, 4 September 1986. Also, Radio SPLA, 1300 GMT, 26 October 1986.

61. Government of Sudan—RRC TCC, "Minutes," 8 September 1986, Khartoum.

62. Ibid.

63. U.S. Department of State, Washington, D.C., Cable 287756, 12 September 1986.

64. United Nations—UNEOS, "'Operation Rainbow' to Fly Relief Food to Southern Sudan," 15 September 1986.

65. "Sudan Rebel Rejects Blame for Famine," *The Washington Post*, 18 September 1986.

66. "Politics in Sudan is Delaying Relief," *The New York Times*.

67. Government of Sudan—RRC, Southern Sudan Emergency Operation, "Status Report No. 12," 12 October 1986, Khartoum.

68. "Sudanese Flights Land Safely," *The Washington Post*, 13 October 1986.

69. Malakal Relief Agencies Coordinating Committee, "Summary of Minutes of the R.A.C.C. in UNAA (Malakal)," 28 September 1986, Malakal.

70. R. Bonner, "A Reporter at Large: Famine," *The New Yorker*, 13 March 1989, p. 88.

71. "Sudan Rebel Rejects Blame for Famine," *The Washington Post*, 14 July 1989.

72. Agence France Press Radio (in English), Paris, 0905 GMT, 12 October 1986; Joint Publication Research Service, Translation NEA 86-135, 27 October 1986.

73. *Al-Tadamun*, 6 December 1986, pp. 23–24; Joint Publications Research Service, Translation, date unknown.

74. Sudanaid, Letter from Rudolf Deng, Aweil, 21 September 1986.

75. U.S. Embassy—Khartoum, Cable 12527, 23 September 1986.

76. U.S. Embassy—Khartoum, Cable 12057, 15 September 1986.

77. Sudanaid, Letter from Rudolf Deng.

78. "Mass Starvation Imminent in Southern Sudan," *Arab News*, 29 August 1986.

79. Sudanaid/SCC, "Emergency Assistance Needs, Bahr el Ghazal and Upper Nile," Khartoum, 28 September 1986.

80. Relief Office, Bahr al-Ghazal Administration, Khartoum, 3 August 1986.

81. *Sudan Times*, Khartoum, 15 October 1986.

82. Government of Sudan—RRC-UNDP-UNEOS, "Southern Sudan: Relief Needs Estimate," Sudan Early Warning System Report, Khartoum, 23 December 1986.

83. USAID-Sudan, "Sudan—Drought and Famine in Africa, 1981–1986, the U.S. Response" (cable), 5 May 1987.

84. Delegation of the European Communities, "Food Aid to Darfur," Khartoum WMB/21/2285, 6 October 1986.

85. U.S. Embassy—Khartoum, Cable 11934, 11 September 1986.

86. Radio SPLA, 1300 GMT, 13 December 1986; Foreign Broadcast Information Service (FBIS), "North Africa," 15 December 1986, p. Q3.

87. SUNA Radio (in Arabic), Khartoum, 1422 GMT, 13 December 1986; FBIS, ibid.

88. Suna Radio, 1450 GMT, 15 December 1986; FBIS, "North Africa," 17 December 1986, p. Q5.

89. *Al-Bayan*, Dubai, 10 December 1986, pp. 1, 12; FBIS, "North Africa," 15 December 1986, p. Q3.

90. FBIS, "North Africa," 12 December 1986, p. Q4.

Chapter 3

1. Government of Sudan—RRC, "Early Warning System Bulletin," vol. 3, no. 4, 15 April 1987, Khartoum.

2. "Leader of Opposition Launches Broadside at Government," *Sudan Times*, 31 January 1989, Khartoum.

3. Government of Sudan—RRC Memorandum, RRC/EXEC/19/6, 21 January 1987.

4. Government of Sudan—RRC TCC, Southern Sudan Emergency Operation, "Minutes," 9 February 1987.

5. Ibid., 23 March 1987.

6. Government of Sudan, the Prime Minister, to The Relief and Rehabilitation Commission, 19 April 1987.

7. Government of Sudan—RRC Memorandum, RRC/EXEC/19/z/22, 11 May 1987.

8. "Opposition to Reappointment of Mr. Azraq," *Forward* (Khartoum), 22 May 1989.

9. Medicines Sans Frontiers/Belgium, "Report of the Raga Exploratory Mission on the Socio-Economic and Medico-Nutritional Situation in Raga District, January to February 1989," Khartoum, 1989.

10. U.S. Embassy—Khartoum, Cable 87928, May 1987.

11. From an anonymous study, "Report on a Visit to Aweil, Wau and Raga, 28–30 April 1987," Khartoum, 1 May 1987.

12. Government of Sudan—RRC/MALT Memorandum, 11 July 1989, Khartoum.

13. P. Symonds, "A Report on the Situation in Raga, Western Bahr al-Ghazal Province, June–August 1987," Khartoum, 12 September 1987.

14. Government of Sudan—RRC Memorandum, RRC/GEN/19/D/3, 9 July 1987, Khartoum.

15. U.S. Embassy—Khartoum, Cable 9188, 29 July 1987.

16. U.S. Embassy—Nairobi, Cable 25863, 30 July 1987.

17. Radio SPLA, 2 and 4 February 1987.

18. R. Hardin, "Life in Sudan Worsened Under Mahdi," *Washington Post*, 1 July 1990.

19. Information on the unofficial census is in the authors' possession.

20. UNICEF-Sudan, "Visit to Kaas/Trip Report," R/87/288, Khartoum, July 1987.

21. U. A. Mahmud and S. A. Baldo, *Al Diein Massacre, Slavery in the Sudan* (Khartoum: Khartoum University Press, 1987), pp. 4–6.

22. Government of Sudan—RRC TCC, "Minutes," Southern Sudan Emergency Operation, 18 May 1987.

23. Ibid., 13 April 1987.

24. Ibid.

25. Ibid., 21 April 1987.

26. USAID-Sudan, "Sudan—Southern Status Report 15" (cable 74691 to AID-Washington), 10 June 1987.

27. UNICEF-Sudan, "Visit to Kaas/Trip Report," R/87/288, Khartoum, July 1987.

28. Mahmud and Baldo, *Al Diein Massacre*, p. 10.

29. "The Running Controversy over Relief Operation in the Southern Sudan: The SPLA," *Sudan Times*, 29 November 1988.

30. "B. The Sudan Relief and Rehabilitation Association (SRRA) 1: Introduction Remarks,"*Sudan Times*, 18 March 1987.

31. Radio SPLA (in English), 1300 GMT, 21 January 1987.

32. "It Is Not for the Army to Question Policy," *Sudan Times*, 10 October 1986.

33. "Sadiq Bows to Peace," *Renewal* (Juba), May 1987.

34. *Guiding Star* (Khartoum), 8 January 1987.

35. *Le Monde*, 20 June 1987.

36. *Al-Tadamun* (London), 10–16 January 1987.

37. *Al-Mussawar* (Cairo), 20 February 1987.

38. "Sudan Enacts State of Emergency to Control Economy," *The Washington Times*, 27 July 1987.

39. "Sudan's Rebel Leader Signals Flexibility in Pursuit of Peace Talks," *Christian Science Monitor*, 14 October 1987.

40. For a history of the displaced persons see M. Burr, *Khartoum's Displaced Persons: A Decade of Despair* (Washington, D.C.: U.S. Committee for Refugees,1990).

41. Sudanaid, Khartoum, "Displaced Southerners in the Three Towns. A Survey Summary," 4 September 1986.

42. Sudan Council of Churches/UNICEF, "Report of MCH Survey Among the Displaced Populations, Khartoum Area," February 1987, Khartoum.

43. E. A. Bassan, "Background Information and Program Recommendation on Displaced People in Khartoum," Khartoum, 30 April 1987.

44. R. McGowan, "Peri-Urban Water Supply; A Brief Glimpse of Refugee/ Displaced Persons Areas Near Omdurman, Sudan," ARD (Adventist Relief)- Khartoum, 13 June 1989.

45. USAID-Sudan, Memorandum (Mackie to Koehring), "Update on Displaced Persons in Khartoum," Khartoum, 6 July 1987.

46. U.S. Department of State, *Country Reports on Human Rights Practice for 1987* (Washington, D.C., February 1988), p. 297.

47. I. Laemerzahl, "Report on the Interviews with PVOs Engaged in Activities to Assist Displaced People in the Khartoum Area," Khartoum, August 1987.

48. "Sudan's Secret Slaughter," *Cultural Survival Quarterly*, vol. 12, no. 2, 1988.

49. "Terror and Hunger Spread as Sudan 'Holy War' Rages," *The Atlanta Journal and Constitution*, 27 June 1988.

50. "Sudan's Secret Slaughter," *Cultural Survival Quarterly*.

51. *Sudan Times*, 23 September 1987.

52. *Al-Ayyam* (Khartoum), 27 September 1989.

53. Radio Message, Acting Governor Darius Beshir, Wau, to World Vision International, Khartoum, 10 December 1987.

54. Data conveyed by 19 January 1988 radio message from Wau to Khartoum.

55. Chairman Rudolf M. Deng, "Quarterly Report (Dec. 1986–Mar. 1987)," Relief Committee, Aweil.

56. Aweil Rice Development Project, "Food Assessment, Aweil," Memorandum K107–289, 25 April 1987.

57. USAID-Sudan, "Sudan—Southern Sudan Status Report 11" (cable from AID-Khartoum to Washington), 18 May 1987.

58. UN Development Program—Khartoum, "Letter to H.E. Mr. Sadiq El Mahdi," 24 June 1987.

59. Relief Office, Bahr al-Ghazal Region, "Report on Relief Work," RO/ OBGR/k/19.A.1., Khartoum, 15 June 1987.

60. See "Fifty People Reportedly Starved to Death in Aweil," *Sudan Times*, 24 July 1987; Government of Sudan—RRC TCC, "Minutes," Southern Sudan Emergency Operation, 2 August 1987; Bahr al-Ghazal Region, "Hunger Situation in Aweil Area," Governor's Office, Khartoum, 24 August 1987.

61. Government of Sudan—RRC TCC, "Minutes," 10 August 1987, Khartoum.

62. UN World Food Program, "Emergency Telex Report No. 130," Khartoum, 12 February 1988.

63. *SPLA/SPLM Newsletter*, no. 13/87, 30 October 1987, pp. 2–4.

64. USAID-Sudan, letter to RRC Commissioner Shawki, 23 March 1987, Khartoum.

65. Ibid., 27 April 1987.

66. Government of Sudan—RRC TCC, "Minutes," Southern Sudan Emergency Operation, 22 June 1987.

67. USAID-Sudan, "Sudan—Southern Sudan Status Report 15, 1987."

68. Government of Sudan—RRC TCC, "Minutes," 21 September 1987, Khartoum.

69. USAID-Sudan, "Sudan—Southern Sudan Status Report 32" (cable 47382 to AID-Washington), 25 October 1987, Khartoum.

70. "Halt Militia Evil Acts," *Renewal* (Juba), May 1987.

71. "Is It a Crime to Be an African in Sudan?" *Renewal* (Juba), July 1987.

72. "SCC Under Attack for Facilitating African Parties for Trip to East Africa," *Sudan Times*, 24 September 1987.

73. "Army Withdraws from Kurmuk," *Sudan Times*, 15 November 1987.

74. "Silence! On negocie malgre les dementis," *Jeune Afrique*, 27 January 1988.

75. "Sudan," *Le Monde*, 20 November 1987.

76. "Tribal Traditions Destroyed by Power of New Weaponry," *Miami Herald*, 11 December 1987.

77. "Emergency Assistance to the Sudan," UN document, A/43/755, New York 22 October 1988, p. 5.

78. Islamic African Relief Agency, "Al-Kurmuk Incident," 29 November 1987, Khartoum.

79. "Ethiopia and Sudan," *Arab News*, 23 November 1987.

80. "Sudan and Ethiopia Back on Speaking Terms," *Middle East International*, 19 December 1987.

81. "Soudan a l'epreuve de la rebellion sudiste," *Le Monde Diplomatique*, June 1989.

82. "Sudan: The Heavy Toll of Civil War," *Middle East International*, 16 April 1988.

83. *SPLA/SPLM Newsletter*, no. 1, 1 January 1988.

Chapter 4

1. UN World Food Program, "Emergency Telex Report," no. 122, Khartoum, 11 December 1987.

2. Ibid.

3. Delegation of the Commission of the European Communities, Sudan, "Western Relief Operation 1987/1988, Draft Report," October 1989, p. 12, Khartoum.

4. U.S. Embassy—Khartoum, Cable 993, 29 January 1988.

5. U.S. Embassy—Khartoum, Cable 352, 11 January 1988.

6. U.S. Embassy—Khartoum, Cable 2673, 7 March 1988.

7. U.S. Embassy—Khartoum, Cable 2881, 9 March 1988.

8. U.S. Embassy—Khartoum, Cable 770, 24 January 1988.

9. USAID-Sudan, "Sudan Status Report 43," (cable to AID-Washington), 14 January 1988; Africa Watch, *Denying "The Honor of Living,"* Sudan: A Human Rights Disaster (New York: 1990), p. 96.

10. World Vision International, "Country Newsletter," no. 2, Khartoum, 28 December 1987.

11. UNICEF, "UNICEF Report: Situation in El Meiram, Abiye District, South Kordofan," Khartoum, 10 October 1987.

12. UN World Food Program, Khartoum, "Emergency Telex Report," no. 127, 22 January 1988.

13. K. Westgate, "Displaced People in Southern Darfur," League of Red Cross Societies, El Fasher, Darfur, February 1988.

14. Bahr al-Ghazal, Acting Governor to H.E. Prime Minister and Minister of Defense, Letter GO/BGR/SCR94.A.1., Wau, 15 January 1988.

15. U.S. Embassy—Khartoum, Cable 993, 29 January 1988.

16. U.S. Embassy—Khartoum, Cable 1551, 9 February 1988.

17. Lakes Province Commissioner's Office, "Statement on Relief Situation in Lakes Province, Bahr el Ghazal Region to the Donor Agencies and the Relief and Rehabilitation Commission," 6 March 1988, Wau, Sudan.

18. Sudan Council of Churches—Khartoum, "Report on Third and Final Distribution of Relief Food by RACC/Malakal," Malakal, 6 July 1988.

19. Upper Nile Region, Relief Agencies Coordinating Committee, "Appeal for Immediate Relief," Malakal, 6 July 1988.

20. "Famine Spectre as Crops Fail in Sudan," The Times, 6 February 1988.

21. U.S. Department of State, Cable 112584, 9 April 1988.

22. Raymond Bonner, "A Reporter at Large: Famine," The New Yorker, 13 March 1989.

23. "One Hundred Thousand Leave Bahr el Ghazal," Sudan Times, 5 May 1988.

24. "How a Youngster Joined the Boys' Republic in the Horn of Africa; In Search of Refuge," The Financial Times, 5 July 1989, p. 4.

25. "Sudanese Flee in Search of Food, Safety," Christian Science Monitor, 29 June 1988.

26. Reuters Library Report, "Ethiopia Braces for Fresh Surge of Sudanese Refugees," 15 November 1988.

27. "Confronting the Mahdi," The Times, 30 January 1989.

28. AID-Washington, AA/AF, "Talking Points," drafted 4 March 1988, p. 13, Washington, D.C.

29. AID-Washington, "FEWS Country Reports: Chad, Mali, Niger and Sudan," Report no. 20, Washington, D.C., February 1988, p. 17.

30. USAID-Sudan, "Sudan—Congressional Hearings: Southern Review and Drought in the West," Cable 2673, 7 March 1988.

31. U.S. Department of State, Cable 58981, 26 February 1988.

32. "Sudan Seizure of Trucks Puts Food Aid at Risk," The Times, 9 February 1988.

33. Ibid.

34. "Sudanese Soldiers Commandeer Food Trucks, Oxfam Says," The Independent, 9 February 1988. The Italian vehicles were never returned; two years later they were seen in army compounds in Malakal, Wau, and Juba.

35. "Statement of the Honorable Charles L. Gladson, Assistant Administrator for Africa, Agency for International Development, in Testimony Before the House Select Committee on Hunger and the House Foreign Affairs Sub-Committee on Africa," 10 March 1988, pp. 3–4, Congressional Record, Washington, D.C.

36. K. Westgate, "Displaced People in Southern Darfur: Situation Report," League of Red Cross and Red Crescent Societies, El Fasher, February 1988.

37. "Sudan Looks at Secession for Rebels," *The Washington Times*, 29 April 1987.

38. Government of Sudan—RRC TCC, "Minutes," 25 April 1988, Khartoum.

39. "While Their People Die of Famine Outside the Grainstore Doors, Bahr al-Ghazal Government Stockpiles Food," *Sudan Times*, 29 March 1988.

40. MSF-Belgium, "Summary Report, Displaced Dinka in South Darfur," Khartoum, 26 September 1988.

41. Kordofan Region, Ministry of Finance and Economy, Food Aid Administration Office, 19 March 1988.

42. UN World Food Program, "Emergency Telex Report #140," Khartoum, 3 May 1988.

43. U.S. Embassy—Khartoum, Cable 3574, 27 March 1988.

44. USAID-Sudan to Undersecretary for Planning, Ministry of Finance and Economic Planning, "Emergency Food Transport," 13 March 1988, Khartoum.

45. UN-UNDP, Office of the UN Resident Coordinator, Letter to H.E. Prime Minister Sadiq al-Mahdi, Khartoum, 27 April 1988.

46. Reuters Library Report, "Aid Workers Say Sudan Famine Is Over—The Vulnerable Are Dead," 12 December 1988.

47. UN World Food Program, "Sudan Sitrep 88/24," Khartoum, 7 July 1988.

48. "Of Sudan's Woes, War Is the Worst," *The New York Times*, 19 October 1988, p. A10.

49. Relief Agencies Coordinating Committee, Upper Nile Region, "Appeal for Immediate Relief," Malakal, 6 July 1988.

50. Joint Relief Committee, radio message to Sudanaid-Juba, Torit, 27 June 1988.

51. "One Hundred Thousand Leave Bahr el Ghazal," *Sudan Times*, 3 May 1988.

52. U.S. Embassy—Khartoum, "Sudan—Field Trip to the Western Sudan," Cable 7212, 21 June 1988.

53. "Terror and Hunger Spread as Sudan 'Holy War' Rages," *The Atlanta Journal and Constitution*, 27 June 1988.

54. UN World Food Program, "Sitrep Sudan 88/24," Khartoum, 7 July 1988.

55. R. Bonner, "A Reporter at Large: Famine."

56. "Selective Starvation in War Zones Triggers Selective Anger Abroad," *The Atlanta Journal and Constitution*, 26 June 1988.

57. Ibid.

58. "Emergency Assistance to the Sudan," UN Document A/43/755, 27 October 1988, p. 5.

59. Bonner, "A Reporter at Large: Famine."

60. U.S. Embassy—Khartoum, Cable 8098, 13 July 1988.

61. UN Food and Agricultural Organization, "Sitrep Sudan, 88/24," 7 July 1988, Rome.

62. Ibid.

63. UN World Food Program, "Displaced Persons in Sudan: Food Need and Availability—Revision as of 4.7.88," Khartoum, 4 July 1988.

64. A copy of the handwritten memorandum is in the authors' possession.

65. U.S. Embassy—Khartoum, Cable 7003, 15 June 1988.

66. UN Multi Donor Mission, "Government of Sudan, Emergency Food Reconstruction Program," 17 October 1988, Khartoum.

67. UN-UNICEF Consultant, "Status Report Displaced People—South Kordofan and Southern Darfur," Khartoum, 1 September 1988.

68. GOS Ministry of Health, Nutrition Department, "Nutrition Monitoring Report #1," Khartoum, 16 October 1988.

69. "Food Relief Trickles into Sudan," *The Washington Post*, 14 August 1987, p. A27.

70. "At the End of the Road is the Graveyard of Hope," *The New York Times*, 4 November 1988.

71. U.S. Department of State, "Khartoum Floods," Cable 256677, 8 August 1988.

72. M. Lejars, C. Carr, and E. de Faramond, "A Project for an Extension of Nutritional and Medical Assistance to El Meiram, Southern Kordofan, Sudan," MSF-France, Khartoum, October 1988.

73. "The Role and Activities of Two French NGOs," *Refugees*, November 1988.

74. USAID-Sudan, "Food Aid for Aweil," letter to the RRC, 21 July 1988, Khartoum.

75. USAID-Sudan, "Re: RRC/19-Z-6, dated 20 July 1988," Khartoum, 3 August 1988.

76. "Relief Workers Bear Witness as Thousands of Refugees Starve in Sudan Town," *The Atlanta Journal and Constitution*, 3 March 1989.

77. CARE International, Sudan, "Urgent Report About Worsening Conditions of Displaced Persons in Abyei and En Nahud Districts," 18 August 1988, Khartoum.

78. Report in the authors' possession, September 1989.

79. CARE International, Sudan, "Urgent Report."

80. Report in the authors' possession, September 1988.

81. "Twenty-One Thousand Dinkas Face Death in Meiram as Misseiria Take Relief Food," *Sudan Times*, 11 September 1988.

82. Reuters, "Agony of the Sudan Sick, Hungry Refugees in a Tent for the Dying," 9 September 1988.

83. Reuters, "Southern Refugees Tell Horror Stories of War and Famine," 9 September 1988.

84. Concern, "Emergency Program, Sudan, 1988," Khartoum, 1989.

85. "Soudan Le calvaire des Dinka," *Jeune Afrique*, 31 August 1988.

86. Aweil Relief Committee Report, dated 21 November 1988, Aweil.

87. Handwritten memorandum in the authors' possession, 1 August 1988.

88. Reuters Library Report, "Hunger, Disease Kill 8,000 in S. Sudan Town," 2 December 1988.

89. "Terror and Hunger Spread as Sudan 'Holy War' Rages," *The Atlanta Journal and Constitution*, 27 June 1988.

90. Government of Sudan-RCC Memorandum, "Kordofan Region," 17 August 1988, handwritten correspondence in the authors' possession, Kadugli.

91. UN-UNICEF Consultant, "Status Report Displaced People."

92. L. Lual Akuey, "Report on the Famine/Expected Famine in the 1988/1989 Bahr el Ghazal Region," Governor's Office, Wau, 22 September 1988.

93. Bishop Nyekindi Joseph, "Hunger Situation in Bahr el Ghazal Region—Wau," 30 September 1988, Wau.

94. "Angelo Beda Speaks on His Visit to Wau," *Heritage* (Khartoum), 3 October 1988.

95. "Week in Politics," *Forward* (Khartoum), 3 April 1988.

96. "The Unsettled Millions," *Africa News* reprinted by U.S. Committee For Refugees, Washington, D.C., 8 August 1988.

97. BBC—Middle East/0489/A/1, 22 June 1989.

Chapter 5

1. UN Development Program, *World Development* (New York: The United Nations Development Program,1989).

2. U.S. Embassy—Khartoum, Cable 11327, 28 September 1988.

3. "Sudan Racked by Famine, Agrees to U.S. Food Airlift," *The New York Times*, 13 October 1988.

4. "The Unsettled Millions," *Africa News* (Reprint), U.S. Committee for Refugees, Washington, D.C., 8 August 1988.

5. Note, for example, "U.S. Policy on Sudan Famine Reflects Split," *The Atlanta Journal and Constitution*, 21 December 1988.

6. M. C. Lejars, C. Carr et al., "A Project Proposal for an Extension of Nutritional and Medical Assistance to Meiram, Southern Kordofan, Sudan," Khartoum, October 1988.

7. "Sudan Racked by Famine, Agrees to U.S. Food Airlift," *The New York Times*, 13 October 1988.

8. Human Rights Watch, "Human Rights in Sudan, Testimony of Holly Burkhalter, Africa Watch, Before the House Foreign Affairs Africa Subcommittee and the Select Committee on Hunger," 2 March 1989, The Congressional Record, 22 June 1989.

9. "Sudan Racked by Famine, Agrees to U.S. Food Airlifts," *The New York Times*, 13 October 1988.

10. M. Philips, "Report on Visit to Abeyi on 9–10 October 1988," MSF-Belgium, Khartoum, 12 October 1988.

11. U.S. Embassy—Khartoum, Cable 13661, 25 November 1988.

12. UNICEF-Sudan, "Note for the Record: Relief Supplies to Abeye," Khartoum, 31 October 1988.

13. "In Southern Sudan, an Airlift of Food Lands in a Town of Misery," *The New York Times*, 16 October 1988.

14. "Airlifted Food Makes Its Tortuous Way," *The International Herald Tribune*, 17 October 1988.

15. "The Hidden Holocaust," *New Statesman and Society*, 23–30 December 1988. Accompanying the article is a photograph of the dead waiting for burial that is as graphic a display of human tragedy as has ever been published.

16. "Food for Sudan Takes Weeks to Affect Famine," *The Washington Times*, 17 October 1988.

17. Quote provided to the authors in 1988. See also *Associated Press*, "Christian, Animist Refugees Wear Out Welcome in Moslem Town," 13 March 1989.

18. Private correspondence dated 31 October 1988; in the authors' possession.

19. Committee to Raise Local Donations for the Displaced and Destitute in Wau, "Report on Emergency Relief Situation in Bahr al Ghazal Region," Wau, 18 September 1988.

20. MSF-France, "A Project Proposal for Emergency Assistance to Aweil Civil Hospital and Nutritional Assistance to Aweil Town," 14 December 1988, Aweil.

21. Private unpublished survey carried out in October 1988, in the authors' possession.

22. Kadugli report, in the authors' possession.

23. USAID-Sudan, Letter to RRC Acting Commissioner Dr. Al-Hag Al-Tayeb, 22 November 1988.

24. AID Office of Foreign Disaster Assistance, "Situation Report No. 12," Washington, D.C., 29 November 1989.

25. "Government Allows Small Airlift to Abiey, but Aweil in Doubt," *Sudan Times*, 16 October 1988.

26. "Sudan Famine Relief Slowed by Civil War," *The Washington Post*, 25 November 1988.

27. "Sudan Accused of Diverting U.S. Supplies for Refugees," *The Atlanta Journal and Constitution*, 23 December 1989.

28. "Red Cross Opens Sudan Relief Drive," *The New York Times*, 5 December 1988.

29. "Sudan: Change of Heart," *Middle East International*, 21 October 1988.

30. Ibid.

31. U.S. Embassy—Rome, Cable 2170, 1 February 1989.

32. Secretariat General Regional Executive Council, "1st Anniversary of the Landing of the 1st Relief Plane," Juba, 28 October 1989.

33. "Starving the South," *Africa Report*, Vol. 1–2, 1989.

34. "Despite International Airlifts, Hunger Persists in Southern Sudan," *The Philadelphia Inquirer*, 6 December 1988.

35. "Federation Joins Food Airlift," Nairobi, *Nation*, 14 November 1988. Also note Lutheran World Federation, "Sudan Airlift: Food, Medicine and Hope," Nairobi, 29 September 1989.

36. "Peace Talks Ring a Bit Hollow for Sudan's Besieged Southerners," *Christian Science Monitor*, 29 November 1988.

37. Ibid.

38. Bishop Taban to Southern Catholic Bishops Conference, 0900 GMT, 28 November 1988.

39. *The Los Angeles Times*, "Sudan Aid Convoy Attacked," 8 December 1988.

40. "Suffering Sudan Needs Our Help," *The Los Angeles Times*, 18 December 1988, part 5, p. 5.

41. Associated Press, "U.N. Says Five African Countries Face Famine," 6 December 1988.

42. M. Burr, "A Working Document: Quantifying Genocide in the Southern Sudan, 1983–1993," U.S. Committee for Refugees, Washington, D.C., October 1993.

43. Committee on Foreign Affairs, U.S. House Select Committee on Hunger, Serial No. 101-1, Washington, D.C., 2 March 1989, p. 35.

44. Associated Press, "Economic, Political Pressures Mount on Government to Make Peace," 10 December 1988.

45. UN Office for Emergencies in Africa, proposal, New York, 5 December 1988.

46. "Sudan Prospects for Peace," *Africa Confidential*, 16 December 1988.

47. "U.S. Relief Effort Blocked in Sudan," *The New York Times*, 28 October 1988.

48. Ibid.

49. "Aid Quagmire in Sudan," *Christian Science Monitor*, 28 November 1988.

50. Ibid.

51. "Dateline Washington, Famine," *States News Service*, 15 November 1988.

52. "In Sudan, Both Sides Use Food as a Weapon," *The Washington Post*, 29 November 1988.

53. "Sudan Policy May Bring More Suffering, House Study Says," *Boston Globe*, 14 December 1988.

54. Ibid.

55. Reuters, "Famine in South Sudan Sensationalized by the Media, Minister Says," 6 December 1988.

56. U.S. Congress, 19 December 1988. Letter to the Honorable Sadiq al-Mahdi, Prime Minister of Sudan, from Congressman Wolpe, Washington, D.C.

57. Ibid.

58. "Thousands Died in Sudan as U.S. Remained Silent," *The Atlanta Journal and Constitution*, 18 December 1988.

59. Comité International de la Croix Rouge, "Report: Emergency Operations in Southern Sudan from December 88 to August 89," Geneva, 13 September 1988.

60. "Sudan, Facing Resistance, Shelves Islamic Law Bill," *The Washington Post*, 7 October 1988.

61. "Economic, Political Pressures Mount on Government to Make Peace," *The Washington Post*, 10 December 1988.

62. "Sudan: Food Deliveries Begin," *Africa News*, 12 December 1988.

63. Reuters, "Sudanese Rebels, Coalition Party Propose Ceasefire," 14 November 1988.

64. Ibid.

65. Reuters Library Report, "Sudan's Chief Backs Peace Deal," 15 November 1988.

66. BBC, ME/0314/A/1, 21 November 1988; see also *SPLA/SPLM Newsletter*, 15 May 1989.

67. "Civil War Peace Plan Puts Strains on Sudan Coalition," *Financial Times*, 17 November 1988.

68. "Time to Call Premier's Bluff," *Sudan Times*, 18 December 1988.

69. Reuters, "Sudanese Politician Gets Hero's Welcome After Peace Accords," 17 November 1988.

70. Ibid.

71. Reuters, "Missile Attack on Minister's Plane May Stiffen Militancy," 19 November 1988.

72. Reuters Library Report, "Sudan Peace Accord Could Trigger Political Storm," 14 November 1988.

73. Reuters Library Report, "Sudan's Main Party Welcomes Peace Plan, Isolating Militants," 18 November 1988.

74. Reuters Library Report, "Mahdi Says Attack Proves Rebels Not Serious About Peace," 20 November 1988.

75. Reuters Library Report, "Sudan Rebels Accuse Peace Plan," 22 November 1988.

76. "Peace Pact Wins Approval of Sudan Cabinet," *The Washington Times*, 2 December 1988.

77. Associated Press, "Premier's Party Approves Peace Agreement," 24 November 1988.

78. Reuters Library Report, "Sudan Peace Pact Remains Paper Commitment," 16 November 1988.

79. Ibid.

80. Reuters Library Report, "Sudan's Government Near Collapse," 22 December 1988.

81. MBBC, E/345/A/1, "Sudan in Brief," 29 December 1988.

82. "The Running Controversy over Relief Operation in Southern Sudan: The SPLA," 29, *Sudan Times*, November 1988.

83. Ibid.

84. Reuters Library Report, "Sudan's Judges Resign, Mahdi Pressured to End War," 2 January 1989.

85. "Famine in Sudan," *The Washington Post*, 3 January 1989.

86. "Sudan Rebels Say They Are Victims of Poison Gas," *The New York Times*, 10 January 1989.

87. Ibid.

88. U.S. House Select Committee on Hunger, "Tragedy in the Sudan," 24 January 1989.

89. U.S. Embassy—Khartoum, Cable 2132, 23 February 1989.

90. "In Sudan Peace Effort, U.S. Meets a Representative of the Guerrillas," *The New York Times*, 1 February 1989.

91. Federal News Service, "State Department Regular Briefing," 1 February 1989.

92. Reuters Library Report, "Washington Wants to Get Food Aid to Rebel-Held Parts of Sudan," 24 January 1989.

93. Ibid.

94. "The Plight of the Displaced in Sudan," *Renewal*, no. 32, Juba, April 1989.

95. "In Sudan Peace Effort," *The New York Times*.

96. BBC, ME/0373/A/1, "Sudan in Brief," 30 January 1989.

97. U.S. Department of State/AFR, "The U.S. and Sudan: Peace and Relief," 7 February 1989, Washington, D.C.

98. "U.S. Offers Help on Alleviating African Conflicts," *The New York Times*, 9 February 1989.

99. "At Last, Plain Words About the Sudan," *The New York Times*, 21 February 1989.

100. "Baker Urges Sudan to Stop Blocking Aid," *The Atlanta Journal and Constitution*, 9 February 1989.

101. "The Famine That Needn't Happen," *The Washington Post,* 22 March 1989.

102. *Al-Ayyam* (Khartoum), 14 February 1989.

103. *Al-Meidan* (Khartoum), 15 February 1989.

104. Omdurman Radio (in Arabic), 1930 GMT, 30 January 1989.

105. U.S. Department of State, Cable 3392, 6 January 1989; Cable 44229, 11 February 1989.

106. International Committee of the Red Cross, "Annual Report, 1988," Geneva, 1989.

107. Concern-Sudan, "Tom Lavin, Malakal Field Visit, 4/15," April 1989, Khartoum; AID-OFDA, "Sudan—Civil Strife/Displaced Persons," Situation Report no. 14, 9 January 1989, Khartoum; Reuters, "Sudan Says Aid Convoy Reaches Cut Off Town," 15 February 1989.

108. "Relief Group in Sudan Gets Boost from Soviets," *The Washington Post,* 3 March 1989.

109. Government of Sudan—RRC, TCC, "Minutes," 20 March 1989, Khartoum .

110. Ibid., 17 October 1988.

111. U.S. Embassy—Khartoum, Cable 1133, 31 January 1989.

112. AID-OFDA, "Sudan—Civil Strife/Displaced Persons," Situation Report no. 18, 23 March 1989, Khartoum.

113. "First U.S. Food Aid Shipped to Rebel-held Sudan," *The Washington Post,* 25 January 1989.

114. "Report Criticizes U.S. for 'Quiet Diplomacy' in Sudan," *The Chicago Tribune,* 16 February 1989.

115. R. P. Winter, "Testimony of Roger P. Winter, Director U.S. Committee for Refugees Before the Senate Committee on Foreign Relations Subcommittee on Africa," 23 February 1989, Washington, D.C.

116. "Can Washington Stop the Starvation?" *Christian Science Monitor,* 28 February 1989.

117. Ibid.

118. UN World Food Program, "Emergency Telex Report—Sudan," Khartoum, 17 February 1989.

119. "Rebels, Sudan to Open Relief Route," *The Washington Post,* 25 March 1989.

Chapter 6

1. Reuters Library Report, "Sudan Rebel Leader Asks Government Troops to Open Dialogue," 1 January 1989.

2. "People of Southern Sudanese Town Are Running Out of Food, Medicine and Hope," *The Los Angeles Times,* 25 December 1988.

3. *Sudan Times,* "Government Launches Diplomatic Initiatives in the Arab World," 6 February 1989.

4. International Press Service, "Sudan: Govt. Faces Crisis as Prime Minister May Step Down," 3 March 1989.

5. "Can Washington Stop the Starvation?" *Christian Science Monitor*, 28 February 1989.

6. *Sudan Times*, "Sadiq Replies to Army Ultimatum with His Own," 28 February 1989.

7. Associated Press, "Prime Minister Threatens to Resign," 27 February 1989.

8. *Sudan Times*, "Sadiq Replies to Army Ultimatum With His Own," 28 February 1989.

9. International Press Service, "Sudan."

10. Reuters Library Report, "Sudan Marks Independence Day Embroiled in Crisis," 1 January 1989.

11. "Decay, Chaos Are Victors in Sudan's 'War with Itself,'" *Baltimore Sun*, 16 April 1989.

12. "Sudan Chief Rides Out Storm," *The Washington Times*, 28 February 1989.

13. *Middle East International*, "Libya: The Colonel Eyes Sudan," 17 March 1989.

14. United Press International, "Khartoum" and "Sudan" reports for 4 March 1989.

15. Reuters, "Sudan Economy Staggers Under Debt, Inflation and War Costs," 15 May 1989.

16. Inter Press Service, "Sudan: Looking to Expatriates to Boost Economy," 25 January 1989.

17. *Al-Ayyam* (Khartoum), 19 April 1989.

18. *Al-Siyassa* (Khartoum), 21 May 1989.

19. Reuters, "Sudan to Reject IMF Cures Even If People Suffer," 18 May 1989.

20. U.S. Department of State, Washington, D.C., Cable 23473, 26 January 1989.

21. United Nations—Khartoum, "High Level Meeting, Government of the Sudan and the United Nations, Khartoum 8–9 March 1989," 15 March 1989; "First U.S. Food Aid Shipped to Rebel-Held Area in Sudan," *The Washington Post*, 17 February 1989.

22. NGO Consortium and MSF-France, "NGO Consortium Submission re Constraints Facing NGOs with Recommended Solutions," 26 February 1989, Khartoum.

23. United Press International, "Sudanese Rebels to Be Consulted on Famine Aid Plan," 9 March 1989.

24. Associated Press, "Donors Pledge Relief Aid," 9 March 1989.

25. Sudan News Agency, "Daily Bulletin," 9 March 1989.

26. "Sudan Signs $250 Million Arms Deal with Libya," *The Washington Post*, 4 March 1989.

27. UNICEF-Nairobi, Cable 700 211554, 22 March 1989; UN-Khartoum, UNDP, "Khartoum Sudan Weekly Report," no. 2, 20–27 March 1989.

28. "Ex-Paratrooper Spurns Rules," *The Los Angeles Times*, 19 March 1989; CBS News, "This Morning," 11 April 1989.

29. Reuters Library Report, "Sudan's Moslem Militants Shun New Government," 14 March 1989.

30. Reuters Library Report, "Mahdi Calls on Rebels to Reply to Peace Overtures," 27 March 1989.

31. "Deputy PM Stresses Confidence in SPLA," 30 *Sudan Times*, March 1989; also note Associated Press, "New Cabinet Endorses Peace Plan," 26 March 1989.

32. "Sudan Leader of Many Hats and Two Worlds," *The New York Times*, 14 March 1990.

33. United Press International, "Sudanese Prime Minister Offers to Meet Rebel Leader," 23 March 1989.

34. "Opposition Denounces Government Policy on Islam," *Sudan Times*, 30 March 1989.

35. United Press International, "AID Appeals for Help in Sudan," 24 March 1989.

36. Associated Press, "Sudanese Emergency Relief Effort to Begin," 25 March 1989.

37. "House Panel Questions U.N. Relief Effort in Sudan," *The New York Times*, 9 April 1989.

38. United Press International, "Parliament Delays Vote on Islamic Law," 10 April 1989.

39. "NIF Leader Declares Jihad," *Sudan Times*, 16 April 1989.

40. Sudan News Agency, "Daily Bulletin," 19 April 1989.

41. *The New York Times*, 19 March 1989.

42. Reuters Library Report, "Sudan Rebel Head Will Let Relief Food Go Through, Congressmen Say," 28 March 1989.

43. Inter Press Service, "U.S. Groups Mobilizing 'National Day of Concern,'" 10 March 1989.

44. From reporting by the Associated Press's Didrikke Schanche, Juba, September 1988, and the *Baltimore Sun*'s J. Eddings, Juba, April 1989.

45. "U.S. Policy on Sudan One of Silence, Contradictions," *The Atlanta Journal and Constitution*, 1 January 1989.

46. "Food Rushed to Sudan as Lives Hang in Balance," *Baltimore Sun*, 18 April 1989.

47. "Starvation as a Political Weapon," *U.S. News and World Report*, 6 February 1989.

48. "Sudan: Food Scramble Is On," *Africa News*, 17 April 1989.

49. "Concern over Sudan Food Crisis," *Newsday*, 17 April 1989.

50. *Sudan Times*, "United States Policy on Sudan," 2 April 1989.

51. *Sudan Times*, "Foreign Affairs Committee Busy on Peace Plans," 27 April 1989.

52. Reuters Library Report, "Mahdi Said Concerned over Effect of Fighting," 25 April 1989.

53. "John Garang: A New Sudan," *Africa Report*, July–August 1989.

54. SPLA General Headquarters (no location given), "Press Statement on Operation Lifeline Sudan," 29 April 1989.

55. "House Panel Questions U.N. Relief Effort," *The New York Times*, 9 April 1989.

56. United Press International, "Rebel Activity Threatens Sudan Relief Effort," 14 April 1989.

57. SPLA/SPLM, "Newsletter: Special Edition," 8 May 1989, London.

58. United Press International, "Report on Sudan," 1 April 1989; Reuters Library Report, "Ethiopian Leader Says He Wants Closer U.S. Relations," 1 April

1989; "Ethiopia Trips Up UN Aid for Sudan," *International Herald Tribune*, 26 April 1989.

59. "SPLA Offers Safe Exit for Sudanese Troops," *The Washington Times*, 3 May 1989.

60. *Al-Siyassa* (Khartoum), 10 May 1989.

61. *New African*, June 1989.

62. Associated Press, "Leader of Sudan's Rebels Making First U.S. Visit," 25 May 1989.

63. *Al-Siyassa* (Khartoum), 31 May 1989.

64. U.S. Information Agency dispatch, Khartoum, 1 (630), 23:30 GMT, 26 May 1989.

65. Reuters, "Sudanese Rebels Welcome American Mediation," 28 January 1989.

66. Reuters Library Report, "Sudan Rebel Leader Says Ceasefire Extended," 1 June 1989.

67. Inter Press Service, "Sudan: To Meet Rebel SPLA in Addis Ababa," 2 June 1989.

68. Federal News Service, "The Brookings Institution Seminar with John Garang," 9 June 1989.

69. Ibid.

70. Ibid.

71. Ibid.

72. "Bitter Historical Split Blocks Solution to Festering Crisis," *Insight*, 17 April 1989.

73. Federal News Service, "The Brookings Institution Seminar."

74. Inter Press Service, "Sudan: Garang Offers to Extend Ceasefire," 7 June 1989.

75. Federal News Service, "News Makers and Policy Makers," 7 June 1989.

76. "Sudan: War and Peace," *Africa Confidential*, 12 May 1989.

77. "Peace at Last?" *New African*, June 1989.

78. *Al-Khartoum, Al-Meidan* (Khartoum), 11 June 1989; *Al-Khartoum*, 14 June 1989.

79. United Press International, "Sudanese Set Three-Month Deadline for Cease-Fire," 12 June 1989.

80. BBC, ME/0489/A/1, 22 June 1989.

81. *Al-Siyassa* (Khartoum), 16 June 1989.

82. Associated Press, "Ousted Sudanese Leader Still Plots to Seize Power," 3 June 1989.

83. *Al-Siyassa* (Khartoum), 23 June 1989.

84. *Al-Siyassa* (Khartoum), 16 June 1989.

85. *Al-Siyassa, Al-Ayyam* (Khartoum), 27 June 1989.

86. *Sudan Times* (from a report in *Al-Ayyam*), 29 June 1989.

87. *Al-Ayyam* (Khartoum), 28 June 1989.

88. *Al-Khartoum* (Khartoum), 28 June 1989.

89. Associated Press, "U.N. Relief Effort Faces Daunting Problems in Sudan," 27 March 1989.

90. B. Wannop, UN-Khartoum, "Report on the First Muglad-Aweil Relief Train," Khartoum, 29 June 1989; "Food Relief Effort Impeded," *The New York Times*, 19 April 1989.

91. Air Serv International, Lehnhart to Charge d'Affaires, Embassy of the Netherlands, Khartoum, 14 March 1989.

92. Reuters Library Report, "Relief Planes Race Against Death in South Sudan," 20 March 1989.

93. Government of Sudan—Council for the South, "Apology," Letter to Ambassador Norman Anderson, PO/SC/SCR/K/19.A.1, 26 April 1989, Khartoum.

94. U.S. Department of State, Cable 136997, 2 May 1989, Khartoum.

95. U.S. Embassy—Sudan, Letter to His Excellency Sayyid al-Sadiq al-Mahdi, Prime Minister, 26 April 1989, Khartoum.

96. UN-Khartoum, "UNDP Emergency Unit Flight Operations, Final Summary," 14 May 1989.

97. UN-Khartoum, "Weekly Report to the Secretary General of UN," 1 May 1989.

98. Associated Press, "U.N. Relief Trains, Barges Delayed Again in Sudan," 15 May 1989.

99. Wannop, "Report."

100. Reuters Library Report, "U.N. Official Relives Execution Threat on Sudan Relief Train," 1 June 1989.

101. Wannop, "Report."

102. U.S. Embassy—Sudan, Cable 5691, 17 May 1989, Khartoum.

103. LICROSS-Sudan, "Monthly Report," May 1989, Khartoum.

104. U.S. Embassy—Kenya, Nairobi, Cable 15297, 26 May 1980; Associated Press, "Gunmen Ambush Second U.N. Convoy in Sudan," 1 May 1989.

105. Prime Minister Sadiq al-Mahdi to U.S. Ambassador, Memorandum CM/SG/PMO/19/A/1, 13 May 1989; UN Operation Lifeline Sudan, "Situation Report no. 2," New York, 2 May 1989.

106. Prime Minister Sadiq al-Mahdi to U.S. Ambassador, Memorandum CM/SG/PMO/19/A/13 May 1989.

107. "John Garang: A New Sudan," *Africa Report*, July–August 1989.

108. "The Shame of Sudan," *The New York Times*, 17 June 1989.

109. "Seeking Peace in the Horn of Africa," *Christian Science Monitor*, 3 March 1989.

110. U.S. Embassy—Kenya, Cable 17931, 16 June 1989, Nairobi.

111. UN-Sudan, "Operation Lifeline Sudan," Situation Report no. 2 (Revision 1), 2 May 1989, Khartoum.

112. Government of Sudan—RRC TCC, "Minutes," 18 June 1989, Khartoum.

Chapter 7

1. Associated Press, "Military Stages Coup in Sudan, Suspends Constitution," 30 June 1989.

2. Reuters Library Report, "Sudan Ruler to Rule with Iron Hand, Vows to End War," 2 July 1989.

3. "Who's in the Sudanese Government," *New Africa*, October 1989, p. 16; "The Coup Makers," *Africa Confidential*, 28 July 1989.

4. BBC, "Sudanese Chairman Interviewed on the Coup," ME/0499/A/1, 4 July 1989.

5. United Press International, "New Sudanese No Stranger to Egypt," 1 July 1989; "Sudanese Military Forces Oust Mahdi Government in Coup," *The Washington Post*, 1 July 1989.

6. United Press International, "Manhunt on for Ousted Leader," 3 July 1989.

7. Radio SPLA, 1300 GMT, 1 September 1989.

8. BBC, "Sudanese RCC Chairman Interviewed on the Coup."

9. "Le Monde—Doubts over Sudan's New Masters," *Manchester Guardian Weekly*, 30 July 1989.

10. "Sudanese Leader Consolidates Support Within Military," *The Washington Post*, 2 July 1989.

11. "The Coup Makers," *Africa Confidential*, 28 July 1989.

12. Foreign Broadcast Information Service, "Al-Bashir on Arrests, Unity with Libya, Egypt," FBIS-NES-89-132, 12 July 1989.

13. *Middle East International*, "Sudan: Pressure Mounts," 17 November 1989.

14. United Press International, "Sudan Coup Reflects Frustration of Middle-Ranking Officers," 30 June 1989; Xinhua General Overseas News Service, "Sudan's Coup Leadership to Offer Civil War Solution Plan," 2 July 1989.

15. Associated Press, "Demonstrators Cheer Junta; Military Ruler Vows No Return to Democracy," 11 July 1989.

16. U.S. Embassy—Khartoum, to Chairman of the Command Council of the Revolution for National Salvation, 5 July 1989.

17. Government of Sudan, Ministry of Foreign Affairs, MFA/PR/2/2/9, 6 July 1989, Khartoum.

18. "The National Salvation Revolution's Program," *Al-Qwat Al-Musalaha*, 3 July 1989.

19. Reuters Library Report, "Sudan's Military Rulers Split over Islamic Laws," 28 August 1989.

20. Xinhua General Overseas News Service, "Mubarak: We Bear No Hand in Sudan's Coup," 11 July 1989, Beijing.

21. Associated Press, "New Military Leader Says He Seeks Peace with Rebels," 1 July 1989.

22. Reuters Library Report, "Sudanese Military Leader Declares Ceasefire in South," 4 July 1989; BBC, "Summary of World Broadcasts: The Middle East, Africa and Latin America," ME/0501, 6 July 1989.

23. BBC, ME/0507/ii, 13 July 1989.

24. "After Coup, Unsettled Sudan Faces Yet Another Fresh Start," *The Washington Post*, 15 July 1989.

25. United Press International, "New Sudanese Leader Open to Rebel Demands," 13 July 1989.

26. Reuters, "Sudan's Ruler Urges Rebel Leader to Attend Khartoum Meeting," 9 September 1989.

27. Reuters Library Report, "Iraqi Arms Said to Transit Jordan," 3 July 1989.

28. Reuters Library Report, "Saudi Joins Arabs in Wishing Sudan Coup Leader Success," 2 July 1989.

29. "Peace Hopes Grow as Sudanese Agree to Meet," *Daily Telegraph*, 28 July 1989.

30. Associated Press, "Military Ruler Returns Home with Good News," 26 July 1989; Reuters, "Improved East-West Ties Prompt African States to Seek Peace," 27 July 1989.

31. Reuters, "Sudanese Leader Extends Cease Fire," 25 July 1989.

32. Associated Press, "Sudan Military Stages Coup, Suspends Constitution," 30 June 1989.

33. "Coup Could Deprive Sudan of American Aid," *The New York Times*, 16 July 1989.

34. United Press International, "Manhunt on for Ousted Sudanese Leader," 3 July 1989.

35. Foreign Broadcast Information Service, Near East and South Asia, "Al-Bashir Interviewed on Politics, Economy," 12 July 1989, Addis Abab'a, Ethiopia.

36. Foreign Broadcast Information Service, NC2607201689, 1535 GMT, Sanaa dateline, "MENA Interviews, Sudanese Interior Minister," MENA, Cairo, 26 July 1989.

37. Foreign Broadcast Information Service, PM260714589, *Al-Madinah*, Jiddah, 19 July 1989.

38. Agence France Press Radio, 1305 GMT, Addis Ababa, 28 July 1989.

39. Agence France Press Radio (in English), 1955 GMT, Paris, 1 August 1989.

40. Radio SPLA (in English), 1300 GMT, 1 August 1989, Naru, Ethiopia.

41. BBC, "Sudan: SPLA Leader on Coup D'Etat," ME/0537/A/1, 14 August 1989, London.

42. "Sudan Peace Talks Break Down," *Financial Times*, 22 July 1989.

43. Reuters Library Report, "Rebel Leader Says Sudan Coup Was Disastrous for Peace," 14 August 1989.

44. Reuters Library Report, "Sudanese Rebel Leader Says Democracy Is the Price for Peace," 15 August 1989.

45. Reuters, "Sudanese Rebels to Meet Envoys from Military Junta," 18 August 1989.

46. Omdurman Radio Domestic Service in Arabic, 1930 GMT, 22 August 1989, Omdurman; Inter Press Service, "Sudan: U.N. Relief Effort Called Successful, but Problems Persist," 15 September 1989.

47. Reuters Library Report, "Talks Between Sudanese Military and Rebels Collapse," 21 August 1989.

48. *Al-Sharq Al-Awsat* (London), 20 September 1989.

49. BBC, ME/0547/A/1, 29 August 1989, London; Agence France Press Radio (in English), 1503 GMT, Paris, 25 July 1989.

50. *Sudanow,* (Khartoum), August 1989.

51. Reuters Library Report, "Sudan Junta's Policies Turn Off Business," 21 August 1989.

52. Reuters Library Report, "Sudan Must Speed Up Economic Reforms, Economists Say," 22 September 1989.

53. *Al-Sudan Al-Hadith* (Khartoum), 20 September 1989.

54. U.S. Department of Agriculture, "World Food Needs and Availabilities, 1989/90: Winter," December 1989, Washington, D.C.

55. U.S. Embassy—Khartoum, Cable 11814, 26 October 1989.

56. Government of Sudan—RRC TCC, "Minutes," 3 July 1989, Khartoum.

57. *Al-Qwat Al-Musalaha* (Khartoum), 6 July 1989.

58. Government of Sudan, Ministry of Foreign Affairs, "Memorandum," MFA/Two Americas/7/I/I, Khartoum, 23 July 1989.

59. "Mickey Leland Made a Difference," *The New York Times*, 15 August 1989.

60. "Mickey Leland," *The Washington Post*, 14 August 1989.

61. U.S. House Committee for Refugees, *Testimony of Roger P. Winter Before the U.S. Senate Committee on Appropriations, Subcommittee on Foreign Operations*, Washington, D.C., 7 May 1990.

62. Copyright CBC and Television Station WETA, date unknown, transcript in the authors' possession, Washington, D.C.

63. Reuters Library Report, "Ethiopia Braces for Fresh Surge of Sudanese Refugees," 15 November 1988.

64. Copyright CBC and Television Station WETA, newscript in the authors' possession, Washington, D.C.

65. UN World Food Program, "Emergency Telex Report," no. 179, 3 March 1989, New York.

66. MSF-Holland, "Wau Emergency Medical and Nutritional Programme Quarterly Report," July–September 1989, Amsterdam.

67. A written report of the incident was received by the authors in early August 1989 and was corroborated by information from Wau citizens.

68. Omdurman Radio, Domestic Service (in Arabic), 1800 GMT, 18 July 1989, Omdurman.

69. Reuters, "Rivalry Forced Him To Quit U.N.," 22 August 1989.

70. Upper Nile, Governor's Office, Decree no. 8/1989, 29 September 1989; Circular GO/REC/UNR.19.A.1, 6 October 1989, Malakal.

71. United Nations—UNDP, Khartoum, Reference RR/89/035, 2 December 1989. See also Government of Sudan—Permanent Mission to the United Nations, "Statement by His Excellency Mr. Amin Magzoub Abdoun," New York, 14 September 1989.

72. Government of the Sudan—RRC-TCC, "Minutes," 1 October 1989, Khartoum.

73. *Newsweek*, 11 September 1989.

74. Sudan News Agency, "Daily Bulletin," 20 August 1989.

75. Ibid., 30 August 1989.

76. Anon., "Aide-Memoire on Announced Plans for Removal of Squatters from Planned Areas of Khartoum," Khartoum, 27 August 1989.

77. OLS Donors Meeting, Khartoum, 23 August 1989; Government of Sudan—RRC TCC, "Minutes," 21 July 1989, Khartoum.

78. Government of Sudan–Ministry of Social Welfare, Zakat and the Displaced, "Working Paper," 29 September 1989, Khartoum.

79. Sudan News Agency, "Daily Bulletin," 10 September 1989; Reuters Library Report, "Sudanese Junta Invites Rebels to Civil War Conference," 6 September 1989.

80. Reuters, "Sudan's Ruler Urges Rebel Leader to Attend Khartoum Meeting," 9 September 1989.

81. Sudan News Agency, "Daily Bulletin," 8 September 1989.

82. Reuters Library Report, "Hopes of Early End to Sudan War Dashed," 8 September 1989.

83. Xinhua General Overseas News Service, "Garang's Conditions for Attending National Peace Dialogue Rejected," 12 September 1989, Beijing.

84. Reuters, "Southern Sudanese Petition for Secession," 3 October 1989.

85. "Interview: Brigadier Kassiano," *Sudanow*, November 1988.

86. BBC World Service (in English), 1530 GMT, 28 September 1989, London.

87. *Al-Sudan Al-Hadith*, 3 October 1989. See M. Burr, *A Working Document: Quantifying Genocide in the Southern Sudan, 1983–1993* (Washington, D.C.: U.S. Committee for Refugees, 1993).

88. "Resolutions, A Summary," *Sudanow*, November 1989.

89. Sudan News Agency, "Daily Bulletin," 25 September 1989, Khartoum.

90. Steering Committee for National Dialogue on Peace Issues, "Final Report and Recommendations," Khartoum, October 1989. Note also Radio SUNA (in English), 1010 GMT, Khartoum, 24 October 1989; Xinhua General Overseas News Service, "Sudan Government Extends Ceasefire," 1 October 1989, Beijing.

91. Sudan News Agency, "Daily Bulletin," 6 October 1989.

92. Ibid., 15 November 1989.

93. Radio Omdurman (in Arabic), 1335 GMT, 24 October 1989, Omdurman.

94. "Conflict in the SPLA," *Sudan Times*, 21 October 1989; Sudan News Agency, "Daily Bulletin," 28 December 1988.

95. U.S. Embassy—Nairobi, Cable 25173, 28 August 1989.

Chapter 8

1. *Al-Qwat Al-Musalaha* (Khartoum), 8 August 1989.

2. Kordofan Political Supervisor Report (in Arabic), "The Displaced at Talodi Village," no. PS/KR/4, October 1989. See also Xinhua General Overseas News Service, "Sudanese Government, Rebels Blamed for Violating Cease-Fire," 8 October 1989, Beijing.

3. "Khalifa: Meeting with SPLM a Success,'" *Al-Sharq Al-Awsat* (London), 20 September 1989.

4. Radio SPLA, 1330 GMT, 1 November 1989, Naru, Ethiopia.

5. *Middle East International*, "Sudan Rebels Advance," 3 November 1989.

6. Radio SPLA, 1330 GMT, 1 November 1989, Naru, Ethiopia.

7. Sudan News Agency, "Daily Bulletin," 1 November 1989; "Army Withdraws from Kurmuk," *Sudan Times*, 15 November 1987; *Al-Sudan Al-Hadith*, 8 November 1989.

8. Omdurman Radio (in English), 0430 GMT, 28 October 1989, Omdurman.

9. Delegation of the European Community, Memorandum, TU/MM/2277/C.16 and T.10 Khartoum, 13 November 1989.

10. *Al-Ingaz Al-Watani*, (Khartoum), 12 November 1989.

11. By March the WFP had lost 13,000 sacks, or 1,150 tons, of grain. Government of Sudan-RRC, Radio Message RM/90/004, Malakal, 1 March 1990.

12. U.S. Information Agency Wireless File, Khartoum, 3 November 1989.

13. U.S. Information Agency Wireless File, Khartoum, "Cheek Sworn In," ZNEA105, 16 October 1989.

14. Comment by Bona Malwal, "Targeted Help in Sudan," *Christian Science Monitor*, 1 November 1989.

15. Radio SPLA, 1300 GMT, 8 November 1989, Naru, Ethiopia.

16. N. Roberts, "Visit to Juba and Yei (1–8 November)," Government of Sudan–RRC, Khartoum, 14 November 1989.

17. Africa Watch Committee, *Denying "The Honor of Living," Sudan: A Human Rights Disaster* (New York: Africa Watch 1990).

18. Government of Sudan—RRC TCC, "Minutes," 20 November 1989, Khartoum.

19. BBC, "Summary of World Broadcasts," ME/0618/B/1, 20 November 1989. See also "Ex-Paratrooper Spurns Rules to Aid the Hungry," *Los Angeles Times*, 19 March 1989.

20. U.S. Embassy—Nairobi, Cable 16297, 26 May 1989.

21. *Al-Sudan Al-Hadith* (Khartoum), 11 and 12 November 1989.

22. Sudan News Agency, "Daily Bulletin," 7 November 1989, Khartoum; "Hundreds of Villagers Reported Slain in the Sudan," *The New York Times*, 7 January 1990.

23. Radio SPLA, 1300 GMT, 8 November 1989.

24. UNICEF, "Operation Lifeline Sudan," Situation Report no. 6, New York, 14 September 1989.

25. Government of Sudan–RCC/UN, "Donors High Technical Meeting," 1 October 1989, Khartoum.

26. UNWFP, "Outline Plan for the Continued Supply of Emergency Food Aid to South Sudan (Only Supply Through Kenya and Uganda)," WFP Nairobi, October, 1989.

27. Reuters Library Report, "Sudan Rebels Say They Seized Three Towns," 9 November 1989.

28. Sudan News Agency, "Daily Bulletin," 8 October 1989.

29. Ibid., 7 June 1990.

30. U.S. Mission to the United Nations, Cable 3102, 26 October 1989, Khartoum via Department of State.

31. A. Swiderski, "Nutritional Surveillance Program in SPLA Controlled Areas of Southern Sudan, July 31–October 14, 1989," International Rescue Committee, Kapoeta, 22 October 1989.

32. UNWFP, "Overall Food Needs 1990," Khartoum, 30 September 1989.

33. El Sayed El Bashra, *An Atlas of Khartoum Conurbation* (Khartoum: University of Khartoum, 1976), p. 75; Government of Sudan—RRC, "RRC News," no. 16, Khartoum, 5 October 1989.

34. UN Department of Public Information, "Secretary General Expresses Concern About Developments Affecting Operation Lifeline Sudan," New York, 8 November 1989.

35. SPLA/SRRA Report, Nairobi Office, 19 June 1990.

36. Reuters Library Report, "U.N. Air Drops Food into Rebel Areas," 19 June 1989.

37. *Al-Ingaz Al-Watani* (Khartoum), 17 November 1989; SUNA Radio (in French), 1520 GMT, Khartoum, 16 November 1989.

38. *Al-Sudan Al-Hadith, Al-Qwat Al-Musalaha* (Khartoum), 16 November 1989.

39. Inter Press Service, "Sudan: Six Million in Western Region Face Starvation," 10 October 1989.

40. Quote provided by two Sudanese, both of whom participated in the meetings.

41. Reuters Library Report, "Sudan Seeks Egypt's Help for Talks with Rebels," 14 November 1989; *Al-Sudan Al-Hadith* (Khartoum), 9 December 1989.

42. *Kenya Times,* 7 November 1989; *Al-Sharq Al-Awsat,* 22 November 1989 (Omdurman).

43. Reuters Library Report, "Uganda Blames Sudan for Air Raid, Says Three Killed," 16 November 1989; "Fear in the South," *New African,* October 1989.

44. "Carter Redux," *The New York Times,* 10 December 1989, Part 6, p. 38.

45. *Al-Sudan Al-Hadith* (Khartoum), 2 December 1989.

46. Radio SPLA, 1300 GMT, 30 November 1989, Naru.

47. *Al-Sudan Al-Hadith* (Khartoum), 2 December 1989.

48. Ibid.

49. *Al-Ingaz Al-Watani* (Khartoum), 19 December 1989.

50. Ibid.

51. Reuters Library Report, "Sudan's Junta Said Planning to Revive Islamic Law," 14 December 1989.

52. Sudan News Agency, "Daily Bulletin," Khartoum, 7 January 1990.

53. Ibid., 13 December 1989.

54. Radio SPLA, Foreign Broadcast Information Service Report EA2212163189, 22 December 1989, Omdurman.

55. BBC, "Sudan Gen. Bashir Addresses Diplomats' Conference on Foreign Policy, Peace Process, Relief Aid," ME/0636/A/1, 11 December 1989.

56. *Al-Sudan Al-Hadith* (Khartoum), 2 September 1990.

57. BBC World Service, 0630 GMT, 7 December 1989.

58. F. M. Deng and P. Gifford, *The Search for Peace and Unity in Sudan* (Washington, D.C.: Wilson Center Press, 1987), pp. 78–89.

59. Ibid., p. 79.

60. "NIF Leader Declares Jihad," *Sudan Times,* 16 April 1989.

61. "Under Bashir's Boot," *New African,* July 1990.

62. Radio SPLA, 1300 GMT, 1 October 1989, Naru.

63. Ibid., 30 September 1989.

64. SUNA Radio (in English), 1615 GMT, Khartoum, 24 October 1989.

65. *Al-Tadamun* (London), 18 December 1989.

66. Associated Press, "Despite Difficulties, Pope Strives for Better Relations with Moslems," 3 October 1989.

67. *Al-Ingaz Al-Watani* (Khartoum), 14 December 1989, Omdurman.

68. Radio SPLA, 1300 GMT, 30 September 1989, Naru.

69. "Sudan: A Government Going Nowhere," *Africa Confidential,* 3 November 1989.

70. Sudan News Agency, "Daily Bulletin," 13 November 1989.

71. Inter Press Service, "Guerrilla Movement Predicts Tough Talks," 28 November 1989.

72. Sudan News Agency, "Daily Bulletin," 13 November 1989.

73. SUNA Radio (in English), 0915 GMT, Khartoum, 27 December 1989.

74. *Al-Ingaz Al-Watani* (Khartoum), 19 December 1989.

75. Sudan News Agency, "Daily Bulletin," 7 January 1990.

76. Ibid., 16 November 1989.

77. U.S. Department of State, *Country Reports on Human Rights Practices for 1989* (Washington, D.C.: Library of Congress, 1990).

78. KUNA (in English), 0855 GMT, Kuwait, 31 October 1989.

79. *Al-Sudan Al-Hadith* (Khartoum), 20 November 1989.

80. Radio Omdurman (in English), 1350 GMT, 23 November 1989.

81. United Nations, letter from Undersecretary Farah to Michael Priestley, New York, 13 December 1989.

82. Human Rights Committee for Sudan, "In Commemoration of the United Nations Human Rights Day, December 10, 1989," 6 December 1989, New York; Anon., "Objet: Liste des hommes politiques detenus dans les prisons de Kober et d'Omdurman," 6 December 1989, Paris.

83. BBC World Service, 1615 GMT, 24 January 1990.

84. The authors have one such list in their possession that includes the names of 115 children, their location, and the Arab family that holds each child captive.

85. "Fear of Lynching and Repression Make Civilians Flee Kadugli," *Sudan Times*, 5 April 1989.

86. Based on correspondence from the Committee of Sons of Daju in the authors' possession and corroborating interviews.

87. *Al-Ingaz Al-Watani* (Khartoum), 5 November 1989.

88. Agence France Press Radio (in English), 1444 GMT, 13 November 1989, Paris.

89. United Press International, "Amnesty International Says Sudan Guilty of Human-Rights Abuses," 11 December 1989.

90. United Press International, from *The New York Times*, "Amnesty Report Cites Sudanese Militias for Killing Civilians," 12 December 1989.

91. United Press International, "Amnesty International Says Sudan Guilty of Human Rights Abuses," 11 December 1989.

92. *Al-Ayyam* (Khartoum), 14 February 1989.

93. *Sudan Times*, 23 April 1989.

94. *Al-Qwat Al-Musalaha* (Khartoum), 8 December 1989; Sudan News Agency, "Daily Bulletin," 8 December 1989.

95. *Al-Sudan Al-Hadith* (Khartoum), 9 December 1989.

96. *Al-Ingaz Al-Watani* (Khartoum),18 December 1989.

97. Catholic Mission, "Statement Related to Nine Months Report on Feeding Center," 31 August 1989.

98. Associated Press, "Corpse Explodes at Airport: Sabotage Feared," 29 December 1989.

99. Radio SPLA, 1300 GMT, 22 December 1989, Omdurman.

100. U.S. Embassy—Khartoum, Cable 13954, 28 December 1989.

101. Associated Press, "Corpse Explodes."

102. Ambassade de France au Soudan, no. 22/MAE, Khartoum, 14 January 1990; Government of Sudan—Ministry of Foreign Affairs, Memorandum MFA/ EO/1/1/31/A., Khartoum, 2 February 1990.

103. UNDP-Khartoum, Priestley Letter to RCC Vice Chairman Al-Zubayr Muhammad Salih, RR/89/035, 2 December 1989.

104. Sudan News Agency, "Daily Bulletin," 31 December 1989; 18 December 1989.

105. Ibid., 31 December 1989; Reuters Library Report, "Sudan's Leader Accuses Relief Workers of Arming Rebels," 31 December 1989.

106. Sudan News Agency, "Daily Bulletin," 6 January 1990.

107. G. Obat, *The Jebelein Massacre* (mimeo.) (Khartoum:1990), p. 8. The name is believed to be a pseudonym for someone who accompanied the NSRCC investigation team to Jebelein in January.

108. Sudan News Agency, "Daily Bulletin," 25 January 1990, Khartoum.

109. "War-Battered South Sudan Senses Peace," *Daily Telegraph*, 3 August 1989, Khartoum.

110. RRC High Technical Committee, "Minutes," 7 January 1990, Khartoum.

111. UN-UNDP, Cable JX/TLX/90/021, Juba, 15 January 1990, Juba.

112. Action Internationale Contre la Faim, "Field Visit Report, Juba-Equatoria," January 1990, Khartoum.

113. Agence France Press Radio (in English), 1144 GMT, 25 January 1990.

Chapter 9

1. Radio Omdurman, 1315 GMT, 3 December 1989, Omdurman.

2. Radio SPLA, 1300 GMT, 27 January 1990, Naru, Ethiopia.

3. BBC World Service, 1700 GMT, 22 January 1990, London; Radio SPLA, 1300 GMT, 27 January 1990, Naru, Ethiopia.

4. *Al-Ingaz Al-Watani* (Khartoum), 30 January 1990; Radio Omdurman, 1300 GMT, 31 January 1990, Omdurman.

5. *Al-Ingaz Al-Watani* (Khartoum), 4 February 1990.

6. National Conference of the Displaced People, "Final Report and Recommendations," Khartoum, 10 February 1990. Also see: M. Burr, *Khartoum's Displaced Persons: A Decade of Despair* (Washington, D.C.: U.S. Committee for Refugees, 1990).

7. *Al-Ingaz Al-Watani* (Khartoum), 11 February 1990.

8. Ibid., 5 February, 18 February, and 20 February 1990; *Al-Qwat Al-Musalaha* (Khartoum), 11 March 1990.

9. UN World Food Program, "Weekly Sitrep 90/8 Covering Period 9–15 March," Khartoum, 15 March 1990.

10. Radio SPLA, 1300 GMT, 16 February 1990, Naru, Ethiopia.

11. Government of Sudan—Ministry of Finance and Economic Planning, "Emergency Grain Supply Programme for Kordofan and Darfur Regions," 18 October 1989; Government of Sudan—RRC, "R.R.C. News," no. 18, 15 February 1990, Omdurman.

12. Catholic Relief Services, "1990 Operational Plan for Emergency Food Assistance in Southern Sudan," Nairobi, December 1989.

13. United Press International, "Sudan Brushes Up Its Image," 2 February 1990.

14. "For the Sudan, Famine Is Almost as Certain as Civil War," *The New York Times*, 4 February 1990, p. E2.

15. Xinhua General Overseas News Service, Beijing, 21 April 1990, quote from *Al-Qabas* (Kuwait).

16. Kordofan Region, "National Dialogue Conference on Peace and Development, Final Report and Recommendations of the Committee for Voluntary Services and Missionary Activity," El Obeid, 3 March 1990.

17. *Al-Sudan Al-Hadith* (Khartoum), 29 January 1990.

18. Radio Omdurman, 1715 GMT, 4 February 1990, Omdurman.

19. Ibid., 29 January 1990.

20. *Al-Qwat Al-Musalaha* (Khartoum), 6 February 1991.

21. "African Dilemma," *The New York Times*, 12 May 1991, p. E3.

22. *Al-Sharq Al-Awsat* (London), 29 March 1990, pp. 1–2.

23. United Press International, "Sudan Rejects U.S. Plan," 5 June 1990.

24. Correspondence in the authors' possession.

25. TASS Telegraph Agency, "UNICEF Calls for Aid to Mozambique and Sudan," 19 April 1990, Moscow.

26. "Sudan's Military Denies Charges of Rights Abuses," Quoted from Africa Watch in the *Christian Science Monitor*, 6 April 1990.

27. "Life in Impoverished Sudan Grows Harsher," *The Washington Post*, 24 May 1990, p. A45.

28. *Sudan Update* (London), 29 June 1990, p. 2.

29. *Al-Qwat Al-Musalaha* (Khartoum), 30 July 1990.

30. United Nations—Khartoum, "UN Operation Lifeline Sudan Sitrep 3/90, June 1–July 1, 1990," August 1990, p. A2.

31. "Sudan Forces Refugees Back to Barren Lands," *The New York Times*, 13 July 1990, p. 2.

32. SRRA-Kapoeta, "Famine Looms in Southern Sudan in 1990–1991, as Rains Are Erratic," July 1990.

33. AID-OFDA, "Sudan—Civil Strife/Displaced Persons," Washington, D.C., 24 August 1990.

34. "Sudan Asserts It Just Helps Refugees Go Back to South," *The New York Times*, 16 August 1990.

35. "Dying by the Thousands," *The New York Times*, 8 June 1990.

36. *Africa Report*, May–June 1990, pp. 23–24.

37. Reuters Library Report, "Sudan Ruler Flies to Cairo," 20 February 1990.

38. SPLA, "Joint Declaration (Draft) Agreement on a Framework for the Peaceful Settlement of Sudan's Conflict," May 1990, Nairobi.

39. *Al-Qwat Al-Musalaha* (Khartoum), 7 May 1990.

40. Government of Sudan, "Joint Declaration (Draft) Agreement on a Framework for the Peaceful Settlement of Sudan's Conflict," May 1990, Nairobi.

41. Inter Press Service, "Sudan Rejects U.S. Peace Proposal," 5 June 1990.

42. United Nation—Khartoum, "UN Operation Lifeline Sitrep 3/90, 1 June–1 July 1990," August 1990.

43. "Genocide and the Horn of Africa," *The Washington Post*, 1 July 1990, p. B7.

44. United Press International, "Sudanese Told to Sacrifice," 12 June 1990.

45. P. Ulrich, Letter to USAID-Sudan, CARE International in Sudan, 7 October 1990.

46. CARE was the largest of the expatriate NGOs, and it was the organization most willing to cooperate with the NSRCC. It would not work in the South, because doing so might jeopardize its program in the North. Beginning in 1989 its work in the North, whether in the distribution of relief food or in the creation of displaced persons' camps in North Kordofan, had been problem-plagued and thus provided a clear caution to any major food distribution program USAID-Sudan might undertake. Founded in response to European needs following World War II, CARE has ceased to be an exclusively U.S. aid agency. Nevertheless, because it had extensive contracts with the Agency for International Development it could usually be counted on when other organizations were uninterested in taking part in a major food distribution program.

47. United Nations—Khartoum, "UN Operation Lifeline Sudan Sitrep 3/90," p. A2.

48. AID, "FEWS Bulletin," Washington, D.C., 31 August 1990; "Pre-Harvest Assessment of Cereal Production," Washington, D.C., October 1990, pp. 32–37.

49. B. D'Silva, "Current Assessment of the Crop Situation in Gezira, Sept. 10–14, 1990," Khartoum, September 1990.

50. AID, "FEWS Bulletin," no. 8, Washington, D.C., 31 August 1990.

51. "Lifesaving Food Barge Stuck in Sudan Quagmire," *The Washington Post*, 6 December 1990, p. A1.

52. See *Middle East International*, "Sudan: Unprecedented Isolation," 28 September 1990, p. 17; *Sudan Update*, 7 September 1990, p. 2; "Shock Treatment for the Economy," *Middle East*, January 1991, p. 36.

53. "Sudan: The Great Hunger," *Africa Confidential*, 9 November 1990, p. 5; *Sudan Democratic Gazette*, October 1990, p. 7.

54. *Colin Legum's Third World Reports* (London:30-I-1991), 2., edited by Colin Legum, Rex Collings.

55. R. Winter and J. Prendergast, "An Embargo for the People of Sudan," *The Washington Post*, 31 October 1990, p. A19.

56. U.S. Embassy—Khartoum, Cable 10122, 26 September 1990.

57. Ibid.

58. U.S. Embassy—Khartoum, Cable 10006, 24 September 1990.

59. U.S. Department of State, Office of the Assistant Secretary/Spokesman, "Statement by Richard Boucher/Deputy Spokesman," Washington, D.C., 28 September 1990.

60. *Al-Sudan Al-Hadith*, 13 October 1990, 16 October 1990; *Al-Ingaz Al-Watani*, 16 October 1990, Khartoum.

61. "West Distorts Food Needs, Sudan Says," *The New York Times*, 31 October 1990, p. A3.

62. W. L. Barclay, "USAID's Contribution to Drought Relief Operations," USAID-Sudan, Khartoum, 20 September 1990.

63. Agency for International Development, "Action Memorandum for the Deputy Administrator—the 1991 Sudan Food Emergency Crisis, State/A.I.D. Policy," 18 October 1990, Khartoum.

64. U.S. Department of State, "Statement by Richard Boucher/Deputy Spokesman: Sudan," Office of the Assistant Secretary/Spokesman, 26 October 1990.

65. *Al-Sudan Al-Hadith* (Khartoum), 27 October 1990.

66. "No Famine in Sudan: Karar Blames Agencies for Supply Shortage," *New Horizon*, Khartoum, 3 November 1990.

67. *Al-Sudan Al-Hadith* (Khartoum), 3 November 1990.

68. *Le Monde*, 5 November 1990, Paris.

69. "Sudan Government Denies New Famine," *The Washington Post*, 2 November 1990; U.S. Embassy—Khartoum, Cable 11266, 29 October 1990.

70. U.S. Department of State, "AF Press Guidance," Washington, D.C., 8 November 1990.

71. "Sudan Government Denies New Famine," *The Washington Times*, 2 November 1990.

72. *Le Monde*, 3 November 1990, Paris.

73. Government of Sudan—Permanent Mission to the United Nation, "Statement on the Food Situation in Sudan," New York, 21 December 1990.

74. *Al-Qwat Al-Musalaha* (Khartoum), 31 December 1990.

75. *Sudan Update* (London), vol. 2, no. 18, 4 March 1991, p. 3.

76. AID Office of Foreign Disaster Assistance, "FEWS Bulletin," 30 January 1991.

77. "Sudan's Government Still Won't Ask for Help as Drought Grows Worse," *The Washington Post*, 23 February 1991, p. A6.

78. Ibid.

79. "Bashir Digs in; Garang Hangs on," *New African*, October 1991.

80. AID-FEWS, "Harvest Assessment of Cereal Production," Washington, D.C., January 1991, p. 39.

81. AID-FEWS, "FEWS Bulletin," Washington, D.C., 30 January 1991.

82. T. Brennan, draft report prepared for the Agency for International Development, Nairobi, May 1991, 56 pp.

83. Ibid.

84. BBC World Service; Foreign Broadcast Information Service, "East Africa," 6 June 1991, Nairobi p. 8.1; "Sudanese Refugees Are Pressed," *Christian Science Monitor*, 11 June 1991, p. 5.

85. *Christian Science Monitor*, 25 June 1991, p. 5; "Sudan: To-ing and Fro-ing," *Middle East International*, 28 June 1991, p. 14.

86. *The Guardian*, 10 May 1991, as quoted in *Sudan Update*, 22 May 1991, pp. 3–4.

87. "Sudan's Junta Fails to Achieve Any Legitimacy," *Baltimore Sun*, 14 July 1991.

88. "Africa Teeters on Famine's Edge," *Christian Science Monitor*, 25 June 1991, p. 4.

89. B. D'Silva, untitled trip report to Darfur, 11–14 July 1991, Khartoum, July 1991.

90. Ibid.

91. *New African*, "Bashir Digs In, Garang Hangs On," October 1991.

92. U.S. House, Committee on Foreign Affairs, *Testimony of Moses Akol, Special Representative, SPLM/Nasir to the Subcommittee on Africa, House Foreign Affairs Committee*, Washington, D.C., 10 March 1993.

93. "Rebel Chief Ousted in Sudan," *The New York Times*, 31 August 1991.

94. "Sudan: SPLA Peace Talks," *Middle East International*, 8 November 1991; "SPLA: War or Peace?" *New African*, November 1991.

95. SPLM/SPLA General Headquarters, "Legal Framework for the Peaceful Resolution of the Civil War in the Sudan (Interim Arrangements)," WP/51/Abuja.TKL, 9 August 1992.

96. AID-Washington, "USAID/Sudan, General Comments—FY 1993 [Annual Budget Submission]," Washington, D.C., 1991.

97. UN High Commission for Refugees, "Information Bulletin No. 7," New York, 17 December 1991, p. 10.

98. Norwegian People's Aid, "NPA Relief Operation in South Sudan, Monthly Report December 1991," Oslo, 14 January 1992.

Conclusion

1. AID-FEWS, "FEWS Bulletin," no. 9/91, Washington, D.C., 20 August 1992.

2. "Civilians Bear the Brunt," *Middle East International*, 20 December 1991, p. 11.

3. "Iran Chief Visits Sudan's Radical Leader," *The Washington Times*, 14 December 1991, p. A2.

4. *Middle East International*, 20 December 1991, p. 11.

5. "Sudanese Talk Peace After Government Offensive," *Africa Report*, November–December 1992, p. 8.

6. Norwegian People's Aid Report, Nairobi, 13 April 1992.

7. AID Cable, U.S. Embassy—Khartoum, Cable 03426, 30 April 1992.

8. S. Lautze, and G. Wagner, "Southern Sudan Relief Operations," USAID-Sudan (Nairobi: 1993).

9. "Controlled Democracy for Sudan," *New African*, April 1992, p. 8.

10. "Beguiling Zealot," *Middle East Times*, 19–25 May 1992, p. 15.

11. Ibid.

12. Lautze and Wagner, "Southern Sudan Relief Operations."

13. "Sudan Talks," *Middle East Times*, 9–15 June 1992.

14. Ibid.

15. "Sudanese Talk Peace," *Africa Report*, November–December 1982.

16. Norwegian People's Aid, "Southern Sudan—Situation Update," Nairobi, 29 June 1992.

17. UNICEF/OLS, "Bi-Monthly Situation Report No. 21, 4–20 July 1992," Nairobi, July 1992.

18. *Sudan Update* (London), 29 August 1992, p. 1.

19. "Gathering Storm," *New African*, January 1993, p. 34.

20. Agence France Press, 7 April 1993, reported in Foreign Broadcast Information Service report, "Arab Africa," Washington, D.C., 7 April 1993.

21. "U.N. Makes Aid Appeal," *The Washington Times*, 8 April 1993, p. A10.

22. "War-Torn Southern Sudan Called 'Another Somalia,'" *The Washington Post*, 12 February 1993.

23. H. J. Cohen, *The Situation in Sudan*, testimony before the U.S. House Foreign Affairs Committee, Subcommittee on Africa, 10 March 1993.

24. M. Burr, "A Working Document: Quantifying Genocide in the Southern Sudan, 1983–1993" (Washington, D.C.: U.S. Committee for Refugees, 1993).

Bibliography

Books

Abdel Ghaffar M. Ahmed and M. Gunnar. *Management of the Crisis in the Sudan.* Bergen, Norway: Centre for Development Studies, University of Bergen, 1989.

Africa Watch. *Denying the Honor of Living, Sudan: A Human Rights Disaster.* New York: Africa Watch Committee III, 1990.

Ahmad, Hassan M. M. *Muslim Brotherhood in Sudan, 1944–1969.* Washington, D.C.: Joint Publications Research Service translation from the Arabic, August 31, 1985.

Ali, Musaddag A. El Haj. *The Redivision of the Southern Sudan, Decentralization in Sudan.* Khartoum: Khartoum University Press Graduate College Publications, No. 20, 1987.

Alier, Abel. *Southern Sudan: Too Many Agreements Dishonored.* Exeter: Ithaca Press, 1990.

Asher, M. *A Desert Dies.* New York: St. Martin's Press, 1986.

Beasley, Ina. *Before the Wind Changed: People Places, and Education in the Sudan.* Oxford; New York: Published for the British Academy by Oxford University Press, 1992.

Beshir, M.O. (ed.). *Southern Sudan: Regionalism & Religion.* Khartoum: U. of Khartoum Press, 1984.

Bienen, Henry. *Armed Forces, Conflict, and Change in Africa.* Boulder, CO: Westview Press, 1989.

Boyles, D. *African Lives.* New York: Weidenfeld and Nicolson, 1988.

Brown, Richard. *Public Debt and Private Wealth: Debt, Capital Flight, and the IMF in Sudan.* New York: St. Martin's Press, 1992.

Brown, Richard. *Sudan's Other Economy: Migrants' Remittances, Capital Flight, and Their Policy Implications.* The Hague, Netherlands: Publications Office, Institute of Social Studies, 1990.

Bucannan-Smith, Margaret. *Food Security Planning in the Wake of an Emergency Relief Operation: The Case of Darfur, Western Sudan.* Brighton, England: IDP Publications, Institute of Development Studies at the University of Sussex, 1990.

Cater, N. *Sudan, The Roots of Famine.* London: Oxfam, 1986.

Collins, Robert. *Shadows in the Grass: Britain in the Southern Sudan, 1918–1956.* New Haven: Yale University Press, 1983.

Collins, Robert. *The Waters of the Nile: Hydropolitics and the Jonglei Canal, 1900–1988.* Oxford, England: Clarendon Press; New York: Oxford University Press, 1990.

Craig, G.M. *The Agriculture of the Sudan.* New York: Oxford University Press, 1991.

Daly, M.W. and Ahmad Alawad Sikainga, (eds.). *Civil War in the Sudan.* London: British Academic Press, 1993.

Deng, Francis M. and P. Gifford. *The Search for Peace and Unity in Sudan.* Washington, D.C.: Wilson Center Press, May 1987.

Deng, Francis M. and Larry Minear. *The Challenge of Famine Relief: Emergency Operations in the Sudan.* Washington, D.C.: The Brookings Institution, 1992.

De Waal, Alex. *Famine that Kills: Darfur, Sudan, 1984–1985.* Oxford, England: Clarendon Press; New York: Oxford University Press, 1989.

Duffield, Mark. *Sudan at the Crossroads: From Emergency Preparedness to Social Security.* Brighton, England: Institute of Development Studies at the University of Sussex, 1990.

Economist Intelligence Unit. *"Sudan in Transition: A Political Risk Analysis,"* Report No. 226, London, 1986.

El-Affendi, Abdelwahab. *Turabi's Revolution: Islam and Power in Sudan.* London: Grey Seal, 1991.

El-Bushra, El-Sayed. *An Atlas of Khartoum Conurbation.* Khartoum: University of Khartoum Press, 1976.

Eprile, C. *War and Peace in the Sudan, 1955–1972.* London: David & Charles, Newton Abbot, 1974.

Ewald, Janet. *Soldiers, Traders, and Slaves: State Formation and Economic Transformation in the Greater Nile Valley, 1700–1885.* Madison: University of Wisconsin Press, 1990.

Farouk El-Baz, Ibrahim A. El-Tayeb, and Mohamed H.A. Hassan. *Desertification in Arid Lands.* Teaneck, N.J.: World Scientific Publishers, 1989.

Fruzzetti, Lina. *Culture and Change Along the Blue Nile: Courts, Markets, and Strategies for Development.* Boulder: Westview Press, 1990.

Garang de Mabior, John. *"Identifying, selecting, and implementing rural development strategies for socio-economic development in the Jonglei Projects Area, Southern Region, Sudan,"* doctoral dissertation: Iowa State University, 1981.

Garang de Mabior, John. *The Call for Democracy in Sudan.* London; New York: Kegan Paul International, 1992.

Hamid, Mohammed Bashir. *The Politics of National Reconciliation in the Sudan.* Washington, D.C.: Center for Contemporary Arab Studies, 1984.

Heiden, David. *Dust to Dust: A Doctor's View of Famine in Africa.* Philadelphia: Temple University Press, 1992.

Hellden, U. *Drought Impact Monitoring: A Remote Sensing Study of Desertification in Kordofan.* Lund, Sweden: Laboratory of Remote Sensing, University of Lund, 1984.

Holt, P. M. and M. W. Daly. *A History of the Sudan.* New York: Longman, 1988.

Human Rights Watch/Africa (formerly Africa Watch). *Civilian Devastation: Abuses by All Parties in the War in Southern Sudan.* New York: Human Rights Watch, June 1994.

International Conference. *The Human Dimension of Africa's Economic Recovery and Development.* New York: H. Zell, 1990.

Khalid, Mansour. *Nimeiri and the Revolution of Dis-May.* London: Kegan Paul International, 1985.

Khalid, Mansour. *The Government They Deserve: The Role of the Elite in Sudan's Political Evolution.* New York: Kegan Paul International, 1990.

Lukudu, S. and P. O. Bulu. *Report on Drought and Hunger Threatened Areas of Equatoria Region.* Equatoria Region, Juba: Ministry of Agriculture and Natural Resources, December 1984.

MacMichael, H. A. *The Tribes of Northern and Central Kordofan.* London: Frank Cass & Co. Ltd., 1967.

Mahmud, U. A. and S. A. Baldo. *The Diein Massacre: Slavery in Sudan.* Khartoum: Khartoum University Press, 1987.

Majok, Damazo. *British Religious and Educational Policy, Southern Sudan: Regionalism & Religion.* Khartoum: University of Khartoum, Graduate College Publications, No. 10, 1984.

Malwal, Bona. *Sudan: A Second Challenge to Nationhood.* New York: Thornton Books, 1985.

Markakis, John. *National and Class Conflict in the Horn of Africa.* Cambridge: Cambridge University Press, 1987.

Maxwell, Simon. *Food Insecurity in North Sudan.* England: Institute of Development Studies at the University of Sussex, 1989.

Minear, Larry. *A Humanitarianism under Siege: A Critical Review of Operation Lifeline Sudan.* Trenton: Red Sea Press, 1991.

Minority Rights Group. *Uganda and Sudan,* London: Report No. 66, December 1984.

Muller, Harald K. *Changing Generations: Dynamics of Generation and Age-Sets in Southeastern Sudan (Toposa) and Northwestern Kenya (Turkana).* Saarbrucken; Fort Lauderdale: Breitenback Publishers, 1989.

Numayri, J. *Al-Hahj Al-Islami Limadha.* Washington, D.C.: Joint Publications Research Service Translation. JPRS-NEA-84-104, August 3, 1984.

Saghayroun, A. A. (ed.). *Population and Development in the Sudan: The Quest for a National Policy.* Khartoum: Khartoum University Press, October 1987.

Sikainga, Ahmad Alawad. *The Western Bahr al-Ghazal under British Rule, 1898–1956.* Athens, Ohio: Ohio University Center for International Studies, 1991.

Sudanaid. *Sudanese Relief & Rehabilitation Programme.* Khartoum, Annual Report, various years.

Sudan National Energy Plan Committee. *The National Energy Plan, 1985–2000.* Khartoum: National Energy Plan Committee, 1985.

Sudan National Population Committee. *Aspects of Population Change and Development in the Sudan.* Khartoum: Khartoum University Press, 1982.

Tesfaye, Teklu. *Drought and Famine Relationships in Sudan: Policy Implications.* Washington, D.C.: International Food Policy Research Institute, 1991.

Thomas, Graham. *Sudan, 1950–1985: Death of a Dream.* London: Darf, 1990.

United States Agency for International Development. *The U.S. Response to the African Famine, 1984–1986.* Washington, D.C.: USAID, November 1986.

United States Congress, House of Representatives, Committee on Foreign Affairs. *Sudan: Problems and Prospects.* Washington, D.C.: 98th Congress, 28 March 1984.

United States Congress, House of Representatives, Committee on Foreign Affairs, Subcommittee on Africa. *War and Famine in the Sudan: Joint Hearing Before the Subcommittee on Africa of the Committee on Foreign Affairs and the International Task Force of the Select Committee on Hunger.* Washington, D.C.: U.S.G.P.O., March 15, 1990.

United States Congress, House of Representatives, Select Committee on Hunger. *Politics of Hunger in the Sudan: Joint Hearing Before the Select Committee on Hunger and the Subcommittee on Foreign Affairs.* Washington, D.C.: U.S.G.P.O., March 2, 1989.

United States Congress, Senate, Committee on Foreign Relations, Subcommittee on African Affairs. *War and Famine in Sudan: Hearing Before the Subcommittee on African Affairs of the Committee on Foreign Relations, United States Senate.* Washington, D.C.: U.S.G.P.O, February 23, 1989

United States Department of Agriculture. *World Food Needs and Availability.* Washington, D.C.: various years.

United States Department of State. *Country Reports on Human Rights and Practices.* Washington, D.C.: various years.

United States Department of State. *World Refugee Report.* Washington D.C.: 1987.

Warburg, Gabriel. *Historical Discord in the Nile Valley.* Evanston, Illinois: Northwestern University Press, 1992.

Woodward, Peter. *Sudan, 1898–1989: The Unstable State.* Boulder: L. Rienner Publishers; London: L. Crook Academic Publishers, 1990.

Woodward, Peter. *Sudan After Nimeiri.* New York: Routledge, 1991.

Articles, Documents, and Pamphlets

Abdalla, Ismail. "Center-Periphery Relations in the Sudan." *Orient*, 33, 1992.

Ammann, Beat. "Sudan: An African Tinderbox." *Swiss Review of World Affairs*, 37, January 1988.

An-Na'im, Abdullahi Ahmed. "Detention Without Trial in the Sudan: The Use and Abuse of Legal Powers." *Columbia Human Rights Law Review*, 17, Spring–Summer 1986.

Annual Report 1993. London: Amnesty International, 1994.

Bienen, Henry. "The Sudan: Military Economic Corporations." *Armed Forces & Society*, 13, Summer 1987.

Bonner, Raymond. "A Reporter at Large: Famine." *The New Yorker*, 65, March 13, 1989.

Burr, Millard. "Khartoum Displaced Persons: A Decade of Despair." Washington, D.C.: *U.S. Committee for Refugees*, August 1990.

Burr, Millard. "A Working Document: Quantifying Genocide in the Southern Sudan 1983–1993." Washington, D.C.: *U.S. Committee for Refugees*, 1993.

Burr, Millard. "Sudan 1990–1992: Food Aid, Famine and Failure." Washington, D.C.: *U.S. Committee for Refugees*, 1993.

Bush, Ray. "Hunger in Sudan: The Case of Darfur." *African Affairs*, 87, January 1988.

Campbell, Colin and Deborah Scroggins. "The Famine Weapon in the Horn of Africa." *Atlanta Journal*, 1988.

Cater, Nick. "The Forgotten Famine." *Africa Report*, 36, May–June 1991.

Deng, Francis M. "The Sudan: Stop the Carnage." *The Brookings Review*, Winter 1994.

De Waal, Alex. "Some Comments on Militias in the Contemporary Sudan." in *Civil War in the Sudan*, (eds.) M. W. Daly and Ahmad Alawad Sikainga, London: British Academic Press, 1993.

"Discovering the South: Sudanese Dilemmas for Islam in Africa." *African Affairs*, 89, July 1990.

Duffield, Mark. "NGOs, Disaster Relief and Asset Transfer in the Horn: Political Survival In a Permanent Emergency." *Development and Change*, 24, 1993.

Duffield, Mark. "The Emergence of Two-Tier Welfare in Africa: Marginalization or an Opportunity for Reform?" *Public Administration and Development*, 12, 1992.

Fluehr-Lobban, Carolyn. "Protracted Civil War in the Sudan: Its Future as a Multi-Religious, Multi-Ethnic State." *Fletcher Forum of World Affairs*, 16, Summer 1992.

"Food Aid." *Courier*, No. 118, November–December 1989.

Henze, Paul. "The Primacy of Economics for the Future of the Horn of Africa." Santa Monica: Rand Corporation, 1992.

"The Horn of Africa: Millions on the Move." *Refugees*, No. 72, February 1990.

Horowitz, Rose. "Special Report: Food For Peace? Food For Profit?" *Journal of Commerce*, December 7, 1988.

House, William. "Population, Poverty, and Underdevelopment in the Southern Sudan." *Journal of Modern African Studies*, 27, 1989.

Hubbard, Mark. "While People Starve." *Africa Report*, May/June 1993.

Johnson, Douglas H. "The Southern Sudan." *London Minority Rights Group*, 1988.

Johnson, Douglas H. "Political Ecology in the Upper Nile: The Twentieth-Century Expansion of the Patrol Economy." *Journal of African History*, 1989.

Johnson, Douglas H. "The Structure of a Legacy: Military Slavery in Northeast Africa." *Ethnohistory* 26, 1989.

Johnson, Douglas H. and Gerard Prunier. "The Foundation and Expansion of the Sudan People's Liberation Army." (eds.) M. W. Daly and Ahmad Alawad Sikainga, London: British Academic Press, 1993.

Lefebvre, Jeffrey. "Globalism and Regionalism: U.S. Arms Transfers to Sudan." *Armed Forces & Society*, 17, Winter 1991.

Legum, Colin. "The Horn of Africa: Prospects for Political Transformation." *Research Institute for the Study of Conflict and Terrorism*, 1992.

Lesch, Ann Mosely. "A View from Khartoum." *Foreign Affairs*, 65, Spring 1987.

Lesch, Ann Mosely. "Confrontation in the Southern Sudan." *Middle East Journal*, 40, Summer 1986.

Makinda, Samuel. "Iran, Sudan and Islam." *World Today*, 49, June 1993.

Makinda, Samuel. "Sudan: Old Wine in New Bottles." *Orbis*, 31, Summer 1987.

Medani, Khalid. "Sudan's Human and Political Crisis." *Current History*, 92, May 1993.

Mikhail, Nabil. "An Interim Report on Sudan's New Regime." *CSIS Africa Notes*, No. 100, July 30, 1989.

Minear, Larry. "A Critical Review of Operation Lifeline Sudan: A Report to the Aid Agencies." Washington, D.C.: *Refugee Policy Group*, 1989.

Mohammed, Nadir. "Militarization in Sudan: Trends and Determinations." *Armed Forces and Society*, 19, Spring 1993.

Novicki, Margaret. "Bishop Paride Taban: Standing Up for the South." *Africa Report*, 36, March–April 1991.

Obat, G. "The Jebelein Massacre" (mimeo). Khartoum: January 1990.

Ottaway, Marina. "Post-Numeiri Sudan: One Year On." *Third World Quarterly*, 9, July 1987.

Prendergast, John. "Facilitating Famine and Civil War in the Sudan." *Transafrica Forum*, 6, Spring-Summer 1989.

Ruiz, Hiram. "Beyond the Headlines: Refugees in the Horn of Africa." Washington, D.C.: American Council for Nationalities Service, 1988.

Salih, Kamal Osman. "The Sudan, 1985–1989: The Fading Democracy." *Journal of Modern African Studies*, 28, June 1990.

Scott-Villiers, Alaster, Patta Scott-Villiers, and Cole. P Dodge. "Repatriation of 150,000 Sudanese Refugees from Ethiopia: The Manipulation of Civilians in a Situation of Civil Conflict." *Disasters*, 17, 1993.

Shields, Todd. "Sudan: A Tragedy in the Making." *Africa Report*, 36, March–April 1991.

Stanfield, Rochelle. "Saving the Sudan." *National Journal*, 20, December 10, 1988.

"Sudan: A Continuing Human Rights Crisis." AI Index: AFR 54/30/92. London: Amnesty International, April 15, 1992.

"Sudan: Deaths and Detentions: the Destruction of Juba." AI Index: AFR 54/26/92. London: Amnesty International, September 23, 1992.

"Sudan: Politics and Society." *Middle East Report*, 21, September–October 1991.

Suliman, Mohamed. "Civil War in the Sudan: From Ethnic to Ecological Conflict." *Ecologist*, 23, May–June 1993.

U.N. Economic and Social Council, Commission on Human Rights, Fiftieth Session. "Situation of Human Rights in the Sudan, Report of the Special Rapporteur, Mr. Gáspár Biró." E/CN.4/1994/48. Geneva: United Nations, February 1, 1994.

"Urgent Action: Sudan." AI Index: AFR 54/14/92. London: Amnesty International, April 6, 1992.

"Urgent Action, Sudan." AI Index: AFR 54/25/92. London: Amnesty International, July 31, 1992.

"Urgent Action: Report, Sudan." AI Index: AFR 54/14/93. London: Amnesty International, April 30, 1993.

U.S. Committee on Foreign Affairs. "Recent Developments in Sudan." March 10, 1993, Washington, D.C.: G.P.O., 1993.

U.S. Congress, House of Representatives, Committee on Foreign Affairs. "Conflict and Famine in the Horn of Africa." May 30, 1992, Washington, D.C.: G.P.O., 1992.

U.S. Congress, House of Representatives, Committee on Foreign Affairs. "Impending Famine and Recent Political Developments in the Sudan." October 25, 1990, Washington, D.C.: G.P.O., 1991.

U.S. Congress, Senate, Committee on Foreign Relations. "Crisis in Sudan." Washington, D.C.: May, 4, 1993.

U.S. General Accounting Office. "Refugees: Living Conditions are Marginal." Washington, D.C., 1991.

Wakoson, Elias N. "The Origin and Development of the Anya-Nya Movement, 1955–1972," in *Southern Sudan: Regionalism & Religion*, Beshir O. (ed.), Khartoum: Graduate College Publications, No. 10: University of Khartoum Press, 1984.

Weiss, Thomas. "Do International Ethics Matter?" *Ethics and International Affairs*, 5, 1991.

Wenyin, D. A. "The Integration of Anyanya into the National Army," in *North-South Relations in the Sudan Since the Addis Ababa Agreement*. Khartoum: University of Khartoum Press, 1988.

Wieu, A.W.R. "Southern Sudan Institutional Structure, Power and Inter-Governmental Relations Yesterday and Today, " in *North-South Relations in the Sudan Since the Addis Ababa Agreement*. Khartoum: University of Khartoum Press, 1988.

Woodward, Peter. "Sudan's New Democracy." *Contemporary Review*, 251, July 1987.

Magazine and Newspaper Articles

"Algeria Breaks Ties with Iran." *The New York Times* 142, March 28, 1993, p. 9(N), p. 12(LC).

"Britain, Retaliating, Expels Sudan's Envoy." *The New York Times* 143, January 5, 1994, p. A4(N).

Caputo, Robert. "Tragedy Stalks the Horn of Africa." *National Geographic* 184, August 1993, p. 88(34).

"Carter Arrives in Sudan (Jimmy Carter)." *The New York Times* 142, August 8, 1993, p. 10(N).

"Carter will Mediate Parley by Warring Sudan Factions." *The New York Times* 143, October 15, 1993, p. A5(L).

"Cold War Forces Called to Clean Up Sudan Mess." *National Catholic Reporter* 30, November 19, 1993, p. 24(1).

Collins, Carole. "Sudan Opposition Debates War." *National Catholic Reporter* 30, November 19, 1993, p. 9(1).

"The Cry of Sudan." *Commonwealth* 119, No. 19, November 6, 1992, p. 3(2).

Dolgoff, Stephanie. "Tears of a Child." *American Photo* 4, September–October 1993, p. 52(2).

Flint, Julie. "Aid Anguish in Sudan." *New Statesman Society* 6, April 30, 1993, p. 10(2).

Flint, Julie. "The Famine Triangle." *New Statesman Society* 6, No. 245, March 26, 1993, p. 14(2).

Flint, Julie. "Anti-Rebel Offensive Creates Sudanese Refugee Crisis." London: *The Guardian*, August 10, 1993

Gargan, Edward. "Sundered by Civil War, Nations on Horn of Africa Melt Away." *The Los Angeles Times*, June 10, 1990, p. 14.

Greenberger, Robert. "Arab Nightmare: Sudan's Links to Iran Cause Growing Worry over Islamic Terrorism; U.S. Is Adding African Nation to List of Outlaw

States; Mideast Stability at Risk; Ties to New York Plot Cited." *The Wall Street Journal*, August 18, 1993, p. A1(W).

Grinker Lori. "Disaster in the Sudan." *The New York Times* 142, February 12, 1993, p. A3.

Hammer, Joshua. "Khartoum Character: A Visit with Sudan's Despot." *The New Republic* 210, February 7, 1994, p. 14(1).

"Humanitarian Crisis in Sudan." *U.S. Department of State Dispatch* 4, May 24, 1993 p. 374(3).

"Islamic Mediator: Sudan." *Economist* (London) 329, December 11, 1993, p. 48(1).

Ibrahim, Youssef. "Arrests Cast Spotlight on Sudan as Staging Ground for Extremists." *The New York Times* 142, June 26, 1993, p. 23.

"Jihad: Sudan." *Economist* (London) 328, August 7, 1993, p. 42(2).

Jordan, Patrick. "A Deadly Silence: Faint Voices on Sudan." *Commonwealth* 120, May 7, 1993, p. 4(2).

"Keep Out: Sudan." *Economist* (London) 326, No. 7801, March 6, 1993, p. 45(1).

Loconte, Joe. "Civil War Brings Suffering to Sudan." *Christianity Today (Washington)* 37, May 17, 1993, p. 82(2).

Lorch, Donatella. "Sudan is Described as Trying to Placate the West." *The New York Times* 142, March 26, 1993, p. A3(N).

Lorch, Donatella. "Fighting in the Sudan's South Halts Famine Relief." *The New York Times* 142, April 18, 1993, 13(N).

Lorch, Donatella. "Drought and Fighting Imperil 2 Million in Sudan." *The New York Times* 143, February 10, 1994, p. A3(N).

"The Lost Years: Sudan." *Economist* 330, February 12, 1994, p. 39(2).

Molotsky, Irvin. "U.S. Expected to Place Sudan on Terrorist List; Evidence of Role in Second Bomb Plot Cited." *The New York Times* 142, August 17, 1993, p. B3(L).

Nachtwey, James. "Slaughter in Slow Motion." *Time (Chicago)* 142, August 23, 1993, p. 46(4).

"Nigeria: Which Way Forward." *U.S. Department of State Dispatch* 4, August 23, 1993, p. 598(2).

"100,000 Flee as Sudan Bombards Rebels in South." *The New York Times* 143, February 6, 1994, p. 4(L).

Prial, Frank. "Sudanese Mission Denies any Tie to Bomb Plot." *The New York Times* 142, August 18, 1993, p. A12(N).

Press, Robert. "Dispute over Becoming Islamic State Prolongs Sudan's Civil War." *Christian Science Monitor*, August 2, 1988, p. 19.

Rosenblatt, Roger. "The Family of Man." *Family Circle* 106, August 10, 1993, p. 148(1).

Rosenblatt, Roger and Sebastiao Salgado. "The Last Place on Earth." *Vanity Fair* 56, July 1993, p. 80(19).

Schmidt, William. "Anglican Prelate Defies Sudan in Trip to South." *The New York Times* 143, December 30, 1993, p. A6(N).

"Situation in Sudan." *U.S. Department of State Dispatch* 4, No. 11, March 15, 1993, p. 153(3)

"Sudan is Expelling the British Ambassador." *The New York Times* 143, December 31, 1993, p. A5(N).

"Sudan is Reported to Arrest Premier Ousted in '89 Coup." 142, April 7, 1993, p. A4(N).

"Sudan's Junta Ends its Rule, Naming Its Leader President." *The New York Times* 143, October 17, 1993, p. 11(L).

"Sudan—The Next Somalia?" *The Christian Century* 110, April 7, 1993, p. 359(2).

"U.N. Condemns Sudan and Iraq over Rights." *The New York Times* 142, March 11, 1993, p. A4(N).

"U.S. to Put Sudan on List of Terrorist Countries." *The Wall Street Journal*, August 17, 1993, p. A13(W).

Walt, Vivienne. "On the Front Lines of Famine." *Vogue* 184, February 1994, p. 128(3).

"Whose Islamic Awakening? A Response." *New Perspectives Quarterly* 10, Summer 1993, p. 45(4).

About the Book and Authors

After a decade of uneasy peace, the historic conflict between the Northern Sudanese, who identify with their Middle Eastern neighbors, and the Southern Sudanese, who are of African heritage, erupted into violent conflict in 1983. This ferocious civil war, with its Arab militias and widespread use of automatic weapons, has devastated the populace. Nature has added to the miseries of war, bringing drought and famine to the already battered victims of violence. Although this regional calamity remains largely unknown to the outside world, the death toll among the Southern Sudanese far exceeds that in both Somalia or Bosnia. Over a million people have either perished or been displaced.

This chilling account of the ravages of drought and civil war is based on a wealth of documents—never made public—from Sudanese government sources, private and foreign governmental aid agencies, research groups, international media, and other organizations involved in famine relief efforts. The authors graphically recount how the attempts of the international agencies and humanitarian organizations to provide food and medical relief have been thwarted by bureaucratic infighting, corruption, greed, and ineptitude.

This rich narrative illustrates with great clarity the convoluted relationship that relief agencies had with the Sudanese government as they tried to negotiate the means of survival for the area's desperate population. It is a sad tale of the tragic human consequences of the failure of conflict resolution, of organizational mismanagement, and of a government hostile toward its own people.

J. Millard Burr is a former relief coordinator for "Operation Lifeline Sudan," U.S. Agency for International Development. **Robert O. Collins** is professor of history at the University of California, Santa Barbara.

Index

CPSIA information can be obtained at www.ICGtesting.com
Printed in the USA
LVOW06s1855141013

356863LV00001B/384/A